AF531108

PROPHECY

VIEWED IN RESPECT TO

ITS DISTINCTIVE NATURE, ITS SPECIAL FUNCTION,

AND

PROPER INTERPRETATION

BY

PATRICK FAIRBAIRN, D.D.

BAKER BOOK HOUSE
Grand Rapids, Michigan

Reprinted 1976 by
Baker Book House
from the edition issued in 1865
by T. and T. Clark

ISBN: 0-8010-3474-4

PREFACE.

THE subject of the present volume is so closely connected with those of some former publications, that it has for long engaged a considerable share of my attention. More recently, however, my thoughts have been, in an especial manner, turned in this particular direction. It has fallen to me, in the discharge of my official duties, to treat of the evidences of revealed religion, and, among others, of the evidence of prophecy. But the whole of this department of theology has been peculiarly affected by the spirit of the age; and a mode of treatment is now required for the several topics it embraces, materially different from what was wont to be pursued even so lately as the earlier part of the present century. Such especially is the case in respect to the subject of prophecy. The claim of the Bible to divine authority, on the ground of its predictions, has now to be maintained from a more internal position than formerly; since objections are laid by the opponents or corrupters of the truth against the argument from prophecy, less on the ground of an alleged weakness in the argument itself, abstractedly considered, than by attempting to extract the element of prophecy from Scripture, in so far as it can be said to carry with it any argumentative value.

Adopt their mode of contemplating the prophetical Scriptures, and you no longer possess the materials necessary for constructing an argument that will serve the cause of Christianity. Contemporaneously, too, with this relative change on the part of the impugners of revelation, modes of interpretation, and views founded on them, have been gaining currency among many students of Scripture, which, if valid, would deprive the argument from prophecy of some of its most important defences. The immediate result of the two tendencies combined has been to involve the subject of prophecy in a medley of confusion, and in great measure to antiquate, even for argumentative purposes, the works which have been framed with an express view to the exhibition of the prophetical argument. In a higher respect, however, this state of things is not to be regretted; since it necessarily forces on the friends of revelation a more fundamental investigation of the whole subject, and cannot fail to lead to the establishment of more correct views respecting the proper function and essential characteristics of prophecy. It is here peculiarly, that this portion of our theological literature has been defective and unsatisfactory.

With the view of contributing to supply this defect, and meeting the new phase of things which has rendered it more clearly manifest, the present volume has been composed. Hence, nearly one half of the volume is devoted to the investigation of the principles of the subject, without which no satisfactory foundation can be laid, nor can any reasonable prospect be entertained, of a general agreement as to the right use and interpretation of prophecy. The latter half, which treats of definite portions of the prophetical Scriptures, as well in regard to past as to prospective fulfilments, is conducted strictly as an application of the principles set forth and maintained in the earlier. In all fairness and propriety, therefore, the one should be examined and weighed before judgment is pronounced upon the other; the course of inquiry should be followed, by which it has been sought to establish the fundamental principles, before the results are looked at, to which, by the application of them, we have been conducted. It has been our object, however, in that part of the volume, which treats of what is fundamental, to interweave with the discussion as many illustrations as possible of particular prophecies, so as, while chiefly occupied with laying the foundation, to make some progress also in raising the superstructure.

The more immediate occasion and design of the work will serve also to account for another characteristic in the form. Writing more especially for those, who wish to study the subject in its essential features, and as connected chiefly with the proper interpretation of Scripture, it has formed no part of my plan to give a complete history of opinion on the topics handled, or to recount at length the views of particular writers. I have aimed at giving the treatise rather an exegetical and positive, than a negative and controversial aspect; and have been at more pains in establishing what I conceive to be the truth, than in noticing every shade and variety of error, that may have appeared in opposition to it. All the leading forms of opinion, of course, are indicated, and wherever necessary for purposes of argument or illustration, references to particular authors are also made; but not unfrequently where views at variance with my own are mentioned, I have purposely refrained from connecting them with the names of individual authors, that the discussion might not be entangled, beyond what was necessary, with personal associations. I need scarcely add, that I have never ascribed to an individual or a party opinions, for which I have not at command the clearest evidence. And in those cases, in which I have adopted from another any view of a passage or a symbol, that may be designated new or peculiar, I have not failed to ascribe it to the proper quarter.

Occasional portions of the volume have appeared already in print, chiefly in periodical publications. But as these form a comparatively small part of the whole, and have also undergone considerable changes and modifications, I have not thought it necessary to distinguish them in any way from the rest. The chapter, however, on the Prophetical Future of Israel, is in no respect a reprint of what appeared as an Appendix on the same subject in the First Edition of the Typology; but is an entirely new investigation. The subject of what is called the Double Sense of Prophecy has been here omitted, because it is formally treated in the First Volume of the Typology (Second Edition), where it is explained as a combination of type with prophecy.

In almost every case, where I have departed from the received text, or from the authorized translation of the Scriptures, I have noticed the difference, and indicated my reasons for so doing. In a few instances, however, such as "a Son of Man" for "the Son of Man," in Dan. vii. 13; Rev. i. 13, and "the kingdom, or sovereignty of the world" for "the kingdoms of the world," becoming Christ's, Rev. xi. 15—where the correct text or rendering is generally known, I have thought it unnecessary to take any particular notice of the diversity.

The four sections of the last chapter are longer than I could have wished; but it was impossible to compress into a shorter compass the discussion of the topics handled in them. Each section, however, contains several breaks, at which the reader may pause in the perusal; and to facilitate his reference to the different topics embraced in them, the Contents of these sections have been exhibited in detail.

CONTENTS.

PART I.

INVESTIGATION OF PRINCIPLES, pp. 1-196.

PART II.

APPLICATION OF PRINCIPLES TO PAST AND PROSPECTIVE FULFILMENTS OF PROPHECY, pp. 197-485.

APPENDICES.

PROPHECY,

VIEWED IN RESPECT TO

ITS DISTINCTIVE NATURE, ITS SPECIAL FUNCTION, AND PROPER INTERPRETATION.

PART I.

INVESTIGATION OF PRINCIPLES.

THE subject of prophecy is one that peculiarly demands, for its successful treatment, a spirit of careful discrimination. From the very nature of the subject, the want of such a spirit must inevitably lead to mistaken views, and even to dangerous results. In what respects do the prophetical portions of Scripture differ from those which are not prophetical? And, again, what specific differences separate between one portion of the prophetical field and another? These are points which call for minute and patient inquiry, as on the right settlement of them much depends for the proper understanding and consistent interpretation of the prophetical Scriptures. There are certain characteristics of a general kind, which belong to prophecy as a whole; and there are, again, subordinate peculiarities, which appear in some of its communications, but are wanting in others. The principle so strongly asserted by the Apostle Peter, that "prophecy came not by the will of man, but holy men of God spake as they were moved by the Holy Ghost," has respect only to one, and, indeed, to the most general, though, at the same time, the most fundamental, property of genuine prophecy—namely, the divinity of its origin. This property it, however, shares in common with every part of God's revealed word; while yet revelation by prophecy possesses features and occupies a place peculiar to itself. Even within the prophetical territory there are important differences, which should not be without their influence on the mode of treatment its several portions receive at our hands. For prophecy is by no means uniform, either as regards the manner in which it came, or the form which it assumed. By much the larger portion of its communications were the utterances of men, who formed a distinct order, and who, in speaking as they were moved by the Holy Ghost, were acting in the discharge of a recognised function in the Church. A certain portion, however, proceeded from persons, who had no proper office of such a kind to fulfil, but were supernaturally endowed for the occasion; while still another portion, without passing through the medium of *any* human instrumentality, was uttered by a voice direct from Heaven. Of those portions, also, of the prophetic Word which were brought through the agency of men, some were communicated in visions, and others when the recipients were in their waking condition and their ordinary frame of mind. Certain parts are written in language comparatively simple; while others are clothed in the richest imagery, or enveloped in the mystery of symbols.

Now, if no regard is paid to such marked distinctions between prophecy in general, and other modes of Divine revelation, and between one portion of prophecy and another; or, if the distinctions are practically overlooked in the mode of interpretation that is adopted, we shall seek in vain to arrive at any safe and satisfactory conclusions, either as regards the design of prophecy in general, or the meaning of its individual parts. It is to want of pains in this preliminary line of inquiry, more than to any other cause, that we ascribe the contradictory views which still continue to be propounded of various predictions, and the manifold uncertainty which now more than ever seems to haunt the prophetical region. In applying our minds, therefore, to this important subject, it will be our duty, in the first instance, to cast our eye over the field of prophecy, with the view of making ourselves accurately acquainted with some of its more prominent and distinctive characteristics. And then on these, as the proper basis of all sound interpretation, we shall endeavour to find our way to such fundamental principles as ought to direct and regulate our inquiries into the several parts of the prophetic volume.

CHAPTER I.

THE PROPER CALLING OF A PROPHET, AND THE ESSENTIAL NATURE OF A PROPHECY.

THE first thing that demands consideration in this survey has respect to the constituent elements of a prophecy, and, in connection with that, the proper calling or function of a prophet. For here, at the very outset, the current language of the world, which so often governs its ideas, is fitted to create a false impression, and impart a misleading bias to our views. In ordinary language, that only is a prophecy which delivers some prediction of the future; while in the original and proper sense this embraces but a part of the idea, and not always even the more principal part. The prophet, as regarded in the light of Scripture, was simply the recipient and bearer of a message from God; and such a message of course was a prophecy, whatever might be its more specific character—whether the disclosure of some important truth, the inculcation of an imperative duty, or a prospective delineation of coming events. A message, however, that bespoke no supernatural insight into the will and purposes of Heaven, could not, except in peculiar circumstances, require a divinely-commissioned person to deliver it. And so, while any communication received directly from above might be called a prophecy, the term was naturally understood only of such communications as inferred a more than ordinary acquaintance with spiritual and Divine things; but these not less when the Word spoken referred to the *higher truths* of God's kingdom, than when it foretold the *future acts* of His providence.

That such actually is the Scriptural idea of a true prophet, and a prophetic Word, is evident alone from the two first occasions on which the subject is formally mentioned. "Restore the man his wife," said the Lord to Abimelech, after he had taken Sarah from Abraham, " for he is a prophet" (Gen. xx. 7). This is absolutely the first time the designation *prophet* is applied to any one in Scripture; and being used without explanation, and with reference to a person, whose peculiar distinction lay in his having been raised to so high a place in the friendship of God, where he enjoyed the privilege of direct intercourse with Heaven, it must have been intended to denote Abraham as possessed of that distinction—to characterise him as one admitted into the secrets, and made acquainted, with the counsels of the Most High. The next occasion is even more precise and definite, as it presents the prophetical agency under the aspect of simply human relations. "Behold," says God to Moses, in Exod. vii. 1, "I have made thee a god to Pharaoh, and Aaron, thy brother, shall be thy prophet." By comparing this declaration with chap. iv. 15, 16, where it is said to Moses, "Thou shalt speak unto Aaron, and put words in his mouth, and he shall be thy spokesman unto the people," it is plain that as Moses was to act God's part in giving the message to Aaron, so in receiving the message, and communicating it to others, Aaron was to do the prophet's part. The prophet, therefore, was one qualified and called to sustain this twofold relation to God and man—on the one side to receive; on the other, to give forth the Word received—to be, in a manner, God's mouth, for the purpose of declaring the truths, and unfolding the secrets, which God might see meet by special revelation to impart to him. This was the peculiar calling of the prophet, and whatever was uttered in the fulfilment of such a calling was a prophecy.[1]

The prophetic writings themselves sufficiently attest this. They give no countenance to the notion that the gift of prophecy was conferred merely for the purpose of announcing beforehand the coming events of Providence. The discourses which actually possess this character never comprise the whole, nor often even the larger portion of the writings which

[1] See Appendix A.

have been left by the prophets to the Church. In these, viewed generally, the grand object seems rather to have been to deal with men, as in God's stead, for the interests of truth and righteousness, and only in so far as might be required for the furtherance of this object, to lay open the prospect of things to come. But the strongest proof is to be found in the case of those who, in the highest and most emphatic sense, had to do the part of a prophet, since it appears to have been with the present, rather than with the future, that their mission called them more immediately to deal. The persons who, above all others, occupied this lofty position, were Moses and Christ. Most commonly, indeed, they are named apart from the prophets, as if something else than prophetical gifts,—something essentially superior to these entered into the revelations brought by their instrumentality to the world: hence such expressions as "Moses and the prophets," "Christ and his holy apostles and prophets." Such representations, however, must be understood as marking only a relative, not an absolute, difference. Moses was, in the strictest sense, a prophet, and is often so described, as in Hosea, chap. xii. 13, "And by a prophet the Lord brought Israel out of Egypt, and by a prophet was he preserved." Not only was he a prophet in the strictest sense, but also in the highest degree; for who, in ancient times, received such free and ample communications from Heaven as were imparted to Moses? Or who, like him, was charged with a commission to order and establish everything in God's kingdom, in its earlier and provisional form, among men? When the time, however, came for that form giving way to another more perfect and complete, then came also the greater than Moses, whom the people of God in every age have recognised as emphatically *the* prophet of the Church, and whom Moses himself descried as destined to arise, and entitled also to obtain, when he should appear, universal homage and respect (Deut. xviii. 15).

Now, it is true, alike of Moses and of Christ, that while, as prophets, they possessed and manifested the profoundest insight into Divine things, the communications they actually made to the Church partook comparatively little of the nature of specific predictions respecting particular personages or events in the future. The whole that either of them uttered of such predictions might be comprised within the limits of a few ordinary chapters. The other and much larger portion of their communications has to do with the great realities of faith and hope, or the principles of truth and duty, which form the basis of their respective dispensations; and is no farther predictive of what was afterwards to happen, than as the present necessarily contained the germ of the future, or the manifestations then given of God's mind and will bespoke the recurrence of like manifestations, and, it may be, still higher ones in the time to come. It could not, indeed, have been otherwise, from the very nature of things. The distinction we now refer to has its foundation, not in accidental circumstances, or individual choice, but in the more essential relations that connect man with God, and the soul of one man with that of another. This we may learn from the world itself. The world also has its prophets,—men in whom it recognises "the vision and faculty divine;" and, among these, some who are regarded as possessing it in a supereminent degree. But to whom does it assign this elevated place? Not to those who labour, even though it should be with superior ingenuity and skill in Nature's corners and byepaths—who, within some narrower range of action, light upon discoveries interesting only to the few, or elaborate works, which can be appreciated by none but persons of exact learning or refined taste. Not such, but the nobler spirits who can venture boldly, and with a step altogether their own, upon the lofty steeps and broad highways of nature: the men who in science attain to the possession of truths which have a world-wide significance and value, or in literature give birth to productions which address themselves to the universal instincts of mankind, touch the springs of thought and feeling in every bosom, and become the common heritage of all generations and all lands. These, in the worldly sphere, are the gifted seers, who have an eye to look into nature's profounder secrets, and a tongue to interpret her meaning, such as is sure to meet with a response from the hearts of her children. And what such men are in respect to human and earthly things, the same in things spiritual and divine was Moses to the Old, and Jesus Christ to the New, Testament Church. Have not they too left behind them—above all, has not Jesus Christ left behind Him—the signature of his peerless elevation, in the incomparable breadth and wide-reaching importance of his revelations? It is not the remoter incidents, or more private details of the Divine economy, which his words disclose, but its grander interests and concerns; not a few streamlets merely that his Divine hand has laid open, but rather the perennial fountain itself of heavenly truth. Of no work could it be said with such manifold reason as of his, that it is not of an age, but for all time; in the heights it reaches, in the depths it explores, in the very form it assumes, it bears the impress of relative perfection and completeness. And it had been a mark, not of a more elevated, but of an inferior prophetical insight, it had stamped his mission as of a subordinate and temporary kind, rather than as one of primary importance and indestructible value, if his communications had turned more upon particular incidents of providence, and the varying evolutions of the world's history.

This signature of relative greatness and superiority in the *nature* of the Divine communications, which came by Christ, and in a measure also by Moses, is accompanied, and, as it were, accredited by another signature in the *mode* of communication. In the case of Moses, a difference in this latter respect was formally established by God himself, and for the express purpose of marking the higher place of power and influence which rightfully belonged to his servant. Rebuking the presumption of Aaron and Miriam, who had become jealous of the pre-eminent rank of their brother, and had been saying to the congregation, "Hath the Lord indeed spoken only by Moses? Hath he not spoken also by us?" the Lord interposed to give an authoritative decision, and said, "Hear now my words, If there be a prophet among you, I the Lord will make myself known to him in a vision, in a dream I will speak to him. Not so my servant Moses: he is faithful in all my house. Mouth to mouth I speak to him, and appearance (*i.e.*, as with open face), and not in dark speeches; and the similitude (form) of the Lord he beholds." (Num. xii. 6-8).[1] With an evident reference to this passage, the singular pre-eminence of Moses is again noticed near the close of his life, Deut. xxxiv. 10, "And there arose not a prophet since in Israel, like unto Moses, whom the Lord knew face to face." There was a certain amount of truth mixed up with the allegation of Aaron and Miriam: they did possess a kind of prophetical character (Exod. xv. 20, 21; Micah vi. 4), though of an inferior description as compared with the prophets generally, and greatly more so when viewed in reference to the position of Moses, betwixt whom and the other prophets a marked distinction is drawn. The distinction bears respect to a difference in the mode of revelation:—in the case of Moses, an open, waking, face to face intercommunion; while with the other prophets communications were to be made by dreams and visions. But this difference in the mode is made to rest upon a distinction in the office. Moses, as the mediator of the old covenant, had devolved on him the care of the whole house or kingdom of God, and consequently required to have the freest intercourse with heaven, and the most explicit instructions, to enable him to order everything aright. But the other and ordinary members of the prophetical order had no such high commission to fulfil. Standing upon the foundation already laid by Moses, and charged to enforce and maintain, but not allowed to remodel or dispense with any of its provisions, they necessarily had but a limited range of operations to mind, and messages of a more special kind to bring. These are the principal points of difference established in this fundamental passage in Numbers, between Moses and the other prophets. But the Jewish doctors are fond of multiplying the marks of superiority in

[1] See Appendix B.

Moses, for the purpose of investing him with a more transcendent glory. Thus Maimonides[1] finds as many as four notes of distinction possessed by Moses, and wanting in the prophets generally:—First, in God's speaking to him without the mediation of an angel, in direct discourse, as one man might do with another; secondly, in his having communications made to him openly, not by way of vision or dream; thirdly, in his being able to hold intercourse with God without suffering such corporeal languishings and faintings of nature as were sometimes at least experienced by men of ordinary prophetical gifts; and, lastly, in his having habitual access to God for supernatural revelations; while to others these came only at distant intervals, and at times also required to be preceded by a season of special preparation. These four grounds of distinction are merely an expansion, by the introduction of related circumstances and effects, of the two points noticed above from the passage in Numbers; they admit of being all comprised in the singular dignity of the office of Moses, and the consequent openness and freedom of his intercourse with heaven. It was in these peculiarly that he rose so much superior to all who succeeded him in the dispensation he introduced.

The privilege of holding free and open communication with heaven in respect to the secret things of God, however it may have distinguished Moses from other prophets, only attained its perfection in Christ, as in Him also the ground on which it rests becomes immeasurably higher and broader. Moses had the honour of being counted faithful as a servant over the house of God; yet it was only as a servant, at a time, too, when the house was comparatively small, and when the service to be done in it had for its highest aim the providing of "a testimony beforehand of those things which were to be spoken after." Christ, however, has the place of a son. It is his to exercise authority and rule in the Divine kingdom, as in his own house; and hence the revelations which came by

[1] Porta Mosis, Pockoke's Works, vol. i. pp. 63, 64.

Him, as in their own nature they were the highest that could be given, so in their form and manner they were the most natural and direct—the freest from whatever partook of outward formality or inward constraint. In Him the Spirit of the Father resided in unrestricted fulness; nay, He himself knew the Father, as one who possessed the same nature with the Father, and had access to his bosom: so that the words He spake, the doctrine He taught, and the works He performed were not more his own than the Father's. (John i. 18; iii. 13, 34; Matt. xi. 27, 29.) Here, therefore, the intercourse with heaven reached the highest degree of closeness and intimacy. It was not so properly God speaking to man, as God speaking in man and through man; and on that account speaking not only with a clearness and comprehension of view, but also with a self-possessed manner and a heaven-like elevation of tone peculiarly his own. To some extent, indeed, though very imperfectly as compared with Christ, the Apostles shared in this higher standing and freer communion, so, however, as to render palpable the difference betwixt them and the prophets of the earlier dispensation. For, excepting on two special occasions, those of which we have the record in the tenth chapter of the Acts and in the Apocalypse, they never appear to have received revelations in a trance or vision; and, like men habitually replenished with the Spirit, they spoke and wrote as if the Lord himself spoke and wrote in them (1 Cor. ii. 12; xiv. 37; 2 Cor. xiii. 3), and hence deemed it unnecessary to preface their discourses with the wonted formula of the prophets, "Thus saith the Lord." As possessed by them the prophetical gift corresponded with the comparative maturity and freedom of their New Testament position; and in the exercise of it, they seemed more like persons in their native element with full scope on every side for the free development of their susceptibilities and powers, than raised for a moment into a region not properly belonging to them.

Thus there were differences between prophet and prophet, and between one kind of prophetical agency and another; and by carefully noting these, we are enabled to draw the line of demarcation between what is essential, and what is merely circumstantial, in the matter.

1. It was, first of all, essential to the prophet, that he should have direct personal communications from above, constituting him, in a sense quite special and peculiar, the medium of intercommunion between heaven and earth; and, consequently, that he should possess a state and temper of soul, such as might form a proper recipiency for the divine communications. In no case could these be dispensed with. Not the actual communications, for on them depended the very substance of the message he had to deliver; not the suitable inward recipiency, for in that stood the capacity to apprehend, and the fidelity to use, what of supernatural insight might be imparted to him. That "vision and faculty divine," of which the world speaks, must have belonged to him, and in another manner than its most gifted seers can attain to; since he had to see what even these could not see, and to hear what they heard not; nay, not only to see and hear, but to give it willing audience in the inmost chamber of his soul. For Scripture knows as little of automaton prophets, as the world knows of automaton orators or poets. Spirit to spirit—a spirit in man rightly attempered and formed to the revelations presented to it by the Spirit of God:—such is the essential law of God's working in his more peculiar, not less than in his more common, operations on the souls of men. The prophet, therefore, was emphatically what he was also often designated, "a man of God." He was one who entered into God's mind, who breathed God's Spirit; whose very heart and soul were imbued with the truth and righteousness of God: so that, when he came forth to speak to his fellow-men, it was to utter feelings of which he was himself profoundly conscious—to proclaim a message which had first given light to his own eyes, and awakened a response in the sanctuary of his own bosom. This much was essential to the proper calling and agency of a prophet, and could not, save in cases altogether exceptional, be dispensed with.[1]

[1] See Appendix C.

But it was not essential—however commonly it may be so represented—that the prophet, when receiving the divine communication, should be agitated and convulsed in the process—should be moved and driven to and fro, as by some overpowering and arbitrary impulse. Such might occasionally have been the case with him; but never in the Hebrew prophet as in the heathen soothsayer (the *μαντίς*), who sought by external appliances to excite his spirit into a kind of sacred phrenzy, and appeared and spoke as one borne away by a really divine fervour. The settled rule in the sphere of Scripture prophecy was, that "the spirits of the prophets are subject to the prophets,"—the higher impulse stimulating their natural powers, and informing their minds with supernatural revelations, but never destroying either their personal freedom, or their proper individuality. And even the regulated excitation of entranced feeling was so far from being essential to the existence of a prophetic agency in its larger sense, that it had the least play in those who occupied the highest standing, and were most plentifully endowed with the prophetic spirit.

2. Secondly, in regard to the communication received by the prophet, it was essential that this should constitute a message respecting the things of God, which it became God, in a supernatural manner, to impart, and His people, through an extraordinary message, to receive. For, otherwise, the necessary condition of the prophet's existence, or the appropriate evidence of his mission, must have been wanting. He would have been like those dreamers, who came forth in the name of the Lord, to speak to the people, though they had seen nothing—nothing, at least, that required the immediate interposition of divine authority, and a direct revelation from heaven.

But it was not essential—it was a matter that depended upon the time and the occasion, whether in the word he spake there might be any explicit announcements of coming events in providence, or, if any, how far they might reach. In a more general sense every prophecy might be said to carry in its bosom a revelation of things to come, as it never failed to disclose the fundamental truths and principles of God's righteous government, and to represent them as the moral hinges on which the events of time and the issues of eternity perpetually turn. In Old Testament times, more especially, it could not fail to have much of a prospective bearing on the future, as every thing then pointed onwards to a more perfect state of things. But in the more specific sense of precise and definite information respecting the future operations of God in the world, prophecy, as we have seen, was far from being uniform. Neither did it always enter into such prospective details, nor, when it did, was the disclosure of these made to assume the appearance of the more direct and primary object it aimed at. It differed essentially from that soothsaying or divination, which prevailed so extensively in the heathen world, and which, by improperly prying into the future, always betokened distrust in God, and naturally allied itself with idolatry. The very criterion laid down by Moses for testing the claims of those who might assume to speak as prophets of the Most High, gave clear indication of this, and marked the relative position which the circumstantial here should bear to the essential in prophecy. If a prophet, it was said, Deut. xiii. 1–5, should arise, and give a sign or wonder which should come to pass; but, at the same time, should seek to draw people away after other gods, and lead them to forsake the worship and service of Jehovah, they were on no account to accredit his testimony, or regard him as a messenger of God, but were rather to suppose that through his plausible pretensions God was making trial of their fidelity. What could have more strikingly shown that the moral and religious element in prophecy, was ever to be viewed as occupying the primary, and the predictive no more than the secondary and subservient place? The ordinary prophet was not to be expected to introduce any thing essentially new. On the contrary, he was to make it patent to all that he stood on the old foundations; and as a true watchman of God, jealous for the honour and glory of Him who laid them, was bound to raise the alarm when he saw them in danger of being destroyed, and freshen up in men's souls the eternal principles of truth and duty in which they consisted. Only as an handmaid to this more determinate part of his function, was the disclosure of future events to be looked for at the hands of the prophet. And a surer sign, either of a false claim to the divine gift, or of a false apprehension and mistaken estimate of the true, could scarcely be named, than the reversing of this scriptural order, by raising the subsidiary element into the place of the principal.

3. Again, and in respect to the last stage of the process, it was essential that the prophet should faithfully record or utter the revelations he obtained. He must not only deliver his message, but deliver it as he had himself received it—like an impartial and incorrupt witness declaring what his eyes had seen, and his ears had heard, in the visions of God. No more in this department of his calling, when dealing with men in behalf of God, was it lawful for him to confer with flesh and blood, than when, in the other, he was dealt with by God in behalf of men. A select ambassador of heaven, he had but one thing, in a manner, to do—to speak what God had put into his heart, without fearing the face of man, or listening to the suggestions of his lower nature. Had this condition failed—as for a moment it did fail in the case of Jonah—the indispensable characteristic of a prophet had been wanting.

But it was not essential, that in this outward communication of the light that shone within him, there should have been any thing like forcible pressure or violence in the tone and manner in which it was done. A certain amount of this there may have been—there occasionally was; yet not "as a form necessarily cleaving to every thing prophetical;" as if the prophetical, "in its works of greater moment and abiding faithfulness, could not possibly exist without it."[1] It could not, indeed, exist without the internal impulse of holy feeling and irrepressible energy of purpose, bearing the prophet's soul aloft, and rendering it superior to all earthly considerations. But this

[1] Ewald, Propheten, p. 8.

may be found in a region of perfect calmness and serenity, nay, found there in the highest degree. It was, in reality, so found for the most part by Moses, but always and entirely by Jesus Christ, whose words, even when laying open the sublimest mysteries, are remarkable for nothing more than the perfect composure and unruffled calmness of spirit which they breathe. Whatever, therefore, might, at any time, appear in the prophet of disturbed feeling or undue excitation, so far from being a necessary accompaniment of his prophetical calling, is rather to be ascribed to his own imperfect elevation of soul, or the embarrassments of his outward condition. If he was himself conscious of some difficulty in fully embracing as his own the word committed to him—or if he had to proclaim that word to a people who were maintaining an attitude of stout-hearted resistance to the will of God, then something of violent agitation, or even of impassioned vehemence in his manner, might not unnaturally be looked for. But it was still only an incidental and separable adjunct, not an essential attribute, of a prophet's calling.

Now, from the whole of the considerations here advanced, and more especially from what has been stated regarding the quite singular nature of the position occupied by Moses and Christ, in respect to the revelation of the Divine will, one can readily understand how they should be so commonly placed apart from the strictly prophetical order. In reality, it was in them that the spirit of prophecy had its noblest exercise, and rose to its highest perfection. But this very perfection threw so wide a gulph between them and the persons who possessed the more ordinary prophetical gifts, that the latter alone came to be regarded as by way of distinction the prophets, and the two others were contemplated as moving in a loftier sphere. Hence, even John the Baptist is called by our Lord, "more than a prophet," though it was in the character of a prophet, that he had been previously announced (Isa. xl. 6, Mal. iv. 5, Luke i. 16, 17); and, beyond doubt, it was the distinctive work of a prophet in which his mission had its fulfilment.

But the same considerations, which account for the usual

restriction of the term prophet to others than Moses and Christ, also explains how the word spoken by these others should partake largely of predictions, and should even thence derive, in the popular conception, its predominant characteristic. It naturally arose from the dependant and supplementary nature of such prophecy, as compared with the revelations brought in by Moses and Christ. In these the more important and fundamental things of the Divine economy had already been established. The truths, on which the respective dispensations were based, might afterwards be reiterated anew, or applied to the different phases of error and corruption which successively arose; germs of spiritual thought implanted there, might be expanded and matured; existing institutions also, after seasons of decay, might have the breath of a new and more vigorous life breathed into them: all this might be done, in connection with the one dispensation or the other, and, to provide for its accomplishment, was always one great design of God in the bestowal of prophetical gifts. But the doing of such work, from its very nature of a subsidiary and ministerial kind, could not of itself, even in the most favourable circumstances, yield so convincing a proof of direct communication with God, and of supernatural insight into the counsels of heaven, as the clear delineation of yet future events in Providence. Nor could the prophets, as the more select agents and witnesses of God among men, be properly qualified for their important mission, unless they had been enabled to direct their eye into the future, and make some disclosure of its coming issues. For, it was to these issues they naturally pointed for the confirmation of the principles they affirmed, and the vindication of the part they took in the ever-proceeding controversy between sin and righteousness. So that, whether we look to the nature of their calling, or to what was needed for its proper authentication, it could scarcely fail that prophecy, in its more regular and wonted ministrations, should partake much of a predictive character, and by indications of supernatural foresight, should often give conclusive evidence of its Divine origin.

It is of prophecy in this more special and restricted sense—

of prophecy as containing announcements, more or less specific, of the future—that the word must be chiefly employed in discussions like the present. In this sense we must, henceforth, be understood to use the term, where no intimation to the contrary is given. It is, undoubtedly, a great limitation of the Scriptural idea, and embraces what is but a particular and subordinate province of the field. This must be carefully borne in mind, if we would either form a correct estimate of the subject itself, or arrive at safe and well-grounded principles of interpretation. To set out with such a definition of prophecy in general as this, that "it is a prediction of some contingent circumstance or event in the future, received by immediate and direct revelation,"[1]—a definition which, if not formally given, is, for the most part, tacitly assumed in works on prophecy—betokens, in the first instance, a partial view of what the prophetic field properly embraces, and it must inevitably lead to practical mistakes in the treatment of particular portions belonging to it.

[1] So Vitringa, Typus Proph. Doc. p. 1.

CHAPTER II.

THE PLACE OF PROPHECY IN HISTORY, AND THE ORGANIC CONNECTION OF THE ONE WITH THE OTHER.

FROM the relation of prophecy in the more restricted, to prophecy in the more general and comprehensive sense, we come, by a very natural transition, to consider the relation of prophecy to history. For the consideration of this point also will be found to turn, in some degree, on the distinction between the two aspects of prophecy already noticed—the fundamental and the subsidiary; and will suggest reflections as to the proper treatment of the prophetic volume very closely allied to some of the considerations urged in the preceding chapter.

The most cursory glance over the pages of Scripture can leave no doubt that prophecy, in so far as it consists in predictions of coming events in providence, exists there in very various and irregular proportions. In the Old Testament—to which alone we shall for the present refer—it appears somewhat like a river, small in its beginnings, and though still proceeding, yet often losing itself for ages under ground, then bursting forth anew with increased volume, and at last rising into a swollen stream—greatest by far when it has come within prospect of its termination. During the whole antediluvian period of the world, it could scarcely be said to exist, excepting at the beginning and the close; and even then only in small amount and apart from any regular official ministration. The first prophecy, called forth by the circumstances of the fall, delineates in graphic, but general and comprehensive outlines, the leading characteristics of the world's history; projects, as it were, the channels alike of evil and of good, in which the stream of events was destined to run, and gives sure prognostication of the final ascendancy of the good over the evil. Indefinite as this prophecy was, it was of unspeakable moment, on account of the promise it embodied to the heart of faith, whereby, in the midst of brooding darkness and wide-wasting destruction, it lighted up the hope of better things to come. As a prediction, however, of contingent events, destined to appear in the future, this primeval word of life is scarcely to be mentioned, since it rather announced great principles of working, and pointed to ultimate results, than defined, beforehand, particular acts of Providence. And this holds yet more of the prophecy of Enoch (Jude v. 14, 15), which may be regarded merely as an application of the prophecy uttered at the fall, to the times of growing apostacy and wickedness in which he lived. It declared the certainty of God's appearing to check the temporary triumph of the adversary, and establish the just. The revelation to Noah of the general deluge, is again but the more specific application of Enoch's announcement, and is, in truth, the first definite prediction we meet with—being required for the support of Noah's faith, amid an almost universal backsliding, and for the direction of his course in respect to the approaching catastrophe.

Subsequently to the deluge, a series of prophecies follow each other at considerable intervals, not unlike in their general character. There is, first, Noah's own prediction respecting the state and prospects of his posterity—a prediction, indeed, considerably more definite in its intimations than that pronounced at the fall; but still, like this, pointing chiefly to the essential principles of the Divine government, and to the relation in which his offspring, by the three lines of descent, should stand to these, and through these to each other. Then, at the distance of some centuries come the revelations to Abraham respecting his seed, and the closely dependant prophecies of Isaac and Jacob to their children—each of them successively growing in precision and definiteness, but dwelling still upon the relative positions and prospects of stems, and races, and tribes, rather than upon individual personages or particular events. The promise of Shiloh, as a centre of unity and peace, to arise out of the tribe of Judah, is the most specific in the series, and for the first time gives prominence to a single individual in the perspective of the more distant future. But, as a whole, those patriarchal prophecies turned mainly on the general points, through what line of descent the more peculiar blessing of the covenant with Abraham was to flow—how, even within this favoured line distinctions of higher and lower, better and worse, should exist, according as the persons concerned might stand related to the moral ends of the covenant; and how, along with the heritage of good promised and secured, there should be also the constant intermingling of struggles, conflicts and sorrows, necessarily calling for the exercise of faith and patience on the part of the true children of the covenant. It holds of these patriarchal predictions, as well as of those which preceded them, that not one of them was given "like an insulated phenomenon, or merely to demonstrate the prescience of their all-wise Creator; but were all by Him engrafted upon the exigency of times and persons, and made to serve as a light of direction to the attentive observers of them, before the event had set the seal to their truth."[1] Their primary and immediate object unquestionably was to give, as the ever-changing circumstances of the world required, counsel or encouragement to the children of promise, in respect to their more peculiar trials and dangers, hopes and obligations. And in so far as they may have tended to produce any other results, the effect could only be regarded as subsidiary and incidental.

Centuries of silence and darkness pass away after the last words of Jacob were uttered, without any addition being made to the prophetic oracles. But the time at length came for carrying into fulfilment the promise of an inheritance

[1] "Davidson on Prophecy," p. 99, who makes this just remark on prophecy in general, without, however, having sufficiently investigated, or freely applied, the principle involved in it.

made to the seed of Abraham; and then, with the appearance and mission of Moses, the well-nigh expiring light of prophecy bursts forth at once into a sudden blaze—but prophecy (as formerly stated) chiefly of the more fundamental and primary kind, dealing less in predictions of coming events than in the great principles of truth and duty, as connected with the introduction of a new phase of the Divine administration. There *were* certain distinct assurances given through Moses to the Israelites regarding their possession of Canaan, and a series of hypothetical predictions uttered regarding the evil and the good that might afterwards befal them there (Lev. xxvi.; Deut. xxviii., xxxiii.)—hypothetical, inasmuch as the blessings and the cursings prospectively announced, were uttered merely as deductions flowing with infallible certainty from the government under which they were placed, and depending for their real character on the course actually pursued by future generations. But, if we except such parts of the writings of Moses, the revelations which came by him cannot be termed prophecies in the sense now understood. The predictions spoken by Balaam—though appearing only as a sort of interlude in the Mosaic record—possess more of the simply predictive element. The circumstances of the time, especially the perilous situation of Israel, required something of this description. And as it could be most effectually done from the camp of the adversary, so the extraordinary course was taken of making use of the heathen diviner to send forth rays of light respecting the future purposes of God, which were to be afterwards expanded into yet more full and explicit delineations.

The age of Moses is succeeded by another long break in the prophetic chain. Persons with prophetic insight occasionally appear during the period of the Judges, but only as rare and glimmering lights, for it was a time for heroic action rather than for lofty utterances. And prophecy, in its formal character, comes into view only in the age of Samuel, with whom properly originates the prophetical order of the Old Testament. And, in the history of this order, it is to be remarked how small a part prediction plays in its earlier operations. The series opens with it in the loud and terrible denunciation of judgment which came forth against the degenerate house of Eli (1 Sam. ii., iii.), and it recurs from time to time afterwards, as in the difficult and perplexing circumstances connected with the elevation of Saul to the throne, the election of David in his stead, and the rending of David's kingdom in the time of Rehoboam. At this period, however, the predictions uttered were manifestly of a quite occasional and circumscribed nature. They gave forth, indeed, a supernatural light, such as was required by the members of the covenant in seasons of emergency and danger, but one that, neither in its reception nor its general diffusion, engaged more than a fragmentary portion of the prophetical activity of the period. This activity, originating in Samuel, and by him organized and perpetuated through regular institutions, called *Schools of the Prophets*, exerted itself mainly as a spirit of revival, and spent its energies greatly more in conducting practical operations, than in searching into or disclosing hidden mysteries. This was what the circumstances of the time especially required. It was not so much new revelations that were needed, as an inworking into the feelings and habits of the people of the revelations which had already been received. The members of the prophetical order, therefore, usually appear as the more select portion of the Levitical and priestly classes, to which also they usually, by birth, belonged. Hence they sometimes took part in the performance of services that were strictly of a priestly character (1 Sam. ix. 13, etc.), but more commonly were employed in holding meetings for devotional exercises and spiritual instruction, in the hope of thereby rekindling the flame of piety, and diffusing the fear of God throughout the land. Such seems to have been the distinctive nature of the prophetic agency for centuries after the age of Samuel. The prophets were, in a peculiar sense, the spiritual watchmen of Judah and Israel—the representatives of divine truth and holiness, whose part it was to keep a wakeful and jealous eye upon the manners of the times, to detect and reprove the symptoms of defection which appeared, and by every means in their power foster and encourage the spirit of real godliness. And such pre-eminently was Elijah, who is therefore taken in Scripture itself as the type of the whole prophetical order in this earlier stage of its development,—a man of heroic energy of action rather than of prolific thought or excellent discourse. The words he spake were few, but they were words spoken as from the secret place of thunder, and seemed more like decrees issuing straight from the presence of the Eternal, than the utterances of one of like passions with ourselves. Appearing at a time when the very foundations were out of course, and the most flagrant enormities were openly practised in the high places of the land, he boldly stood forth in the name of God, as a wrestler in the cause of righteousness—not so much to plead for it, as to avenge and vindicate it, as if the time had come for deciding the controversy by deeds rather than by words. For this gigantic work power was given him to smite the earth with plagues, and to torment those who dwelt on it, and who were corrupting it by their wicked deeds (Rev. xi.). But when the results aimed at by this severe and stern agency were in a good measure accomplished, when by terrible things in righteousness the daring of the adversary had been quelled, and an open field had been won for active operations, his mission called him to work of another kind—such work as was fitly symbolised by the still small voice at Horeb, in which now, and not in the whirlwind, the earthquake or the fire, the Lord made Himself known to His servant. Enough, it was virtually said to the prophet, of such overawing displays of power as have hitherto been put forth. They have already served their more immediate purpose, but work of a more peaceful and regenerative nature still remains to be done. The decayed schools of the prophets must be revived, and spiritual labours prosecuted, if haply through such instrumentality the hearts of the children may be quickened into newness of life, and turned back to the Lord their God. And so, after he had by patient and faithful exertion approved himself in this part also of his prophetical mission, he was received up to heaven in a chariot of glory.

The only remarkable divergence from the general course which appears in this great series of prophetical agency, after the pattern of Samuel, is that of David's circle—including, beside himself, Nathan, Solomon, and the more distinguished men of certain Levite families, who took part in the composition of the Psalms. So far this collateral branch of prophecy corresponds with the main stem, that here also the grand aim was of a practical kind. It had for its direct object the infusing of new life and vigour into the Mosaic institutions, and promoting, among all classes of the people, the cultivation of that righteousness which they were given to plant and nourish. But, with this general resemblance, the agency of David and his coadjutors differed from that of the contemporary prophetical order, in the more judicial character of the measures employed on the side of righteousness, and also in the frequent composition of inspired writings. Here there was not only action, but action pursuing its ends through the channels of constituted government, with the view of purging out evil from the kingdom, and rendering it in reality, what it was in name, a commonwealth of saints. And, along with this, sometimes also without it, there was ever and anon flowing the pure stream of didactic and devotional poetry. Popular and sacred song, chaunted first upon the lyre of the son of Jesse, and afterwards continued by a noble band of like-minded companions and followers, breathed forth in lofty strains the spiritual essence of the solemnities of Zion, which it also touchingly inwrought with the feelings of a profound and widely-spread personal experience. By consecrating such productions to the interest of religion, and even associating them, as was usually done, with the service of the sanctuary, the believing Israelite was supplied with forms of thought and feeling suited to all the moods of his soul, and the diversified circumstances of his condition. And to these spiritual songs, so fragrant with the odour of Divine truth and sanctified experience, were added others (indited after the promise brought by Nathan to David, respecting the perpetuity of the kingdom in David's line), usually designated, by way of eminence, the Messianic Psalms, which, with the other elements, combine also the predictive, by pointing to the greater personage and nobler results in which the kingdom was to find its ultimate completion. Of both parts of the Psalmodic poetry, it may be said, that the primary tendency and design was to inspirit the entire framework of the ancient economy with the measure of life, of which it was susceptible, and to carry its members to the highest degree of light and purity it might be possible for them to reach under that provisional state of things.

In process of time, however, it became evident that all these extraordinary efforts, both by the prophetical order generally, and in the collateral line of operations originated by David, could not avail to stem the tide of corruption, and raise the affairs of the old economy to the desired elevation, or even to save them from fatal disorder and ruin. Too manifestly the external fabric of its institutions must be taken down, and the kingdom of God among men cast in another mould. As soon as this melancholy result came distinctly into view, then began the later, and, as regards specific predictions, the more fully developed stage of ancient prophecy. It commenced with Hosea and Amos (if not with Jonah), in the kingdom of Israel, and with Joel and Isaiah, in that of Judah—and had its distinctive characteristic in this, that while the prophets did not cease to lift their voice against prevailing evils, and strive for a return to the old paths, yet, seeing every thing as it then stood tottering to its foundation, they chiefly directed their eye to the more distant future, and disclosed the purposes of God respecting the higher development of the divine kingdom now in prospect, along with the destinies awaiting the earthly states and dominions which had disputed, or might yet dispute, with it the claim for empire. In this period, as the prophetical writings were greatly more numerous than in any previous one, so, from the very nature of the case, they go more into details about the future, and supply our amplest materials for comparing the anticipations of prophecy with the subsequent events of history.

In this brief survey, we have purposely confined our view to the more general features of the subject, such as may be perceived on the most cursory inspection, and about which there can scarcely be any difference of opinion. The more minute investigations connected with its several parts, will be matter for future inquiry and consideration. Meanwhile, from the outline itself, various thoughts naturally suggest themselves as to the relations of prophecy to history, and these of some importance for a correct appreciation of the nature and function of prophecy.

1. First of all, it is obvious, that the prophecy of Scripture is closely interwoven with its history. So far from standing by itself in a sort of isolation and independence, it is in connection with the facts of history that prophetical revelations took at once their rise and their form. It is so in whichever light the revelations of prophecy be contemplated—whether in the higher and more enlarged sense of Divine communications respecting the mind and purposes of God, or in the more limited sense of predictions of things to come. As prophecy, however, in this latter sense, appears in Scripture as only a particular and comparatively subordinate department of a wider field, it naturally enters less in this sense than in the other, into the bulk and texture of sacred history. Prophetic communications and prophetic agency occur often in the greatest frequency, and tell with the most powerful effect upon the course of events, when little is to be met with of predictions—at least of clear and definite predictions—of coming events in providence.

But even in this narrower sense—the one also with which we have now more especially to do—the connection between prophecy and history is alike close and pervading. A prophetic thread runs through the whole of the inspired records, and binds together both ends of revelation. To a certain extent this is not peculiar to the Bible, but belongs to it in common with the products of human thought and observation, which record the facts of providence, or unfold the principles on which they proceed. For, as has been justly said,[1] "prophecy is not an anomaly; it springs from the nature of Jehovah, the self-existent and eternal, who gives continuity to existence, and perpetuity to knowledge. Philosophy is prophetic as well as religion—the fact discovered to-day becomes the prediction of that which will take place under exactly similar circumstances when ages have rolled away, as long as the present system of creation remains."[2] True, as far as it goes; though not by any means the whole truth as regards the Word of God; since it places the prophetic element in the supernatural sphere simply on a footing with what may be found in the natural, and makes no account of the more peculiar points of contact which Scripture presents between heaven and earth, and the more vital links with which the present is there bound with the future. While there is a common agreement, there is also a specific difference; on the side of Scripture there is a marked relative superiority. We would not ignore the truth so happily and profoundly uttered by the poet, that

> "There is a history in all men's lives,
> Figuring the nature of the times deceased;
> The which observed, a man may prophesy
> With a near aim of the main chance of things,
> As yet not come to life, which in their seeds
> And weak beginnings lie intreasured."

But sacred history furnishes other materials of a prophetic

[1] Douglas on the Structure of Prophecy, p. 4.

[2] On this ground Coleridge said admirably of Burke—"He possessed, and had sedulously sharpened, the eye which sees all things, actions, and events, in relation to the laws that determine their existence, and circumscribe their possibility. He referred habitually to principles. He was a scientific statesman; and therefore a seer. For every principle contains in itself the germs of a prophecy; and as the prophetic power is the essential principle of science, so the fulfilment of its oracles supplies the outward, and (to men in general) the only test of its claim to the title."—Biog. Lit., I., p. 195.

nature than are to be found in "men's lives," or in the common operations of providence. For God is in the Church as He is not in the world; and the history which records the manifestations He gives of Himself in the former, has aspects to unfold of His perfections and character, which will be sought for in vain amidst the lights of natural science, or the annals of earthly transactions. The fundamental difference lies in this—that in the Church there is the revelation of God's grace; and grace from its very nature is instinct with the spirit of prophecy. What is it, indeed, but the exhibition of Divine mercy, in a way of righteousness, for the prospective recovery and blessing of the fallen? Of necessity, therefore, it anticipates not only a future, but a future better than the present: it awakens desire and hope in respect to things not seen as yet, and points expectation onward to their coming realisation. Hence the first manifestation of grace is also the first prophecy; a prophecy, indeed, vague and indeterminate as to particular personages or events, but perfectly explicit as regards the certainty of a good in prospect, purposed by God, to be looked and waited for by man. And continually as the work of grace proceeded on its course—as it brought its plans and operations more fully within the reach of men's discernment, and the region of their responsibilities—especially from the time its professed recipients were taken to be the members of a visible kingdom, and had their expectations of coming good associated with the affairs of a local territory and complicated earthly relationships, it was impossible but that with the growth of the historical element, the prophetical also should increase, and should, in many respects, become more varied and definite in its prospective intimations of the future.

Prophecy, therefore, being from the very first inseparably linked with the plan of grace unfolded in Scripture, is, at the same time, the necessary concomitant of sacred history. The two mutually act and re-act on each other. Prophecy gives birth to the history; the history in turn, as it moves onward to its destined completion, at once fulfils prophecies already given, and calls forth farther revelations. And so far from possessing the character of an excrescence, or existing merely as an anomaly in the procedure of God toward men, prophecy cannot even be rightly understood, unless viewed in relation to the order of the Divine dispensations, and its actual place in history.

Let it not, however, be inferred from this mutual interconnection, that prophecy and history are altogether alike in nature; or in such a sense assimilated, that by the rule and measure of the one, we must determine the import and bearing of the other. Such, too often, has been the manner of dealing with the subject by those who have perceived and exhibited the connection; as if, on the one side, prophecy could not rise above history—nor, on the other, history be more precise and determinate than prophecy. However closely related the two are to each other, they still have their own distinctive characteristics, and through these, their respective ends to serve. History is the occasion of prophecy, but not its measure; for prophecy rises above history, borne aloft by wings, which carry it far beyond the present, and which it derives, not from the past occurrences of which history takes cognizance, but from Him to whom the future and the past are alike known. It is the communication of so much of His own supernatural light, as He sees fit to let down upon the dark movements of history, to show whither they are conducting. For the most part, the persons who live in the midst of events, are the least capable of understanding aright the character of their age. But God is elevated above it, and, by the word of prophecy, He so informs the minds of his people in respect to the end, that they come also to know better than they could otherwise have done, the beginning and the middle. And as prophecy, from its intimate connection with history, has its regular progress and development, there are two considerations that ought not to be forgotten in any attempts to ascertain its proper nature and import. The one is, that the meaning of a prophecy is not to be restrained and limited by conclusions deduced simply from the historical circumstances out of which it may have sprung, but from the words of the prophecy itself; since the circumstances only prompt and fashion the words, but by no means hold them restricted within the same compass. And along with this, there is the further consideration, that since prophecy has God, and not history, for its author—has only been conceived in the lap of history, but not properly produced by it—it must ever have in it something divinely rich and great, reaching, not only beyond the things presently existing, but also, it may be, beyond what even, with the help of these, it might be possible beforehand adequately to conceive.[1]

2. These remarks, however, only touch the more obvious and formal part of the connection of prophecy with history. The connection goes much farther and deeper. For, we observe, secondly, that the sacred history itself is deeply pervaded by the prophetic element. Not only is it to be viewed as the germinant soil out of which predictions were ever springing forth, but in the very facts and statements it records, predictions, though of a somewhat concealed and general kind, lie imbedded. The historical transactions of Scripture are part of a great plan, which stretches from the fall of man to the final consummation of all things in glory; and in so far as they reveal the mind of God toward man, they carry a respect to the future not less than to the present. Their having such a prospective significance rests on the fundamental principle, that in His character and purposes, God is unchangeably the same; so that, seeing the end from the beginning, and planning all with infinite wisdom, as parts of a progressive and consistent whole, the truths embodied in the transactions of one period necessarily retained their efficacy, and reappeared in the corresponding transactions of another. Hence, the freedom, and the frequency also, with which prophecy, in its delineations of the future, serves itself of the antecedent facts and

[1] In these closing remarks I have adopted the thoughts, though not the precise words of Delitzsch, in his Biblish-Proph. Theologie, p. 184, where he opposes the view of Hofmann, that history must be made the measure and rule of prophecy. Another, and, in this country, a more common form of the historical interpretation of prophecy, will fall to be noticed afterwards, when we come to treat of the prophetic style.

characters of history. As—to point only to a few examples out of many—when the Psalmist announces in Ps. cx., a royal priest after the order of Melchizedec, which implied, that the relations of Melchizedec's time and person, should somehow revive again in the future; or, when, by a mode of representation common to all the prophets, the successive stages of Israel's history are described as experiences once more to be undergone (Hos. ii., Ezek. iv. xx., etc.). Hence, too, the use perpetually made by the apostles of the notices of patriarchal and Israelitish history, as a kind of preparatory exhibition of the truths and relations of the gospel (Rom. iv. 4, 17; 1 Cor. x. 1-11; Rev. iv. 1-6, etc.); and by our Lord himself, who so often appears retracing the footsteps of His forefathers after the flesh—re-echoing from His own bosom the recorded utterances of their faith and hope—and appropriating to Himself the words that had been addressed to them, of counsel and encouragement, (Matt. iv. 1-10; Luke xxiii. 46, etc.).

Nor is even this the whole; for, the more important and characteristic features of the ancient dispensation—the erection of the tabernacle in the wilderness, with its complicated ritual of worship—the conquest and possession of Canaan—the institution of the earthly kingdom, and the building of the temple on Mount Zion—what are they all but so many prophetic forms and symbols of things to come? In themselves they were but imperfect and provisional means, incapable, from their very nature, of reaching their proper end, and ever, in a manner, proclaiming the necessity of a higher order of things to substantiate and perfect their design. And so, when the higher things actually came—when Christ's work and kingdom entered among men, they did not assume the aspect of something absolutely new, but appeared rather as the natural result and completion of the old—the working out of the plan of God in accordance with its Divine and spiritual nature, and establishing it on its immoveable foundations.

Indeed, it is as true of the history, as of the prophecy of Old Testament Scripture, that it points to the incarnation and work of Christ for man's redemption as its great terminating object. *There* alone it finds its proper explanation and its adequate result. It records manifestations on the part of God, and experiences on the part of His people, which, in respect to that ulterior event, are all anticipative and preparatory; since in them God was ever manifesting Himself under the limits and conditions, sometimes also in the form, of humanity, for the purpose of saving men from the evils and dangers of sin; while yet the salvation, which might effectually and for ever accomplish this, is never reached, and remains still an object of desire and hope. Those Divine theophanies, therefore, with the human experiences of grace and redemption connected with them—from the walking of God in Eden, when He came to reveal the purpose of salvation, to the last appearances of the angel of the covenant to counsel and comfort the released exiles of Babylon—the whole of these, when rightly understood, are so many converging lines that meet in the God-man and His redemptive work, as their common centre. They are a prophecy in action of that personal union of the divine and human in Christ, by which alone the gulph between God and man could be closed, and the breath of a new and higher life infused into the fallen. Viewed apart from this consummating process, they seem like the disjointed materials and fragmentary projections of some vast building, which cannot attain to proper harmony and completeness, till the Great Architect comes to finish the work. But let them be viewed, as they should be, in their relation and subservience to what was to come, and then they will be seen to give evidence throughout of the presiding agency of God, planning and directing all with infinite skill, so as to render the past a suitable and growing preparation for the future, and present in the antecedent history of redemption the prelude of redemption itself. But for this redemption, foreseen and contemplated by the mind of God, there could as little have been such an antecedent history, as there could have been a volume of prophecy springing out of it, having for its pervading and animating spirit the testimony of Jesus.

Thus it appears that the Old Testament is impregnated

throughout with the prophetical element, and not as by caprice or accident, but from the very aim and character of its revelations. The more specific and formal predictions it contains, do not stand out in solitary grandeur by themselves, like eminences rising abruptly from a surrounding level; they are only the higher elevations, the occasional mountain-peaks, from which the eye of faith was allowed at times to descry more clearly the shadows of the coming age. But all around also, there were prospective contrivances and points of contact between the present and the future. "As, in a writer of genius, his individual, great thoughts appear like lilies on the surface of the water, groundless and rootless, and yet are sustained by one common soil, so also the individual prophets of God's people are not to be regarded as scattered manifestations of the Divine Spirit, but rooted in one common soil,—namely, in the prophetic subsistence of the nation itself, and its institutions."[1] Besides, there were occasional arrangements and transactions, in which the prophetical element assumed a somewhat more distinct shape, and which, consequently, held a closer affinity with the announcements of prophecy. Such, for example, were the things accomplished in Abraham, as the head of that covenant, which was to diffuse life and blessing through all the families of mankind. Occupying this high position, a position that so manifestly linked together the present and the future, he was constituted by God, in the truest sense, a representative man, in whose calling and course of life there was to be a real significance for others down to the latest generations. There, as in a glass, the children of the covenant, of every age, were to find a prospective exhibition of the things which concerned their relation to God—what they were as children of nature, what they become as partakers of grace, what they are called to strive after, and what they may expect to be, as the heirs of blessing. And so again, at a later period, in the case of David, who was also the head of a covenant, and, indeed, of the same covenant, only

[1] Tholuck, Comm. on Hebrews, Diss. i.

made to assume a form more immediately adapted to the working out and administration of the blessing. All the lines of his eventful history pointed, like prophetic signs, to the future, and were by himself employed, through the direction of the Spirit, as the materials of many vivid delineations that had for their object the person and kingdom of Messiah. Daniel's history, too, was in the closest manner connected with his prophecy. The one may fitly be called a type of the other, and on that account, doubtless, occupies so large a place in his book. The grand aim of the revelations communicated by him, was to unfold the progress of the kingdom of God from deep depression, and through manifold struggles, to the supreme place of honour and glory, and Daniel himself is first made to pass through like experiences to a corresponding elevation. The Hebrew captive became at length the real head of the wisdom and destinies of Babylon, an embodied symbol of the ultimate transference of the kingdom, and power, and glory, of the world, to the saints of the Most High. Generally, indeed, it might be said of the prophets that their personal history was ordered so as to form a typical accompaniment to the prophecies they delivered.

Nor, among those prophetical elements and affinities interwoven with the history and institutions of the Old Testament, should we omit to notice a class of persons who made a near approach to the prophetical order, and might not unfitly be designated prophets in action. We refer to the Nazarites, who, in one passage, are named along with the prophets, as if there were no very marked distinction between them: "And I raised up of your sons for prophets, and of your young men for Nazarites" (Amos ii. 11). The Nazarites were simply the separated ones, persons who stood apart from the mass of the community, as under a special vow or act of consecration to the Lord. Individually, and for a set time or purpose, they were to give a living exhibition of that holy surrender and devotedness to God which should ever have been exemplified by the covenant-people as a whole. They were, therefore, a kind of election within the election. And the peculiar restraints and services imposed on them had this alone for their object: To present the Nazarites as pattern-men, withdrawn from everything fitted, whether by undue exhilaration or by mournful sadness, to mar their communion with the pure and blessed life of God. According as they abounded in Israel, there were to be found among the people so many embodied lessons, or palpable manifestations of that covenant faithfulness, which it was always the first part of a prophet's calling, as well as the sum of Israel's duty, to illustrate and maintain. But it was possible for the Nazarite to be brought into still closer resemblance to the prophet. There might be circumstances connected with his vow of separation to the Lord, which served to mark him out as a special gift of heaven, or, in some more peculiar sense, a witness of the truth of God. That such was, occasionally, at least, the case, may naturally be inferred from the language of Amos, in which the Nazarites are mentioned as among the singular proofs furnished by God of His goodness to His people. They are also referred to by Jeremiah in a way that seems to betoken the high place they held among the peculiar lights and instruments of blessing in Israel. "Her Nazarites," he says (Lam. iv. 7), "were purer than snow, they were whiter than milk, they were more ruddy in body than rubies, their polishing was of sapphire." And in two very remarkable cases, those of Samuel and John the Baptist, cases in which instruction by action was to go hand in hand with that of direct teaching, the obligation of the Nazarite vow was by Divine ordination made coeval with birth, and associated also with the higher gifts and calling of a prophet.

The most singular example, however, of the whole class, and the one that, in its simply Nazaritish character, bore most distinctly the aspect of a prophecy, is that of Samson—in itself a kind of sacred enigma. Not, however, an inexplicable enigma, if viewed in connection with the circumstances of the time, and with due regard to its prophetical character. The time was one of backsliding and rebuke. The marvellous story begins immediately after it has been said, that "the children of Israel did evil again in the sight of the Lord, and the Lord delivered them into the hand of the Philistines forty years." Judges had been raised up for their deliverance before, with only a partial and temporary success, for the root of the evil was never properly reached. But the Lord now bethought Him of trying, as His chosen instrument of working, a Nazarite, wonderful in his very birth, and wonderful still more for the singular gift with which he was endowed,—yet trying him not solely, nor even chiefly, for the purpose of breaking the Philistine yoke, but for what was more urgently needed, the imparting of a proper insight into God's mind, and awakening a right spirit of devotedness to His fear. It was this which alone could re-establish the people in honour and blessing, as the oppression and miseries that lay upon them were the result merely of broken vows, and unfaithful dealing in the covenant of God. And how could the requisite instruction be more touchingly and impressively conveyed to them, than by such a marvellous and mournful story as presents itself in the life of Samson? A child is supernaturally promised and given, expressly on account of the exigency of the times—the child of a mother laid, for the occasion, under the restrictions of the Nazarite vow, and himself appointed to be a Nazarite from his birth—one so emphatically called to separate himself to the Lord, that to every thoughtful mind he must have readily seemed a personified Israel, the peculiar representative of a people standing under covenant to God. "The child grew, and the Lord blessed him; and the Spirit of the Lord began to move him at times;" but only, it would seem, in the lower sphere of operations, in the display of supernatural bodily might, and the performance of astonishing feats of strength and prowess. We can descry, through those fitful and terrific movements of his early life, a zeal glowing in the breast of this young Nazarite, capable of daring and accomplishing the greatest things. But we watch in vain to see it rising to the proper height; it looks more like the earth-sprung zeal of patriotism, than that of a holy and self-denying regard to the glory of God. Ready to seize on every opportunity to afflict the Philistines as enemies, it burns not against them as the servants of idolatry and corruption; and so, while at one moment he rushes on them in his fury, at another he takes them to his familiar embrace, and is even bent on having one of their daughters for his wife. It was precisely the defect and failing of his people. To them, too, collectively belonged a noble superiority in outward standing and privilege above their idolatrous neighbours. They were a people of relatively high endowments, and were bound together by a strong international and patriotic spirit. But they lacked the true zeal of God, and hence were ever ready to lose sight of what was in itself their grand distinction, and the foundation of all that they possessed of good—their divine call to the knowledge and service of Jehovah. For such a people to lose this was, in a manner, to lose all, since, by losing it, they necessarily became false witnesses of God, and were justly surrendered by Him to the powers of evil, which they should have held in subjection.

The moral weakness, therefore, which appeared in Samson, was but a reflection of the hereditary and prevailing evil in Israel. And God did with it in the present case as He ever in effect does with evil of that description, when unrighteously clung to: He shut it up to a particular channel, allowed it to take only that course which might render the example of this externally strong, but internally feeble, Nazarite, a more exact and instructive image of the people whom he represented. Hence, as one carried away by a resistless impulse, he must go to woo and wed among the uncircumcised Philistines, ally himself to the daughter of a strange god, nay, suffer himself to become the weak tool of this woman's treachery and caprice, so as to betray, at her solicitation, the secret of his strength, and part with the symbol of his consecration to God. How light did it show him to have made of his heaven-imposed vow of separation to the Lord! And how bitterly was his own measure meted back to him, when, after being caught in the toils of the deceiver, he was delivered over as a laughing-stock to his enemies, and was trodden under foot of men! *There*, in black night and abject humiliation, the riddle might have ended; it *would* have ended there, if the fall of Israel were like the fall of the world—a fall without the hope of recovery. But it is not so; through the loving-kindness and mercy of God other things were still in reserve for them. Therefore, when the cold winter of desolation had passed over the son of Manoah, and amid the shame and wretchedness of his captivity, the Nazarite's heart returns to him, the freshness of another spring returns along with it; he again raises himself up with the might of a giant, and with one terrible blow brings confusion on the pride and glory of his adversaries. An acted prophecy throughout—only, in the earlier part, bearing more immediate reference to the things which had been taking place in Israel's experience, and, in the later, to the expectation that might be cherished of a brighter future. With the solemnity of a sign from heaven it proclaimed, that for the seed of Israel every thing in evil or in good depended upon the part they acted in respect to the covenant of God; and it should have been heard by the men of that generation, proclaiming this the more loudly, as *their* failure to recognise aright the divine mission of Samson, and stand by him at the outset of his career, had manifestly contributed not a little to *his* failure in the work of deliverance he should have accomplished. There was hope, however, still—hope in his death; and if their repentings did but kindle together, and their faith revive after the manner of his, they might yet ride upon the high places of the earth, and become even more than conquerors.[1]

[1] When the history of Samson is understood in the light presented above, no difficulty need be felt about the statement in Judges xiv. 4, that it was of the Lord he sought a wife from the Philistines. It was of the Lord, in the same sense, that the act of David in numbering Israel was so (2 Sam. xxiv. 1). In both cases alike, as in many others of a similar kind, there was a wrong bias or disposition already working in the soul, sure to take *some* outward direction in the way of evil; and God so ordered matters, as to make it take *that* direction which He saw to be the best fitted for displaying its own nature, or subserving the purposes He meant to accomplish in connection with it. For another quite parallel case see 1 Kings xii. 15.

This branch of our subject, however, has been pursued far enough. We have seen that not a few points of contact exist between the prophecy of Scripture and its history; and how naturally, how necessarily even, the one grows out of the other, and how closely, in several respects, it is interwoven with it. So that while there are specific differences, it is impossible but that there must also be general agreements, and particularly in regard to the place they respectively hold in the great plan of God's moral government. Prophecy and history alike occupy but different provinces in the evolution of this Divine plan—provinces that continually overlap and interpenetrate one another; and the relation they bear to it, is the aspect in which both should always be primarily and chiefly contemplated. Their common and more direct object is to make known God's purposes of grace and principles of dealing towards men; the one by narration of the past, the other by connecting the past with the future.

CHAPTER III.

THE PROPER SPHERE OF PROPHECY—THE CHURCH.

By the sphere of prophecy, we mean the parties for whom it was directly given, and the objects it more immediately contemplated. The subject is very closely connected with the topics which have already been discussed, and the correct view may be said to be involved in the preceding remarks. But it is a matter of too much moment to be settled merely by implication; the more especially as conclusions naturally flow from it, which ought to exercise an important bearing on the interpretation of prophecy.

It is of prophecy in the stricter sense that we now speak—prophecy as containing pre-intimations of things to come—not only a distinct branch, but the most special and peculiar branch of God's communications to men. This alone determines it to have been, in its leading aim and object for the good of the Church. If prophesying, in other respects, was "not for them that believe not, but for them that believe" (1 Cor. xiv. 22), it must have been so more especially in this; only in an incidental and remote manner could it have been intended to bear upon those without. For it was the revelation of the Lord's secret in regard to the future movements of His providence, which belongs peculiarly to them that fear Him (Ps. xxv. 14). Not such a revelation, however, for the purpose of gratifying the curiosity of those who might seek needlessly to pry into the future, but for the higher end of furnishing, especially in times of darkness and perplexity, the light that might be required for present faith and duty. It is not God's *common* method, nor, indeed, would it be consistent with His wisdom, to lay open His hidden counsel respecting things destined to come to pass, even to the children of His covenant: for such knowledge, if imparted with any measure of fulness and precision, would be a most dangerous possession, and would inevitably tend to destroy the simplicity of their trust in God, and beget an unhealthy craving after human calculations and worldly expedients. It is only, therefore, within certain limits, or in cases that may be deemed somewhat exceptional, that God can grant, even to His chosen, a prophetical insight into future events. In so far as this may be needful to awaken or sustain hope in times of darkness and discouragement—to inspire confidence in the midst of general backsliding and rebuke—at the approach of imminent danger to the life of faith, to give due intimation of the brooding evil—at such times, and for such purposes, God's merciful regard to the safety and well-being of His people may fitly lead Him to provide them with an occasional and partial disclosure of the future; but the same regard would equally constrain Him to withhold it, when not necessary for the moral ends of His government.

Apparent exceptions to this view present themselves in the cases of Balaam and Daniel, both of whom primarily disclosed to the enemies of God's kingdom, the things destined to come to pass. Both, however, occupied a kind of exceptional position. They stood apart, not only from the prophetical order of men in Israel, but also from the common affairs of the church. Hence the writings of Daniel, notwithstanding their high prophetical character, have had a place assigned them in the Jewish canon, distinct from the writings of strictly prophetical men. But in regard to the point immediately before us, the grounds of exception are more apparent than real. For, in the case of both Balaam and Daniel, it was mainly for the light and encouragement of the church, that the word of prophecy came by them; only, the circumstances of the times were such as to render the camp of the enemy the most appropriate watch-tower, where it should have been received, and primarily made known. At both periods, Israel had come into direct collision with the kingdoms of the world—in the one case as a new, in the other as a small and shattered power, standing over against others of mighty prowess, and, as might seem, of all-prevailing energy. The subject for consideration, then, came to be, not what it usually was with the prophets, Israel in its relation to the worldly powers, but rather the worldly powers in their relation to Israel.[1] The providence of God had ordered matters so as, for the time, to give these powers the predominant rank in the world's affairs; and it was meet that the word which announced the evanescence of their glory, and their ultimate subjection to the kingdom of God, should proceed from a divine seer on their own territory. There was thus extracted from the domain of the earthly, a testimony on behalf of the spiritual and divine. And to render the witness still more striking and impressive, it was ordered in the latter of the two cases referred to, that Nebuchadnezzar, the head and representative of the worldly kingdom, should, by receiving a divine dream himself, herald the final downfal of the one, and the eternal ascendancy of the other (chap. ii.). The actual revelation, however, came from Daniel, the representative at Babylon of the divine kingdom; and though the general outline of the future was presented in his interpretation of Nebuchadnezzar's dream, yet the more inward and special delineation of the respective natures of the earthly and the heavenly kingdoms, of the relations that were to subsist between the two, of the death-like struggles through which, both in the nearer and the more distant future, the kingdom of God was to make its way to a secure position, and a universal dominion—all this, which forms the great burden of Daniel's prophecies (chap. vii.–xii.), and which it was his more especial calling to disclose, was given through him directly for the support and encouragement of the church, amid the deep depression and gloom which both then and afterwards hung around her condition. Here also, therefore, the general principle holds, that prophecy, as the revelation of things to come, in all its leading phases, is

[1] See Auberlen's "Der Prophet Daniel und die Offenbarung Johannes," p. 22.

God's communication to the church; and that for spiritual ends—for the especial purpose of preparing and fitting her for the more trying emergencies of a struggling and perplexed condition.

1. And this, first of all, accounts quite naturally for the very unequal, and apparently irregular, distribution of prophecy. Being intended, in its more immediate aim, to counsel and direct the church, in respect to evils in her condition, too great for ordinary light and privilege, it was fitly made to vary, both in form and quantity, according to the exigencies of the times. Hence, prophetic revelations were much longer continued, and more widely diffused in the earlier ages of the church's history than now; for believers then possessed so imperfect an insight into the scheme and purposes of God, that they required more full and frequent glimpses into the future to sustain their faith, and guide their course of procedure. Hence also, when toward the close of the Theocracy, error and corruption became unusually prevalent and strong—when on account of these, it was necessary to allow a cloud of darkness to settle upon the outward position and prospects of the church, and every thing began to wear a frowning aspect; it was then more especially that the spirit of prophecy needed to multiply, and that it actually did multiply, its announcements—pouring in rays of heaven's light amid nature's gloom, and doing so the more, as the gloom became deeper, and difficulties thickened around the walk of faith. In perfect accordance with this more immediate and special design of prophecy, not only are there comparatively few prophetic delineations in New Testament Scripture, but the portions which more peculiarly belong to this class (viz., our Lord's predictions respecting the destruction of Jerusalem and the end of the world, St Paul's description of the great apostacy, and the mystic visions of alternate suffering and triumph in the Apocalypse), all proceed on the anticipation of distressing and perilous times to the church, and are obviously designed to provide her beforehand, with the necessary materials of light and comfort.[1]

[1] In what has now been stated regarding prophecy, we have a ready

Now, since this is the primary design of prophecy in its more specific announcements—since in these it has respect more immediately to the church of God, and speaks peculiarly for her direction and support in times of danger or distress—it is clear we should not expect prophecy to be framed, as if its argumentative value were the main service it was intended to render. Whatever it may be fitted to yield of this description, is rather to be regarded as an incidental result, than its direct and proper aim. It speaks, for the most part, in a tone of confidence and sympathy, as to those who should be disposed to receive and profit by the communications it addressed to them, not with a view to meet, on the field of controversy, persons on the look out for grounds of objection to the truth of God. The moral position of such persons is entirely wrong; and it is only what might be expected, that various things respecting prophecy and its fulfilment, should afford ground for doubt or cavil to *them*, which appear full of light and satisfaction to the children of God. The eye of the one class is evil, and so abides in darkness; while in the other it is single, and receives in simplicity the testimony of truth.

2. The same consideration, which accounts for the somewhat irregular distribution of prophecy, also serves to explain a peculiarity, which not unfrequently appears in the form of its announcements. This peculiarity consists in the *minatory* aspect given to many predictions which are really pregnant with blessing; or their indirectly announcing good to the church, by directly denouncing evil upon the adversary. In all cases of this sort it is the relation implied or indicated

explanation of a notice in New Testament history, as this notice, in turn, incidentally confirms the statement just made. In Acts iv. 36, the surname of Barnabas, given to the good Levite, Joseph, is explained as meaning "son of consolation" (υἱὸς παρακλήσεως), while more strictly it is "son of prophecy" (בַּר נְבוּאָה). It implied, that prophecy, in its primary and leading design, was what we have represented, the light and comfort of the church in her times of trouble and perplexity. And had prophecy been viewed more in this scriptural aspect, and less as a weapon of defence against unbelievers, the explanation of this name would have appeared more easy and natural than it has usually done.

between the two parties, which determines the form of the prediction; this being such as to render the infliction of evil on the one necessary to the accomplishing of deliverance for the other. Every such prediction, therefore, is in truth a word of promise addressed to the church, assuring her, under covert of the spoliation or defeat of the enemies of her peace, of her own coming safety or enlargement.

The very first promise belongs to this category. It assumes in both its parts the form of a threatening—a threatening of partial injury to be brought on the woman's seed by the seed of the tempter, and of the utter destruction of the tempter's seed by that of the woman. In itself, a most significant fact, and indicating, from the outset, how necessarily and how much the salvation of an elect church was to proceed by the avenging of evil, and the overthrow of an adverse power! In the same light are we to view the denunciations of coming judgment and desolation, which, in the later prophets, are so often given forth against Egypt, Assyria, Babylon, and other heathen kingdoms. The relation in which these powers stood at the time to the church of God, as her dangerous rivals or cruel oppressors, made it impossible to give her the promise of good she needed, without, at the same time, foretelling their coming ruin; for it was only by the fall of the one, that the other could rise to the ascendant. Even the more particular and detailed representations of Daniel respecting the successive monarchies of the world, had the same ultimate design; the terminating point of his visions (as we have already stated), was to impress upon the minds of believing men the temporary nature of the earthly, under every phase it might assume, and with whatever weapons it might arm itself; its doom still was, to pass away, that the eternal might remain. Nor is it otherwise in the case of the Apocalyptic sketches of the New Testament. The plagues of judgment, the vials of wrath, the woes, calamities, and desolations, with which they so greatly abound, are all of the nature of promises to the party more properly contemplated by the spirit of prophecy; for the revelation they contain of the world's doom, is given for the especial purpose of enabling the church to reckon on her abiding security and final triumph. They are but another form of the message "Comfort ye, comfort ye, my people, saith your God."

3. It is of more importance, however, to notice another point connected with the revelations of prophecy, and which is also a simple deduction from the view under consideration, of its more immediate purpose and design. From the relation of prophecy to the church, a very large portion of its announcements naturally consists of direct promises of good things to come; and addressed, as these necessarily are, to the church in the strictest sense, they can only be expected to meet with fulfilment in so far as the church is true to her calling, or in the experience of the church as composed of sincere and faithful members of the covenant. It could not be otherwise, if prophecy really is—what we have found it to be—the more special and peculiar revelation of God's purposes of mercy to His people in times of comparative darkness, or extraordinary trouble and perplexity. In that case, whatever it contained of comfort and encouragement, must have been designed for genuine believers—for them alone; because such only are the proper subjects of blessing. It were, therefore, to turn prophecy out of its proper direction—to draw it into a sphere that does not rightfully belong to it, if we should view the promises of blessing it embodies, as bearing respect to men in their natural condition: if, for example, we should regard them as the settled heritage of the Jews, in their simply natural descent and national capacity, apart from the spiritual element of the church, or the seed of true believers, which that nation contained in its bosom. This were, indeed, to invert the relative order and position of things; it were to convert the incidental and formal in Israel's condition into the substantive part, leaving all that is inward and spiritual as a kind of separable adjunct. It were to exhibit God's election of Israel to the prominent place they held, and their title to Divine favour and blessing, as a thing by itself, and for itself—a piece of mysterious favouritism, or freak of arbitrary will and power; instead

of being, as the whole tenor alike of the historical and the prophetical Scriptures manifests, a concentrated display of his principles of truth and grace, in order to work with the greater effect upon the world at large.[1] So far from its being the case, that the promises in Isaiah and the other prophets were all made to the Jews as a nation, it were nearer the truth to say, that no promises were made to them, simply in that capacity. The promises, in which they were more peculiarly interested, were made to Abraham and his seed; but to his seed only in the sense explained by the Apostle (Rom. iv. ix.; Gal. iii.); that is, to those who might spring from Abraham's loins, in so far—but in so far only—as they stood also in his faith and walked in his footsteps; and along with these, to all who should possess the same spiritual standing, whether they might belong or not to the number of his natural offspring. The possession of the spiritual element was thus, in every age, stamped as the essential thing, as the vital bond of connection, according to the pregnant saying of Augustine, Fides Abrahae semen est Abrahae (Op. x., p. 2593). When the lineal descendants were found devoid of this, they were not recognized by God as the heirs of promise, or as having any title to blessing. They then wanted the heart of the parent, which was unspeakably more important than bearing his name, or having a portion of his blood in their veins. Their condition did not essentially differ from that of the heathen. How clearly was this indicated by the prophet Isaiah, when at the beginning of his book, though described as "the vision he saw respecting Judah and Jerusalem," he breaks forth in an address to "the rulers of Sodom and the people of Gomorrah." Not only had they become like heathens in God's sight, but like that portion of the heathen, who, from having been pre-eminent in guilt, were made also pre-eminent in punishment; not Abraham's seed, therefore, in the proper sense, but a generation of vipers. In like manner, Ezekiel advances it as a specific charge, against the children of Israel, that they had "brought strangers, un-

[1] See this point more fully treated in Typology of Scripture, vol. i. p. 338 sq.

circumcised in heart, and uncircumcised in flesh, to be in God's sanctuary, to pollute it" (chap. xliv. 7), describing a corrupt priesthood as uncircumcised heathen, because such morally was their position in the sight of God. So, again Amos in chap. ix. 7, "Are ye not as the children of the Ethiopians unto me, O children of Israel? saith the Lord. Have not I brought up Israel out of the land of Egypt? and the Philistines from Caphtor, and the Syrians from Kir?" That is, the doing of the one, as matters *now* stand, is to be regarded as entirely of a piece with the doing of the other. Since Israel has descended *spiritually* to a level with the nations of the earth, the removal of their forefathers from Egypt, and their settlement in the land of Canaan, has also become a merely political and worldly change, similar to what has occurred among other tribes and races of men. It involves no distinctive privilege; it secures no real blessing. The promise is not for persons in such a condition, but only for the children of faith, the true seed of Abraham.

The rule for promised blessing, however, does not hold of threatened evil. The prophets could not, in accordance with the principles of the Divine government, have assured the Israelitish people, in the mass, and irrespective of their spiritual condition, of future good; but there was nothing to prevent the same prophets from threatening the people with the most general and overwhelming judgments. The two cases are essentially different. True believers alone are in any case the proper subjects of promise; but sinners of every name are exposed to the judgments of heaven, and those who have sinned, as Israel did, against covenant light and engagements, only render themselves the heirs of a heavier condemnation. Hence the groundlessness of the complaint which is sometimes heard respecting the seed of Israel, as if a certain degree of harshness were shown them when their connection with the severity of God is represented as more marked and general than their connection with his goodness —when the prospects of blessing unfolded by the prophets are held to have been the heritage only of the *spiritual* portion of the people, while the calamities threatened are found to have had a collective and national fulfilment. Such a complaint, if traced to its source, would resolve itself into a dissatisfaction with the principles of the Divine administration; since, according to these, individuals or communities, merely as such, may become the subjects of threatened evil, there being always enough of sin in the general mass, enough even in the better portion, to account for every visitation of evil that may be sent; while, on the other hand, no tokens of the Divine favour, no blessing either temporal or eternal, can be made sure to any, unless they may become partakers of the grace and salvation of God.

It is true that the promises of blessing held out to Israel by the prophets are often couched in terms not less comprehensive than the threatenings of evil; they are addressed to the people in their completeness, as if all were alike interested in them. This arose from the desire felt by God's servants to treat Israel according to their proper ideal, as a people called to the knowledge and service of Jehovah—an ideal which they were reminded by this very mode of address *ought* to have been realised in the entire community. The same thing precisely occurs in New Testament Scripture. In the epistles addressed to particular churches, these are designated according to their Christian profession, as standing in the faith and purity of the gospel, and as so standing, have many rich and precious promises conveyed to them; but without prejudice to the truth that there might be, nay, not without many indications of the fact that there were, amongst them persons who were not conformed to the doctrine, and who could have no part in the blessing. The principle which underlies one and all of these promises is, that as it is Christ who gave them confirmation for his people, so it is such only as really are his people who are entitled to look for their fulfilment. But for those who are without the faith of Christ, so far from their having an interest in any promises of grace, they still have the wrath of God abiding upon them.

It is proper to add, that the converse of the principle here affirmed respecting the promissory element in the prophecies of Scripture, or the positive aspect of the truth it contains, also demands consideration, and is, indeed, one on which both the comfort of believers and the practical value of the prophetic Scriptures greatly depend. If, on the one hand, the promises of future good they disclose are only for the children of faith, who constitute the real members of the covenant, on the other hand, it is to be remembered, they are for all such. To the latest generations, and to the utmost bounds of the world, these may claim an interest in them. Not always, indeed, as to the mere form of the promised good (which changes with circumstances of place and time), but invariably as to its substance. For "the word of God lives and abides for ever;" if, as a word of blessing, for *none but* the true seed, yet assuredly for *all* the seed, of every kindred, and tribe, and tongue. Believing Gentiles are therefore designated "heirs according to the promise" (Gal. iii. 29)—the promise, namely, given originally to Abraham, and which may justly be said to comprehend every other in its bosom. And both our Lord himself and his Apostles continually inculcate and act upon the principle, that the child of faith, wherever he is, and in whatever region he resides, has a personal interest in every word of encouragement and hope which has been delivered to the church of God. (Matt. iv. 4; Acts ii. 39; 2 Cor. vi. 2; Heb. vi. 17, 18, etc.) How could it possibly be otherwise? This word is the testimony of an unchangeable God—the expression of his own unalterable nature. Distance of space or time, therefore, can make no material alteration respecting it. It is as veritable in its announcements, and as fresh in its spirit, for the believer now, as if it had been uttered for the first time in his own day, and even had come direct to his own ear. So that, on sure and solid grounds, grounds that are rooted in the very being and character of God, we may affirm believers of every name to be substantially on a footing as regards the word of promise; to all of them it speaks one language, and lays open to them the same inheritance of blessing.

But the principle which thus binds the individual believer of one time with the believer of another, is, of course, equally valid in a collective respect; it establishes the unbroken continuity of the church, and the essential oneness of her relation to the promises of God. These promises have, indeed, to do with different covenants and successive dispensations, but not by any means with diverse churches, one having a right to this, and another to that, part of its provisions. There is in reality but one church, pervaded by one organic life, and only so far differing at one time from what it was at another, as it has had to pass through successive stages of development, and to adapt itself to circumstances full of change and progress. Hence, as Owen justly remarked, in one of the shortest, but, at the same time, one of the most solid and well-digested of his Preliminary Dissertations to his "Commentary on the Hebrews" (Exer. vi.), "At the coming of the Messiah, there was not one church taken away, and another set up in its room; but the church continued the same, in those that were the children of Abraham according to the faith. The Christian church is not another church, but the very same that was before the coming of Christ, having the same faith with it, and interested in the same covenant. The olive tree was the same; only some branches were broken and others grafted into it: the Jews fell, and the Gentiles came in their room. And this doth and must determine the difference between the Jews and Christians about the promises of the Old Testament. They are all made unto the church. No individual hath any interest in them, but by virtue of his membership with the church. This church is, and always was, one and the same. With whomsoever it remains, the promises are theirs; and that, not by application or analogy, but directly and properly. They belong as immediately at this day, either to Jews or Christians, as they did of old to any. The question is, with whom is this church, which is founded on the promised seed in the covenant; for where it is, there is Zion, Jerusalem, Israel, Jacob, the temple of God."[1]

[1] See also "Typology of Scripture," vol. i., pp. 171-177.

4. A still further deduction, and one of much importance to the right interpretation of prophecy, remains to be drawn from the consideration of its proper sphere and intention. Since prophecy is mainly and essentially a revelation of God's mind and will to his church, and that more especially for the direction and encouragement of her members in times of darkness and perplexity, we may confidently infer that the *ethical* or moral element, not the simply *natural*, must predominate in its announcements respecting the future. It *may*, and to a certain extent *must*, foretell events in Providence with sufficient distinctness to enable those who have witnessed or become cognisant of their occurrence, to identify them with its prior intimations; for otherwise the church could never assure herself that the hopes and expectations it had awakened in her bosom had found their realisation. In regard, for example, to the Messiah, to whom, most of all, prophecy was intended to bear witness, it was necessary that it should describe Him by such marks and characteristics as would enable those who waited for His coming to recognize Him when he did come, as the same that had been promised to the fathers. In like manner, the predictions that bore on the destinies of the covenant-people, and the hostile kingdoms around them, must, in order to serve the purposes for which they were given, have spoken with sufficient plainness, at least, of the grand results concerning each of them, in which the course of Providence was to issue. But it could not be in any case the mere occurrences themselves, as objects of natural curiosity or ordinary facts of history, in respect to which they were so announced beforehand, or were afterwards to be marked as fulfilments of prophecy. For then they should have belonged, not to the province of religion, or to the sphere of the church, but to the region of nature and the world. It is in the moral element that the church moves; and the prominent point in all prophetic intimations respecting her state and destiny, must be something of a moral kind —something that, in one respect or another, tends to exhibit the principles of the Divine administration in its dealings

with men as subjects of a moral government. Prophecy, therefore, as has been justly said, "is not merely the divination of future events; these events, however important, are but points in the immense map of God's designs. It is the weakness of the human mind to desire to pry into futurity without a moral aim. God's aim, on the contrary, is to raise us above the whirl of passing events, and to fix our attentive gaze on the Divine hand, which is moving all the complicated wheels of Providence."[1] And moving them, it might have been added, for the great end of displaying His moral attributes, and accomplishing the purposes of His grace in behalf of His church and people. Everything in the Divine plan is subordinate to this, and must also be subordinate in the prophetic word, which is but the partial disclosure of that plan, before the time has come for its actual evolution in Providence.

If due weight is given to the consideration now advanced, it will exercise an important influence on our interpretations of prophecy. It will lead us to view every thing, not through a natural, but through an ethical, medium. In the predictions, for example, respecting states and kingdoms, it will dispose us to look not so much to the land or territory they occupied, or the external changes these might undergo, as to the rational beings composing them, who alone were proper subjects of a moral treatment. Hence, when the predictions took the form, as they very commonly did, of denunciations of coming evil, they are to be understood more especially of the people whose sins had provoked the threatened doom, and of the territories they occupied, only in so far as the external aspect of these might be made visibly to reflect the prostrate condition of their owners. To have respect to the territories, rather than to the people who inhabited them, were to look at the prophecies and their fulfilment in a simply natural light. It were to make account of the relation in which they stood to the omniscience and power of God, but to lose sight of their

[1] "Douglas on the Structure of Prophecy," p. 8.

connection with His moral government. This, however, as we have stated, was invariably the point of highest moment. The primary question was how the states referred to stood related, now, in guilt, and, prospectively, in punishment, to the righteousness of heaven. "It is not, therefore," to use the words of Arnold, who correctly exhibits the general purport of this portion of the prophetical Scriptures, "it is not as if the *places* were accursed for ever; or as if the language of utter vengeance, which we find in prophecy, was applicable to the soil of Mesopotamia or Eden; but the people, the race, the language, the institutions, the religion, all that constitutes national personality, are passed away from the earth. And if Mesopotamia were to be civilized and fertilized to-morrow, and a city with the name of Babylon re-built, yet it could not be the old Babylon (of Scripture); for that has become extinct for ever." Viewed thus, in their predominantly moral bearing, such prophecies will be found to have met with the fullest verification; while, otherwise, as will afterwards appear, the verification is at best broken and incomplete.

Nor is this all. For, by keeping thus prominently in view the moral element in prophecy and its primary destination to subserve spiritual interests, we escape from what, more than any thing else, has impoverished much of our prophetical literature, and we may almost say, has stricken it with the curse of barrenness:—namely, the disposition to treat the subject of prophecy merely as a branch of the evidences, and make account of nothing but what it contains of the miraculous. Somewhat of the miraculous, undoubtedly, belongs to every prophecy of Scripture; since it necessarily betokens a supernatural insight into the counsels of heaven, and a power not granted to men in general, of penetrating through the veil of the future. This, however, is only a part, not the whole; it is not even the more essential and prominent part; and to isolate and magnify it, as if it were alone entitled to regard, is most unduly to contract the boundaries of the field, and leave unexplored its hidden riches. Even in the case of miracles themselves, the too exclusive regard to the miraculous element has proved a source of weakness and danger. It has presented them to men's view, merely on their natural side, apart from their moral use as manifestations of the character of God —has treated them, not as themselves integral parts of a revelation, but only as evidences of a revelation; and the natural result has been, that being under-estimated by the defenders of the faith, they have been but more rudely disparaged and assailed by its opponents. It is, in truth, to use the words of Archdeacon Hare, "the theological parallel to the materialist hypothesis, that all our knowledge is derived from our senses."[1]

The mistake is, if possible, still worse in regard to prophecy, which purports to be a disclosure of the very heart of God. When considered merely as a Divine act of foresight, it is but an evidence of his foreknowledge, which, even in its highest exercise, is still only a *natural* attribute, standing in no necessary connection with spiritual aims and purposes. But what, if not to exhibit these, is the great design of all the revelations of Scripture? They are given to tell, not that God is, but *what* he is—what in the elements of His character, in the principles of His government, in His purposes of mercy or of judgment toward men. So that to contemplate the revelations of prophecy in their relation merely to the Divine foresight, is to view them apart from what has ever been the higher aim of God's direct communications to men. And not only so, but the further error is naturally fallen into, of expecting prophecy to be more full and explicit in its announcements regarding future events, than from its inherent nature and immediate uses it could properly be. Valued only for the evidences it contains of Divine foresight, a mode of interpretation is in danger of being adopted, which, in its craving for specific predictions, would confound the characteristics of prophecy and history. How far this has actually been the case, will appear when we come to treat of the proper style and diction of prophecy.

[1] Mission of the Comforter, p. 354.

CHAPTER IV.

THE RELATION OF PROPHECY TO HUMAN FREEDOM AND BEHAVIOUR; WITH A CONSIDERATION OF THE QUESTION, HOW FAR PROPHECY IS ABSOLUTE OR CONDITIONAL IN ITS ANNOUNCEMENTS.

From the proper sphere of prophecy, we pass to the consideration of its proper bearing on those who are the subjects of it, with respect to their liberty of thought, or their actual course of behaviour. It indicates the future; does it in every case absolutely determine this? Does it leave no room for human freedom to work, and human repentance or perversity to alter its prospective exhibition of things to come? In a word, is it the characteristic of prophecy, in giving intimation of the future, to announce definitely what shall be—or are its announcements to some extent conditional, depending on the line of conduct that may be pursued by those whom they respect?

This is a point of great importance for the sound interpretation of some parts of the prophetical writings; and a point that has been decided in the most contradictory manner. Sometimes the decision made, has been arrived at more on philosophical, than on religious grounds. The earlier Socinians, for example, holding strongly to the principle of human freedom, as always requiring for its exercise, the perfect liberty of choosing an opposite, maintained on this ground, the impossibility of absolutely determining beforehand, and consequently also of foreknowing, with certainty, the actions of men. In their view, every thing was contingent, even in its relation to the Divine mind, and prophecy could rise no higher than to the office of presenting a general outline or probable prognostication of future events. The necessitarian school of Christian philosophers from Leibnitz downwards, take up the opposite position ; and, on the ground that all actions and events are foreseen by God, and certain of them also foretold, conclude them to be also absolutely determined, and deny the possibility of any real liberty to act contrary to that foreknowledge and predetermination. According to this view, the prophetic intimation becomes an absolute element, to which the moral agency of man is placed in unconditional subjection. We abstain, however, from entering upon such speculations ; and the rather, as they have, not only in the past, proved barren of all profitable results, but in themselves, proceed upon assumptions respecting the Divine foreknowledge, in its relation to human freedom, which are entirely gratuitous, and may justly be characterized as an intruding into those things, which man, in his present state, neither has seen, nor can see.

But among strictly scriptural interpreters, we have also two antagonistic modes of representation, the one maintaining the conditional character of the prophetic announcements, and the other asserting their absolute and unchangeable fixedness. Of the first class—to say nothing of the older Calvinistic writers, who used to press the distinction between God's secret and revealed will, between his *real* intention or decree, which remains, like himself, fixed and immutable, and his *declared* purpose, which may vary from time to time with the changeful conditions of men—to say nothing of these, we have, in the present day, such men as Köster and Olshausen holding, on grounds connected with men's rational freedom and responsibility, and God's methods of dealing with them, that all prophecies are conditional. Thus Olshausen on Matt. xxiv. says, "As everything future, even that which proceeds from the freedom of the creature, when viewed in relation to the Divine knowledge, can only be regarded as *necessary ;* so everything future, as far as it concerns man, can only be regarded as *conditional* upon the use of his freedom. As obstinate perseverance in sin hastens destruction, so genuine repentance may avert it.

This is illustrated in the Old Testament in the prophet Jonah, by the history of Nineveh; and intimated in the New Testament by Paul, when—like Abraham praying for Sodom—he describes the elements of good existing in the world as exercising a restraint upon the judgments of God (2 Thess. ii. 7); and in the second epistle of Peter, the delay of the Lord's coming is viewed as an act of Divine long-suffering, designed to afford men space for repentance. Accordingly," he adds, "when the Redeemer promises the near approach of his coming, this announcement is to be taken with the restriction (to be understood in connection with all predictions of judgments), 'All this will come to pass, unless men avert the wrath of God by sincere repentance.' None of the predictions of Divine judgments are bare historical proclamations of what is to take place; they are alarums calling men to repentance—of which it may be said, that they announce something for the very purpose, that what *is* announced may *not* come to pass."

Hengstenberg rejects this view of prophecy, and espouses the opposite. "Beyond all doubt," he says, "when the prophet denounces the divine judgments, he proceeds on the assumption that the people will not repent—an assumption which he knows from God to be true. Were the people to repent the prediction would fail; but because they will not, it is uttered *absolutely*. It does not follow, however, that the prophet's warnings and exhortations are useless. These 'serve for a witness against them;' and, besides, amid the ruin of the mass, individuals might be saved. Viewing prophecies as conditional predictions nullifies them. The Mosaic criterion (Deut. xviii. 22), that he was a false prophet, who predicted 'things which followed not nor came to pass,' would then be of no value, since recourse might always be had to the excuse, that the case had been altered by the fulfilling of the condition. The fear of introducing fatalism, if the prophecies are not taken in a conditional sense, is unfounded; for God's omniscience, his foreknowledge, does not establish fatalism, and from omniscience simply is the prescience of the prophets to be derived. The prophets feel themselves so closely united to God, that the words of Jehovah are given as their own, and that to them is often ascribed what God does, which proves their own consciousness to have been entirely absorbed into that of God." (Kitto's Cyclopedia, Art. Prophecy.)

These two forms of representation may both be characterised as extremes, and neither of them can be fully carried out in the interpretation of the prophecies—although the one, which supposes them to be conditional, if understood within certain limits, approaches nearest to the truth. One does not see how the ethical element could have been allowed that scope in prophecy which we have already seen to belong to it, unless the historical result had been made to *some* extent to depend on the manner in which those might act to whom the prophecy came ; since such persons might be, and often actually were, as much the subjects of moral treatment, in respect to the announcements of prophecy, as in respect to the commands of law, or the revelations of grace. The case alone of Nineveh under the preaching of Jonah, puts it beyond a doubt, that such a conditional element as we suppose, might find a place in the domain of prophecy. Never did its announcements of coming evil assume a more absolute and definite form, than when Jonah proclaimed in the streets of that great city that in forty days it should be overthrown. And yet, by operating in the way of moral suasion on the hearts of the people, the predicted event did not take place; in other words, the prophecy, notwithstanding its apparent absoluteness, was found to have in it a latent conditionality. Precisely similar was the case of Hezekiah in his sickness. The prophet Isaiah came to him with a formal message, "Thus saith the Lord, Set thine house in order, for thou shalt die and not live." Yet, on account of the deep humiliation and earnest prayer of Hezekiah, the word was recalled, and a prolongation of life granted to him. The Mosaic criterion, interpreted after the fashion of Hengstenberg, and applied here, or to the case of Jonah, would oblige us to hold, that there was no true prophecy. And if the introduction of a conditional principle might occasionally afford some excuse to a mere pretender, for evading the condemnation due to him on the failure of his prediction, might even sometimes render it a matter of doubt how far a *divine* prediction should be expected to have a fulfilment according to its terms, on the other hand, the absolute rejection of such a principle can have no other result, than that of excluding from the rank of genuine predictions a considerable portion of the prophetic word itself, and also of most unduly contracting the ethical import and bearing of prophecy. Its single quality as a prediction—the merely natural element in it—would thus be made to carry it over everything besides.

But the chief error, we conceive, in these conflicting views respecting prophecy, is the disposition they exhibit to generalise too far, to extend to the whole prophetical field principles that are properly applicable only to a part. There is manifestly need for discrimination, as prophecy, in regard to the real absoluteness of its terms, must materially depend upon the nature of the subjects it refers to, and the kind of results it contemplates. It may, in this respect, be divided into two great classes, the one having more especial reference to the divine purposes in behalf of men, and the other to the divine procedure towards men.

I. The first class consists of such prophecies as have respect, more immediately and directly, to the divine purposes in behalf of men. As the ultimate ground and reason of these purposes must be in God himself, it is evident there can be no room for the operation of any conditional element, excepting, it may be, in respect to the time and mode of their accomplishment. Whether sooner or later, whether in this particular manner, or in some other—as regards such points, the issue might be made in part to depend upon the conduct of men and the state of the world. Possibly, even, predictions respecting them may be given at one period which shall be modified at another; but the things themselves, having the root of their being in the determinations of the mind of God, must be of an absolute character, and the announcement, when once made regarding them, can never be recalled.

As examples of this great class of prophecies, we may refer to the original promise of salvation, by the triumph of the woman's seed over the tempter; to the promise given to Abraham, that through his seed the blessing should come to the world; to the farther limitation, as regards the fulfilment of the promise, by its immediate connection with a distinguished personage of the tribe of Judah, and the seed-royal of the house of David; to the intimations given of this personage Himself as to the constitution of His person, the nature of His work on earth, the character of His administration, the final results and triumphs of His kingdom, and the several dooms of those rival powers or dominions which were successively to contend with the cause of Heaven for the mastery. In regard to such things, as purposed in the divine mind, and announced in the prophetic word, there could be no room for any such conditional element as might in the least bear upon the question whether they should actually come to pass or not, for they were matters entering into the very core of the divine government of the world, and were the settled results of the eternal principles on which all was to proceed. In regard to them, we have simply to do with the omniscience of God in foreseeing, His veracity in declaring, and His overruling providence in directing, what should come to pass.

The utmost that can be conceived of anything conditional, in respect to the class of predictions now under consideration, is, that in the *time* and *mode* of their accomplishment they may in a degree have been made to turn upon the course of things in the world. The prophecies, for example, relating to the second coming of the Lord, involving, as they do, the execution of overwhelming judgments on the ungodliness of the world, may be regarded, with Olshausen, as protracted beyond what the natural import of the language might have seemed to indicate, on account of the forbearance of God waiting for the conversion of men. It is true that in none of those prophecies was the time of the event accurately defined. Our Lord purposely left it in concealment; and we by no means concur in the opinion of several recent commentators, German or Germanized, that the apostles intended, in anything they said of it, to intimate their expectation of its arrival in their own life-time. We see no grounds for maintaining such a position. Yet when spoken of, as it often is, of being "near," of "drawing nigh," or being "at hand," while now so many centuries have elapsed without its taking place, we can scarcely help admitting (however we may choose to express it) that some after-respect has been had to moral considerations as influencing the time of the predicted event; in other words, that there has been the operation of a conditional element to the effect of delaying longer than the original predictions might have led us to expect the actual occurrence of the event predicted. Indeed, the explanation of the Apostle Peter seems plainly to proceed upon such a mode of viewing the matter.[1]

A more striking and palpable example, however, of the partial dependance of this class of prophecies on the actual course of events in the world, may be found in the predictions bearing on the divine purpose to connect the peculiar blessing for mankind with the royal house of David. The appointment in favour of that house to bear rule among men, for the purpose of securing and dispensing the blessings of salvation, was irrevocably fixed from the time that Nathan delivered to David the prophecy in 2 Sam. vii. 1–17. And presently a series of predictions, founded on it, began to be delivered to the church, in which the eye of faith was pointed to the bright visions in prospect, and especially to the peculiar child of promise, in whom the chain of royal successors was to terminate, and who was to hold the sceptre of the kingdom for ever. But while the appointment itself was absolute, and the original prophecy respecting it was so far absolute, too, that it expressed no condition which might seem to indicate a possible interruption to the promised good, David himself knew perfectly well,

[1] See part ii., chap. 2, sec. 3.

that there was an implied condition, and that the prophecy must be read in connection with the whole plan and purposes of God in the administration of the affairs of His church. Therefore, in his last words, he left, as a testimony to all his seed, the description of the ruler, such as he knew the word of promise contemplated, and God designed, to be alone entitled to possess the throne: "He must be just, ruling in the fear of God." Not only so, but in his more specific charge to Solomon he expressly hung his expectation of the fulfilment of the word spoken, though spoken in a comparatively absolute manner, on the faithful adherence among his descendants to the law and testimony of God. For, after enjoining Solomon to walk in the ways and keep the statutes of God, he adds, as a reason for the charge, "that the Lord may continue His word, which He spake concerning me, saying, If thy children take heed to their way, to walk before me in truth, with all their heart, and with all their soul, there shall not fail thee a man on the throne of Israel" (1 Kings ii. 4). But when this fundamental condition was slighted, as it began to be, in the time of Solomon himself, the prophecy suffered forthwith a capital abridgement, so that the very language was now used respecting the house of David which had formerly been uttered of the house of Saul ("I will rend the kingdom from thee, and give it to thy servant," 1 Kings xi. 11, compared with 1 Sam. xv. 28), with this difference only, that so much was still left to the house of David as might save the prophecy from entire failure. And when, in process of time, the obstinate and incorrigible wickedness of the royal line led to still farther entrenchments on the promised good—when that stately and glorious house of David, as it appears in the original prophecy, had shrunk into a frail tabernacle; and even that tabernacle was made to fall down, rent and shattered on the earth, according to the figure of the prophet Amos, chap. ix. 11—then darkness seized the hearts of God's people, and fearful misgivings arose in their minds regarding the Divine faithfulness. The painful question was stirred in their bosoms, "Has His promise failed for evermore?" The thought even sometimes pressed upon them, "He has made void the covenant of His servant." And in Ps. lxxxix., we have a remarkable and interesting specimen of the manner in which faith struggled with these doubts regarding the Divine faithfulness as to this portion of His revealed purposes.

Still, as the event proved, all this respected only the mode and time of fulfilment. The prophecy, in its main theme, remained sure and steadfast. But the course of behaviour with which it was met on the part of those immediately concerned, led to breaks, to a temporary suspension, and a protracted delay in the accomplishment of the Divine purpose, very different from what was originally indicated in the word of Nathan. And so far—within these limits—it is perfectly legitimate and proper to say, that there was something conditional in the prophecy; not, indeed, so as to affect the great purpose itself of which the prophecy spake, and which could have its ultimate reason only in the sovereign will of God, but so as most materially to tell on the way in which the purpose travelled toward its accomplishment. Conditional it was to the extent of admitting some modification as to the how and when of its proper fulfilment, though not to the extent of hindering it from having such a fulfilment.

II. We leave, however, this class of prophecies, in which the conditional element, from their very nature, must necessarily be limited, and scarcely requires to be brought into particular notice as an element of importance in the interpretation of prophecy. But it is otherwise with the class of prophecies, which bear more directly upon men's responsibilities and duties—those which disclose, by way of promise or threatening, the course to be pursued by the Divine procedure toward men. Here, in point of fact, the conditional character of prophecy has often been prominently exhibited, and must always, we conceive, virtually, if not formally and expressly, enter into its announcements of things to come. This conditionality rests upon two great and fundamental principles. The first of which is, that in God's prophetical revelations of His mode of dealing with men, as in His revelations generally, all is based on an ethical foundation, and directed to an ethical aim; so that the prediction should never be viewed apart from the moral considerations on account of, or in connection with, which it was uttered. And the other principle is, that in giving intimations to men or communities of approaching good or evil, God speaks, as in other parts of Scripture, in an anthropomorphic manner; He addresses the subjects of His threatening or promise, more from a human than from a divine point of view; in other words, He adopts that mode of representation which is most natural to men, and which is best adapted for impressing and influencing their minds.

Let us take as an illustration of the proper working of these principles, the striking case of Nineveh, already referred to. After having sent His prophet to announce the destruction of Nineveh in a specified time, the Lord suffered the prophecy to fall into abeyance, refrained from executing the threatened doom, or, in the language of Scripture, He repented of the evil He said He would do to the city, because of the moral change that had meanwhile taken place among its inhabitants, as manifested in their turning from their evil ways. Why, we naturally ask, such a change in the mind of God? Why such a difference in His actual, from his previously meditated and announced, procedure? Simply, we answer, on the ground of the *first* principle mentioned above, from the predominantly ethical character of God's revelations and dealings; on account of which these must be all framed so as to convey just impressions of sin and righteousness, and preserve a proper correspondence between men's behaviour toward God, and His dealings toward them. The character of His administration, in itself, is such, that where sin is perseveringly and obstinately indulged in, it inevitably brings upon itself a doom of evil: while, on the other hand, if it is repented of and forsaken, the doom is averted, and a heritage of blessing substituted in its place. But alternations of this sort, so far from bespeaking God to be capricious in His ways, and changeable in the principles of His government, rather serve to manifest Him, in what alone is essential, as unalterably the same. Directing His procedure in accordance with the principles of righteousness, He *must* change His dealings toward men, when their relation to Him has become changed; since, otherwise, there would be only an *apparent* uniformity, but a *real* diversity. So, long ago, Abraham perceived when in his pleading for Sodom, he said, "That be far from Thee, to slay the righteous with the wicked, and that the righteous should be as the wicked; shall not the Judge of all the earth do right?" And so, also, the prophet Ezekiel met the captious spirits of his day, who, from looking more to the appearances than to the realities of things, complained of inequalities in the Divine administration, "Hear, now, O Israel, is not my way equal? Are not your ways unequal? When a righteous man turneth away from his righteousness, and committeth iniquities, and dieth in them; for his iniquity that he hath done shall he die. Again, when the wicked man turneth away from his wickedness that he hath committed, and doeth that which is lawful and right, he shall save his soul alive" (Ezek. xviii. 25–27). Hence, when Nineveh ceased from being a theatre where wickedness of every form was running riot, and became a place where the name of God was feared, and His authority respected, the measures of the Divine government fitly partook of a corresponding change; the people having passed into another condition, it was meet that they should be subjected to other treatment. And to have dealt with repenting, as it had been purposed to do with corrupt and profligate, Nineveh, would have been to disregard the essential distinctions between right and wrong in behaviour, and to make it fare with the righteous even as with the wicked.

It is with reference to these eternal principles of righteousness, that the declarations in Scripture are made, which deny the possibility of change in the administration of God: Such, for example, as is found in the word of Balaam, "God is not a man, that He should lie, neither the Son of man, that He should repent; hath He said, and shall He not do it? hath He spoken, and shall He not make it good?" (Num. xxiii. 19).

Or, in the word of Samuel, which is but a resumption, and fresh application of that of Balaam, "The Strength of Israel will not lie nor repent; for He is not a man, that He should repent" (1 Sam. xv. 29). Testimonies of this sort uniformly bear respect to such revealed purposes of God, as are inseparably connected with His inherent and immutable righteousness, and consequently admit of no change in the direction of His dealings. To purposes of that description belonged, as we have already stated, His fixed determination to connect, with the seed of Israel, His peculiar blessing. The covenant of God was with them, and in the time of Balaam, they stood, as a people, within the bonds of the covenant. And standing there, the faithfulness of God was pledged, to secure them against the assaults of any adversary, or the enchantments of any diviner. But when they fell from the obligations of the covenant—as thousands of them did, shortly after the word of Balaam was uttered, and in later times, the great mass of the people—then God made them to know, what He Himself called, His breach of promise (Numb. xiv. 34; Zech. xi. 10); He changed the blessing into a curse. In such a case, as in the reverse one of Nineveh, the change of dealing on the part of God, was necessitated by a change of relation, on men's part, to Him; and He could only maintain uniformity of action in the essential principles of His moral government, by giving a new turn to the course of His external administration.

But, such being the case, why, it may be asked, should not the prophetic word be always framed, so as to meet a possible change of this description? If it is to be understood conditionally, why should it not also speak conditionally? Why, to refer again to the case of Nineveh, instead of declaring absolutely, that the city should be overthrown in forty days, should it not rather have taken the form of announcing such a doom, in case the people did not repent? We reply, on the ground of the *second* principle, previously mentioned, that in this, as in His revelations generally, God spake as from the human point of view; He took up the case of the city as it stood at the time, and pronounced without qualification or reserve, its appropriate doom; knowing, perhaps, that the very absoluteness and precision of the form was the best fitted, it may be the *only* one actually calculated to arouse slumbering consciences, and lead to serious repentance. No doubt, if the thing done, had involved any breach of righteous principle—if the throwing of Jonah's message into such a form, had been a mere stroke of policy, inconsistent with the truth of things, in that case, however adapted to the higher end in view, it could not have been employed with the sanction and approval of God. But who would venture on such an affirmation? who has any right to say, that the predicted overthrow of wicked Nineveh would not have actually taken place, if Nineveh had persevered in its wickedness? There may have been, and doubtless were, instruments of destruction at hand, ready to do the work of judgment, if the Divine purpose had required them to do it. What we have here to do with, is simply the prophet's message, which must be held to have been a genuine and truthful utterance of God's mind and purpose toward Nineveh, in the circumstances of its existing position—as the place where sin had attained an enormous height, and cried in Heaven's ear for immediate vengeance. But when that position was shifted, when sin was repented of and abandoned, then another state of things, and one not contemplated in the message, came into being; the *cause* of the threatened evil had gone, and there was room now for the principle entering, "The curse causeless shall not come."

Indeed, the form, as to its main features, has a substantial parallel in the first great act in the drama of God's administration toward fallen man. The constitution of grace introduced at the fall, proceeded on the assumption, that not only was the human race to perpetuate its existence, but, that in its history, the good, upon the whole, was to prevail. What was then said and done, contained a matter-of-fact promise or prediction, that God should still have His delights with the children of men. Yet, when the era of the deluge approaches, we meet with the very strong declaration—the strongest in the whole Bible, as to a change of feeling or purpose in the mind of God, "It repented the Lord that He had made man upon the earth, and it grieved Him at His heart" (Gen. vi. 6). In this declaration, to use the words of Calvin, God is represented as "clothing Himself with our affections, that He might the more effectually penetrate our hearts, and impress us with His abhorrence of sin. It is as if He had said, 'This is not my workmanship; this is not the being I formed after my own image, and replenished with such noble endowments; I disdain to acknowledge such a corrupt and degenerate creature as my offspring.'" Or, as Hengstenberg puts it, with a more especial respect to God's end in creating man, "The words have respect, merely to the destination of man, to glorify God with a free and willing mind. Were this man's only, as it certainly is his original destination, God must have repented that He had made the degenerate race of mankind. What God would have done had this point alone come into consideration, He is here represented as having actually done, in order to impress upon the hearts of man, how great their corruption was, and how deep was God's abhorrence of their sin."[1] Whatever precise turn we may give to our explanation of the passage, there can be no doubt, that as a representation of the mind of God toward mankind at the close of the antediluvian period, it exhibits a very marked change as compared with what appeared at the beginning; and a change, which finds its justification in the two principles we have enunciated: first, that in God's revelations of Himself, whether *pro*spective or *retro*-spective, the ethical design and tendency ever has the foremost place; and secondly, that for the purpose more especially of effecting His aim in this, He discloses His character and purposes in a human manner, as the only way by which He can be properly understood, or can effectually reach our hearts.

So much is this the case, and so certainly does the truth involved in it underlie the whole prophetic testimony, in so far, at least, as this touches on the dangers or the expectations of men, that the prophet Jeremiah has formally announced it

[1] Authentie ii., p. 453.

as a definite principle of prophetical interpretation: "At what instant I shall speak concerning a nation, and concerning a kingdom, to pluck up, and to pull down, and to destroy; if that nation, against whom I have pronounced, turn from their evil, I will repent of the evil that I thought to do unto them. And at what instant I shall speak concerning a nation, and concerning a kingdom, to build and to plant; if it do evil in my sight, that it obey not my voice, then I will repent of the good wherewith I said I would benefit them" (Jer. xviii. 7–10). It may be the case that, for the most part, in the prospective delineations of good and evil which are given in prophecy, there was to be no such moral change in the subjects of them, as would call for the application of this principle in the interpretation of their import. More especially might this be expected to be generally the case in respect to the denunciations of coming judgment, which, being usually pronounced against inveterate adversaries of the truth, were but too unlikely, in most cases, to tell with a wholesome and reformatory influence on the subjects of them. Yet still even these the prophet Jeremiah teaches us to regard, as, in the first instance, in their more direct and primary object, intimations of God's displeasure on account of sin, and contingently only predictions of what should actually occur in providence. They did not, in any case, become, of necessity, events in history. Their doing so was a contingency depending on the spiritual state and behaviour of those over whom the threatenings of judgment were suspended. And to take such prophetic burdens in the fixed and absolute sense of announcements of evil, that *must* be executed as described, is plainly to overlook an essential element in the structure of prophecy, and possibly also to involve ourselves in inextricable difficulties as to its proper fulfilment.

How it would have happened, with such a mode of interpretation, in the case of Jonah's prophetic judgment against Nineveh, is obvious at first sight. But let us take another example, and one which has respect not to open and inveterate adversaries, but to parties standing within the bonds of the covenant, in whose case there was less to interfere with the moral action of the prophecy as a revelation of the mind and character of God. We shall take the prophetic utterance in the last words of Jacob on Levi and Simeon: "Cursed be their anger, for it was fierce; and their wrath, for it was cruel: I will divide them in Jacob, and scatter them in Israel." (Gen. xlix. 7.) As the language itself bears, this was of the nature of a curse. Only, indeed, *comparatively* so, for being themselves children of the covenant, and viewed as heads of a covenant-offspring, they still had a share in the blessing connected with the covenant, and are hence said to have been blessed by the patriarch, along with their brethren (ver. 28). But the sentence of judgment pronounced upon them, which took a form so strikingly retributive—destining them, in consequence of their former *union* in iniquity, to future *separation* and *scattering* in the land of their inheritance—this prophetic sentence of judgment evidently proceeded on the footing of a moral connection, which runs through the whole of Jacob's prophecy respecting the heads of the future Israel,—a connection, first of all, between righteousness and blessing, sin and punishment, and, still further, between the condition of the parents and the offspring as subjects respectively of the one or of the other. In the different sections of the covenant people there was to be a descending impulse in evil or good, to be transmitted from those patriarchal heads to their future descendants; and this was dwelt upon with such peculiar emphasis at that formative period of their history, for the purpose of stamping it indelibly upon the minds of the people, how essentially moral was the foundation on which the provisions of the covenant rested. So far as Simeon was concerned, the prophetic threatening of the dying parent appears to have produced no beneficial effect of a moral kind, and the germ of coming evil it contained took its natural course of development. Of all the tribes, that of Simeon suffered most severely from the divine judgments on the way to Canaan, implying, of course, that among its members there had been a sad pre-eminence in transgression; and in so enfeebled a condition did it enter the sacred territory, that, instead of having a separate province of its own, a portion was allotted it within the inheritance of the tribe of Judah (Joshua xix. 1). It was so shattered and dispersed, that it never properly attained to a distinct tribal standing, but became merged, as it would seem, in Judah; and its people are, doubtless, those more particularly referred to in 1 Kings xii. 17, as "the children of Israel that dwelt in the cities of Judah," who adhered to Rehoboam. Matters, however, turned out differently with Levi. From whatever cause it might be, probably from nothing more than a consideration of the solemn words of the dying patriarch, this tribe became distinguished for its piety and zeal in the cause of God; and on this account it was honoured above all the others, first by providing the great Deliverer and Lawgiver of the nation, and then by furnishing for the service of God the stated ministers of religion. In their case, therefore, while the dispersion in Israel, threatened in the prophetic judgment, might be said to be carried into effect, since the priests and Levites were in reality dispersed among the other tribes for the better discharge of their spiritual functions, yet, in accordance with their altered condition, the act came to assume a new character. What was originally announced as a brand of dishonour on the tribe of Levi, was at length turned into a mark of distinction; and if it served to render the sons of Levi politically weak, it provided for them, at the same time, the opportunity of becoming morally strong, assigned them, in fact, the place of highest influence so long as they were faithful to their high charge as the spiritual teachers and guides of Israel. The dispersion, indeed, was such that it could only become a source of weakness, if the great ends for which it was more immediately appointed were allowed to fall into abeyance. But the change thus put on the original prophecy, the new form and aspect given to the divine procedure toward the tribe of Levi, in consequence of the marked change in a moral respect its members afterwards underwent, is a striking exemplification of the principle of Jeremiah, as to the dependence in prophecies of this nature for the actual results on the spiritual state and conduct of the parties concerned.

If, in such cases, however, of threatened judgment, we find the principle strikingly exemplified, not less certainly may we expect to see it acted on in the opposite class of cases,—in those, namely, in which the theme of prophecy was of a blissful tendency. If a change in man's spiritual relation to God, from bad to good, necessitates a corresponding change in the manifestations he gives of himself to them, an alteration in the reverse order, from good to bad, must, in like manner, draw after it a partial or total suspension of God's intention to do them good. So that if the *threatened judgments* of the prophetic word, then also its *promised blessings*, are to be regarded, not as primarily and absolutely predictions of coming events, but rather as exhibitions of the Lord's goodness, prospective indications of his desire and purpose to bless the persons or communities addressed, yet capable of being checked, or even altogether cancelled, in the event of a perverse and rebellious disposition being manifested by men. The word of Jeremiah makes express mention of this class of cases, as well as the other. And the Apostle Paul re-announces the principle with special emphasis on this particular branch of its application, when he says, at the close of his reasoning on the case of the Jewish people, "Behold, therefore, the goodness and the severity of God: on them which fell severity, but toward thee goodness, *if thou continue in his goodness; otherwise, thou shalt also be cut off*" (Rom. xi. 22),—that is, the prophetic intimations of future blessing are to be understood as valid only so long as the spiritual relation contemplated in them abides. When that ceases, a new and different state of things has entered which the promise did not contemplate, and to which it cannot in justice be applied.

There is no want of cases of this description. They are even more numerous than those of the former class, and are to be found both in the larger and in the more limited sphere of things. Thus, in respect to a single family, a very emphatic seal was set on the principle by the dealings adopted with the house of Eli, when, for its profligacy, the right to minister in the priest's office was taken from it: "Wherefore, the Lord God of Israel saith, I said, indeed (viz., to Phinehas, their ancestor), that thy house, and the house of thy father, should walk before me for ever. But now the Lord saith, Be it far from me; for them that honour me I will honour, and they that despise me shall be lightly esteemed" (1 Sam. ii. 30). God never meant that the promise of blessing should hold good in all circumstances. Like the revelations, generally, of His mind and will, it was linked inseparably to His own moral nature; and as the degenerate offspring had abandoned the spiritual position of their forefather, the ground no longer existed on which the promised heritage of blessing proceeded. We have even, if possible, a still more specific case in New Testament Scripture, in the prophecy of future honour and blessing uttered by our Lord to the apostles. When speaking to the twelve, he said, "Verily I say unto you, that ye which have followed me, in the regeneration—when the Son of Man shall sit in the throne of His glory—ye also shall sit upon twelve thrones, judging the twelve tribes of Israel" (Matt. xix. 28). Yet one of these twelve was Judas, of whom the Lord knew, even then, that he should have no part in the matter, and that another should take his place. On a larger scale, the history of Israel is replete with changes and vicissitudes of a similar kind. Thus, when Moses was sent to them in Egypt, he came with a message from the Lord, that their groanings had been heard, and that now the promise given to their fathers, respecting the possession of the land of Canaan, was to be carried into effect. The message proceeded on the supposition, as was afterwards expressly declared (Ex. xix. 5, etc.), that they would hearken to the voice and obey the call of God. But failing, as the great majority of them did, to verify this supposition, the promised good was in their case never realized. So, again, the prophecies, which were uttered before they entered Canaan, respecting the portion of good things awaiting them there—that it should be to them "a land flowing with milk and honey"—that they should dwell in it alone among the nations, replenished with the favour of Heaven, and enjoying it as an everlasting possession:—Such prophecies as these, which were, in other words, promises of grace and goodness, could not be more than partially verified, because the children of the covenant were ever falling from the state of filial reverence and love, which was pre-supposed as the ground of all inheritance of blessing.

To sum up, then, upon this branch of our subject: When the predictions recorded in Scripture relate to things which belong peculiarly to God—when it is simply God's omniscience in foreseeing, His veracity in declaring, and His over-ruling providence in directing coming events that is concerned—then, undoubtedly, the predictions are to be regarded as of an absolute character—they foretell what infallibly shall come to pass. But when, on the other hand, the word of prophecy takes the shape, as it so often does, of threatenings of judgment, or promises of good things to come, the prophetic element is not the first and the determinate thing which must, at all events, develope itself, but rather that which is secondary and dependent. It always implies, if it does not expressly declare, a certain state of mind and course of behaviour as the ground of its prospective intimations. And before we inquire whether any events in Providence precisely correspond with those previously announced in the prophecy, there is a primary question to be settled, How far does the spiritual condition of the parties interested agree with what is implied or expressed in the prophetic announcement? Nor is this dependancė of such portions of prophecy on the condition of those, who are the subjects of them, a mere expedient devised to meet a difficulty in interpretation. On the contrary, it rests on a principle which is essentially connected with the nature of God, and therefore cannot but pervade the revelations he gives of his mind and will in Scripture. *There*, from first to last, all is predominantly of a moral or spiritual, as contradistinguished from a simply natural character; and in nothing more does the religion of the Bible, in its entire compass, differ from the religions of the world, than in the place it assigns to the principles of righteousness. These it constantly sets in the foremost rank, and subordinates to them all divine arrangements and purposes. It knows nothing of results in good or evil, coming as merely natural processes of development, but ever brings into account the eternal distinctions between sin and holiness, which have their root in the character of God. It was the capital error of the covenant people that they so often forgot this. Holding their position and their prospects formally in connection with their descent from Abraham, this simply natural element was ever apt to assume too high a place in their minds, and in their reckoning imparted an absolute and unconditional character to the promises of God. For *them*, a most pernicious and fatal mistake in experience, as it must also be for *us* in interpretation, if we should tread in their footsteps. We want the key to a right interpretation of all prophetic utterances of good and evil, unless we read them in the light of God's righteousness. And we shall certainly misunderstand both Him and them, if we suppose that, when He most loudly threatens visitations of evil, He shall execute the threatening where repentance, meanwhile, has taken place, or that He can continue to bless those who may have hardened their hearts in sin, however expressly and copiously He may have promised to do them good.

CHAPTER V.

THE PROPHETIC STYLE AND DICTION.

We proceed now to the consideration of a topic which bears even more closely and directly upon the interpretation of the prophetic Scriptures, than those hitherto discussed. We mean the appropriate style and diction of prophecy. The subject calls for the more particular and careful treatment, as it has been associated with many fanciful notions, and is now, more than ever, mixed up with modes of interpretation altogether groundless and indefensible. We shall, therefore, need to go at much greater length into this department of our inquiry, than has been necessary in regard to any of the points, which have already passed under our notice. And for the sake of greater distinctness, we shall view the subject in a negative light, before we look at it positively; in other words, we shall first endeavour to show, and that in opposition to prevailing errors, what is not the proper style and diction of prophecy, and then establish some of its more fundamental and essential characteristics, with the deductions that naturally arise from them.

SECTION I.

NEGATIVELY: WHAT IS NOT THE CHARACTER OF THE PROPHETIC STYLE AND DICTION.

By looking at the matter in this negative aspect, we have respect more particularly to one of the results growing out of the too exclusive contemplation of prophecy on its merely natural side, and in its apologetic use, as an argument for the defence of the Bible. Writing, as the exponent of an age and a class by whom this was very commonly done, Bishop Butler gave expression to the sentiment, which has since been many a time repeated, "Prophecy is nothing but the history of events before they come to pass."[1] Of course, if it be nothing but that, it should be written like that: as the *character* of both is the same, there can be no reason why the *style* of both should not also be substantially the same. Proceeding, therefore, on this ground, and carrying out the principle to its legitimate conclusions, two schools of prophetic interpretation have sprung up, having one starting-point in common, but wide as the poles asunder as to the goal, to which they deem the light of prophecy fitted to conduct us. The more Christian section reason thus: since prophecy is but history anticipated, all it reveals of the future must be taken as literally as history itself; every word must have its simple meaning attached to it—that and no more; so that the degree of fulfilment which has been given to any prophecy of Scripture, is to be ascertained and measured by the adaptation of what is written to events subsequently occurring, viewed simply in the light of a pre-historical intimation of them; whatever has not been so fulfilled must be regarded as still waiting for its accomplishment in the future. And as this view seemed to betoken a high regard for the exact and perfect truthfulness of the prophetic record, so by pressing the literality of some of its announcements, it appeared for a time to gain in value, and to furnish new weapons for the confutation of the adversary. Hence the popularity of such works on prophecy as have been written to show what numerous and exact correspondences can be pointed out in the past or present state of the world, with the prophetic delineations of Scripture, and how often the language of prophecy has proved like that of history, by receiving the most close and palpable verifications.

[1] Analogy, Part II., chap. 7.

We are far from wishing to undervalue works of this description, or denying that they have rendered any service to the cause of divine truth. They have unquestionably contributed to awaken a more lively interest in this portion of the word of God, and have also helped to diffuse a more general and intelligent belief in its verity, by fixing attention on certain undeniable fulfilments of its predictions. But it is perfectly possible that the efforts in this direction may have somewhat overshot their proper mark; that the advantage obtained on one side may have been pushed so far as to create a disadvantage on another; that the evidence of a close and literal fulfilment of particular prophecies, by being carried beyond its due limits, may have given rise to views and expectations respecting the structure and design of prophecy in general, which are neither warrantable in themselves, nor capable of being vindicated by a reference to historical results. Such, indeed, has proved to be the case. This principle of regarding prophecy as merely anticipative history, will not stand, by any fair construction, with some of the recorded examples of fulfilled prophecy mentioned in New Testament Scripture. It would oblige us to consider these as little better than fanciful or arbitrary accommodations. And even in the midst of those, which to a certain extent admit of being read in the exact and literal style of history, there often occur passages which have obviously received no fulfilment of a similar description. The consequence has been, that the number of fulfilled prophecies has been constantly lessening in the hands of this school of interpreters. Not a few that at one period were held to have received their accomplishment, have latterly, by the more stringent and uniform application of the principle of historic literality, been thrown into the class, which are to stand over for their fulfilment till the time of the end. And of those, which seem to have found their verification in the facts of gospel history, a considerable portion are allowed to have had only a kind of preliminary fulfilment —such a fulfilment as is at most but a prelude and earnest of the proper one.

It is no new thing for extremes to meet; and so far there is a coincidence between this school of interpreters, and another of a very different spirit, that they both agree in reducing very much the number of fulfilled prophecies. This latter class, however, hold, that there are few, if any, to be fulfilled, scarcely, indeed, any that can be fitly characterized as history written beforehand, while the others do not question their existence, but only, in the case of the greater part, transfer the period of their fulfilment to the yet undeveloped future. On the hypothetical ground, that, in so far as prophecy may be descriptive of coming events in Providence, it must be written like history, the school we now refer to, think, some that they can find very little, others almost nothing so written among the prophecies of Scripture; and so, practically, they come in great measure to change the idea of prophecy—to deny, that its object was to give any precise or definite outline of the future, and to regard it rather as the varied expression of men's fears or longings as to what might be found therein. Thus, Schleiermacher, who may be said, if not to have originated, at least to have rendered current, this mode of thinking regarding prophecy, was of opinion, that in Old Testament Scripture there are no actual predictions of the Messiah; nothing more than indistinct longings, expressions on the part of pious men of their felt need of redemption—such also, only more intense and earnest, as some, even among the heathen, were conscious of. It were certainly wrong to say, that Dr Arnold, in this country, went so far as this, in disavowing the predictive character of Scriptural prophecy; yet, there are some passages in his writings, which seem to come very near to it. "If you put," he writes in a letter to Dr Hawkins, written about two years before his death, "If you put, as you may do, Christ for abstract good, and Satan for abstract evil, I do not think, that the notion is so startling, that they are the main and only proper subjects of prophecy, and that, in all other cases, the language is, in some part or other, hyperbolical—hyperbolical, I mean, and not merely figurative. Nor can I conceive how, on any other supposition, the repeated applications of the Old Testament language to our Lord, not only by others, but by Himself, can be understood to be other than arbitrary." This evacuating, on Arnold's part, of nearly all that was properly predictive in prophecy, and in respect to what one might look for distinct and circumstantial fulfilments in Providence, was, in one sense, a revulsion from the common practice of assimilating prophecy to history. He held them to be essentially different in their characteristic features and objects; but did so in a way, which, at the same time, left little for it to do in foretelling things to come—in short, lessened the predictive element in it in proportion as he magnified its dissimilarity to the historical. In reality, therefore, there are here also the same fundamental ideas, only differently assorted and made to work to a different result. It is supposed, that prophecy to be, in the ordinary sense, predictive in character, must be historical in style; and that it possesses little of the one, because it partakes little of the other.

There are not wanting persons, however, bearing the Christian name, but possessing little of the Christian spirit, who would rob prophecy altogether of its predictive character, on the ground of its containing no historical delineations of the future, which lie beyond the reach of human foresight. Thus, Theodore Parker affirms, "The writings of the prophets contain nothing above the reach of the human faculties. Here are noble and spirit-stirring appeals to men's conscience, patriotism, honour, and religion; beautiful poetic descriptions, odes, hymns, expressions of faith almost beyond praise. But the mark of human infirmity is on them all, and proofs or signs of miraculous inspiration are not found in them." That they commonly prefaced their declarations by, "Thus saith the Lord," merely arose, we are informed, from the prevalent Jewish feeling, which regarded every manifestation of religious and moral power as the direct gift of God. But it is denied, that any of them ever uttered "a distinct, definite, and unambiguous prediction of any future event that has since taken place, which a man, without a miracle, could not equally well predict." And in regard, particularly to Messianic prophecy, we have the bold assertion, "it has never been shewn that there is, in the whole of the Old Testament, one single instance, that, in the plain and natural sense of the words, foretells the birth, life, or death of Jesus of Nazareth."[1] This might seem to be going far enough in the depreciation of the prophetic Scriptures, in their predictive character, but there is a phase beyond it still. For, Mr Foxton, in what he calls his "Popular Christianity," not only maintains that there *are* no proper predictions of things to come in Scripture, but that there *cannot* be. He holds the doctrine of prophecy to be "directly at variance with the theory of Providence,"—the theory, namely, of a providence proceeding entirely according to general laws, as opposed to any particular interpositions of Divine power. The farthest he can go is to admit, that men of superior intellect and sagacity, who have acquired more than ordinary insight into the laws of nature and God's dealings in providence, may sometimes have uttered what, in common language, might be called predictions. Thus, "the prophecy of Christ, concerning the destruction of Jerusalem, recorded by St Matthew, may be interpreted as a simple instance of political foresight into an event extremely probable in the existing condition of his country. And the same may be said generally of the predictions of the earlier Jewish prophets respecting the probable fortunes of their nation. The prophecies of the advent of Christ, when stript of the ingenious explanations, forced constructions, and subtle spirit of adaptation displayed by critics and commentators, are nothing more than instances of a speculative expectation of those reformations of society, which the periodical appearance of men of genius, after long periods of corruption, always renders probable in the history of nations."[2]

[1] Absolute Religion, p. 205-9.

[2] Popular Christianity, p. 120. We take no notice of some of the more offensive things in this volume; as when the prophets of the Old Testament are spoken of as having visions precisely akin to those of Swedenborg of Sweden, Jacob Behmen of Germany, and James Nayler of England.

Such are the extremes to which, in different hands, the tendency has run, to place prophecy, in so far as it may be predictive, on a level with history, as to style and diction. On the one hand, some finding little or nothing, as they conceive, of such prophecy in the Bible, altogether, or very nearly deny it the possession of predictions in the proper sense; while others maintain, that they abound, indeed, in sufficient number, but that comparatively few have, as yet, been properly fulfilled. It becomes us, therefore, to look well to the foundation, out of which such tendencies and results have grown; and we shall do so with more especial reference to those, who appear to take up in good faith, the historical view of prophecy, and regard it as necessary to the strict veracity of God's word.

The great argument of the persons, who advocate this view, is the exact fulfilment of many prophecies already accomplished, and especially of those which pointed to the appearance and history of Christ on earth. Never, it is alleged, were facts more literally described than those which were foretold to take place, and actually have taken place, in connection with the events of gospel history. But if the principle of literal exactness, or historical precision holds there, why should it not be understood as holding also in other parts of prophetical Scripture? What can a departure from it be but a corruption of the simplicity of the divine word? And so, since throughout we have to do with plain historical description on the one side, and corresponding matters of fact upon the other, "the vision which Isaiah (for example) saw concerning Judah and Jerusalem," the heading of his whole book, must be viewed as bearing immediate respect only to the Jewish people, and their land and city. So also in regard to what is written generally in the prophetic word, Edom is to be taken literally of Edom, Moab of Moab, Egypt of Egypt, Zion of Zion, and Jerusalem of Jerusalem.

Now, if the ground on which this stringent literality is contended for were real; if the sense, which past fulfilments of prophecy appear to have put on the predictions of Scripture, were uniformly that alone of the historical and literal; then, we should not hesitate to regard it as a settled point, that the past should in this respect rule the future, and that for prophecy in general, what remains to be fulfilled, as well as what has already been fulfilled, all must be understood and interpreted like history. But is it so in reality? Let us put the principle to the test; let us try it even with the first prophecy uttered in the ears of fallen man. Addressing the serpent the Lord said, "And I will put enmity between thee and the woman, and between they seed and her seed: it shall bruise thy head, and thou shalt bruise his heel." Here, the seed of the woman beyond all doubt is the woman's offspring—a child of promise, or, collectively (as the word *seed* is commonly taken), a line of children to be born of her; and, consequently, the serpent—if all must be taken in the prosaic style, and read as history—can only be that creature of the field then present, and its seed the offspring, which might afterwards by natural generation proceed from it. The prophecy, therefore, speaks merely of the injuries to be received from serpents on the one side, and of the killing of serpents on the other: and any member of Eve's future family, who might have the fortune to kill a serpent, should, by so doing, verify the prophecy. For, taking all in a simply historical aspect, as the woman's seed must be one or more of human-kind, so the serpent and his seed can only comprehend what is of the serpent-kind. Such is a fair application of the principle of a bald and naked literalism; and the fruitful result it enables us to extract from the primeval promise to a fallen world, is an assurance of man's relative superiority to the most subtle of beasts, and the ultimate destruction of the serpent-brood! Could the lowest rationalism find any thing more suited to its purpose? Or, could the pitiable condition of the parents of the human family, and the great necessities of their fallen state, have been more bitterly mocked? It would truly have been giving them a serpent for bread.[1]

[1] This is really all that Hofmann finds in the original promise, the spirit of literalism in him leading to the same result as the spirit of ra-

Those who can rest in such a conclusion, and see nothing in it at variance with the character of God and the general tenor of his revelations to men, are not to be reasoned with, but must be held naturally or morally incompetent to deal with matters of such a kind. We, therefore, affirm, that the simply literal for prophecy will not do at the very outset; and that to apply it to the first prophetic announcement connected with the hopes of mankind, were only to burlesque the occasion of its deliverance. Let it be, that some respect was therein had to the natural enmity, which was henceforth to subsist between the serpent-brood and the human family; still, when the whole circumstances of the case are taken into account, this cannot now, nor could it ever, be regarded as more than a sign or emblem of the spiritual truth, which lay underneath, and which alone constitutes its prophetic import for Adam and his offspring. "The warfare," as has been justly remarked,[1] "which the human race have carried on and successfully with the serpent-brood, has been merely a repetition by emblems of the predicted warfare, which the spiritual seed have been carrying on against the spiritual old serpent, who is the devil—which prediction received its highest accomplishment, when Christ at his crucifixion and resurrection triumphed over Satan; when the conqueror bruised Satan's head after the tempter had bruised the victor's heel." How, indeed, could a thoughtful mind rest satisfied with any other than a spiritual interpretation of the prophecy? It was not a physical, but a spiritual conquest, which the tempter had achieved,

tionalism in others. He asks, if there was no matter of joy in these words of God for man? And answers, "Nothing, but that it was not quite over with them. They were to live for a time, and perpetuate their nature in offspring like themselves" (Weissagung and Erfullung, i. p. 76). The simple prolongation of existence as opposed to utter destruction, was all they had given them to hope for! Such literalism finds a fitting parallel in the rationalist Credner's view of Joel ii. 28, who thinks that the *all flesh*, on which the Spirit is to be poured out, must mean absolutely all, beasts as well as men, yea even locusts.

[1] The Structure of Prophecy by James Douglas, Esq. of Cavers, p. 28.

and which, according to the principles of the divine government, drew after it the heritage of natural evil that rushed in upon the world. Could it be seriously imagined, that the successful warfare which was now with divine help to be waged, and the final victory that was to be won by the woman's seed, should be of an inferior kind to that accomplished by the serpent? The good promised should in that case have been no proper reversion of the evil. Even the language by its poetical colouring naturally carries the mind to this higher aspect of things, and lodges a silent protest against the notion of a flat and prosaic literalism. To bruise a serpent's head is a natural expression for putting it to death, making a final end of its power to injure or destroy; but who ever heard of a serpent, in the natural sense, bruising a person's heel? To speak thus is not to speak in the style of history, as if the object were to give a naked unvarnished account of a specific result hereafter to be expected; not this, but rather a picturing out, by means of existing relations, and with a measure of poetic freedom, of the general nature of what was in prospect, as to the relative positions of the contending parties, and the final issue of the struggle.

Rightly viewed, therefore, this first prophecy is an instructive example, not in favour of, but against, the idea of prophecy being *merely* history written beforehand. It is a sign and witness set up at the very threshold of the prophetic territory, showing how much prophecy, in the general form of its announcements, might be expected to take its hue and aspect from the occasion and circumstances that gave rise to it—how it would serve itself of things seen and present, as a symbolical cover, under which to exhibit a perspective of things which were to be hereafter—and how, even when there might be a *certain* fulfilment of what was written according to the letter, the terms of the prediction might yet be such as to make it evident that something of a higher kind was required properly to verify its meaning. Such plainly was the case with respect to the prediction at the fall; and in proof that it must be so read and understood, some of the later intimations of prophecy, which are founded upon the address to the serpent, vary the precise form of the representation which they give of the ultimate termination of the conflict. Thus Isaiah, when descanting on the peace and blessedness of Messiah's kingdom, tells us not of the serpent's head being bruised, but of his power to hurt being destroyed; of dust being his meat, and of the child playing upon his hole (chap. xi. 8, 9; lxv. 25). It is the same truth, again, that appears at the close of the Revelation, under the still different form of chaining the old serpent, and casting him into the bottomless pit, that he might not deceive the nations any more (Rev. xx. 2, 3),—his power to deceive in the one case corresponding to his liberty to bruise the heel in the other, and his being chained and imprisoned in the bottomless pit to the threatened bruising of his head.

The introduction of type into the scheme of God's revelations brought another peculiarity into the region of prophecy, and still farther increased its tendency to diverge from the simple and direct style of historical narration. Every type was, so far, a prophecy, that under the form of sensible things, and by means of present outward relations, it gave promise of other things yet to come, corresponding in design, but higher and better in kind. And hence, when a prophetic word accompanied the type, or pointed to the things which it prefigured, it naturally foretold the antitypical under the aspect, or even by the name, of the typical. At the time the first promise was given, nothing of a properly typical nature yet existed to weave into the prophetic delineation. There was only the loss of Nature's heritage of good, and in that loss the triumph of the principle of evil; so that in the prospect held out of an ultimate recovery, there was room only for a symbolical use of what was, or had been, to image what should hereafter be. But as the scheme of Providence proceeded on its course, bringing, from time to time, its temporary and partial provisions of blessing, these commonly became to men of prophetic insight the form under which the better and more enduring reality presented itself to their view, as well as the pledge of its certain realization. We have elsewhere treated of this at large, and need not enter into detail concerning it here.[1] But as an evidence how materially the diction thus formed differed from that proper to history, we may refer to the single example of Ezekiel xxxiv. 24, "And I, the Lord, will be their God, and my servant, David, a prince among them"—where, assuredly, another personage must be understood than the historical David; one who, in that greater and more glorious future, would hold relatively to the kingdom of God the same place which had been held by the Son of Jesse in the best period of the past. In any other way it is impossible to extract a suitable meaning from the prediction, and to avoid putting on it a sense that is utterly incongruous or puerile.

Nor is this all. There are many passages in the prophets in which the application to them of a strict and historical literalism would not only evacuate their proper meaning, but render them absolutely ridiculous and inconsistent one with another. Nothing, surely, can be more evident to a simple reader of the prophetic writings than that one of their great objects, the burden not of one or two only, but of many of their predictions respecting Messiah, was to have the hearts of men prepared for His coming by a genuine repentance and moral reformation. But take the prophecy on this subject in Isaiah xl., and we shall find that, according to the principle now under consideration, it is something quite different which was announced as going to precede the Lord's advent. Referring to the words of the prophet, and describing his own mission, the Baptist said: "I am the voice of one crying in the wilderness, Prepare ye the way of the Lord. Make straight in the desert a highway for our God; every valley shall be exalted, and every mountain and hill shall be laid low; and the crooked shall be made straight, and the rough places plain." The language, it will be observed, understood as a naked and historical delineation of what should take place before the Lord's personal appearance, speaks only of external changes and re-

[1] Typology of Scripture, vol. i. p. 100 sq.

forms on the earth's surface, such as might more suitably adapt it to purposes of travel. And as no beneficial improvements of that description, in the Baptist's time, nor even to the present day, have been accomplished in Palestine, the opinion has been avowed by the advocates of historical simplicity and directness in prophecy that the prediction still remains unfulfilled—that, in its leading import, it must refer not to the first, but to the second advent. And the thought has even been suggested whether it may not refer to that great improvement of modern times, the levelling of hills, the elevating of valleys, and straitening of paths, by means of railroads? A happy thought, no doubt, if the object for which the Spirit of prophecy had kindled the bosom of Isaiah had been to light the way to inventions in art and science, or, if the essential condition of the Lord's coming to dwell among His people was their providing for Him the means of an easy and rapid conveyance in an earthly chariot! But before this can be admitted, we must entirely change our ideas of the Bible, and the purport of Messiah's appearance among men.

We shall refer to another prediction of Isaiah, found at the commencement of the second chapter, where, in speaking of the glory of the latter days, he says, "It shall come to pass that the mountain of the Lord's house shall be established on the top of the mountains, and shall be exalted above the hills; and all nations shall flow unto it." It is spoken absolutely, and, therefore, if taken as an historical delineation, must be regarded as importing that the little elevation of the temple-mount shall be projected upwards, and made to overtop in height the loftiest of the Himmalayas—and that, too, for the purpose of increasing its attraction as a centre of religious intercourse to the world, and drawing men in crowds toward it from the most distant regions. What a mighty revolution —what an inversion even of the natural state of things, this would imply, it is needless to point out. Yet the interpretation now given has often been adopted, as conveying the real meaning of the prophecy, if not to the extent of making Zion absolutely the loftiest summit on the earth's surface, at least to the extent of its elevation above all the hills in that region of the earth. So common, indeed, had this view of the literal elevation of Mount Zion in the latter days, become in the time of Edward Irving, that we find him excusing himself from not implicitly adopting it. He expresses, indeed, his belief that there would be "some remarkable geographical changes on the face of the earth, and especially in the Holy Land"—so that he was "far from slighting the more literal interpretation of the passage;" yet, withal, "he inclines to think that the glory of Zion, in the eye of the prophet, standeth rather in this,—that it shall acquire such a celebrity in those days as shall bring low the most noted of the mountains of the earth, and the eyes of all men upon it, being the centre of the worship of the whole world." Even the better sort of Jewish rabbies read with a less fleshly eye the meaning of the prophet. "It does not mean," says Kimchi, "that the mountain shall be raised in bulk, but that the nations shall exalt and honour it, and shall go there to worship the Lord." But we have a surer interpreter here than either Jewish rabbies or Christian divines. For the prophet Ezekiel, evidently referring to this prediction of Isaiah, connects it with circumstances which *oblige* us to understand the relative elevation of the sacred mount, as of a *spiritual*, not of a *natural*, kind, and as verified in what already *has been*, not in what is *yet to be*. Representing the seed of David as the subject of promise, under the image of a twig of a lofty cedar, and contrasting what the Lord would do to this, with what was to become of the twig cropped from the same cedar by the king of Babylon, the prophet says in the name of the Lord, "I also will take of the highest branch of the high cedar, and will set it; I will crop off from the top of his young twigs a tender one, and will plant it upon an high mountain and eminent: in the mountain of the height of Israel will I plant it; and it shall bring forth boughs, and bear fruit, and be a goodly cedar; and under it shall dwell all fowl of every wing; in the shadow of the branches thereof shall they dwell" (chap. xvii. 22, 23). There cannot be the smallest possible doubt that the young and tender twig here mentioned represents Jesus of Nazareth, the branch, as he is elsewhere called, out of the roots of Jesse, and represents Him in His *first* appearance among men, when he came in the low condition of a servant, to lay through suffering and blood the foundation of His everlasting kingdom. For, it is of the *planting* of the twig that the prophet speaks, and of its original littleness when so planted, as compared with its future growth, and ultimate peerless elevation. Yet even of those very beginnings of the Messiah's work and kingdom, it is said, that they were to take place on "an high mountain and eminent," on "the mountain of the height (the mountain-height) of Israel." So that, as seen in prophetic vision, the elevation had already taken place when Christ appeared in the flesh, the little hill of Zion had even then become an enormous mountain; in other words, it was not the natural, but the spiritual, aspect of things which was present to the eye of the prophets, when they made use of such designations. All Israel was in their view a height, because distinguished and set up above the nations by its sacred privileges;[1] Mount Zion was the loftiest elevation in that height, because *there* was the seat and centre of what rendered Israel pre-eminent among the nations; and when seen as the place where God, manifest in the flesh, was to accomplish the great redemption, and unspeakably enhance the good, by turning what before was shadow into substance, then its moral grandeur indeed appeared transcendent, and all that might be called great and lofty in the world shrank into littleness as compared with it. Here now was the world's centre—the glory that eclipsed every other.

If it were necessary to our argument, and would not lead us too far from our present purpose, we might strengthen the ground of this interpretation, by showing how commonly in prophetic language powers or kingdoms, as such, are spoken of under the image of mountains—mountains varying in height or stability according to the character and position of

[1] See Ezekiel xxxiv. 14, and the note there in my Commentary.

the kingdoms themselves. We merely refer to the fact (giving a few instances in the note[1]), and shall find occasion when we come to treat of the *positive* aspect of the subject, to shew the essential connection of such a style of representation with the usual form in which prophetic insight was given. But from the examples already adduced, it is manifest, that if we would not render prophecy in some parts utterly fantastical, and in others plainly inconsistent and contradictory, we need other rules to guide our interpretations, than that of a strict adherence to historical simplicity. Prophecy *cannot* be always read merely as history antedated. And the absolute impossibility of making out, on such a principle, a prophetic harmony, or, to state it positively, the inevitable confusion and discord it would introduce into the prophetic record, may be further seen by a comparison of the diverse and, historically considered, antithetical representations, that are given of the religious changes that were to come in with the gospel dispensation. Sometimes this appears as a revival and perfecting of the old, and sometimes, again, as the entire supplanting of it by something higher and better. Thus Isaiah, in certain places, speaks of the future glory as consisting in the full re-establishment of the old things, the erection of the temple in surpassing magnificence, the rigorous enforcement of its ritual, and the vieing of all nations with each other to frequent its courts and celebrate its services (chap. lx.; lvi. 7, 8; lxvi. 21–23); while, in other places, he pours contempt upon the old, as not worthy to be mentioned, treats the erection of a material temple, like that which formerly existed, as a thing no longer to be thought of, and holds out promises of blessing, which imply the abolition of the ordinances introduced by Moses (chap. lxv. 17; lxvi. 1–3; lvi. 3–5). In like manner, Jeremiah, setting forth, at chap. iii. 16, the superiority of the latter days, affirms that the time was coming when they should no more remember or speak of the ark of the covenant, nor make such a thing—meaning,

[1] See Appendix D.

that the peculiar sacredness and glory belonging to it should then be more widely diffused, not confined to so limited a spot. In another place (chap. xxxi. 31), he tells us of the supplanting of the old covenant entirely by a new one, founded on better promises; and yet, passages again occur in which he depicts the full and perfect re-establishment of the ancient order of things, as the glory of those latter days (chap. xxx. 18–22; xxxiii. 15–22). To mention no more, Ezekiel's last vision of the brighter future presents all under the aspect of a re-edified temple, perfect in its structure and arrangements; while, in St John's last vision, it takes the form of a holy city, complete in its proportions, and composed of the most precious materials, but having in it no temple. There *is* a principle, we may be well assured, which is quite sufficient to harmonise these different representations, and render them perfectly consistent with one another; but no skill or sophistry can ever persuade simple and unprejudiced men, that such a harmonising principle is to be found in reading the whole as one would read history—taking all as matter-of-fact descriptions of gospel times, or the millennial age. On that principle, the contradiction is necessarily real, and we have no alternative, according to it, but that of holding by one portion of the prophetic future, and letting go another.

Nor would such be the result merely with what may be still regarded as the prophetic future, and in respect to which endless and fanciful conjectures, for reconciling things which differ, may be thrown out; it would hold equally with what once was a prophetic future, but is now the historical past or present; for many of the representations we have noticed point to the New Testament dispensation generally, and necessarily bear respect to what has already come to pass. Indeed, it is difficult to say what a fair and uniform application of the principle of historical interpretation to the style of prophecy would leave us of prophetical fulfilments. Micah, for example, predicted that out of Bethlehem was to come forth He that was to be Ruler in Israel, the Messiah, as King of Zion. But it is held as a settled point by those who read prophecy like history, that Messiah has not yet appeared in the character of the King of Zion, or Ruler in Israel; so that, we should suppose, the predicted coming out of Bethlehem, in the proper sense, had yet to take place. In like manner it must be maintained that he shall yet have to make good the prophecy of Zechariah, by riding into Jerusalem on an ass, since it was distinctively as the King of Jerusalem, that the act in question was to be performed by Him. We are afraid, indeed, that on this principle a large portion of Christ's earthly career, which the Evangelists have described as finished, and finished in accordance with the intimations of prophecy, must be regarded as still future. For when, according to one prophecy of Isaiah, was He actually anointed, or oiled, to preach the gospel to the poor? or, according to another, was precisely His back given to the smiters? Where do we read, in literal conformity with the Psalmist's words respecting Him, of His ears having been bored; or of His sinking in deep waters, where there was no standing; or of His being heard from the horns of the unicorns? Such things, and others of a like nature, were written concerning Messiah in the Psalms and prophets; and if all were to be ruled by a principle of historical literalism, the conclusion seems inevitable that the predicted humiliation of the Messiah has been accomplished but in part by Jesus of Nazareth—a conclusion which could be hailed with satisfaction only by unbelieving Jews, as it is also one that is the legitimate result of their own carnal principles of interpretation.[1]

To conclude on this point, we object to the treatment of prophecy as merely anticipated history, or to the strictly literal principle of prophetical interpretation:—First, because, in point of fact, this principle is not justified by all the applications made of prophecy in New Testament Scripture, nor by the course of Providence in certain cases, at least, which may confidently be reckoned those of fulfilled prophecy; secondly, because it would necessitate, if uniformly applied and carried

[1] See Appendix E.

out, the belief of many things utterly extravagant or absurd, as necessary to verify the prophetic word; and finally, because it would render one part of this word manifestly inconsistent with another.

These objections, it is to be understood, are not urged against the *existence* of an historical element in prophecy, but only against the *mode* of ascertaining it—against the principle, that prophecy in its predictive character is written substantially in the style and diction of history. While we contend against its being so written, or interpreted as if such had been the case, we still strenuously maintain, that if understood in its proper nature, and interpreted in a manner agreeable to that, it will be found in many of its announcements capable of yielding clear and specific historical results. The prophecy, for example, of Ezekiel, recently referred to, not less certainly foretells the appearance of the King of Zion in a state of deep humiliation, the founding of His kingdom amid circumstances outwardly mean, yet of vast spiritual moment, and its subsequent growth to universal sovereignty, that it represents all under the image of a slender twig planted on the summit of Israel, and rising and expanding till it overtopt all the trees of the field. In such a representation there are unquestionably involved conditions of an historical kind, which required to be met by definite corresponding facts in providence—such facts precisely as are recorded in the gospel history. At the same time, the prophecy differs materially in the form it assumes, from that of historical narration, and, as regards the events actually in prospect, plainly exhibits these in an aspect that must have appeared somewhat obscure, till it was shone upon and informed by the events themselves. But then, something of this kind was necessary to the very evidence which was to be furnished to the truth of Scripture by fulfilments of prophecy. A certain veil required to hang over the prophetic field, up to the time that its predictions passed into realities; otherwise, there would have been room for the allegation, that the palpable clearness of the prophecy had prompted the efforts that led to its fulfilment. The allegation, in fact, *has* been made, in respect to some of the most important parts of the prophetic Scriptures. Lord Bolingbroke did not scruple to assert, that Jesus Christ brought about his own death by a series of preconcerted measures, merely to give his disciples the advantage of an appeal to the old prophecies. "This was ridiculous enough (to use the words of Dr Chalmers[1]); but it serves to show, with what facility an infidel might have evaded the whole argument, had these prophecies been free from all that obscurity which is now complained of. The best form (he adds) for the purposes of argument, in which a prophecy can be delivered, is to be so obscure, as to leave the event, or rather its main circumstances, unintelligible before the fulfilment, and so clear as to be intelligible after it." It may be said, indeed, that the problem to be solved by prophecy was to speak of the future in such a way as to admit of its being fulfilled, before its import was distinctly perceived by the persons taking part in the fulfilling of it, and yet to leave no proper room to doubt, that the things they did constituted the actual future pointed to in the prophecy. It were not easy to conceive a train of circumstances, in which these conditions were more remarkably met, than in those connected with the personal appearance and history of Christ in the world. Throughout the whole of it, prophecies were continually passing into fulfilment, and for the most part, actually did so before they either were or could be brought into remembrance by those who were taking part in the transactions. So far from its being the prediction which led to the doing of the things which accomplished it, it was the doing of the things which first suggested the prediction, and brought to light what had previously lain in a neglected obscurity. In this peculiarity, therefore, of the structure of prophecy, this felicitous combination of light and shade, we have a signal proof of the unsearchable wisdom of God, in directing those who uttered its predictions.

[1] Works, vol. iii. p. 347.

It is proper, however, to add, that while the style of prophecy always to some extent differs from that proper to history, it is not itself uniform in this respect, but is subject to change. It purposely spake of the future in "divers manners," accommodating itself to the diversified circumstances in which it was given, and the more specific objects it contemplated. In the comparative fulness and frequency of its communications, as we had occasion formerly to remark (ch. ii.), it varied exceedingly from time to time, and, as a general rule, increased in proportion to the dangers and difficulties of the period, or the magnitude of the subjects involved. The same considerations naturally had some influence also on the form of the prophetic announcements, as to their approaching nearer to the directness and circumstantiality of history, or receding farther from it. Sometimes general intimations regarding the course and issues of things might be enough for the support of faith, and the ordinary discharge of duty; while more full and explicit announcements of coming events might be called for in circumstances of an unusually perplexing or perilous nature. It was in such circumstances that Elijah had to do the work of a prophet in Israel. Spiritual wickedness in high places had assumed so bold a front, that there was the most imminent danger of overwhelming ruin; and the prophet coming forth as a mighty wrestler with the evil, there is an awful force and directness in his words—he speaks as already standing amid the scenes, which he perceived to be at hand. In like manner Jeremiah, though cast in a different mould from Elijah, yet because placed in circumstances of similar backsliding and rebuke, speaks often in the plainest terms of approaching events; and in those portions of his writings that relate to the nearer future,—such, for example, as chap. xxiv., xxv., xxxi., l., li.,—has greatly more of the historical element than in such as point to times subsequent to the return from Babylon. Matters of fact abound in the one, while they are scarcely to be found in the other. So also in the Messianic prophecies, as a class, the same diversity is observable; there is more that is general in the earlier part, more that is specific in the later. By far the most explicit and circumstantial predictions were reserved for the time, when the old covenant and its earthly kingdom were tottering to their foundations, or existing only in an impaired and enfeebled condition. The heart of faith required then more special supports to bear it up; and suiting itself to the necessities of the case, the Spirit of prophecy began to disclose with greater freedom and distinctness the things which concerned Messiah's appearance and kingdom, and gave the picture of the coming future, if we may so speak, more of an historical setting.

Nor was this gradual approach to historical distinctness required, merely for those who lived in the latter days of the Hebrew commonwealth; it was also necessary for the generation that should witness the coming of the Messiah, and those of after times. As He was to present Himself to their acceptance in the character of a *promised* Redeemer, certain marks, of an external kind, to be verified amid the transactions of history, were necessary to assure them, that He who should come, actually did come. The vision, in this respect, must be written so plain, that no sincere inquirer could fail to perceive the correspondence between the promise and the fulfilment. But this it could only be by touching at many points on the common relations and circumstances of life, such as are patent to the observation and level to the capacities of the simpler order of minds. In such a matter, men could not be left to grope their way to the truth, by the help merely of internal considerations or general characteristics. So that, however the prophecies which went before, may have differed in their style of delineation from the histories which followed after, the coming of Messiah, they must still, to accomplish the purpose they had in view, have borne distinct reference, and furnished a kind of pre-historical testimony, to certain things that should hereafter appear in the outward domain of history.

If due weight be given to the considerations now stated, there will be no need for holding some of the prophecies in Daniel (especially chap. viii. and xi.), on account of their historical details, to be at variance with the essential character of prophecy, and, therefore, liable to the suspicion of having been written after the events they refer to. This objection was raised so early as the third century by Porphyry, has frequently been revived in modern times, and has even, quite recently, been advanced in this country by Dr Arnold, in his discourses on prophecy. He holds, that delineations like these, cast so much in the mould of history, and finding their verification in the affairs of the Alexandrian and Maccabean periods, are alien to the nature of prophecy, and must have been written after the events had taken place. We need not say, that such an opinion is fraught with most serious consequences in regard to the character and integrity of the Old Testament canon; as it admits of no doubt, that the book of Daniel, with those portions included, had its place in the Jewish Scriptures, when these were acknowledged, as of Divine authority, by our Lord and his Apostles, and were declared to have been all given by inspiration of God. The argument for the inspiration of the Scriptures of the Old Testament, as they now exist, would be shaken to its foundation, if the portions of Daniel referred to, were displaced from the rank of genuine prophecies.

But as there is no valid reason of an external kind for such a rejection, neither can one be found in the internal objection derived from the historical aspect of the predictions. It is not denied, that there is somewhat peculiar in the form of those predictions, a form that assimilates them more to the detailed and prosaic style of history, than is usual in prophecies, which relate to a future at some distance from the speaker. Yet it is to be remembered, we have the advantage of reading them after the fulfilment, at least of the *larger* portion, of what they foretold; whereas Daniel himself, and those to whom the word originally came, lived even before the national revolutions had taken place, which rendered the fulfilment possible. Hence, he speaks of the vision, in its most historical parts, as being perfectly dark to himself and others (chap. viii. 27; xii. 4, 8, 9). And so different, after all, is this prophetico-historical delineation of things to come, from history in the proper sense, that, as Hengstenberg has remarked,[1] no one ignorant of the history, and with only this prophetical outline in his hand, could make his way to any precise and circumstantial account of the events; nor even yet are we free from all difficulties in the interpretation; there is still room at several points, from the mode of representation employed, for difference of opinion. And then, when we look at the circumstances of the period, for whose instruction and comfort this portion of Daniel's prophecies was more especially intended—that, namely, stretching from the rebuilding of Jerusalem to the coming of Messiah—we can easily discern an adequate reason for that nearer approximation to the historical style, which unquestionably characterizes the predictions. Two leading peculiarities distinguished the period. It was, in the first instance, one of great feebleness and depression, and subject throughout to many trying and perplexing difficulties, which could not fail to put faith many times to the stretch. The people, too, returning from Babylon, with high hopes of the revival of their ancient glory, were the more likely, from the painful contrast which the realities of their position presented, to become disaffected and downcast in their minds. For long the infant colony in Judea had to struggle for its very existence, against the insidious attacks of powerful and envious neighbours. And though its affairs became more settled and prosperous during the ascendancy of the Persian kings, and of Alexander, yet, soon again, the tide of fortune turned, and a period came, of which Calvin has said, that "if ever there were times of distress, such as might tempt men to imagine, that God was asleep in heaven, and had become forgetful of the human race, it was certainly then, when the revolutions that took place were so frequent and so various."

Another peculiarity, however, added very materially to the trials connected with these circumstances of outward trouble, and rendered some special support and consolation necessary. For, during the whole of the post-Babylonian period, the

[1] Authentie des Daniel, p. 190.

theocratic constitution existed in a kind of anomalous and shattered condition. The original ark of the covenant, the centre of the whole polity, was gone, and the Shekinah, and the answering by Urim and Thummim, and even the kingly rule and government, though it had been secured by covenant in perpetuity to the house of David. It was to contend, at fearful odds, with the difficulties of their position, as compared with former times, when the members of the ancient covenant had to pass through deep waters shorn of these distinctive badges of a proper covenant relationship. Yet this was not all; for during that period all sensible tokens of God's immediate presence were wanting. There was no longer any vision; the spirit of prophecy was silent; and with a closed record, and destitute of any miraculous agency, the people were left to hold on their course, as they best could, with no more than the settled and ordinary means of grace placed at their command.

Taking, then, into account the entire circumstances of the period between the return from Babylon and the coming of Christ, is it to be wondered at? might it not rather be expected, from the whole character of God's dealings with His people, that His foreseeing and watchful guardianship should make some suitable provision for such a time of need? It would have been precisely such a provision, if, along with the prophecies pointing the eye of hope to Messiah's appearance and kingdom, there were also furnished to the hand of faith a more than usually explicit pre-intimation of the changes and vicissitudes that should arise during the intervening period; in particular, during that portion of it when the conflict with sin and error was to be the hottest. For this would, in great measure, compensate for the failure of the prophetic office, through which, in earlier times, direction was given in emergencies, and a sensible connection maintained between the hand of God and the events which befel His people. With such a comparatively detailed exhibition of the coming future in the prophetic record, the children of faith could feel that they were not left alone in their struggles, but that the eye of

God still directed every movement, and had descried, as formerly, the end from the beginning. And, finally, if such a provision, by means of prophetic delineations, was to be made, Daniel, of all the prophets during the captivity, or immediately subsequent to it (as Hengstenberg has already noted), was precisely the one fitted for the purpose. "In the impartation of prophetical gifts, God always acts in adaptation to human powers and susceptibilities. A man, therefore, like Daniel, who had spent his life in the highest employments of the state, must have been peculiarly fitted for apprehending aright communications, which had reference chiefly to political revolutions. The other prophets held not only the prophetical gift, but also the prophetical office; their utterances bore a distinct reference to their contemporaries. But, with such a relation, the communication of so long a series of special revelations was scarcely compatible. These were necessarily destined, as, indeed, is expressly said in this book, more for the future than for the present; while a prevailing destination for the present naturally carries along with it a direct monitory tendency, and, at the same time, an elevated, predominantly poetical style of discourse, which might easily have proved prejudicial to the requisite precision and clearness in a case like this. . . . . Now, Daniel was no prophet, so far as office was concerned. Hence, in the prophecies communicated through him, comparatively little respect required to be had to the necessities of the existing generation, and their capacity of spiritual apprehension. Nor would an elevated poetical diction have here been in its place, as for himself only, in the first instance, did he desire and receive explanations. And in so wonderful a manner had he been accredited by God, that men could not venture, on account of what might appear of darkness in his revelations, to withhold an acknowledgment of their Divine character, and were only the more careful in comparing the prophecy with the fulfilment. Of this, the Books of the Maccabees and Josephus contain indisputable proofs."[1]

[1] Die Authentie des Daniel, p. 193.

On the whole, therefore, we conclude that there are material differences in form and style between history and prophecy, as the distinctive aims and provinces of each are also different; but, at the same time, that prophecy approximates more nearly to the manner of history at one time than another, varying considerably in this respect, according to the circumstances in which it was given, and the more specific purposes it was intended to serve.

SECTION II.

THE PROPHETIC STYLE AND DICTION VIEWED POSITIVELY—ITS MORE DISTINCTIVE PECULIARITIES.

The Ground of those Peculiarities, in the Mode of Revelation by Vision.

At an early stage of our investigations, we had occasion to notice the regular and settled method by which Divine communications were made to those who were prophets in the ordinary sense, as contra-distinguished from the revelations given by Moses, and afterwards by Christ. In the latter cases, the intercourse with Heaven was maintained, while the mind continued in its habitual state, and the Divine message was received by a face to face communication. But, in the case of the prophets generally, it was to be otherwise; the Lord was to "make Himself known to them in a vision, to speak to them in a dream" (Numb. xii. 6). The Jewish doctors were wont to make some distinction between these two—the prophetic vision and the prophetic dream. They generally regarded the vision as superior to the dream, as representing things more to the life, and seizing upon the prophet while he was awake, though it often declined into a true dream, as in the case of Abraham (Gen. xv. 12). The difference, however, as Mr Smith, of Cambridge, long since remarked,[1] seems rather to lie in the circumstantials than in anything essential; only, as the term *vision* pointed to what was seen, the *dream* must be understood as referring more particularly to what was spoken and heard; as, indeed, the passage itself indicates, "*make known* in a vision," "*speak* in a dream." But, in regard to the state marked by these expressions, the older Jewish interpreters described it as one in which the imaginative faculty was set forth as a stage on which certain *visa* and *simulacra* (appearances and images) were represented to the understandings of the prophets, as they are in our common dreams; only, that in their case the understanding was always kept awake, and strongly acted on by God in the midst of those apparitions, that it might see the intelligible mysteries in them. And the Jewish writers regarded this as constituting the specific difference between the more ordinary prophetic illumination and the Mosaic degree, that in the latter the impressions of things were made nakedly to the understanding, without any schemes or pictures exhibited upon the phantasy.[2] This ancient view of the prophetical state is, beyond doubt, substantially correct. It supposes the prophet, when borne away by the impulse of God's Spirit, to have been transported out of his natural condition, into a higher, a spiritually ecstatic state, in which, losing the sense and consciousness of external objects, he was rendered capable of holding direct intercourse with heaven; and surrendering himself wholly to the divine impressions conveyed to his soul, for the moment he ceased from his ordinary agency, and, as one released from the common conditions of flesh and blood, entered into the purely spiritual sphere to see the vision and hear the words of the Almighty. It was his, therefore, in a degree altogether supernatural, to possess and exercise the faculty, which the soul ever in some degree exerts in its intenser frames of thought and feeling, which it is the part especially of the poet's soul, in its loftier moods, to exert,—the faculty of withdrawing within itself, closing its

[1] Discourse on Prophecy, chap. ii. [2] See Smith, as above.

eyes and ears against external impressions, and living as in a world of its own. Like this in kind, but far higher in degree, was the ecstacy of the divine seer, which transferred the conscious exercise of his powers to the region of spiritual things, and placed him in direct and free communion with God.

The Fathers seem to have been afraid of altogether granting this concerning the ancient prophets, from its appearing to place them in a dangerous resemblance to the heathen diviners, and the rhapsodical Montanists. A sharp distinction was drawn between the ecstacies of such persons, speaking in a kind of sacred fury, and the conscious spiritual elevation of the true prophet. Miltiades is even reported by Eusebius to have written a book on the theme, that a prophet must not speak in ecstacy.[1] In this, however, they did not mean to deny, that the prophets were in a supernaturally raised and elevated frame when they received their revelations; but only, that the excitation under which they thought and felt, was not that sort of irresistible agency claimed by Montanism, and assumed in heathen divination, which left no room for human individuality, and impelled those who experienced it to utter what had no place in their own understandings. This appears to have been all they meant, as may be learned from Jerome's more explicit statement, in his preface to Habakkuk, where he vindicates the prophets from assimilation with Montanists, by asserting that they were not madmen, as if they had spoken without intelligence, and had no power over themselves, either to speak or to remain silent. The jealousy of the Fathers in this direction naturally led them to contract somewhat unduly the difference between the ordinary frame of the prophets, and that to which they were raised when presented with the visions of God. And, certainly, in their interpretations of the prophetical writings, they often exhibit grievous failures in the correct appreciation of the prophetical state, in its bearing on the prophetical style. But, on the other hand, some modern writers on prophecy—among others,

[1] Hist. Eccl. v. 17, and the same sentiments are expressed by Epiphanius, Adv. Haeres. Mont., chap. 2, Jerome, Praef. in Isaiam, Nahum, etc.

Hengstenberg, in the first edition of his Christology—seem to go to the opposite extreme, in making the ecstacy of the prophets approach too closely to the μανία, the sacred fury of the diviners. Such, undoubtedly, is the impression produced, when it is said of them in that state, that "they lost their consciousness," that "their rational powers were suspended," that they were "completely passive under an overpowering influence of the Spirit of God." They were, indeed, borne aloft by an impulse which lifted them above themselves, but, at the same time, an impulse which destroyed nothing they possessed, which left unimpaired their native susceptibilities, and wrought in accordance with their personal characteristics. So far from their own intelligence and agency being suspended, everything in their perceptive and emotional nature moved then with living energy and freedom; they saw, they heard, they felt, they spake, not less than if all had come from the spontaneous workings of their own minds, but with a clearness of insight, and a glow of sentiment, which of themselves they would have been impotent to reach.

We must here hold fast by the principle, which lies at the foundation of all right views of the Divine agency in the soul, and the overlooking of which, more than anything else, has bred perplexity and error on the whole subject of God's inspired communications to men—that *the supernatural ever bases itself on the natural.* Grace, in all its acts and provisions, comes not to mar or destroy, but only to quicken, and exalt, and perfect nature. And the Spirit of Grace, alike in his more peculiar, and in his more common, operations upon the soul, ever has respect to its essential powers and properties, and adapts himself, even in his loftiest communications, not only to the general laws of thought, which regulate the workings of the human mind, but also to the various idiosyncrasies and acquired habits of individual minds. While it was altogether of the Spirit, therefore, and through a supernatural exercise of his power, that prophetical men were raised into the ecstatical condition, in which they received the vision of things to come, still no more when in that condition than in their ordinary frame, did the Spirit suspend or control their mental faculties. On the contrary, he employed these faculties as his instruments of working, and, in doing so, gave the freest scope to their powers of thought and utterance, and even to their more remarkable peculiarities. We see the undoubted proof of this, in the diversities of manner which characterise the prophetical, equally with the other portions of inspired Scripture, and which not only shed over them the charm of an instructive and pleasing variety, but also endow them with a singular adaptation to the different tastes and capacities of men. We see it again in the use made by one prophet of the writings of another—a use made more frequently by none than by those who most distinctly relate what passed before them in the visions of God, and which, as often as employed, plainly bespoke the intelligent exercise of the mind's natural and acquired endowments. We see it even in the form and materials of the visions themselves, which so uniformly bear the impress of the cast of mind, and the individual relations, of the persons who saw them. How strikingly, for example, do these differ in Ezekiel from the kind of visions reported in Isaiah! And again, in Daniel, how widely different from what are found in the prophets generally of the Old Testament! The point of view from which *their* visions proceeded, was the church or kingdom of God, from which they looked forth at times, now to this, now to that region of the heathen world, and disclosed something of their approaching future. But Daniel stood in the centre, not of the church's, but of the world's power and glory, and at that remarkable phase of its history, when no longer isolated and independent states, but huge and aspiring world-monarchies, began to strive for the mastery. Accordingly, it is the worldly power in this concentrated and all-embracing form, which has the prominent place assigned it in the visions of Daniel—a reflection of the prophet's own peculiar position, and political environments; and in that characteristic feature of them we perceive the free operation of the *natural* element, as in the wonderful insight they display concerning the future movements of Providence, we discern the *divine* element, that wrought on the occasion. Nay, a farther and more specific distinction may here be noted, illustrative of the principle under consideration. For, in the two classes of visions in the book of Daniel—in the visions of Nebuchadnezzar as compared with those of Daniel, we mark a characteristic difference, such as might well have been expected, if the native bent and the special relations of each were allowed to come into play. As presented to the view of Nebuchadnezzar, the worldly power was seen only in its *external* aspect—under the form of a colossal image, possessing the likeness of a man, and in its more conspicuous parts composed of the shining and precious metals; while the divine kingdom appeared in the meaner aspect of a stone, without ornament or beauty—with nothing, indeed, to distinguish it but its resistless energy and perpetual duration. Daniel's visions, on the other hand, direct the eye into the *interior* of things, strip the earthly kingdoms of their false glory, by exhibiting them under the aspects of wild beasts and nameless monsters (such as were everywhere to be seen in the grotesque sculptures and painted entablatures of Babylon), and reserve the *human* form, in conformity with its divine original and true idea, to stand as the representative of the kingdom of God, which is composed of the saints of the Most High, and holds the truth that is destined to prevail over all error and ungodliness of men. In such natural and striking diversities as these, who can fail to see an indication of the different frames of mind in the subjects of the revelation—a difference stamping itself on their respective visions, though the visions themselves, in each case, came from a higher source? It is thus that the Spirit of God, in his most peculiar workings, shows how thoroughly he knows man's frame, and how, in his supernatural gifts and operations, he takes the natural as the ground and basis of all that is imparted and done. So that, when raised by the Spirit into an ecstatical condition, the prophets did not lose either their personal consciousness, or any distinctive characteristic they possessed of thought and feeling; the faculties of their intellectual and moral being were allowed their proper scope and exercise, and the ideas and imagery they employed came in perfect accordance with the mind's ordinary habits and associations.

At the same time, it is not less clear, that the state itself, in which the prophets received their revelations, was essentially a supernatural one. It was in the most peculiar sense a spiritual state, in which the soul was carried by a divine impulse above the region of sense, and, with powers and sensibilities strung for the occasion, was brought into immediate contact with the things of the Spirit. This is evident even from the most common expressions used to denote the prophetical state; such as, "I was in the Spirit and heard," "The hand of the Lord was upon me," "The Spirit of the Lord came upon me," etc. The apostle Paul, speaking of what he experienced in that state (2 Cor. xii.), describes himself as unable to tell whether he was in the body or out of the body—so completely was the spiritual part of his being transferred to that higher sphere, and so thoroughly was it for the time loosed from the ordinary conditions of flesh and blood. Its activities were all absorbed by what was presented to it in the invisible world. In like manner, it is said of the apostle Peter, when going to receive in vision a special revelation concerning the admission of the Gentiles into the church, that an ecstacy fell upon him (ἐπέπεσεν ἐπ' ἀυτὸν ἔκστασις, Acts x. 10). And the same apostle, when speaking of the prophetic impulse generally (2 Pet. i. 21), describes it as carrying those who were the subjects of it out of their usual condition, raising them into a rapt and excited state, in which the human in them was borne aloft, and, in a manner, lost in the divine: "Not by man's will was prophecy at any time brought (or borne) in, but borne by the Holy Spirit, holy men of God spake."[1] Hence, also, the occasional excitation of manner, which appeared in the utterance of the prophecy, after the strictly prophetical state had passed away (2 Kings ix. 11; 1 Sam. xix. 24).

[1] See Appendix F.

Now, since the prophets, when under divine illumination, were thus raised to the higher sphere of the Spirit, having their agency for the time being transferred to that sphere, it is but natural to suppose, that whatever they relate as having been spoken or done, was spoken and done simply in the Spirit—a real transaction, indeed, but a transaction in vision. Whether the prophet on any particular occasion might, or might not, expressly state, that the things he saw, heard, or did, took place when he was in ecstacy or vision, the original appointment in respect to prophetical communications, that it was in vision they were to be imparted, left it to be inferred, that according to the rule such was actually the case, and that, if at any time, the rule was departed from, and the transactions occurred in the external world, very express and unequivocal intimation would require to be given. There can be no doubt, that the more intelligent portion of the Jewish interpreters perfectly understood this, and, by just inference, we may suppose also the better informed Israelites of earlier times. Maimonides gives a clear deliverance upon the subject in his *More Nevochim.* "Know, therefore," says he, "that as it is in a dream, a man thinks that he has been in this or that country, that he has married a wife, and continued there for some certain time—that by this wife he has had a son of such a name, of such a disposition, and the like; precisely so was it with the prophetical parables, as to what the prophets see or do in a prophetical vision. For, whatever those parables inform us concerning any action the prophet does, or concerning the space of time between one action and another, or going from one place to another, all is in prophetical vision. Nor were those actions real to sense, although some particularities may be distinctly reckoned up in the writings of the prophets. Since it was well known, that all was done in a prophetical vision, it was not necessary, in the rehearsing of every particularity, to reiterate that it was in a prophetical vision, as it was also needless to inculcate that it was in a dream. But now (he adds) the vulgar sort of men think, that all such actions, journeys, questions, and answers, were really and sensibly performed, and not in a prophetical vision."

It were well, if we could say with Maimonides, that it is only the vulgar sort of men, in present times, who understand the narrations referred to in this realistic manner. The greater part of our popular writers on prophecy take them generally in this sense, and not a few also of our more eminent commentators. Horsley contends at great length, in the introduction to his Commentary on Hosea, for the necessity of interpreting the instruction given to the prophet in the first chapter, to marry an unchaste woman, and the successive births of children by her, of transactions in real life—a view that was held also by Augustine and many of the fathers in former days, by many Lutheran and reformed divines, and is still also held by Hofmann. Even Dr Alexander of Princeton, who usually exhibits a correct discrimination and sound judgment in his Commentary on Isaiah, at chap. xx. 2, where the prophet is commanded by the word of the Lord, to loose the sackcloth from off his loins, and pull off his shoes from his feet, and go naked and barefoot three years as a sign and wonder respecting Egypt and Ethiopia, regards the account as descriptive of what actually took place in public. Nor are there wanting some, who insist upon a like actual accomplishment of Ezekiel's appointment (chap. iv.), to lie 390 days at a stretch upon one side, and forty days upon another, for a sign to Israel and Judah—all the while fixed down with bands to prevent him from turning from the one side to the other—his arm, too, constantly uncovered, as in the act of prophesying evil—and his food consisting of the meanest provisions, and baked with what both nature and the law held to be abominable. One might have thought, that the absolute physical impossibility involved in such cases, if transferred to the world of sense—the palpable indecency of food so repulsive, and nakedness so startling and long-continued (for there is nothing in either case in the descriptions given to qualify the full import of the language), might alone have been regarded as a clear indication, that the spirit of holiness and purity could never have intended the instructions to take effect in the sphere of ordinary life.

In so far as the things reported to have been enjoined upon the prophet and done by him, were of an absurd and fanatical, or of an unbecoming and illegal character, it has been alleged, that if the action were such in real life, it could not be otherwise when transferred to an ideal region, and done in the Spirit—the impropriety would still follow the prophet in his visions, and would only have been justified there by the special appointment of God, which might equally have warranted it in real life. But the two cases are entirely different. An internal action, it would be readily understood, was prescribed and accomplished simply for purposes of instruction—as a representative type merely of things that had happened, or were going to happen on the outward theatre of the world; in order that the characters and procedure it personated, whether good or bad, might be more distinctly realised, and forcibly impressed upon the heart and conscience. If done, however, on the territory of every-day life, it could not be considered in such a light. The things belonging to it then necessarily became more than types; they must have had a personal, before they could possess a didactic import; and by multitudes would undoubtedly have been looked at in their more immediate and obvious aspect, without a thought of any thing farther or higher. Pursuing a course in itself objectionable, the prophet (who should have stood pre-eminent for sanctity and worth, whose prime characteristic was to be conformity to the law of God) would inevitably have been subjected to suspicion, or covered with shame in the very act of fulfilling his mission. He must, to all human appearance, have descended to a level with the heated enthusiast, who in the fervour of his inflated zeal, or the rashness of his presumption, tramples upon law and order. But, to use the language of Calvin on the case of Hosea, "It seems not to be consistent with reason, that God should voluntarily have rendered his prophet contemptible; for how could he ever have appeared in public after such ignominy had been inflicted upon him? If he had married such a wife as is described, he ought rather to have hidden himself all his life-time, than have assumed the prophetic office." Besides, many of the actions were of a kind to have lost rather than gained in impressiveness by being outwardly transacted: some, as in the case of the siege conducted by Ezekiel with tiles (chap. iv.), being of so diminutive a nature, and others (like the same prophet's lying hundreds of days upon his side, or the details of Hosea's marriage-relation, or Jeremiah's going to hide his girdle by the river Euphrates, and returning after many days to find it marred), being spread over so wide a space, occupying so long a time, or requiring to be performed (if performed at all) in so secret a manner, that no one could in any proper sense be cognisant of the performance. If presented all at once as an acted lesson—a rehearsal of what had taken place in that ideal world, where the prophet in his entranced condition lived and moved as in the presence of God, then the action being seen in its completeness might immediately produce its proper effect. But if seen only in fragments, as it must have been if outwardly performed, the action as a whole should have been in great measure unintelligible, and, in a moral respect, could have conveyed no certain and definite impressions. It was, after all, by the narrative of the story with its accompanying explanations, that the desired result in either case must have been reached.

To all this the farther consideration may be added in respect to the argument derived from the moral impropriety of certain of the actions, that as those typical actions of the prophets in general stood in a close relation to parabolical representations, and were essentially, indeed, of the same description, so, in these also, we find an occasional use made of circumstances, which the Lord never could have directly countenanced in any real transaction. Such, for example, is the parabolical representation in the twenty-third chapter of Ezekiel, where the story of Israel's calling, guilt, and punishment is exhibited under the figure of two women, both of them received into marriage relationship to God, and acting unfaithfully to the marriage vow. Such also, in the parables of the

New Testament, are those of the unjust steward (the type in a particular aspect of true wisdom), and of the unmerciful servant; in both of which, things in themselves morally improper, form, to some extent, the basis of representations pertaining to the kingdom of God. In these cases, the Lord showed that He could make an *ideal* use of earthly relations and doings, to image the truths of His kingdom, such as on the territory of real life He could have commissioned no one to employ; and so was it precisely in respect to the ideal world of prophetic revelation. *There*, simply because it *was* ideal, and intended to present a faithful image of the actual world, in its guilt and punishment, as well as its privileges and hopes, scenes behoved to be occasionally enacted with the Divine sanction, which could have had no place in the outward history of God's true servants. Understood to be representative and teaching actions in the purely spiritual sphere, nothing they might contain of an unbecoming nature, could produce the pernicious effect, which must have attended it, had it obtruded itself on the senses; it was for the mind alone to contemplate, and it would naturally do so with a respect to the moral bearing of the representation.

It is humiliating to reflect, how clearly the right principle of interpretation, on this point, was perceived, and deduced from its proper foundation—revelation by vision—by Mr Smith of Cambridge, two centuries ago, and how often it is missed or but partially apprehended now. He states, that "though it be not always positively laid down in the prophetical narrations, that the transactions were in a vision, yet the nature and scope of prophecy required, that things should be acted in imagination (the imagination being the prophetical scene or stage, on which all apparitions were made to the prophet), and we should rather expect some positive declaration to assure us, that they were performed in the history, if indeed it were so. The things which God would have revealed to the prophet, were acted over symbolically in his imagination, as in a masque, in which divers persons are brought in, among whom the prophet himself bears a part; sometimes by speaking and reciting things done, or propounding questions, sometimes by acting that part in the drama which was appointed him by others. It is, therefore, no wonder to hear of those things being done, which, indeed, have no historical or real verity; the scope of all being to represent something strongly to the prophet's understanding, and sufficiently to inform it in the substance of those things, in which he was to instruct those to whom he was sent. And so, sometimes, we have only the intelligible matter of prophecies delivered to us nakedly, without the imaginary ceremonies or solemnities."

But have we not, it may be asked, undeniable evidence, that the symbolical actions ascribed to the prophets were sometimes, at least, performed on the outward theatre of life? Allowing this, however, to have been the case, it cannot materially affect the general result. The normal state of the prophets, when they were receiving Divine communications, was that of ecstacy, and while in ecstacy, their proper sphere was not the external, but the internal world—the region of spirit as contradistinguished from that of sense and time. And though there might be symbolical actions, performed by them also in real life, yet the circumstances are such as to warrant our expecting clear evidence of their having been so, and even then regarding them as exceptions to the general rule. There are recorded examples of this description—cases, in which the action has a place in the narrative of sacred history, and is surrounded by other historical transactions. In such cases, undoubtedly, it must be held to be of the same character with the rest, and, like them, accomplished on the visible theatre of earthly affairs: as in the notice (1 Kings xx. 35–43), of the prophet, who disfigured his person, and requested others to smite him, as a sign of the Lord's judgment on the Syrians; or in the account given by Jeremiah (chap. xxviii.), of the yoke upon his neck, seized and broken before the people by the false prophet Hananiah. The action with the yoke there is imbedded in details of history, and must necessarily be understood as itself of the same class. Indeed, it is only the circumstance, which incidentally comes out, of Jeremiah having a yoke upon his neck, which can properly be regarded as a symbolical action of the kind under consideration, and which seems to have been done by him as a realistic fulfilment of the word that came to him in the preceding chapter, "Make thee bonds and yokes, and put them upon thy neck." In New Testament times also, we have the undoubted case of Agabus, binding himself with a girdle, as a symbolical pre-intimation of the approaching imprisonment of St Paul. Such recorded actions, however, differ from those previously referred to, and, indeed, from the mass of symbolical actions described in the prophetical writings, in that they appear, not in the account of a Divine message communicated by God to the prophet, but as parts of an historical narrative, where all must necessarily have been of a homogeneous nature. They differ also from the greater portion in being so obviously aud transparently typical in their character, that their symbolical import could scarcely fail to be apprehended at the very first, and perceived to be the sole reason of their appointment.

The general conclusion, then, we would draw from what we have stated, may be thrown into the following principle of interpretation: As, according to the rule, Divine communications were to be made to the prophets in ecstacy or vision, *so whenever we have to do merely with the record of these communications, the actions related, as well as the things seen and heard, should be understood to have occurred in the spiritual sphere of prophetic revelation; and outward reality is to be predicated of any of them, only when the account given is such as to place the symbolical act in undoubted connection with the facts of history.* Or, it may be put thus: The actions are to be held as having taken place in the spiritual sphere alone, if they occur simply in the account of God's communications to the prophet; but in actual life, if they are found in the narration of the prophet's dealings with the people. In the one case, the mere publication of the account constituted the message from God, while, in the other, an embodied representation was given of it in the outward act. Such a rule may leave us in some doubt as to certain cases in the history of prophetical agency, but they will be found to be extremely few. It may not, perhaps, conclusively determine whether all the transactions recorded in Isaiah, chap. vii. and viii., respecting the prophet's two sons by the prophetess, and the messages given him to Ahab and his people, belong to the spiritual alone, or also to the actual sphere, though the natural impression from the narrative is that they belong to the former;—since the whole account seems to refer merely to the Lord's communication to the prophet, and the going to the *prophetess*, to have sons by her, involved in the transactions, would infer, if understood otherwise than as an ideal matter, an impurity not to be named or thought of in such a connection. In like manner, the account in Jeremiah, chap. xviii. and xix., of that prophet's being instructed to go to the potter's house, in the valley of the Son of Hinnom, and there see and speak several things, may not, with perfect certainty, be assigned to either the ideal or the actual sphere by the application of our principle; yet, as in the case previously noticed, the presumption manifestly is on the ideal side, since the whole narrative carries the aspect simply of what passed in the region of the prophet's communings with God, and appears to relate to the message he got to deliver, not to the actual delivering of it. For almost every other case the rule laid down will be found sufficient. In particular, it will certainly lead us to regard the many symbolical actions in Zechariah and Ezekiel as having taken place in vision—not excepting that in Ezekiel xxiv., respecting the death of the prophet's wife, and the charge to refrain from mourning on account of her. For the entire chapter is in the form of a direct communication to the prophet, conveying instruction he was to impart to the people; and so at verse 25, immediately after the account of the action, and without a break, the Lord is represented as continuing his address to the prophet, and saying, "And thou, Son of Man, shall it not be in the day that I take from them their strength," etc.[1]

[1] This case, and others in Ezekiel, may be seen examined at some length in my Commentary on that Prophet.—See also Appendix G.

It is only necessary to add, farther, that the mode of revelation by vision, which was common to all the prophets in the strictest sense, appears, like other supernatural gifts, to have existed in different degrees of power and completeness; but it rose to its highest form in the case of those who may be called, by way of eminence, apocalyptists. These were, more especially Daniel in the Old Testament, and the Apostle John in the New. Not that there was anything absolutely peculiar to these two prophets, for every real prophet is, so far, an apocalyptist, that it is given him in some measure to take off the veil (ἀποκαλυτεῖν) from things spiritual and divine. But the persons in question were called to do this in a somewhat peculiar and superabundant measure. Both of them were placed, by the events of God's providence, in a remote and isolated position, so as to be precluded from speaking directly to the church then present, and they had, by way of compensation, the honour assigned them of speaking more specially and peculiarly than others to the church of the future. In respect to this future they stood upon a loftier altitude, and had visions of things to come more explicit, more detailed and consecutive, than were afforded to any of the other prophets. The perspective of the church's history was, in a manner, mapped out before them; in particular, as regards the long-continued and bloody struggle between Christian truth and antichristian error, and its final termination on the side of righteousness. In Daniel this great struggle first assumes its more definite and concrete shape, as a mortal conflict between two kingdoms, with their appropriate heads and vital agencies; and the theme is resumed by the apostle, in connection, at once, with a larger battle-field and mightier forces, and conducted to its final close. Hence, also, from the more distinctly marked apocalyptic character of the two books, it is first in Daniel that several distinct phases of the kingdom of God are brought out—that mention is made of a typical as well as of an antitypical antichrist—and of an earlier appearance of Messiah, in humiliation, to suffer and die, quite apart from another, in power, dominion, and glory; while it is by St John that the interval is properly filled up, which separates between the first and second advents of Christ. These men, therefore, were emphatically the church's apocalyptists, and had most of those visions which unveiled her future fortunes and destiny.

SECTION III.

First Peculiarity of the Style and Diction of Prophecy—Poetical Elevation.

THAT a poetical element enters largely into the composition of the prophetical writings requires no proof. The fact is on all hands admitted; and the only points respecting it that can be termed disputable, or that call for explanation, are the grounds of its existence, and the effect it should exercise on the interpretation of the writings themselves. It was the fashion at no remote period, with Biblical scholars, to regard these writings of the prophets as if they simply belonged to the poetical remains of the Hebrews. Some of the ancient nations, among others the Hebrews, had but one name for poet and prophet (vates); and it was thought that, with the Hebrews also, every prophet must be a poet, and every poet to some extent a prophet. It hence naturally arose, that the measure in which the prophetical gift was possessed, was supposed to be in proportion to the degree in which the poetical property was displayed, and the prophetical books were assigned to a golden or a silver age, according to their rank as poetical compositions. The more exact and discriminating spirit of recent times has led in this, as in other things, to a juster perception of the essential characteristics respectively belonging to the prophetical and the poetical departments—to a discernment of the differences, as well as the agreements subsisting between them, even on the part of those who are still disposed to look at the sacred writings too much in the light of human productions. Thus Ewald, in the present day, devotes two entirely separate publications to what, in the last century, was comprised in one, both by Lowth in this country, and by Herder in Germany. Instead of a single work on Hebrew poetry, including the writings of the prophets as a part of the whole, he treats in one work of the poetical, and in another of the prophetical portions of the Old Testament. In his introduction to the prophetical books, Ewald also correctly distinguishes between the manner proper to the prophet, and that of the poet. "The distinctive characteristic," he says, "of the prophetical representation lies peculiarly in this, that it is not confined to any precise mode; but as its aim rises above all kinds of human discourse, so it avails itself of all, according as they are best adapted to that aim. The poet has his definite manner, and cannot so readily change and vary it, for his immediate aim is not to work upon others; he must satisfy himself, and the requirements of his own art. But the prophet will and must work upon others—nay, work upon them in the most direct and impressive manner; and so for him every method and form of representation is right which carries him straitest to his end."[1]

This strong practical tendency in the prophets operated in various ways to check and regulate the poetical element in their writings, as it did, indeed, in the inspired productions generally. Their primary aim throughout, as we have had occasion once and again to notice, is of a moral kind; to influence the heart and conscience is their main object. Even in the more strictly poetical portions, therefore, the imaginative faculty could never be allowed uncontrolled play, as it may be in the higher productions of human genius; nor, like these, could it clothe itself in external forms of a very artificial and complicated nature. All had to be kept subservient to the higher ends of spiritual instruction, and only such peculiarities in rythm and structure could be employed as were compatible with the simple measures of Hebrew parallelism. The very structure of Scripture as a book, the comparative free-

[1] Propheten i., p. 31.

dom and simplicity even of its artificial forms, bears evidence to the deep-toned ethical spirit that pervades it.

But this is said merely of the restraint, under which the poetical element was necessarily held in Scripture, not of its entire suppression. The regulated use of that element, so far from being inconsistent with, was fitted materially to promote the spiritual ends of the word of God. Poetry of a certain kind is proverbially a powerful instrument for swaying the hearts and moulding the manners of a people. And, accordingly, when a form of instruction was to be prepared by Moses, which might go down to succeeding generations, and work with special and sanctifying energy upon the minds of all, a sublime and stirring lyrical song was the result, instinct throughout with the fire and elevation of poetry (Deut. xxxii.). But in its ordinary functions—in that function more especially, in which it had to do with the varying aspects of the times, and the pre-intimation in connection with them, of things to come—prophecy was too directly and energetically practical in its aim, to admit so much of a poetical nature, as might be proper in a sacred ode or song. And a comparison of such portions of Scripture with those which are more strictly prophetical—of the last chapter of Habakkuk, for example (though this also is prophetical), with the two preceding chapters in the same book—will show at once, in how subdued a form the poetical spirit usually works in the prophetical portions, as compared with the others, and how much they partake of the direct and simple style proper to oratory. Not only so, but as a large proportion of the communications of prophecy came in the guise of symbolical actions, the mere description of these actions would manifestly be, for such parts, the appropriate form; as in such cases, the poetical element consisted in the things described, rather than in the mode of depicting them. And, generally, the more nearly prophecy approached in its character to history, it always of necessity partook less of the higher characteristics of poetry.

Such, however, it must be understood, were differences in degree, not in kind. Prophecy, in the more distinctive sense, never altogether lost a poetical impress, whether in the form of its representations, or in the language in which it clothed them. And in the larger and more important part of its communications, it stands more nearly allied to the poetical, than to any other species of composition which we can name. Nor did this arise fortuitously, or depend merely upon the choice, the individual temperament, or the natural endowments of the persons employed in inditing it; for in the prophetical writings the simplest narratives, and the most practical addresses are often found in close juxtaposition with highly coloured and wrought-up descriptions. *Now* the language bespeaks the profoundest repose, and again the most powerful emotions; in one part, a spirit of calm reflection seems to breathe in it; in another, it indicates a state of lofty excitation. And here, especially, is to be sought the ground of the poetical element in prophecy. It was in vision that the prophet received the revelations given to him, and in uttering them, he naturally spoke as in an ecstatic or elevated frame of mind—the same in kind with that of the poet's, however superior in the spiritual insight connected with it. So that what has been finely said of the one, may be understood also of the other. It is "of imagination all compact;" and being so,

> "The poet's eye, in a fine frenzy rolling,
> Doth glance from heaven to earth, from earth to heaven;
> And, as imagination bodies forth
> The forms of things unknown, the poet's pen
> Turns them to shapes, and gives to airy nothing
> A local habitation, and a name." [1]

For here again the great law of the Spirit's working comes into operation—the supernatural bases itself on the natural. In the gifts of grace generally, and still more in those possessed and exercised by prophetical men, while the Spirit carries the soul above nature, He does not set it on modes of thought and speech, which are at variance with its own constitutional ten-

[1] Midsummer's Night's Dream, Act v., sc. 1.

dencies. Under the Divine afflatus, the mind acts with as much freedom and spontaneity as when left to the unassisted operation of its own powers. And, as might be expected, when the minds of prophetical men were raised, through the Spirit, to that state of ecstatical elevation, in which they saw the vision, and heard the words of the Almighty, they naturally disclosed the revelations they obtained, in a tone of corresponding elevation. Thoughts conceived, messages taking shape in such a frame, could not possibly keep the level of ordinary discourse, or even in language follow the beaten track. They must rise above the common and familiar, because the subjective condition of the speaker was above it.

Bishop Lowth, in his work on Hebrew poetry, failed to connect properly the character of the prophetical diction with the nature of the prophetical state; but he describes, with his usual taste and discrimination, the influence of the poetical excitation on the language of those who experienced it. "The first," he says in his *Third Prelection*, "the first and chief source of the poetical diction is the powerful excitation of the mind. For what else is that phrenzy peculiar to poets which the Greeks, ascribing it to a Divine afflatus, called ἐνθουσιασμός, than a manner of discourse, prompted by the very condition of nature, and exhibiting the true and exact image of a mind moved by some powerful impulse!—since it lays open, as it were, the innermost depths and recesses of the mind, and shows its profoundest feelings in their most troubled, agitated, and disjointed state. Hence, sudden exclamations, frequent interrogatives, addresses even to inanimate objects; for, to those who are much moved themselves, every thing around appears to participate in the same commotion." And in regard to the style, "It is the tendency of all poetry, and especially of the Hebrew, anxiously to avoid familiar language, and as well in the choice of words, as in the structure of sentences, to cultivate a certain peculiar and polished form of speech."

This description applies, of course, only in part to the writings of the prophets; for, as has been already stated, from the nature and objects of their calling, the prophets were not limited either to one form of representation, or to one species of diction. In those parts, for example, which consisted in the rehearsal of symbolical actions performed in vision before the Lord, the prophet's excitation, as well as the divine communication, appeared in the actions themselves; and the narrative style, with some slight deviations, was the one naturally adopted. In other parts, the symptoms of poetical elevation might be expected to vary, as it suited the occasion and object of the revelation to restrain or foster the ecstatical impulse. But, looking to the prophetical discourse generally, and making no account of extremes either way, it has, beyond doubt, a form and impress of its own. "On the one hand," to use again the words of Ewald,[1] "it was too elevated in its matter and tone for sinking down to simple prose; and, on the other hand, too much destined for working immediately upon the life, to depart so far and wide from ordinary discourse, as to assume a complete poetical form. Therefore it moves between the two, and in such a manner that internally it always appears aspiring and reaching after poetic elevation, while externally it acts with more freedom and familiarity, in order to operate directly upon the life, and, at the same time, not altogether lose the quality of oratorical fulness and flexibility. From the intermingling of these two forces has arisen its quite peculiar form. This form is of a determinate and settled nature, and, in particular, is fully established in the form of the words, the structure of the sentences, and the development of the whole after its parts; rising, however, as might be expected, from its intermediate character, in some prophets more, in others less, to a proper poetical elevation."

Ewald goes into some details, in proof of these linguistic peculiarities, and points out certain characteristic differences and agreements, first in the selection of words, and then in the use of parallelisms and strophe-arrangements, between

[1] Propheten i., p. 46.

the prophetical diction and that of poetry strictly so called. Comparatively little, however, can be made within a brief compass, of such an investigation; as the usages of which it makes account, when viewed singly, can scarcely be said to indicate results quite uniform and conclusive. In the general it may, doubtless, be asserted, without any chance of contradiction from those who are intimately acquainted with the books of the Old Testament, that whatever distinguishes Hebrew poetry from Hebrew prose, is found, though after a somewhat modified manner, in the prophetical writings. In these also, rare expressions and forms of words are often put in the room of those which were in common use, the concrete are preferred to the abstract, the tone is grave, elevated, sonorous, and the sentences are, for the most part, regular and harmonious, but occasionally also concise and abrupt.

Apart, however, from such peculiarities in the use of words and the structure of periods, the poetical elevation appears in the strongly idealistic or imaginative form, which the delineations and addresses of the prophets very commonly assume. Instead of speaking in the severe and exact style of history, they delight rather to throw around the actual world, the life and lustre of a higher sphere; so that symbols to their view often take the place of realities; inanimate objects appear with the properties of sentient beings; the past seems to live again in the future; and, overleaping the gulph of ages, the dead of former generations are seen still prolonging their existence, and consciously intermingling in the affairs of men. Examples of such forms of poetical licence will readily suggest themselves to those who are in any measure conversant with the prophetical writings. It is scarcely possible, indeed, to look into any portion of these, without lighting on some of them. As when—to point only to a few specimens—Zechariah symbolizes the power of the world, in its opposition to the kingdom of God, as a great mountain, and then addresses it as a real and sensible object, capable of thought and feeling, "Who art thou, O great mountain? Before Zerubbabel thou shalt become a plain" (chap. iv. 7); or when Joel identifies the invading host of the Chaldeans with the ravages of a horde of locusts, describing the operations of the one under those of the other (chap. i., ii.); or when Hosea (chap. ii.), and Ezekiel (chap. iv., xx.), represent the memorable period of chastisement appointed in former times to the covenant-people in the wilderness, as coming back again in their future history; or when, as in numberless passages, the patriarchal heads of the Israelitish nation, or Zion and Jerusalem, their religious and political centre, are addressed as living personalities, present to the mind and eye of the prophet. We refrain here from entering into any particular examination of such cases, the rather as those of them, which involve any peculiar difficulty in the interpretation, either have been already, or will yet be, considered in another connection. We shall, however, briefly advert to two passages, which are both, in respect to form, examples of the same kind of idealism, and have also both suffered from the same mistaken disposition to get rid of the poetical element in prophecy, and substitute for it the historical. One of these is Jer. xxxi. 15, "Thus saith the Lord, a voice was heard in Ramah, lamentation and bitter weeping, Rachel, weeping for her children, refused to be comforted, because they were not." It is the passage itself, not the application made of it to an event in gospel history, of which we have now to speak;[1] and, in particular, the singular personification embodied in it of Rachel. This is to be explained from the poetical elevation of the prophet, in connection with the circumstances of the time. It was at Ramah, as we learn from Jer. xl. 1, that the Chaldean conqueror assembled the last band of Jewish captives, preparatory to their being sent away after the others, to the land of the enemy. And as their going thither had, to the eye of sense, all the appearance of a perpetual exile—as with them, indeed, the last hope of Israel's existence as a nation seemed to expire, the ancestral mother of the tribe, within whose bounds the captives were assembled, is by a strikingly bold, yet

[1] See the passage, considered in that respect, in "Typology of Scripture," vol. i. p. 406.

touching, impersonation, conceived of as present at the scene, and as raising a loud wail of distress, cherishing even an inconsolable grief, because getting there, as she naturally, though falsely imagined, the last look of her hapless offspring. This peculiar form is employed merely as a cover, under which to give a more impressive exhibition of the apparently hopeless prostration to which matters had been reduced, and the prospect which, in spite of it, the power and faithfulness of God did not hesitate to unfold, of better days to come. But no one, surely, needs to be told, that it is a form very different from what is wont to be found, or could with any propriety be used, in history—a form, indeed, conceived in the very highest style of poetry.

In this respect the other passage also is essentially alike, and differs only in softening a little the bolder features of the image. It is the last prediction of the Old Testament, "Behold I will send you Elijah the prophet, before the coming of the great and dreadful day of the Lord, and he shall turn the heart of the fathers to the children, and the heart of the children to their fathers, lest I come and smite the earth with a curse." Here again the past and the future are contemplated as at once present to the eye of the prophet; generations far asunder in point of time appear together upon the same scene —on the one side, the godly fathers of the Jewish people, on the other their degenerate offspring in the days of the prophet and subsequent times: the two alienated from each other, on account of the entirely different feeling respectively entertained by them toward the covenant of God; and, to effect a proper reconciliation between them, and have all, if possible, prepared for the coming of the Lord, the sending anew of Him who was pre-eminently the prophet of reformation, the man, whose whole striving in a like degenerate age was directed to the object of having the hearts of the people turned back again to the God of their fathers, in whom, as the only proper centre of union the hearts of fathers and children could meet and embrace each other. Thus understood, the meaning of the passage is plain; and the mode of representation is so natural, so accordant with the genius of prophecy, in spirit also so entirely at one with the tendency of the writings of Malachi, which perpetually aim at the restoration of a backsliding people to the bond of the covenant and the piety of better times, that it at once commends itself to our approval. But it is altogether of a piece. The poetical element, which moulds it into such a peculiar form, belongs to one part as well as to another; it is throughout an ideal representation. And we should no more imagine, that for its fulfilment the literal Elijah was at some future time to resume his place among men as a preacher of repentance, than that the pious forefathers of Israel were personally to arise from the dead and receive with a hearty embrace their converted children, or (to recur to the prophecy of Jeremiah) that Rachel was actually heard in the neighbourhood of Ramah, bewailing her loss of children. In truth, neither Elijah nor the fathers seemed to need resuscitation for such a purpose; they are viewed as still living and present—the one ready to be sent on a fresh mission of reform, and the other to welcome those on whom it should take practical effect.

These remarks and illustrations may suffice in regard to the ground of the poetical element in prophecy, and the indications in form and language, which are there given of it. They apply chiefly to the prophetical writings of the Old Testament, as these constitute by far the largest portion of the revelations, which were received in the ecstatical state, the real source of the poetical element in prophecy. There is only one Book of the New Testament which had its origin in such a state—the revelation of St John. And there can be no question that it is beyond comparison the most poetical Book of the New Testament. Though belonging to an age in many respects unlike that of the ancient prophets, and consisting chiefly of narrations of what was seen and heard in the spiritual sphere, yet both in its general diction, and in the attributes of its particular style, it bears the evident marks of the poetical impress. Indeed, it is on this ground we are to explain, and *can* explain with perfect satisfaction, the characteristic differences between the apocalypse and the other writings of John himself,—differences, which have been of late diligently searched out and magnified, for the purpose of connecting the apocalypse with another and inferior authorship than that of the apostle. Its more Hebraistic style; its scenic representations and fragmentary-like form; its disuse of expressions common in the other writings of the apostle, and frequent resort to other expressions seldom or never found there; its many solecisms, full toned periods, perpetual recurrence to objects in the natural world (seas, hills, trees, sun, moon, stars, and such like), as forms, under which to present others somewhat resembling them in the political and moral world—are all to be traced to that one source; and, when properly viewed, they are a proof of the divine origin and genuine apostolicity of the Book.[1]

The age of the apocalypse, we have said, was a very different one from that of the Old Testament prophets. It differed primarily in the comparative completeness of its revelations, which, by unfolding the redemption itself that had been so long waited for, has rendered the dispensation of the gospel pre-eminent in light and truth. And this principally it was that gave rise to another difference, which appears on the very face of the New, as compared with the Old Testament revelations, that they have greatly less of the predictive in matter, and still less of the poetical in form. An incidental allusion is made to this difference in the Second Epistle of Peter, chap. ii. 1, where the apostle draws attention to a resemblance that was to exist between Old and New Testament times, but so as, at the same time, to indicate a difference: "There were false *prophets* also among the people, even as there shall be false *teachers* among you"—implying that teachers now were to occupy relatively the same place, that prophets did under the preceding dispensation. The fundamental reason of this comparative diminution of the prophetic element in New Testament scripture, and by consequence

[1] See Hengstenberg on the Revelation, vol. ii., p. 436, sq. Trans.

also of the poetical, lies in this—that the ecstatic, which properly belongs to a supernatural and temporary state of things, has lost its more immediate and necessary ground, by the bringing in of the greater things of the gospel. All has now reached a higher elevation. What before was supernatural, has become, in a manner, natural; and things once but dimly descried on the lofty watch-tower of prophetic vision, are seen as in the clear light of day by the ordinary disciples of Jesus. Placed on such a high vantage-ground, the Church of Christ no longer depends for her stability and encouragement, as the church of old did, on such partial and fitful glimpses into the future, as holy seers might at times be permitted to enjoy. And far more elevating and powerful in their influence on the soul than the glowing effusions of Hebrew poesy, are the sublime and simple records of the gospel. In the wonderful facts there presented, with the many soul-inspiring truths and ennobling prospects, inseparably connected with them, are treasured materials in ample abundance, such as a sanctified imagination might work into the finest creations of poetry. But this it was rather for the church herself to do in the course of ages by the hand of her more gifted sons, than to have it done once for all, and stereotyped for ever by the pen of prophets and apostles on the page of inspiration; the more so as the things themselves were not for a single land or people, but the common heritage of mankind. Better that these materials of sacred song should for the most part be left by inspired men in their native simplicity, to be used, according to the free, transfusive, and world-embracing spirit of the gospel, by the people of every age and clime, and, like the flower-seeds of nature, expanded into manifold and ever-varying forms of beauty. Such, indeed, has been the result. The gospel age has been a new era for poetry as well as history. The really sovereign songs of modern times are those which have drawn their inspiration from the New Testament; although we may still indulge the hope, to which expression has been given by one who has a right to speak on such a theme (the late Professor Wilson), that "the time will come, when Christian Poetry will be deeper and higher far than any that has ever yet been known among men, and that as the Dayspring from on high which has visited us, spreads wider and wider over the earth, the soul of the world, dreaming of things to come, shall assuredly see more glorified visions than have yet been submitted to her ken."

Thus all is found to be in its proper place; and here, too, as was meet, the New Testament scriptures bear on them the stamp of relative perfection. In them living realities take the place of prophetic visions; and vivid exhibitions of heavenly things at once supplant and transcend the former poetical elevation. As Christ was in himself unspeakably greater than Moses, so by Him came such full revelations of grace and truth, that he needed not, like the ancient lawgiver, to supplant the imperfection of his direct teaching, by the stirring notes of a prophetico-poetical song; and not in ecstatic visions, which veiled as much as disclosed the truth, but in greatest plainness of speech, his apostles laid open to the church the mysteries of the kingdom. One book alone was given in vision, and written in the obscurer characters of prophetic symbol—fulfilling by its very existence the double purpose of being a witness to the church of her still imperfect and militant condition, and a pledge of the brighter and better future, that is preparing to complete her destiny.

SECTION IV.

Second Peculiarity of the Prophetic Style and Diction—Figurative Representation.

A CERTAIN freedom and fertility in the employment of figurative representations is an undoubted characteristic of the prophetical writings. But the ground of this peculiarity, instead of being traced to its source in the mode of prophetic revelation, is too often ascribed to merely partial and secondary influences. With many it has seemed enough to say that the persons through whom the word of prophecy came were Asiatics, and so naturally adopted the rich and gorgeous style which is agreeable to an eastern imagination—forgetting that the same book, which in some parts is so remarkably distinguished by its use of figure, is in others not less distinguished by its severe simplicity and directness. The explanation of Warburton, and his follower, Hurd, cannot be pronounced much more successful. These writers carry us back to the original imperfection of human language. They tell us of its comparatively small stock of words, which obliged men to resort, by way of compensation, to external signs and representative actions; descant upon its prevailing tendency, from the want of cultivation and refinement, to make use of material images, which again was greatly strengthened and long perpetuated by the practice first of picture-writing, then of symbolic characters formed into a regular system of representative signs, and known by the name of hieroglyphics. This highly ornamental, or hieroglyphic style of thought and expression, we are told, sprung up in Egypt, and from that as its centre gradually diffused itself throughout the East; so that it became with the Israelites, as well as the oriental nations generally, the common and approved garb in which they clothed their ideas, at least in their more formal and laboured compositions. "What, then, could be more natural," asks Hurd, "than that a mode of expression which was so well known, so commonly practised, and so much revered—which was employed in the theology of the eastern world, in its poetry, its philosophy, and all the subliner forms of composition—should be that in which the sacred writers conveyed their highest and most important revelations to mankind? If we consider how ancient, how general, how widely diffused this symbolic style has been, and still is, in the world—how necessary it is to rude nations, and how taking to the most refined—how large a proportion of the globe this practice had overrun before, and at the time of writing the prophecies—and what vast regions of the east and south, not yet professing the faith, but hereafter, as we presume, to be enlightened by it, the same practice at this day overspreads—when we consider all this, we shall cease, perhaps, to admire that the style in question was adopted rather than any other." [1]

There had been no need for this apologetic strain, or the reference, on which it is based, to the original imperfection of language, if due regard had been paid to the distinctive nature of the mode of revelation by which prophecy usually came. Nor does it fairly meet the point at issue. It draws no line of demarcation between the different kinds of composition in Scripture; and if well-founded, as applied to the prophetical, should have been scarcely less so in regard to the historical and didactic portions of the Bible. Seeking to account for the peculiarity under consideration in the common characteristics of human thought and speech, it obviously establishes nothing for one species of writing any more than for another, and consequently leaves the specific point of the prevailing use of figure in prophecy without any adequate explanation. The whole that can justly be attributed to the circumstances above noticed is, that a certain subsidiary influence may have been exerted by them, and that in such kinds of composition as properly admitted of the use of figure, the associations and habits of the time may have afforded greater licence for its employment than could otherwise have been taken.

The fundamental reason, however, of the figurative style, which is so prominent a characteristic of prophecy, must be sought in the mode of revelation by vision. In the higher species of prophecy, which was connected with no ecstatic elevation on the part of the writer, but with his ordinary frame of mind—that, namely, of which the most eminent examples are to be found in Moses and Christ—the language employed does not in general differ from the style of ordinary discourse. But prophecy, in the more special and peculiar

[1] Hurd on the Prophecies, ser. ix.; also, Warburton's Legation of Moses, B. IV., sec. 4. The same track is still occasionally followed; among others, by Dr Turner of America, in his recently published Discourses on Prophecy, p. 103-5.

sense, having been not only framed on purpose to veil while it announced the future, but also communicated in vision to the prophets, must have largely consisted of figurative representations; for, as in vision, it is the imaginative faculty that is more immediately called into play, images were necessary to make on it the fitting impressions, and these impressions could only be conveyed to others by means of figurative representations. Hence the two—prophetical visions and figurative representations—are coupled together by the prophet Hosea, as the proper co-relatives of each other: "I have also spoken by the prophets, and I have multiplied visions and used similitudes by the ministry of the prophets" (chap. xii. 10).

Thus the predominant form of prophetic revelations was conditioned by the mode in which they were wont to be communicated. That they were received by the prophet in vision bespoke the sensuous character of the representations made to him, and the prevailing use in them of images and figures. Yet this did not take place always in the same manner, or to the same extent. In accordance with the diversified circumstances in which prophecy was given, and its skilful adaptation to the present or prospective condition of the church, the figurative element might be greater at one period and less at another; and hence, indeed, the tendency, formerly noticed, in certain prophecies to approximate to the style of history. But there could never be more than an approximation in this direction, so long as prophecy came by vision. Otherwise, vision and reality should have lost their distinctive places, and violence must have been done to the mind of the prophet when being made the subject and channel of divine communications. If the process was conducted intelligently and rationally, there must always have been something of imagery presented to the imagination. And even in the kind of imagery selected, it is but reasonable to infer that the same respect would be had to the ordinary laws of human thought, and that the images would be formed, in objects of the past or present, familiar to the individual—since thus alone could they either have presented themselves in a natural manner to the prophet's imagination, or have been adapted to the apprehension of those for whom, more immediately, the revelations were imparted. It is only by things known, however relatively imperfect, that the mind can picture to itself such as are unknown; and in foreshadowing things that are yet to be, it must avail itself of those which have already been. In any other way, to have conveyed to the prophets an insight into the coming issues of Providence, would have required, not a supernatural working merely upon the human faculties, but the super-addition to them of a new sense, or the coercion of an irrational force.[1]

1. Now, this natural, and, as it may fitly be called, necessary tendency in prophetical men to resort to known and familiar things for figurative representations of what was to come, took a twofold direction; it led them to draw chiefly from two sources. The first comprehends the various objects belonging to *the world of nature*. Of these objects themselves it is not necessary to treat at much length; for, that they were frequently used as images of things bearing some resemblance to them in the history of God's kingdom among men, has never been disputed; nor is the use generally such as to give

[1] The mental law here spoken of, having respect to the operations of mind generally, holds equally in the philosophical as in the religious province. Hence it is laid down as a fundamental principle in the Novum Organum of Bacon, Axiom 34, B. i. : "Nor is it an easy matter to deliver and explain our sentiments, for those things which are in themselves new can yet be only understood from some analogy to what is old." In other words, when attempting to conceive things not yet perceived or known, the mind necessarily shapes its conceptions by the forms of which it is cognizant in the present or the past. As a principle to be taken into account in the interpretation of prophecy, it was most distinctly enunciated by one who failed egregiously in the proper application of it :—"The prophets were taught the future by means of emblems, as a blind man is taught arithmetic by means of counters. They never speak in the spiritual mood, because they never saw in that mood. Everything which the Spirit manifests to them was by these emblems, and is expressed in these the great historical events and epochs of their nation.—*Irving's Preface to Ben Ezra*, page 193.

rise to much diversity of opinion respecting it. In the great majority of cases where any difference exists, it turns less upon the import of the images themselves, than upon the specific application to be made of the sense expressed by them, in the passages where they occur. No competent interpreter will doubt, that on the ground of a certain analogy between the symbols and the things symbolized—the metals in Nebuchadnezzar's vision, and the wild beasts in Daniel's (chap. ii., vii., viii.), denoted certain ruling powers and kingdoms. As little will he doubt that, both in the prophecies of Old Testament Scripture, and in the book of Revelation, mountains are a common designation for worldly kingdoms, stars for ruling powers, roaring and troubled seas for tumultuous nations, trees for the higher, as grass for the lower, grades of society, running streams for the means of life and refreshment, the bow in the cloud for the return of mercy and loving-kindness after floods of judgment—and many more of a like kind. The spiritual import of such symbols is generally rendered plain enough by the connection in which they stand, and a comparison of one passage with another. Nor are there wanting works which give, in a compendious and accessible form, a particular explanation of the symbols in the prophetic imagery derived from natural objects, and which may be referred to by those who wish to study the subject in detail.[1] We refrain, therefore, from entering into minute investigations regarding it; but there are two points to which we must particularly advert, as they form the fundamental conditions on which the use of natural symbols in prophecy is founded, and must, therefore, be kept steadily in view by all who would succeed in the interpretation of the prophetical Scriptures.

(1.) The first of these conditions is, that the image must

[1] Two of the latest in this country are Wemyss' "Clavis Symbolica," and "Mills' Sacred Symbology," both useful works, and, for the most part, agreeing in their explanation of the symbols, but occasionally differing from each other, and (as we believe) from the correct view itself, in the application and use made of particular images.

be contemplated in its broader and commoner aspects, as it would naturally present itself to the view of persons generally acquainted with the works and ways of God, not as connected with any smaller incidents or recondite uses, known only to the few. The reason of this is obvious. For if symbolical language is to convey any definite or certain meaning, it must proceed on a consideration of the objects employed as symbols, such as is commonly known and understood; and to depart from this common ground, and make account of things entirely incidental and peculiar, could only give occasion to subtleties and refinements, which must render certainty unattainable. Even analogies, which might readily enough have presented themselves to people in certain times or circumstances, but belonging rather to the profane than to the sacred territory, must here be left out of view; for they necessarily want those characteristics which fit them for serving as the elements of a Biblical symbolical language, such as might be distinctly apprehended, and generally acquiesced in. Let us take as an example the warlike attire of the first rider in the Apocalypse (chap. vi. 2), who is described as appearing with a bow, and going forth conquering and to conquer. From the frequent use of the bow in ancient war, its early consecration in poetry and the arts, as a common accompaniment or emblem of martial skill and prowess, and, more particularly from its use in Ps. xlv., in connection with that glorious King, who, in the cause of truth and righteousness, was to ride forth prosperously, sending his arrows into the hearts of his enemies, and bringing the people under Him:—from such considerations, which are obvious and patent to all, one can easily understand how appropriately the bow might be selected, in a book of symbols, as the distinctive badge of a hero, or of the cause identified with the Hero, whose singular destiny it was to go forth conquering and to conquer, —whose career of conquest was only to cease, when all power and authority had been made subject to Him. But the matter assumes another aspect—it is withdrawn from the broad field of nature and of history, to the obscure and narrow corner of antiquarian research, when, as with some recent writers, the key to its precise import and application is sought in the remote ancestry of a single individual. By this class of interpreters, the symbol is identified in the first instance with the reign of Nerva, but extended also to that of his four immediate successors, on the special ground that Nerva himself, who stands at the head of the group, though his family had been long domesticated in Italy, yet was by descent connected with Crete, his great-great-great-grandfather having been born there; and, in Crete, the bow was used as a sort of national emblem! As if the readiest thought about a public man, and the mark by which he might be most aptly characterised, yea, and with him a line of successors, who, in this precise point, differed from their head, was the relation in which he happened to stand, through the ascending links of several generations, to a comparatively unimportant island! With a licence to ransack antiquity for such incidents to determine the meaning and application of prophetic symbols, who should be able to foretell what may one day be extracted from them! Or who could assure himself, that he had really ascertained their import? But, indeed, such modes of explanation may be left to themselves; and when the principles of prophetical interpretation are better understood, they will be seen to carry their own refutation along with them.

(2.) The other condition with which the use and interpretation of prophetic symbols must be associated, is that of a consistent and uniform manner of applying them; not shifting from the symbolical to the literal, without any apparent indication of a change in the original, or from one aspect of the symbolical to another essentially different, but adhering to a regular and harmonious treatment of the objects introduced into the representation. This also is necessary; for, without such a consistence and regularity in the employment of symbols, there could be no certainty in the interpretations put upon them; all would become arbitrary and doubtful. Thus, if in the second chapter of Isaiah, the mountain of the Lord's house is to be understood in a moral sense, understood symbolically, of the seat of the divine kingdom,[1] then the other mountains mentioned in connection with it, over which it was to be exalted, must also be understood of kingdoms, the rival powers and monarchies of the world. So, in the sixty-third chapter of the same prophet, if the Edom there mentioned, on whom the Lord's vengeance is exercised, is the "country spiritually called Edom," really some modern hostile power, the people in whose behalf the work is done must also be those spiritually called Israel—the true church. Or, take an image that occurs with great frequency in the prophetic Scriptures—that, namely, of *falling*, used in reference to a person or a kingdom, and denoting, when so used, the destruction of a power, or the overthrow of a dominion; as, when the proclamation is heard, "Babylon is fallen." There can be no doubt, that such is the import of the expression in ancient prophecy, and also in the eighteenth chapter of Revelation, where the subject of discourse is the complete overthrow of the power there designated by the name of Babylon. But the same sense should manifestly be retained in other passages of the book; at chap. xi. 13, for example, where, speaking of the same power under the image of a city, it is said, that on the occasion of a mighty earthquake, the tenth part of the city fell. Whatever may be there intended by the tenth part of the city, consistency in the use of terms requires that the falling should denote an overthrow; and, so understood, the idea conveyed by it cannot well accord with that, which is so commonly found in the passage, of the detachment of a kingdom of Europe from the Romish apostacy by the reception of the Protestant faith. Nor does the description in other respects appear to suit this interpretation; for it is immediately added, "seven thousand were slain in the earthquake, and the remnant (those, namely, who remained in the city) were affrighted, and gave glory to the God of heaven." So that neither does the *kind* of falling implied in this interpretation agree with that actually con-

[1] See Part I., chap. iii.

veyed by the expression (the event supposed, indeed, might more properly be termed a rising than a falling, as regards the particular kingdom), nor did the other results connected with it at all correspond in nature and magnitude to those unfolded in the apocalyptic vision.

Many similar violations of the very simple and necessary condition we have specified, might be selected from some of the more popular and current works on the Apocalypse. In particular, they often err by confounding together symbol and reality. Thus, while Babylon is uniformly understood, in the mystical sense of the Papal system, with its centre of power and influence at Rome, the Euphrates (chap. ix. 14), the river on which it should stand, if the image is consistently employed, is taken as the actual Assyrian river, or (if viewed symbolically), as the designation, not of a Romish, but of a Mahommedan power, having its seat where the literal Euphrates flows. In like manner, the burning mountain of the second trumpet is viewed as symbolizing Genseric the Vandal; but the sea, into which that mountain is cast, is supposed to be, not the symbol of something else, but the veritable sea of the Roman empire in its coasts and harbours. So, again, Attila is regarded as the scourge that corresponds to the burning star of the third trumpet, while the fountains and rivers it falls upon, are held to be, not what resemble the objects denoted by these terms, but the objects themselves—the Danube, the Rhine, and the Po, with the countries to which they belong. We are not to be understood as indicating any opinion, as to whether the historical events now referred to, were contemplated in the visions, with which they have thus been associated, but are merely expressing our conviction, that there is an obvious flaw in such a mode of interpretation. It is impossible that the symbolical representations of Scripture can be written in so confused and arbitrary a style; and if those were in reality the events in which the prophetic visions found their accomplishment, it will assuredly be practicable to establish the connection between the prophecy and its fulfilment without so palpably travestying the ordinary laws of language.

It belongs also to the same fundamental condition, as to the use of figurative representations in prophecy, that the figurative character of the description, in its general features, not less than in the particular images it employs, should be preserved throughout. The examples of false interpretation just noticed, refer to particular images, and show the uncertainty and confusion that inevitably arise, when they are dealt with in an arbitrary and variable manner. But there ought to be the like consistence and uniformity observed in respect also to the general features of a prophetical delineation; since we cannot suppose that the vision shifted from a symbolical or ideal description in one part to a plain matter-of-fact description in another. We might, indeed, expect occasional notes and indications derived from the actual world as prospectively contemplated by the prophet, rather than from the ideal world in which he was for the time living, furnishing a kind of key for the more certain explanation of the figurative delineation, and giving some indication of the more prominent acts in the historical drama to which it pointed. This, we say, might not unnaturally be expected; for such ideal delineations in prophecy, viewed in respect to the things they represented, must always have been of a somewhat enigmatical nature. They necessarily, to some extent, veiled, while they exhibited the coming reality; and so required, in part, to borrow from the reality to prevent the veil from altogether hiding its proper character. Such, no doubt, is the case in the description given by Joel (chap. i. ii.), of the threatened judgment of God under the image of locusts invading the land, and spreading terror and desolation through all its borders. In several parts of the description, traits are introduced which appear so strange and exaggerated, if understood merely of the natural plague of locusts, that we cannot but regard them as designed, like so many rays of light let in from the actual world, to render the veil transparent, and discover the much more fearful reality which it imaged—namely, the desolation to be produced by the Chaldean army. Of this sort, in particular, are the statements made respecting the unparalleled greatness of the calamity to be produced by the locust-army—its coming was to be emphatically the day of the Lord, and in itself an evil of unheard-of magnitude (chap. i. 2, 3, 15); so also what is said of the effects of the visitation, which are described as nothing less than the loss of all the outward signs of a covenant relationship to God (ver. 8, 9); then again, the designation of the instruments of vengeance as a nation (ver. 6), and their subsequent identification with the mighty conqueror from the north (chap. ii. 20), nay, with the heathen generally, deliverance from whose oppressive and ignominious yoke is represented as all one with preservation from the threatened calamity (ver. 17). Such things are undoubtedly to be regarded as realistic features, introduced on purpose to show that the description *was* an ideal one, and should be understood throughout only as intended to present an imperfect image of the transactions really predicted. Similar things are to be found in other parts of the prophetic writings—for example, in the description of Ezekiel's temple and its accompaniments—which, in like manner, serve to break the shell of the ideal covering, and render manifest the proper greatness of the reality that lies beneath.[1]

So far, we admit, it was probable, and, in a sense, necessary, that the realistic should intermingle with the ideal, or the actual with the symbolical in prophetical delineations. But it was still within very narrow limits, that this either was, or could be done; so far only as might be required to indicate the kind of realization that was to be expected, or the manner in which it was to be brought about. In the general, however, the description must be uniform; it could not otherwise be intelligible, and if constructed on a figurative basis, one and the same character must be sustained throughout. For example, the vision which Isaiah is reported to have seen respecting Babylon, and which forms the most imaginative

[1] In the case of Ezekiel's temple the vast dimensions of the temple and city may be referred to in proof, the alterations at several points introduced into the Old Testament ritual, and the river flowing from the temple to the Dead Sea—but see our Exposition of the Book of Ezekiel.

and picturesque delineation in his whole writings (chap. xiii. xiv.)—a delineation which condenses into one vivid picture the history of ages, and draws together all that can be conceived most terrible and affecting of things in heaven, things on earth, and even things under the earth, to portray the doomed and prostrate condition of the self-exalting, God-dishonouring kingdom:—in the whole of this pictorial representation, there is to be sought, according to its predominant character, not the exact and literal description of the future, but rather such an ideal picture, as might present the most distinct and lively image of its nature. This is so plain as to admit of no doubt in regard to certain parts of the representation—those, which speak of the sun being darkened, and the stars of heaven ceasing to give their light, of the fir-trees rejoicing, and the cedars of Lebanon lifting up their voice, of the humbled monarch himself descending into the shades of the mighty dead, and being there greeted with taunts from those, over whom he was wont to domineer, as now brought down to a level with themselves. Every one perceives, that in all this, there is merely an ideal or figurative representation of the awful reverse, the utterly remediless desolation and ruin, which awaited Babylon as a kingdom. And why should not the same view be taken of the other parts? It is one end that is aimed at throughout, and the means employed to reach it could, with no propriety, be diverse in their character. Even the mention of the Medes, in connection with the coming vengeance (chap. xiii. 17), can only be regarded as an historical trait introduced for the purpose formerly stated—to mark more definitely the nature of the events predicted, together with the nearness and certainty of the change they were to bring. And what is said in the remaining details of the shepherds making their folds there, and of wild beasts of the desert—owls and dragons, and all kinds of doleful creatures—making it their haunt, was necessary (like the monarch's ideal descent into the nether world, and hearing the shout of triumph raised over his downfal), to complete the picture of thorough desolation, and exhibit Babylon as an utterly extinct empire. This was the real object of the representation; and the actual appearance of some of the things specified in the condition of Babylon as a mere city or province, served but to exhibit, how the doom of Babylon as an empire—the only doom properly announced in the prophecy—had already passed into accomplishment. In the execution of this doom, the prediction was verified; and the signs of local wretchedness and desolation, which in process of time, settled upon the very city and neighbourhood, less properly fulfilled what was spoken, than sealed the fulfilment, and rendered it palpable to the most careless observer.

(3.) But beside this sustained and pervading ideality in many of the figurative delineations of prophecy, which are drawn from natural objects, there is another element to be taken into account—not always, indeed, as an indispensable condition, on which they proceed, yet still as a very common characteristic, giving a distinctive form and colour to the representation. We allude to the prophet's subjective state and position, while the objects in the divine vision were passing before his illuminated eye. If the prophet simply described what he saw as a calm observer, the subjective element would, of course, be kept in abeyance. But this was not usually the case. More commonly his personal feelings were called into exercise, and were allowed to give their tone and impress to the description. Hence the perceptible differences in manner among the prophetical writers, who, even in narrating what occurred in vision retain severally their individual characteristics of thought and expression. Hence, also, the apparently exaggerated descriptions, which are sometimes given of the changes predicted to take place in the world—as in the vision of Isaiah respecting Babylon just referred to, when he says, "The stars of heaven and the constellations thereof, do not give their light, the sun is darkened in his going forth, and the moon does not cause her light to shine." Or in what Jeremiah saw, when he was assured of the approaching dissolution of the Jewish state, "I beheld the earth, and lo! it was without form and void: and the heavens, and they had no light. I beheld the mountains, and all the hills moved lightly" (chap. iv. 23, 24). Or, again, in Joel's memorable description of the wonders that were to appear in the latter days, according to which the sun was to be turned into darkness, and the moon into blood, before the great and terrible day of the Lord (chap. ii. 30, 31). Such passages in the prophetical writings are not to be regarded simply as high-wrought descriptions in the peculiar style of oriental poetry, possessing but a slender foundation of nature to rest upon. On the contrary, they have their correspondence in the literature of all nations, and their justification in the natural workings of the human mind; we mean its workings, when under circumstances which tend to bring the faculty of imagination into vigorous play, as it often *was* brought with the prophets when receiving in ecstacy divine revelations. For, it is the characteristic of this faculty, when possessed in great strength, and operated upon by stirring events, such as mighty revolutions and distressing calamities, that it fuses every object by its intense radiation, and brings them into harmony with its own prevailing passion or feeling. It leads the person who is under its sway to regard himself as the centre of all that is proceeding around him, even to see "the history of his own most secret emotions written on the very rocks." So that, if working in connection with a bosom greatly troubled and agitated, it will transfer that trouble and agitation to the objects, which it happens for the time to be contemplating. Such precisely is the exhibition—an exhibition not to be apologised for, but justly reckoned among the finest creations of Shakespeare's genius—given of the workings of Macbeth's mind, when on the eve of perpetrating the horrid murder.[1]

[1] The words of Macbeth, more particularly referred to, are the following:—

> "Is this a dagger which I see before me,
> The handle toward my hand! Come, let me clutch thee:—
> I have thee not, and yet I see thee still.
> Art thou, fatal vision, sensible
> To feeling, as to sight? Or art thou but

"Standing on the very brink of hell, and about to plunge into it, he sees the reflection of his own chaotic feelings in all things. Order is turned into disorder; law is suspended; every natural, every social tie is cracking; he is hurling an innocent man, his king, his guest, into the jaws of death; death is in all his thoughts. To him, therefore, with the deepest truth, 'o'er the one half world nature seems dead;' even as also the instrument with which the crime was to be perpetrated, rises in palpable form before him, though it was 'only a dagger of the mind, a false creation, proceeding from the heat-oppressed brain.'"[1]

Nor are such things to be met with in poetry alone; they are not wanting even in prose compositions, when the subject is of a kind fitted to work powerfully on the imagination, and agitate the bosom. The mind then cannot refrain in its historical delineations of what is taking place, from throwing around the world of outward realities the aspect of its own inward experience; as (to refer to a familiar example) in the descriptions given by contemporary writers of the fearful irruptions of the northern barbarians into the south of Europe, which they were wont to characterize as torrents, conflagrations, and even earthquakes. "Such," says Guizot, when speaking of these descriptions, "is the instinctive poetry of the human mind, that it receives from facts an impression, which is [often] livelier and greater than are the facts themselves; they are for it but matter, which it fashions and forms, a theme upon which it exercises itself, and over which it spreads beauties and effects, which were not really there." And on this ground, combined with the excitation naturally

A dagger of the mind: a false creation,
Proceeding from the heat-oppressed brain?
——————— There's no such thing:
It is the bloody business, which informs
Thus to mine eyes.—Now o'er the one half world
Nature seems dead, and wicked dreams abuse
The curtained sleeper," etc.

[1] Guesses at Truth, i. p. 63.

produced by a sense of personal interest in the events described, he justly infers that in the light of history the accounts referred to must be understood with some qualification; they must be considered as to a certain extent pictures of the imagination, though raised, doubtless, on a dreadful substratum of historical reality.[1] Need we wonder, then, that the prophets, when depicting scenes of uproar and convulsion, should often have done so in language that reflected the agitation or distress experienced in their own bosoms? Being descriptions of what was seen in vision, they *are* pictures of the imagination; they are ideal scenes, though scenes, which *appeared* real to the prophet who lived in them, and which in due time, also, as regards the substance of the delineation, were to *become* real in the historical future. What, therefore, is actually meant by the constellations of heaven disappearing, or by the sun being turned into darkness, and the moon into blood, is that everything would appear to men's view in a convulsed state; such terror should everywhere strike their minds, as would make all things in nature seem to be out of course, and the very instruments of life and blessing would wear the aspect of messengers of wrath. This is the case to some extent in every manifestation of the Lord for judgment; but not till his appearance for what shall be emphatically the world's judgment shall it rise to its proper consummation.

2. As yet we have noticed only one of the sources from which the prophets drew the materials of their figurative representations of the future,—namely, the visible world of nature. But there was another, and one more frequently resorted to in those prophecies, which bore respect to the person and kingdom of Messiah; one, therefore, that we have more especially to do with, when considering the word of prophecy with reference to Christian times. This other and very fertile source of prophetic imagery consisted of the things which belonged to the *history of God's dealings with his church and people*—the things, as they are very commonly called, of the Old

[1] History of Civilization in France, Sect. viii.

Covenant, though including also what pertained to earlier times. The higher and better things to come, which it was the calling of the prophets to announce beforehand, were to be but the fuller development of those which existed in the past, or a grander exemplification of the truths and principles they embodied. The two stood related to each other, partly as the beginning to the end, partly, also, as the shell to the kernel; and in a doctrinal respect alone it was of great importance to have this relative connection and dependence maintained—so to exhibit and foretell the better future, as not to lose sight of its organic union and fundamental correspondence with the past. This, of itself, must have led to the various use of the former things which lay within the ken of the prophets, and of those whom they immediately addressed, as a fitting medium through which to point men's hopes and expectations toward what was to be hereafter. And not only so, but as God, when revealing himself in vision to the prophets, did not work *magically*, though he wrought *supernaturally* upon their minds—as in all that they saw and felt there was the free and conscious exercise of their mental faculties—and, finally, as it is only from things known, existing in the present or past, that the mind can image to itself, or describe intelligibly to others, the things which are still unknown and future: —On these grounds it was a matter of necessity that the materials of what the prophets uttered respecting the appearance and kingdom of Messiah should be drawn chiefly from the affairs of past and preparatory dispensations. It was only by the help of the lower and ascertained class of objects and relations that they could attain to any definite idea of the higher things in prospect; even as still it is only from God having let himself down to the sphere of humanity, having clothed himself in human form, acted under the impulse of human affections, and spoken of himself and heavenly things in modes of speech derived from the familiar objects of sense and time, that we can rise to the apprehension of what is really spiritual and divine. And, as in these latter, so, beyond doubt in the other, the prophetical representations, there must be a large intermixture of the figurative. What they presented could not be the very image or naked reality of the things in prospect, but only such a view of them as could be given through imperfect forms, and by means of partial and glimpse-like visions; so that in them the dim shadow of the past ever, as it were, projected itself into the future, and spread like a veil or masque over the prospect that lay before.

The necessity we here speak of was one that arose from the very position of the prophets, and the mode in which an insight was granted them into a future, which, in many respects, was higher and greater than anything that had hitherto appeared —a future which one of the most distinguished of those prophets announced would be such as "the world had not heard, nor perceived by the ear, neither had the eye seen." Before Isaiah and the later prophets (to whom we now more particularly refer) came upon the stage of sacred history, several of the most prominent features in this grander future had been brought out with a considerable degree of distinctness. Plain and repeated intimations had already been given of a personal Messiah, who should come to fulfil the promises made to the fathers; of the connection in which he was to stand with the house of David; of his peculiar relation also to the Godhead, qualifying him for higher work than David himself could perform; and, in the accomplishment of that work, of His destination, like David, first to severe trials and deep humiliation, then to pre-eminent greatness and glory. Such points in the prophetic future had been rendered familiar to men's thoughts and expectations, even before the commonwealth of Israel took the downward course, which began with the division into two kingdoms. But, for the filling up of the prospect by more special predictions, for the investing of those primary and essential features with the properties of flesh and blood— in short, for the delineation of the Messianic future in its more distinctive characteristics and varied results, everything had yet to be done by Isaiah and the prophets of a later period. Nor, according to the fixed laws of human thought, could it have been done otherwise than under the form and aspect of things previously existing; for, if revealed in another and more direct manner, the distinction must have been practically abolished between vision and reality; and the prophets, whose part it was only to descry and herald from afar the better things to come, would, contrary to the progressive character of the Divine plan, have been placed on a footing as to light and privilege with Christ and the apostles, by whom the better things themselves were introduced. There had been no room, in the case supposed, for the marked difference between the revelations of the old and the new dispensations; nor could it have been said of the one period as compared with the other, "The darkness is past, and the true light now shineth."

In this, no doubt, it is implied that the revelations by prophecy, respecting the gospel age and its realities, were necessarily defective as to clearness and precision, and are not capable of bearing so exact an interpretation, or yielding so explicit a meaning, in respect to the affairs of Christ's kingdom, as is conveyed by the writings of the New Testament. But such, precisely, is the result that was to be expected, from the place and calling of the Old Testament prophets. Though high in one respect, they were subordinate in another. Indeed, they were subordinate in reference to the past, as well as to the future—subordinate even to Moses, so that they could not alter in any particular the polity introduced by him; and the primary and most fundamental test of their divine commission was the conformity of their teaching to that of the lawgiver. The whole they could do in the way of advance was to hold out the prospect and kindle the desire of another and better state of things. But if inferior to Moses as regards the revelation of the mysteries of God's kingdom, how much more in comparison of Christ? Even John the Baptist was more than a prophet, because he stood within the actual dawn of Christ's day; and yet such was the brightness which characterised this day, that John himself was less than the least of those who fully shared in its privileges. Nor was this the case merely in the general, but on specific points also it is expressly asserted that the revelations of Old Testament prophecy were much inferior in distinctness to those brought by the ambassadors of Christ. Thus the Apostle Paul, when discoursing of what he calls "the mystery of Christ," says: "It was not made known in other ages to the sons of men, as it is now revealed unto the holy apostles and prophets by the Spirit, that the Gentiles should be fellow-heirs, and of the same body, and partakers of his promise in Christ by the gospel" (Eph. iii. 5, 6). Here the apostles and prophets of the New Testament are placed above the prophets of the Old, distinctly on the ground that in the matter referred to they had more clear and explicit revelations given them. Nay, it is on these apostles and prophets of the new covenant that the entire temple of the Christian church is reared; not on them as apart from Christ, but as connected with Christ, and under Christ; as charged by Him with the whole ordering and establishing of the church in its institutions, privileges, government, and progress. Could such things have been said and done, if the revelations by the ancient prophets, respecting the work and kingdom of Christ, had not been dim and imperfect, as compared with the announcements of the gospel? And if those prophets received nothing in vision which could interfere with and unsettle what had been imparted to Moses, when God spake with him face to face, what an anomaly would it not be if their word were to be called in to supersede, or even to explicate and determine more perfectly, the word that came by Christian apostles and prophets! This were truly to invert the natural order of things—to imagine one could find in twilight-gloom what is not to be perceived amid the sunshine of noon-day. There cannot be a surer canon of interpretation, than that *everything which affects the constitution and destiny of the New Testament Church has its clearest determination in New Testament Scripture.*

This canon, with the grounds on which it is based, strikes at the root of many false conclusions drawn mainly from ancient prophecy, respecting the events of the latter days—conclusions which always implicitly, and sometimes even avowedly, give to the Old the ascendancy over the New; and, on the principle, which has its grand embodiment in Popery, would send the world back to the age of comparative darkness and imperfection for the type of its normal and perfected condition.[1] But, by the positions we have been establishing in respect to the essential nature of Old Testament prophecy, and the mode of its revelations, we are carried farther than this; we are enabled also to perceive the fallacy of a conception which, from an early period, has been prevalent in the church, as to the kind of insight possessed by the ancient prophets into the realities of the gospel dispensation. It has been very commonly supposed, that these were presented to them in their proper character, and that they saw them much as they are now seen amid the revelations of the gospel. Hence the prophecies, in which they gave utterance to the knowledge they obtained, according to a happy simile of Tholuck, came to be regarded as "an image of history, thrown by means of a concave mirror from the future into the past;"[2] that is, the character and events of the prophetic future were supposed to be exhibited in a kind of reflex manner to the eye of the prophet, and though in less definite lines, yet precisely in the form of the historical reality. It was the same misconception which prevailed in regard to the Old Testament types, and which, by perpetually stirring the question, What under this and that particular ordinance did ancient believers perceive of Christ's person or work? gave a wrong direction to men's inquiries, and perpetuated the existence of an entirely fanciful and arbitrary typological system. This error we have endeavoured to expose elsewhere,[3] and the similar error in respect to the prophecies of

[1] The late Mr Irving only spoke out distinctly on this subject what is implied in many current interpretations, when he said, "My idea is, that not the Old Testament, but the New Testament dispensation, hath an end; and then the other resumes its course under Christ and his bride, which is his church." All who hold, that there is to be a return to the old sacrificial worship, must concur in this opinion, whether they give expression to it or not.

[2] Commentary on the Hebrews, Diss. i.

[3] See Typology of Scripture, vol. i. p. 143.

the Old Testament, admits still more readily of exposure; it flows as a necessary deduction from the fundamental principles of the subject. For, if the revelations given of Christian times by the prophets of the former dispensation, occupied, like the prophets themselves, only a subsidiary position in respect to Moses, and a preliminary one in respect to Christ and his apostles—if, on this account, they disclose simply what was exhibited to them in vision, and heard in dream, not perceived amid the realities of waking life; then there must have been a specific and characteristic inferiority in the nature of the prophetic, as compared with the apostolic revelations. And that inferiority must, according to the known laws of human thought, to which the Spirit ever adapts himself in his operations, have mainly stood in the more ideal and figurative character of the prophetic announcements. The prophets necessarily thought and spake of the future under the conditions of their own historical position; so that it was not the image of the future which threw itself back upon the past, but rather the image of the past which threw itself forward into the future—the things which were, and had been, gave their form to the things which were yet to be. The substance of the Messianic prophecies, as Tholuck has again happily said, "is the Psyche of the New Testament, hidden under the chrysalis envelopment of the Old Testament. But, as the latter is still a Psyche, even while concealed under its thick covering, so also the prophecies wear an envelope, which they can be divested of only by him, who perceives their historical fulfilment. Hence, the prophets delineate the blessings of the New Covenant, in colours taken from the Old Testament theocracy."

Now, that such actually was the case—that the Old Testament predictions of gospel times did usually partake of an Old Testament colouring, may be made plain by a few examples bearing on the very heart and centre of the new economy, in which we have the benefit of an inspired interpretation, and about which, therefore, there is no proper room for dispute. Such are some of the predictions, which went before, respecting Christ's personal appearance and work—those more especially which bore respect to his threefold office, and which usually present what he was to be and do under an Old Testament aspect. Thus in Isa. lxi. 1, the Messiah, in his prophetical office, is represented as "*anointed* to preach good tidings to the meek," with reference to the consecrating oil, which in the case of such persons as were designated to special prophetical service, was wont to be employed (1 Kings xix. 16); although not the outward form, but the spiritual reality alone, was to be found in Christ. In like manner, as Priest, He is described as "opening a fountain for sin and uncleanness," "anointing a holy of holies," "pouring out his soul unto death," (as in the ordinary victims, the animal soul, the life-blood), and thereby "making it an offering for sin," (Zech. xiii. 1; Dan. ix. 24; Isa. liii. 10, 12)—all of them expressing Old Testament acts, and therefore neither having, nor capable of having, a formal, though they certainly had a most real, fulfilment; the words were accomplished—not in the letter, which from the nature of things they could not be, but in spirit and in truth. So, again, as King, it was predicted of Messiah, that He should spring forth as a stem out of the root of Jesse, a branch of the royal stock of David, that he should sit upon David's throne, and should build (in some higher sense than the returned captives were building) the temple of the Lord (Isa. ix. 7; xi. 1; Zech. vi. 12, 13, etc.). And, in perfect accordance with the meaning of these predictions, but with little agreement as to the outward form of things, He is represented in Gospel history as coming into the world to occupy the throne of His father David (Luke i. 32); nay, as allowing himself to be proclaimed its present occupant (Mark xi. 9, 10; Luke xix. 38; Matt. xxi. 5); and, after His ascension, the apostles, in the most explicit manner, declare Him to have entered on the fulfilment of the prophecies, which spake of His kingly glory, openly announce Him as having already become a Prince and a Saviour, even represent Him as having been anointed in terms of the

Second Psalm (Acts ii. 33, etc.; iv. 25–27; v. 31); and speak of Him as thus constituted head over all things, that He might carry forward the building of a great spiritual temple to the Lord (Eph. ii. 20–22; 1 Pet. ii. 5, etc.). It is impossible, by any fair construction of the language in these cases, to understand it of anything but an actual and present fulfilment of the prophecies referred to, an occupation, at that very time, of the predicted throne, and a prosecution of the work properly belonging to it; while between the form of the predictions, and the manner of their accomplishment, there were as many formal differences as there were essential agreements. For those, who might insist upon a literal conformity to the pattern of David's throne and kingdom, there could have appeared no fulfilment.[1] And, indeed, whence arose all the misapprehensions of the disciples themselves about the work and kingdom of Christ, and the difficulty of having them brought to a right understanding of the prophecies concerning Him? Did it not spring from this very source, the predominantly outward and shadowy form of the things predicted, the shell of which they were long unable to break, and get at the kernel which lay within? The gospel history would be an inexplicable riddle, if prophecy had not in general presented the new things of the kingdom under the veil of the old.

It is much the same when we pass from the personal work of Christ to that which more immediately concerns its application and fruits among men, the work of the Spirit. Of this, beyond doubt, the prophet Ezekiel speaks, when he makes promise of a sprinkling with clean water (chap. xxxvi. 25), in language derived from the corporeal lustrations of the old covenant; and the fulfilment alike of the prophetic word, and of the legal type, is indicated in those passages of the New Testament which describe believers as "washed," as "clean," or even as having "their bodies washed with pure

[1] For a more particular examination of the prophecies respecting Christ's occupation of the throne of David, see part ii., chap. 2.

water," though what was really meant is the purifying of their consciences from the guilt and pollution of sin. But one of the most striking examples of this species of prophecy and its fulfilment, connected with the work of the Spirit, is to be found at the very commencement of the Spirit's dispensation. On the day of Pentecost, the Apostle Peter, accounting for what was at the time proceeding, said: "This is that which was spoken by the prophet Joel: And it shall come to pass in the last days, saith God, I will pour out of my Spirit upon all flesh; and your sons and your daughters shall prophesy, and your young men shall see visions, and your old men shall dream dreams; and on my servants and on my handmaidens I will pour in those days of my Spirit, and they shall prophesy," etc. It were against all probability to suppose that the apostle meant to speak of this prophecy as having found a complete fulfilment in the events of that particular day, or as being in any measure exhausted by these. But, beyond all question, he does claim for it an actual fulfilment in the filling of the apostles with the Holy Ghost, and their speaking in a supernatural manner of the things of salvation. This must, in the apostle's estimation, have answered to the prediction of Joel respecting the outpouring of the Spirit, and the results in which it was to appear; for there precisely lay the occasion for citing the prophecy, and the point on which its testimony was needed. Yet here, also, the form in the two cases materially differs; it is old in the one, and new in the other. The prophecy, viewed in respect to its substance, makes promise of a far freer and larger communication of the Spirit than had hitherto been known; but it does this under the peculiar form of a quite general seeing of visions and hearing of dreams, because such, when Joel lived, was the mode in which the more special gifts of the Spirit manifested themselves. In that manner alone could he conceive of so plentiful a communication of the Spirit taking place. But by the time the prophecy entered on its proper fulfilment, this form of the Spirit's working had been well-nigh supplanted by another; the great realities of Christ's kingdom were now brought to the light of day, and were discoursed of in plain and direct terms. This was the only kind of speaking in the Spirit which appeared on the day of Pentecost, or was commonly practised in the New Testament church; so that while the substance remained, the form in which it was wrapt necessarily disappeared. The promised gift of the Spirit was conferred, but with a mode of operation higher than that of which the prophet Joel was himself cognizant.

Various other subjects of prophecy might be referred to as exemplifying the principle under consideration, but we simply point to an additional class of prophecies. In not one merely, but in a whole series of passages, the predictive assurances given to Abraham and the patriarchs respecting a seed of blessing, are applied, first, indeed, to Christ (in whom they were verified as to the form, as well as the substance), but also to believers generally in Him, without respect to their genealogical descent, if only they had through the Spirit become members of the family of God. These, also, are held in a legitimate and proper sense—in a sense included in the prophecy, and verifying it—to be of the seed promised to Abraham (Luke xix. 9; Rom. iv.; Gal. iii. iv.).

Now, in all these cases we have examples, about which there can be no reasonable doubt—examples resting for their proof on inspired authority—of precisely such figurative representations in the prophets of the Old Testament as the nature of their position might have led us to expect. They are, one and all, examples of prophecies which received their accomplishment as regards the substance, but not as regards the form, for another state of things had entered which rendered this impracticable. But if so in such cases, why not also in others? There is, doubtless, a general uniformity in the style of prophecies coming by vision, as well as in any other department of sacred writing. And specific examples, such as those noticed, ought to be viewed as so many illustrations, or light in an embodied form, let in by the Spirit of God upon some of the more select portions of the field, to guide us to a correct knowledge and understanding of the rest. Nor are there wanting collateral considerations to confirm and strengthen the conclusion.

(1.) First of all, there is the consideration that the symbolical prophecies contained in the manifold types of the Old Testament were of a similar nature, and had a similar fulfilment. They were every one of them made good as to their predictive import by the realities of the gospel, but in forms differing as much from the typical representations of them as the realities themselves were higher and better than their temporary substitutes. Since the very body of the religious dispensation under which the prophets lived was of such a nature, and carried in its bosom the prospect of such a realisation in the future, could it be otherwise than reasonable and proper that the Spirit of prophecy, when giving intimations of the same future, should to a large extent have assimilated them in form and manner to the other?

(2). A second consideration is found in the circumstance, that even before the introduction of the gospel era, and in respect to changes far less fundamental and peculiar than that, ancient prophecy did certainly predict events in the manner now specified; it announced things to come under the formal aspect of a recurrence of those which had already happened, although the later proved not to be a repetition of the earlier, but only of a like nature. Thus, Hosea, when foretelling the approaching bondage and captivity of Israel, represents it as a returning again into Egypt—because, there the great example of such a state presented itself in the past. But to show it was the Egypt-state, and not the actual country of Egypt, to which the prophet referred, he afterwards names Assyria as the region, where the humiliating discipline was to be experienced, and even with an apparent contradiction of the former announcement, declares they should not return to Egypt (chap. viii. 13; ix. 3; xi. 5). Another period in Israel's earlier history, the sojourn in the wilderness, is represented both by Hosea (chap. ii.), and Ezekiel (chap. iv., xx.), as destined to recur in the future; again, the people were to be led back into the wilderness, or be subjected to the memorable forty years' chastisement on account of sin, that they might be prepared for future mercies; but the subsequent mention in Hosea of Assyria, as the more immediate place of discipline, and Ezekiel's designation of the wilderness, as that "of the peoples," plainly indicate, that something quite different from a bald repetition of former events was intended. In Obadiah's prophecy respecting Edom and Israel, the period of the Judges, in like manner, is taken as the form under which to predict the future ascendancy of Israel; saviours were to come up on mount Zion, judging the mount of Esau, and bringing deliverance to Israel (ver. 17, 21, compared with Judges ii. 16; iii. 9). And still more strikingly in the description given in Hab. iii., of God's manifestation of Himself for judgment, is the history of the past taken as a vehicle for revealing what was to take place in the approaching future. We have there, not an historical narration of what had been done in former times, but a lyrical-prophetical delineation of what might be looked for, when God came forth, as He was on the eve of doing, to punish sin, first among the backsliding Jews, and then among the proud and lordly Chaldeans. Even Delitzsch with all his Jewish leanings and love for prophetical literalism, feels constrained to adopt this view of the description; he does not suppose, that, according to its real import, God was actually going to come from Teman, to shake the tents of Cushan, to make the land of Midian tremble, and such like. No, he says, most properly, "The prophet borrows from the ancient wonders of God, and the descriptions given of them (viz., as to his conducting the covenant people through the wilderness), the traits and features of his delineation of a corresponding future, justly considering the one as the type of the other. He forms thence the delineation of a great day of judgment, which was to combine in itself the severe and awful, yet salutary judicial manifestations of God for His people, which have ever and anon been taking place, of a deliverance outshining the typical deliverance out of Egypt. This close pre-established connection between the past and the predicted future, is the reason why the prophet makes Teman and the mountains of Paran, the starting point of the theophany, and represents the tribes on both sides of the Red Sea, as in terror and confusion." For the principle of this interpretation, the authority of Crucius is quoted, who says, "Since future things could not yet be narrated historically, which could not indeed have been done with propriety, a tropical mode of speech is employed, in which figurative terms are borrowed from things which happened at the departure from Egypt and the entrance into the land of Canaan, and which are fitly taken as images of things that were still to happen."[1]

(3). Still farther, there is the consideration, that in the language also of the New Testament, and of Christian discourse generally, the same practice is constantly followed—the practice of expressing new things in a phraseology derived from the old; while yet no one dreams of a formal resemblance between the things themselves, or an interpretation of the language according to the letter. At the very commencement of the gospel, our Lord, pointing to the free intercommunion between heaven and earth, which was to be the result of His mediation, describes it to Nathaniel in the words of Jacob's vision, "Hereafter ye shall see heaven open, and the angels of God ascending and descending on the Son of Man"—not that Jesus was ever to present the appearance of a ladder for that purpose, such as Jacob saw in his vision, but that in the new and higher sphere of his kingdom, there should be a like medium of communication established, and the agency of a like intercourse maintained. In a similar manner, the death of Christ is often spoken of under the old sacrificial form of the shedding of the blood, and the inward application of His atonement to the soul, is termed the sprinkling of His blood upon

[1] Der Prophet Habakkuk Ausgelegt, p. 139. Various other predictions might have been given, beside those specified; such as Ezek. xxix. 11, 12, where the forty years' chastisement of the wilderness is threatened even against Egypt; and Zech. v. 5-11, where a second exile to the land of Shinar or Babylon is spoken of as in reserve for the covenant people because of the sins that were beginning to appear among them: a repetition of the old calamity is taken to indicate fresh judgments.

the conscience, and baptism is designated his circumcision; and never, scarcely, is a prayer offered, or a Christian discourse heard without the free use in it of words that belong to the old covenant—such as altar, priest, sacrifices, Zion, Jerusalem, Canaan. Here, again, the instinctive poetry of the human mind, discovers itself in its fondness for the sensible and concrete, for the hallowed, though, in themselves, imperfect symbols of the past, in order to express its spiritual thoughts and feelings, instead of looking at the direct and naked reality. It is a continuing to do from choice what the prophets, who lived before the reality appeared, did from necessity. And it were even more incongruous to insist on an outward and formal agreement between *their* representations of gospel times, and the events that verified them, than inversely to demand the same in respect to the similar, but now less absolutely needed, representations of gospel realities under the antiquated forms of the old covenant.

Thus, every thing, both of a direct and of a collateral kind —considerations grounded in the proper nature and function of prophecy, in the light thrown upon the style of its predictions by the applications made of them in New Testament Scripture, in the typical character of the old dispensation, and the predilection for symbolical modes of speech as well among Christians now, as with prophets of former times—all seem to point to, and establish, the conclusion, that in the announcements of ancient prophecy, respecting the work and kingdom of Christ, there must have been a prevailing and characteristic tendency to exhibit the new under the image of the old. Whence it follows, that since the new has come, what appears of the old, in the prophetical delineations, must be interpreted in the light of the new—they must be set loose from their earthly and now obsolete form, and seen in the position and aspect of things pertaining to the kingdom of heaven. By being so considered, they are only made to keep pace with the progressive march of God's dispensations; and their proper import is no more lost, than our Lord's proper personality was lost, when on the mount of transfiguration, He was enveloped in the glory of the kingdom, or than the essence of Judaism was lost, when its prophetic symbols passed into the abiding realities of the gospel. All take a simultaneous and corresponding rise. And so far from evacuating the meaning of Old Testament predictions, when we transfer what they say of Zion or Jerusalem, of the temple and its sacrificial worship, of a ransomed people and their inheritance of blessing, to the church of the New Testament with its clearer light, its ample privileges and elevating prospects, we throw into them fresh life and meaning, illuminate their darker side, and render them, like the whole economy to which they belonged, in the strictest sense, "the testimony of Jesus."

The whole, however, of this line of thought is to be understood only of the general and prevailing character of the Old Testament predictions regarding Messianic times; and it must be taken in connection with what was formerly stated (in the first section of this chapter) of the variable and elastic nature of prophecy, whereby it could adapt itself to different circumstances, and approximate more to the style of history at one time than another. For though communicated in vision, and always to a certain extent partaking of the characteristics of that mode of revelation, yet, by means of spoken explanations and continuous statements (as in Daniel's later prophecies through the revealing angel), it was capable of assuming more of an historical character, than would have been practicable in a simple vision. Nor should its frequent combination with type be overlooked, especially with type as exhibited in the representative life of David and the history of Israel; since thus a variety of personal and local traits naturally came to be interwoven with its delineations of the future. These were so many tangible links connecting the new with the old, and served as special helps to a weak faith and a feeble discernment at the beginning of the gospel, that it might the more readily assure itself of the certainty of those things which it was called to embrace. And yet even these stood so intimately connected with things of a higher kind, they were so closely entwined with more profound marks of verisimilitude, as to render it scarcely possible for those, who perceived the external points of agreement, to avoid discerning others of a more inward and spiritual nature. In Christ's birth at Bethlehem, for example, or his temporary asylum in Egypt, or the actual piercing of his side with a spear, while there was a formal agreement with the prophecies mentioned in connection with those events by the evangelists, there was manifestly something more; in that outward verification no intelligent believer could fail to perceive the sign and index of a deeper fulfilment, which was at the same time accomplished, and which reached to the inner mysteries of the kingdom.[1]

It is in this typico-historical element more especially, so widely diffused through Old Testament prophecy, that we are furnished with a safeguard against the rationalistic tendency to carry to excess its figurative character, and are enabled to resist the temptation, presented by apparent contrarieties between prophecy and history, of attempting to resolve all its announcements into vague generalities. Real contrarieties are not to be found, if only the language of prophecy is understood and interpreted in accordance with its distinctive nature. But, certainly, there may be no difficulty in finding apparent ones, if the same principles of interpretation are indiscriminately applied to prophecy and history. And it is the practice alike of infidels and rationalists to make diligent search for contrarieties of this description, which they take to be real, and thence argue against every thing specific and supernatural in prophecy. We shall be prepared and fortified against this error, if we keep properly in view the connection between prophecy and type, and the comparative approach that might be made, particularly in this direction, to a measure of historical distinctness. For, on account of this connection, it necessarily moved within definite relations, which had their historical basis in the past, and must likewise have a historical basis in the future; it embraced transactions, which had their points

[1] For the illustration and proof of this, see Typology of Scripture, Book. I. chap. iv., and Appendix B on the Old Testament in the New.

of contact with the world, as those also had, which corresponded to them in the earlier dispensations. So that in perfect accordance with its figurative character, as bearing respect to events, which were to constitute an extraordinary era, and introduce an immense rise in the divine economy, prophecy might, and actually did, contain a considerable variety of particulars, which were capable of receiving a plain and palpable verification.

SECTION V.

Third Peculiarity of the Prophetic Style and Diction—the Exhibition of Events as Present, or Successive only in Relation to each other, rather than as linked to definite Historical Epochs.

THE scenical nature of the mode in which prophetic revelations were given, naturally brought along with it this additional peculiarity. The prophet was in spirit transported into the midst of the representations which emblematically unfolded the coming future, and depicted them as they passed in vision before the eye of his mind. Some of these, as in a picture or panoramic exhibition, might appear nearer, others more remote; one series of actions might be seen to terminate and another to begin; but they must have been continuously present to the prophet, or have stood related to each other as successive operations in the same line of things. "The prophets," says Crusius, "by the divine light which illuminated them, for the most part beheld things to come much as we look upon a starry sky. For, while we see the stars above us, we are incapable of rightly discerning at how great a distance they are from us, or which are nearer, and which more remote." So also, Bishop Horsley, in the main correctly, though not without a certain tendency to excess, "If you have observed, that this is the constant style of prophecy—that when a long train of distant events are predicted, rising naturally in succession one out of another, and all tending to one great end, the whole time of these events is never set out in parcels, by assigning the distinct epoch in each; but the whole is usually described as an instant—as what it is in the sight of God; and the whole train is exhibited in one scene without any marks of succession: if you consider that prophecy, were it more regularly arranged, and digested in chronological order, would be an anticipated history of the world, which would in a great measure defeat the very end of prophecy—which is to demonstrate the weakness and ignorance of man, as well as the sovereignty and universal rule of Providence: if you take these things into consideration, you will, perhaps, be inclined to think, that they may best interpret the ancient prophecies concerning the Messiah, who refer to two different and distant times, as two distinct events, His coming to make reconciliation for iniquity, and his coming to cut off the incorrigibly wicked."[1]

The tendency to excess in this passage betrays itself chiefly in the application made of the principle at the close. For, if that application were altogether correct, it might seem as if there were not only an indistinctness, as to time, in the prophetic delineations, but an absolute confusion—a juxtaposition of things in the prophecy, such as could scarcely fail to beget a false expectation in regard to the historical fulfilment. If Malachi, for example, at the beginning of chap. iii., on which Bishop Horsley more immediately grounds his remarks, had described the first coming of the Messiah, and then instantly started off to what was to take place at His second coming, we are at a loss to see how the prophecy could have been of any service in bearing testimony to the claims of Jesus. For, in such a case, the question must instantly have arisen, why should the results specified have stood so entirely disjoined in fact from the coming, with which they are prophetically asso-

[1] Works, vol. i., p. 83.

ciated? One can easily conceive, that the results indicated may not have been accomplished at once, or may have received nothing more than an initiatory accomplishment at the period of the first advent; but to have conjoined with this advent results, which were not to come then into operation at all, nor till another advent separated from it by the distance of centuries, must inevitably have tended to give rise to false anticipations beforehand, and created afterwards a most embarassing perplexity. It was not necessary, however—and here lay the ground of Horsley's partial misapprehension—that the first coming of the Messiah should always be specially connected with the work of reconciliation, as if that were its only object, and as if the first coming were to have nothing in common with the second. There was to be, in many respects, a fundamental agreement between them; and, in particular, the work of judgment, which is to have its consummation at the second, began also to take effect at the period of the first coming. It is true, that the more immediate and ostensible purpose, for which our Lord came into the world, was not to condemn, but to save it. Yet he himself testifies, "For judgment am I come into this world, that they which see not might see, and that they which see might be made blind." So, even at the period of his birth it had been announced by the aged Simeon, when he said, "This child is set for the fall and for the rising again of many in Israel;" and again by the Baptist, when he spoke of the coming Saviour as one "whose fan was in his hand, and he would thoroughly purge his floor," or, shifting the image, "who would lay the axe to the root of the tree." Indeed, the work of judgment is inseparable from the manifestation of the truth; when the one is brought to bear upon the hearts and consciences of men, the other infallibly takes effect upon their condition. And, therefore, in the prophecy of Malachi respecting the coming of the Lord, there is no need for any formal separation between what is designated the first and the second advent; the judicial procedure, with which it is associated, belongs to the one as well as to the other; only, in the first, there was necessarily a reserve and a limit in its operations, while in the second it will be complete and final.

It is a *relative* merely, not a *total*, disregard of time that was proper to the scenical representations of prophecy. An exact and detailed chronological order was incompatible with its nature, yet not such an order as might be required to mark the comparative distance or progression of events. There is a perspective also in the delineations of prophecy. Hence the language of Balaam, "I see him, but not now; I behold him, but not nigh" (Numb. xxiv. 17). A glorious personage rose upon his view, but one descried as at a remote point on the field of vision, because not to appear for ages to come on the theatre of the world's history. Hence, also, Daniel's successive monarchies; successive, and yet in a manner co-existent, for only with the establishment of the last do the others seem finally to disappear. More commonly, however, the description of the future is presented in a kind of continuity—exhibited under some particular phase, and in that carried onwards to its proper consummation. Thus, in the prophecy of Isaiah, respecting Babylon, formerly referred to, the whole drama of her coming downfal and ruin is set forth in an unbroken delineation, which in one rapid sketch embraces the history of ages, and connects, with the first stroke of vengeance inflicted by the Medes, the last sad proofs of her prostrate condition. A representation, precisely similar, is given by Jeremiah respecting the same proud city (chap. l. and li.); and by Ezekiel respecting Tyre, Egypt, and Assyria (chap. xxvi.–xxxii.) Many, also, of the prophecies given of Christ, and His times, possess the same character; they comprise the entire outline of the history in the particular aspect or class of relations under which they present it. Striking examples of this are to be found in such Psalms as the ii., xlv., lxxii., cx., or in the eleventh chapter of Isaiah, where, after having depicted, in the chapter preceding, the discomfiture and overthrow of the Assyrian power, which was then the peculiar rival and enemy of the kingdom of God, he breaks forth into the description of a new and very different scene in the land of the covenant. This scene began with the appearance as of a tender shoot out of the decayed stem of Jesse, by which, beyond doubt, is to be understood the Messiah in His original humiliation and outward littleness. But presently the personage thus appearing in comparative insignificance rises to the highest place of power and authority, shows Himself to be possessed of the noblest qualities and endowments; and, in the exercise of these, proceeds onward, till every enemy is subdued, unrighteousness in every form is put down, and universal harmony and blessing is restored. In this delineation everything is left indefinite as to time. The preceding downfal of Assyria, with which it is connected, merely furnishes the occasion for bringing out the contrast that should, in this respect, be found to exist between the worldly and the divine kingdom—the one being destined to pass from its peerless height of grandeur to utter annihilation; the other to rise from the lowest depression to universal dominion and imperishable glory. But while the delineation is indefinite as to time, in the nature of the things described it is comparatively distinct and complete; and as regards the particular aspect under which the things of God's kingdom are here contemplated, the prospective outline reaches from the commencement to the close. In like manner, in the second part of Isaiah's writings, amid all the phases presented of the Redeemer's history and work, the progress of His cause, and the triumphs of His kingdom, no notes of time are anywhere given; each successive scene is described as in itself complete, and the order of events no farther indicated than that some things were to stand in a relation of priority to others. The same substantially may be said of the prophets generally, more especially when they discourse of the coming events of the gospel. They knew that it was of the remoter future that they spake, although, we are informed, they had to make diligent inquiry before even this could be rightly ascertained (2 Pet. i. 10, 11). As much also is implied in the general nature of the formula with which their predictions of the Messianic times are usually introduced, the things spoken of are announced merely for "the latter days," so that it is clear the prophetic Spirit could have no intention of marking out distinctly beforehand the times and seasons of the "world to come."

Yet here also the accommodating and variable nature of prophecy discovered itself; for, as vision and dream commonly went together in the imparting of the revelation, so in the dream words might be heard with reference to the time, defining more or less exactly the period of the transactions which presented themselves in the vision. Such actually was the case in respect to *some* of the predictions; they were associated with certain prophetic periods. Occasionally this was done when a test of prophetic verity had to be given. The test was made, wholly or in part, to consist of a particular event happening within a specific time, as when Isaiah foretold the destruction of the kingdom of Israel in threescore and five years, or when Elijah declared that for three whole years there should be no rain in Israel. Such signs, however, were but rarely given; and when they were, they rather belonged to the nature of wonders or miracles, than to prophecy in its more regular operations. But beside this, in times of peculiar difficulty and depression, the introduction of the element of time might be necessary to afford the consolation which was required for the people of God. Above all others, in ancient times the period of the Babylonish captivity was of that description. Everything seemed then verging to utter ruin; and not merely a prospective deliverance, but a deliverance within some definite period was needed to re-assure and strengthen the heart of faith. It is, accordingly, at this period that we have one of the most specific announcements as to time in Old Testament prophecy—in the intimation that at the end of seventy years the season of captivity and desolation should expire (Jer. xxv. 11). Yet even here the period was not exactly determined; for as the captivity was effected at three successive stages, from any one of which the seventy years might, with some appearance of probability, have been dated, the expiry of the period by no means lay upon the surface, and Daniel himself only ascertained it by searching into books (chap. ix. 2). A much greater obscurity, however, must necessarily have hung over the mystical notes of time in some of Daniel's own visions—the seventy weeks that were determined upon His people and the holy city; the fourfold succession of worldly monarchies, with the setting up, during the last of them, of the kingdom of heaven; the time, times, and the dividing of time, during which the power represented by the little horn was to prevail; and the several other numbers which afterwards occur in connection with the later visions of his book. Such indications of time obviously bear obscurity and indistinctness upon their very front. They were intended to conceal not less than to disclose; and while, on the one hand, they set a limit to the prevalence of evil, or fixed a period for the accomplishment of promised good, on the other hand they so determined this as to require the most careful inquiry and patient consideration of the march of Providence, before ultimate assurance could be attained respecting it. Daniel expressly testifies he did not himself understand what he heard of some of those numbers (chap. viii. 27; xii. 8). And yet such helps did they furnish to an inquiring faith, and such checks did they set to artful imposture, that through them, and similar landmarks in the prophetic word, general expectation was awakened at the time of Christ's appearance; the history of the period, the more it is examined and understood, the more it is found to possess points of coincidence with the notes of time and circumstance in prophecy; and presently after, the relative position of things became so completely changed, that a proper agreement between the two ceased to be any longer possible.

This aversion of prophecy to clearly defined historical periods—its tendency to exhibit coming events under relations in space or time, or, as successive only, without being on either hand definitely bounded—appears also in New Testament predictions. It appears in the discourses of Christ himself, in whom the Spirit resided above measure, and who received no revelations in dream or vision. He gives certain signs of the approaching destruction of Jerusalem, and of His own personal return to the world, by the careful consideration of which His followers might not be taken unawares by either event; but the precise period in both cases is altogether indeterminate. Nay, so essential did He deem it to the spiritual interests of His church to have the time so left, as regards the great object now of the church's expectation, His own second coming, that He refrained from knowing it Himself when on earth. He *voluntarily* refrained from doing so; for, beyond doubt, He might have had the knowledge of that also, if He had so willed it, since, as the Son in the highest sense, He knew the Father (Matt. xi. 27); nay, had all things of the Father's delivered into His hand (John xvi. 15). But He did not will it; He purposely restrained the intercommunion between the divine and human natures, that He might exhibit Himself an example to His people, as not seeking to know what were not proper to be known, even by the most perfect, in a state of humiliation and trial. Therefore, he said, "Of that day and hour knoweth no man, no, not the angels which are in heaven; neither the Son, but the Father" (Mark xiii. 32). Not only so, but when the disciples showed, at their last interview with their Master, that they had failed to profit aright by this declaration, and came to Him with the question whether He was then going to restore the kingdom to Israel, He rebuked their curiosity by the answer, "It is not for you to know the times or the seasons which the Father has put in His own power." This specific announcement, delivered in a face to face communication, we may be sure, from the fundamental laws of prophetic revelation, could not be annulled by any subsequent information on the subject, communicated in vision. *It fixed, from the first, the abiding condition of the church as regards the knowledge of coming epochs in her history.* It did so, more especially in regard to the great epoch of her Lord's personal return. And whatever insight the visions of the Apocalypse might be intended to give in respect to the *kind* and *order* of events which were to fill up the intervening space, it were unreasonable to expect that they should be such as to throw any determinate light upon the *precise period* of the end. Interpretations pretending to derive from them light of this description, betray, in the very pretension, their own vanity, and cannot fail, as often as renewed, to afford fresh proof of the folly of attempting to penetrate a veil which God has wisely resolved to hang over the events of the future.

Let it not, however, be supposed, that the revelations of prophecy contain no materials for aiding our inquiries concerning the probable approach of the greater movements and issues of Providence. There is here also a growing light, which will be found sufficient for all practical purposes, if it is carefully sought for and applied. The events of gospel history separated between things which had not been accurately discriminated, in respect to time, on the page of prophecy; and the visions of the Apocalypse were, no doubt, designed to light up more clearly the prospect of the future, by exhibiting it in successive and contemporaneous forms of development. It is only by the facts and revelations of the New Testament, that ancient prophecy has been found conclusively to require for its complete verification, two disparate manifestations of Godhead—the one in humiliation, the other in glory. And had we not possessed the visions of the Apocalypse, we could hardly have imagined the interval between the commencement of Messiah's reign, and its proper consummation, was to be so great, or that it was to admit of so complicated a drama of good and evil, of such manifold and successive waves of sin and judgment, trial and victory. On this account alone the book occupies a most important place, and fills what would otherwise be a grievous blank in the general scheme of revelation. But from its very structure, and more especially from the mystical numbers it employs, and the absence of any explicit information as to the relation of the different visions it unfolds to each other, it is plain, that nothing more than probable grounds of expectation beforehand, or moral certainty afterwards, should be looked for in respect to the events of which it speaks.

Should this be reckoned strange? Should it be viewed as

derogating to some extent from the honour and usefulness of the prophetic word? Should we not rather esteem it matter of just admiration, that men, who were endowed with such profound insight into the future, should in this particular have been led to place so peculiar a reserve on their communications? Here, especially, the impatient curiosity of the human mind is ever and anon going in quest of specific information; and the world's prophets seldom want the will, however often they prove destitute of the power to gratify it. But we have only to search the records of divination, to learn what disastrous results have followed its presumptuous attempts in this direction—even when, by a fortunate coincidence, the prognostications have found a verification in Providence; and what numberless confirmations they have afforded of the saying:—

> "Oftentimes, to win us to our harm,
> The instruments of darkness tell us truths!"

Most commonly, indeed, it is falsehoods under the colour of truths, that have been told. Yet even truths, when told out of their proper place and time, respecting the future, have ever proved among the deadliest snares to human virtue. In greatest mercy, therefore, as well as wisdom, God has restrained his servants from breaking too rashly the seal of the future. He has permitted them to impart only such a measure of knowledge concerning things to come, as might not be out of proportion to our other endowments. In special emergencies, when more than common light was needed for direction and encouragement, he has disclosed something even of the times and seasons of coming events. But as comparatively little could have been communicated on such points with safety, so it has always been done with the most sparing hand, and seldom without a covering of secrecy. And in nothing, perhaps, more than in this wonderful combination of darkness and light observable in the prophetic word—in the clear foreknowledge it displays on the one hand, of the greater things to come in Providence, coupled, on the other, with only such indications of time and place as might be sufficient to stimulate inquiry, and ultimately dispel doubt, may we discern the directing agency of Him who knows our frame, and knows as well what is fit to be withheld, as what to be imparted in supernatural communications.

CHAPTER VI.

THE INTER-CONNECTED AND PROGRESSIVE CHARACTER OF PROPHECY.

VERY considerable misapprehensions have arisen, and both partial and mistaken views have been propounded respecting particular prophecies, by considering them singly and apart, without regard to the place they hold in the general scheme of prophetical development. Their relation to such a scheme was not a matter of accident, but one of wise and orderly adjustment—not, indeed, on the part of the prophets, who uttered the predictions, but of the inspiring Spirit from whom the communications really proceeded. The prophets themselves spake as they were moved, and as the circumstances of the time required; but both in the personal qualifications of the prophets, and in the particular messages they were commissioned to deliver, a regard was had to the prophecies which had been previously uttered, to the more or less complete fulfilment they had received, and the farther progress that remained to be made. The testimony of prophecy, therefore, like the testimony of history, is a chain composed of many links, each running into others before and after it, and by the introduction of some fresh particulars, or some different aspect of the truth, contributing at once to the elucidation of the past, and to a more explicit representation of the future.

This unity of plan and mutual inter-connection of parts, with progressive action on the whole, is precisely what was to have been expected in prophecy, on the supposition of its being the product of one and the same Spirit, operating in connection with a gradual and growing development of the divine purpose in respect to the world's redemption. In such a case, it is but natural to infer, from what appears in the divine works generally, that as the end would be contemplated from the beginning, so the whole burden of prophecy would be comprised even in its earlier utterances, but only that it might be afterwards expanded into such variety of parts, as was required by the manifold and ever-changing phases of the world's history, and the onward progress of the scheme of God. So it was in reality, as the following brief, but comprehensive, sketch, very strikingly unfolds:—"At first, the word of God is as a seed, it may be of the oak, or of any other plant, in which the whole majestic form and various parts of the future lie undisclosed, ready to reveal themselves when the times and the seasons, and other conditions which God has appointed to determine its being, shall have taken their course. And there is no break, nor leap, nor start in its course, which proceeds by a slow, and sweet, and beautiful progression, to perfect that purpose or word of God, which said at the beginning, 'Let the earth bring forth grass, the herb yielding seed, and the fruit-tree yielding fruit, after its kind, whose seed is in itself.' So the first great promise made in Eden, contains the whole of the revelation and prophecy of God, in an embryo state: first, the enmity between the seed of the woman and the seed of the serpent, which has produced all the persecutions endured by the church from the world, since the time of righteous Abel, until this hour, and which she shall endure till the resurrection. The second part of it, 'Thou shalt bruise his heel,' has been likewise developing itself during the whole of the same long period, in which the heel, or lowest part of the church's body, that is, our carnal, natural life, has been vexed and crucified by him during life, and lies bruised unto dust in the grave; but, at the resurrection, the church shall bruise his head, casting him out of his usurped domination, and reigning over him for ever and ever. Therefore it is written, both of Christ and of His church, that they shall rule the nations with a rod of iron, and dash them in pieces like a potter's vessel, and have all their enemies under their footstool. We have not room to trace the progress of this seed sown in paradise, as it is developed in the progress of revelation, and shoots its roots into the soil of the fallen world, and spreads its branches into the atmosphere of time, until it shall possess the whole earth; yet in order to show how true the principle is, let us trace it out a little. We have the promise to Abraham still made of a seed, and now all nations are to inherit the blessing, in whose right their father Abraham is enfeoffed in a country by the divine word. In the mouth of David, the promise is still of a seed to come, which has now attained the high stature of a triumphant and universal king of Judah by pre-eminence, of all the earth by equal privilege; in this same character of a king, the child is made known to the immediate precursors of His birth, Zacharias, Elizabeth, Mary, John; in the same character to Simeon, though now His sufferings and the calling of the Gentiles be hinted as first to happen, which He labours all His life long to make intelligible to Nicodemus, to His apostles, and all His disciples. In no other character does Peter declare Him, after the day of Pentecost, and James in the council of Jerusalem, and the two shining ones on Mount Olivet, and Paul and all the apostles, than as THE KING, who ascended on high without seeing corruption, waiting and expecting, till the Father shall accomplish the times and the seasons, and bring in the days of refreshing spoken of by all the prophets, the restitution of all things waited for by the whole creation of God. In no other way does John see Him in the Apocalypse, than as a child, the seed of a woman, caught up to God, and His throne, and there abiding until, after certain sore warfares and persecutions of His church, He comes again with many crowns upon His head, and followed by all the armies of heaven, in order to break the confederacy of Satan's powers, to bind the old serpent himself, and cast him into the bottom-less pit, with all the nations that forget God. There is such a soft, sweet, and silent development of this one seed sown in paradise, and which in its growth doth change the earth into paradise again, reproducing that *kind* of blessedness which the world was then deprived of, that this alone has ever to thoughtful men marked revelation as a divine work, comprehending the restitution, regeneration, and complete blessedness of man and his habitation. Like the stately branching oak, which begins in an acorn, and of which the end and purpose is, to generate an acorn, while, during the progress of its stately growth, it covers every beast of the earth with its kindly shade, and nestles every bird of heaven in its ample branches; so this promise was sown in the soil of a perfect and perfectly blessed state, while man still dwelt in paradise, and its end is to produce perfectly blessed men, dwelling in paradise again; while, during all the ages of its growth, it should bless the immortal spirits of men with salvation, and its leaves be for the healing of the nations." [1]

In this outline, which we present, chiefly because of the happy manner in which it connects together the beginning and the end, and exhibits the analogy that subsists between God's method of working in nature and in grace, only some of the more obvious links are noticed; when the matter is looked at more closely, far more is discovered of the progressive unfolding of the first promise, and the inter-connection between it and subsequent prophecies, and of these again with each other. Before we reach the time of Abraham, reference is made to it in the benediction of Noah upon Shem, which defines to some extent the line through which the blessing was to come upon the world—it was to be directly in connection with Shem, and mediately, through a participation with that line, upon the other branches of the human family. Then the revelation to Abraham may be said to combine together the word of Noah and the original promise; it makes promise of a seed of blessing, which was to spread and prosper and have the ascendancy in the world, and defines still more exactly the line by which it should proceed; singling out the family of Abraham, setting it in the highest place, and linking

[1] Irving's Preface to Ben-Ezra, p. lxxi., etc.

indissolubly with it the better destinies of the world. Along with the promise of the land of Canaan for a possession to his seed, or, as it was afterwards defined, to a select portion of his seed, after the flesh, the word given to Abraham was, "I will make of thee a great nation, and I will bless thee, and make thy name great, and thou shalt be a blessing. And I will bless them that bless thee, and curse him that curseth thee, and in thee all the families of the earth shall be blessed."

This great promise to Abraham was in one sense only a limitation of the original promise; it merely chalked out a particular channel, through which divine grace should flow in raising up a spiritual seed, to resist and baffle and drive out the tempter; yet in the actual form which it gave to the expected good, more especially in the relations it established with a view to the accomplishment of what was promised, it became a germinant word for all future prophecy before the coming of Christ. From henceforth prophecy takes what may be called the Abrahamic type. Connecting, as this fundamental promise did, the particular with the general—the hope of the world with a chosen family and a local territory, the same particularism ever after adheres to prophecy; it moves continually within the relations, which date their commencement from the call of the Father of the faithful. The relations are variously modified; new elements are ever and anon intermingled with them to make out the progressive exhibition of the future; but only as gradual developments of what already existed, additional branches springing out of the old stock, and clustering around it, not the production of a stock altogether new. Thus, the prophetic disclosures successively made to Isaac and Jacob are little more than renewals of the original promise to Abraham, with certain indications regarding the mode in which it was to proceed to its accomplishment. Even the remarkable prophecy of Jacob, "The sceptre shall not depart from Judah, nor a lawgiver from between his feet, until Shiloh (the peaceful one) come; and unto Him shall the gathering of the peoples be," is merely a step forward in the same line; it simply associates the divine purpose, as disclosed to Abraham, primarily with the tribal ascendancy of Judah, and ultimately with a distinguished individual of that tribe, in whom the fulness of power and blessing was to reach its culminating point, and diffuse itself throughout the nations of the earth. Balaam ere long catches up the strain of the dying patriarch, and, along with other expansions of the Abrahamic promise, proclaims the rise of the bright day-star, of which Jacob spoke—the glorious and mighty Lord, who should rule with resistless might, but rule only to subdue the evil and establish the good. The current grows in volume as it proceeds. The house of David comes into view as the election within the election, the seed out of all the tribes of Israel and the families of Judah, which, by virtue of its peculiar relationship to God, was to attain to the ascendancy in the affairs of men, and carry the blessings of salvation and peace to the remotest habitations. Here, again, a fresh start is taken by the prophetic word, another stage is reached; and the settlement of the power and the glory for ever in connection with the house of David, as disclosed in the fundamental prophecy of Nathan (2 Sam. vii.), appears at once as a certain consummation of the earlier predictions given to Abraham and his posterity, and the seed-corn of other predictions that point to a still brighter and greater future. Hence these other predictions have respect alike to the more general and the more special relations indicated in what had been spoken and done; they point back sometimes to the less definite covenant of blessing made with Abraham, sometimes to the more personal and specific form it assumed in connection with the house and lineage of David; and not unfrequently the language carries a distinct reference to both together. The Messianic psalms, and the later Messianic prophecies generally, are constructed mainly on the basis of Nathan's prophecy and the relations it introduced respecting the kingdom, yet not so as to lose sight of the earlier promise, and the fulfilment it was to receive in the fulfilment of the other. Thus, in the seventy-second Psalm, which is throughout a prophecy of Him, who was to be emphatically the King, and of the character of His kingdom, it is said at ver. 17, with evident reference to the Abrahamic promise, "And they shall bless themselves in Him, all nations shall call Him blessed;" and, again, in Psalm xxii. 27, "All the ends of the world shall remember, and turn unto the Lord; and all the *families* of the Gentiles shall worship before Him." It is as much as to say, then shall the blessing of Abraham have come upon the Gentiles. In Jer. xxxiii. 22, the promise of a continued and flourishing condition to the house and kingdom of David is thrown—doubtless for the purpose of marking more distinctly the connection between the two—into the peculiar form of the Abrahamic promise, "As the host of heaven cannot be numbered, neither the sand of the sea measured, so will I multiply the seed of David my servant"—although the covenant with David had respect, not so properly to a numerous offspring, as to a perpetual and glorious succession in the kingdom. And in Zech. xiv. 16–19, which obviously has respect to the closing issues of Messiah's kingdom on earth, the word of promise to Abraham as to those being blessed who blessed him, and cursed who cursed him, and all the families of the earth being at last blessed in him, is taken up and applied in Zechariah's peculiar manner; the nations, as in the old promise, have the designation of "all the families of the earth," and they are represented as going to be blessed or cursed, according as they did or did not go to worship before the Lord with His covenant people.[1]

Such examples show very distinctly the consecutive, as well as progressive nature of prophecy—how tenaciously it adheres to the old channels, and maintains the original impress, and proceeds by way of development under relations already settled and known, not by the introduction of others essentially different and new. They show, that as regards the great stream of prophecy, the past never properly dies; it is perpetually resumed and carried forward in the future. Earlier develop-

[1] See this subject of the developments of the earlier prophecies ably handled in Hengstenberg's Christology, vol. i., new edition.

ments become only the historical basis, out of which spring the announcement of more matured and diversified results. It is thus that the historical goes along with the prophetical, the one ever furnishing, by its fresh evolutions, the occasion and groundwork on which the other proceeds to unfold some further aspect of the scheme of God. And instructive, as well as interesting, is it to mark how the history was moulded, sometimes even into peculiar and unexpected shapes, to open the way and provide the materials for the progressive informations of prophecy. The circumstances of David's time were remarkable illustrations of this, which were all divinely ordered, so as to make the beginning prophetic of the end. Even the changes to the worse, that afterwards arose—the falling down, as it is called, of the tabernacle of David, or the decaying of his once stately tree, till it had become like a scathed and branchless stump—though singularly trying to faith in the meantime, was improved by the Spirit of prophecy to the end of bringing out more distinctly and graphically, than might otherwise have been possible, the deep humiliation and adverse circumstances amid which the kingdom was ultimately to rise from the dust and advance toward its perfected condition. But, perhaps, the most striking example to be found of this moulding of the historical relations and occurrences, to admit of prophecy, without essentially altering the form of its representations, progressively adapting these to the approaching future, is furnished by the changes—in themselves changes to the worse, that entered after the return from Babylon. Various points might be mentioned in this connection, but one very particularly indicates the foreseeing eye, and presiding agency of God. An anomalous and, as regards the history of the period, an almost inexplicable state of things then began. While the work of God generally was revived among the covenant people, and the house of David did not want a worthy representative in the person of Zerubbabel, yet that house itself did not revive in the same proportion as the rest; it even fell, after a little, into complete abeyance; and, notwithstanding, that the hopes of the people were all suspended on the appearance of a glorious personage of the seed-royal, it was not the *royal* but the *priestly* line that rose to the place of power and authority in Judah. This was, no doubt, partly ordained to the end, that when the promised child appeared, the hand of God might be more evidently seen in His rise to the possession of the kingdom. But it was partly also, and, indeed, more immediately appointed for another purpose—for the purpose of directing the thoughts and expectations of the church to the *priestly* element in Messiah's character, which in the prophecies founded on the relations of David's time, had been somewhat obscured by the kingly. The reverse now takes place; the kingly drops out of sight, and the priestly rises in its stead. Hence, in the prophecies of this period, those of Zechariah, Haggai, and Malachi, a quite peculiar place is given to the priesthood; and though Zerubbabel is once and again mentioned as the representative of the royal house, yet it is Joshua, the high-priest, who is formally exalted to the head of the covenant people, and is even taken as a type to foreshadow the future Joshua or Saviour-king. In the third chapter of Zechariah, after being set up as a type of the people, first clothed in filthy garments, then in others fair and comely—a sign of forgiveness and acceptance—a charge is addressed to Joshua, to walk in the ways of God, coupled with the assurance, that if he did thus walk, it would be given him to "judge the house of the Lord and keep His courts"—in other words, to have regal as well as priestly power. And then, after declaring Joshua and his fellows, in this, to be men of wonder or signs, the prophet goes on to read the import of the transaction, by making promise of the *Branch*, the Lord's anointed already promised under that name, by whom the iniquity of the people was really to be purged away, and who, as the true Shiloh, would give them to sit in peace, every man under his vine and under his fig-tree. In like manner, in the sixth chapter, Joshua is expressly set forth, with crowns upon his head, as the representative of "the Man whose name is the BRANCH," of whom it is said, "He shall build the temple of the Lord," build it, namely, in the true and proper sense, as contradistinguished from that inferior and shadowy sense, in which Joshua and his companions were then doing it. "And," it is added, "He shall bear the glory, and shall sit and rule upon His throne; and He shall be a priest upon His throne; and the counsel of peace shall be between them both." In Malachi also, it is the state and calling of the priesthood that are peculiarly dwelt upon, and the most explicit prophecy that is given of the coming Messiah, represents Him as going to establish the covenant which the sons of Levi were violating, and accomplish a work of thorough purification upon the members of the covenant.

Thus was it wisely ordered by the providence of God, that in the last announcements of prophecy, that aspect of the Messiah's character and mission should be the most distinctly, as from the turn given to affairs it was also quite naturally, brought out, which was the first to be formally established, and which was to constitute the ground-work of all that should follow. It was nothing absolutely new, however; but only a more palpable and prominent exhibition of what had been frequently indicated in earlier, and was involved even in the earliest, prophetical announcements. And so, when prophecy enters on its proper fulfilment, the whole appear to have simultaneously reached their end; the relations, whether more general or more particular, under which the future had been predicted, are once for all established in the higher sphere of gospel realities, so that the end may be said to embrace the beginning. When Christ enters the world, He is made known as pre-eminently the seed of Abraham, through whom the blessing, so long promised, comes upon the Gentiles; as the son of David, who appears to rectify every evil, and set up the throne of the kingdom in righteousness and truth; as the high-priest, also, who bears away the iniquity of His people, and in His own blood, lays the foundation of His kingdom—receives the crown of glory in the heavenly places, because He has suffered unto death in the earthly. His followers become Abraham's children, the true Israelites, fellow-citizens with the saints and of the household of God, a chosen generation, a royal priesthood, ministering before God in light and purity in the midst of surrounding Gentiles (1 Pet. ii. 5, 12 : 3 John 7), at death going to Abraham's bosom, at the regeneration sitting down with Abraham, Isaac, and Jacob in the kingdom of God, nay, at the restitution of all things, entering paradise as the woman's victorious seed, and taking their place beside the tree of life, and the river, clear as crystal, that proceeds from the throne of God and the Lamb. In reality, and looking to the order of nature, Christ is the root of all; in Him and from Him the whole proceeds; and so it is declared in Scripture with the greatest plainness and frequency. But out of regard to the historical element, which plays so important a part in the revelations of Scripture, the older relations are still preserved in the word of promise, in order to connect prophecy with its fulfilment, and to render manifest the consecutive as well as progressive character of its revelations.

But it is clear that if this holds in regard to one class of relations, it must equally do so in regard to another. The manner and style of prophecy must be uniform, if it is to be intelligible. The relations we have referred to, as embodied in its representations—progressively embodied, as its views of the future came to be progressively unfolded—are those of a *personal and social* kind; but, in intimate connection with these, there were also *local* relations, which stand side by side with the other in the delineations of prophecy. They were not merely poetical beings in connection with whom it revealed the future; they had their place amid the realities of sense and time. Eve was connected with a paradise of life and blessing before her fall, as with a cursed and troubled earth afterwards; and the prophecies respecting her victorious seed point to the uplifting of this curse, and the return to that paradise again. Abraham, with his immediate offspring, Isaac and Jacob, were also connected, by promise, with a specific territory; and the covenant made with Abraham as distinctly and properly includes an inheritance of blessing, as a seed of blessing that should become co-extensive with the families of the earth. In the history and prophecy alike, the two are bound up inseparably together. Circumcision was appointed as the seal of the covenant, without the remotest hint of a division in respect to these objects, so that it can only be characterised as a fiction of modern times to connect it with the one of these more than with the other. We must here also proclaim the word, "What God hath joined together, let no man put asunder." Certainly the prophets of the Old Testament did not do so. As they employ the *personal* and *social* relations of Abraham and his posterity to unfold the character and purposes of the great scheme of God, so with these they ever conjoin the *territorial;* and Canaan, Jerusalem, Zion, are at every step mixed up with Abraham, Sarah, Isaac, Jacob, David, Solomon, and others, in the prospective exhibition of the better things to come. What, under the one class of relations, is represented as the blessing of Abraham diffusing itself to all the families of the earth, appears, under the other, as the King of Zion having the heathen for His heritage, or reigning in peace and righteousness to the ends of the earth; or as Israel being third with Egypt and Assyria, a blessing in the midst of the earth (Isa. xix. 24); or as people out of Egypt, Babylon, Ethiopia, and other countries, going to be born in Zion, and many representations of a like nature. Nor is it otherwise when we pass to writers of the New Testament. They tell us, indeed, that baptism has taken the place of circumcision, but in its entireness, not in respect merely to a part of its symbolical and sealing import. They speak, with reference to Christians generally, of *our* fathers having passed under the cloud and through the sea. They designate believers, not only Abraham's children, but heirs also with him, according to the promise—heirs, namely, of what he himself was heir of. They represent the oath, which ultimately confirmed the covenant with Abraham, as added, that "*we* might have a strong consolation, who have fled for refuge to the hope set before us;" and describe the members of Christ's church as having now come to Mount Zion, the city of the living God, the heavenly Jerusalem.

Yes, and shall we not thank God that it is so; that the evidence on each side is so clear and decisive; and that on the warrant of inspired prophecy going before, and an infallible interpretation coming after, we can assure ourselves of a personal interest in all that was written in former revelations, without being obliged to grope our way between certain things that are for *us*, and certain other things with which we have no proper concern? All hangs harmoniously together. The same word that, as addressed to men of former generations, tells us of the way to a sonship condition, lays open, at the same time, the prospect of a sonship inheritance. And speaking, as it does, of things to come, through the existing relations of those by whom it came—their territorial as well as personal and social relations—we may, and we *ought* to see in one and all of them alike, the hidden purpose of God's grace, in its completeness, struggling into light, and in the present and visible sphere of things giving open pledge and testimony of the glorious heritage of life and blessing, destined for those upon whom the ends of the world have come.[1]

[1] On the ground of these considerations we object to the division of the prophecies of the Old Testament into those of a simply temporal kind, which belonged to Abraham and his family; and those of a spiritual kind, in which the people of God generally have an interest. Sherlock, in his Discourses on Prophecy, exhibits this division. One portion, he says, "relates to the temporal state and condition of the Jews, and was in order to the administration and execution, on God's part, of the temporal government given to Abraham and his natural descendants. These prophecies, relating to the things of this life, concern us but little; but there are others in which we are highly concerned," etc. But Davison carries out this division more formally. He regards prophecy as taking, from the call of Abraham, a double course—falling into two distinct lines, "one of them exclusive and particular to his family; the other extending to all the nations of the earth." He holds the two to "be exceedingly distinct in their extent and in their kind, and their distinction was marked from the beginning" (p. 83). We take this to be a superficial view of the matter. The outward and temporal did not exist by itself or for itself, but for the higher spiritual things connected with it, and as the necessary means for securing their attainment. To separate such things which God has bound so closely together, and draw a broad line of demar-

We have hitherto spoken of the mutual inter-connection and progressive character of the prophetical writings together, the one as the natural result and sequel of the other. There might, however, be a connection without an actual progression. One prophecy might either in regard to its subject, or to the form of representation it employed, have a respect to, and even be in a sense dependent upon, an earlier prophecy. And, in so far as such may be the case, it must be proper to keep it in view as an important element in the interpretation of prophecy, since a later prophecy of that description, even when it does not add anything material to the earlier, and brings out no new aspect of the future, cannot fail to be of service in confirming or elucidating what has preceded. The reference in Zechariah, already noticed, to the prophecy of Isaiah, respecting the branch that was to spring out of the stem of David, would have been of value (to say nothing of the intimation coupled with it of the priestly character of Him in whom it was to be realised), were it only for the familiarity it bespeaks with the earlier prophecy, and the explanation it puts upon the term *branch*, as indicative of small beginnings, but such as were to grow to the greatest magnitude.

The passages in which one prophet substantially adopts the representation, or quotes the language of another, are of considerable number and variety. We can only refer to a few of the more obvious examples. Thus, in Isa. ii. 1–4, we have, with only a few verbal differences, the same prediction respecting the exaltation of the house of the Lord in the latter days, and the general resort of the nations to it, that occurs in Micah iv. 1–3; the ideas, the language, the structure of the periods are so nearly alike, that there can be no doubt of the one having given rise to the other; and there are pretty strong grounds for the conclusion, that it appeared first in the pro-

cation between them, is false in principle, and sure to lead to erroneous results. If believers in Christ are Abraham's children, and heirs according to His promise, they are assuredly interested in all that was said or promised to him. And the outward and temporal can never stand alone; rightly considered, it will be seen to have a spiritual element pervading and animating it.

phecies of Micah. The prophecies of Balaam, as they refer more than once to earlier predictions, so are they again among the most frequently referred to and quoted in subsequent prophecies. Micah, for example, distinctly points to them, in chap. vi. 5, and calls upon the people to remember them. Habakkuk at chap. i. 3, "why dost thou show me iniquity, and cause me to behold violence?" and again, at ver. 13, "Thou art of purer eyes than to behold evil, and canst not look on evil," evidently uses language derived from Numb. xxiii. 21, where Balaam speaks of God as "not beholding iniquity in Jacob, nor seeing perverseness in Israel." Balaam had said (Numb. xxiv. 17), of the star that was to arise out of Jacob, that "He should smite the corners of Moab, and destroy all the children of Sheth;" and Jeremiah (chap. xlviii. 45), says, "a flame shall devour the corner of Moab, and the crown of the head of the children of noise"—partly quoting the former words, and by a slight change (much slighter than the translation might seem to imply), giving the meaning more distinctly of the rest—the children of Sheth in Balaam, becoming the children of noise or tumult in Jeremiah. There are many similar examples in Jeremiah, who, more than any of the prophets, adopts the language of his predecessors: thus, in chap. xvii. 8, his description of the man, whose hope is in the Lord ("He shall be as a tree planted by the waters, and spreadeth out her roots by the river, and shall not see when heat cometh, but her leaf shall be green"), is very much an adoption with some amplifications of the Psalmist's description of the righteous in the first Psalm; and the prophecy in Jer. xlix. 7–32, of Edom, is in many parts the same, with what is found in Obadiah, or differs from it only in unimportant particulars. Obadiah had said, "The pride of thine heart hath deceived thee, thou that dwellest in the clefts of the rock, whose habitation is high; that saith in his heart, Who shall bring me to the ground? Though thou exalt thyself as the eagle, and though thou set thy nest among the stars, thence will I bring thee down, saith the Lord." Jeremiah says, "Thy terribleness hath deceived thee, the pride of thine heart, O thou that dwellest in the clefts of the rock, that holdest the height of the hill; though thou shouldest make thy nest as high as the eagle, I will bring thee down from thence, saith the Lord." Several other specimens might be given from the same prophecies. And Obadiah, who here is followed, himself also follows Joel in various expressions; as when he says, "They have cast lots upon Jerusalem" (ver. 11), while Joel had said, "They cast lots upon my people" (chap. iii. 3): or, "Thy reward shall return upon thine own head" (ver 15), and "Upon Mount Zion shall be deliverance" (ver. 17), where the words are in each case taken from Joel chap. iii. 4, 7; ii. 32. But it is needless to multiply examples farther.

Now, at first thought, such appropriations by one prophet of the words and ideas of another, may seem scarcely to consist with the raised and elevated condition of those who saw the vision of God, and spake as they were moved by the Holy Ghost. It may seem to throw around such portions of the prophetic word, an appearance of art and labour; and exhibit them in a dangerous resemblance to the productions in human literature of those who endeavour to make up for the want of original genius, by availing themselves of the ideas and expressions of more gifted intellects. Such actually has been the interpretation sometimes put upon the matter. And yet, that it is manifestly not the right one, is evident alone from the order in which the citations and references by one prophet from another, appear in the examples we have adduced. If an Isaiah could take from a Micah, a Habakkuk from a Balaam, a Jeremiah from an Obadiah, it is clear, that some other principle must be sought to account for the dependence, than any native inferiority of mental powers, or the decay of prophetic gifts.

In the way of explanation, it must be remembered, that the revelations of the prophets, if not formally given over, like the Psalms of David, to persons charged with the service of God in the sanctuary, were usually made public as soon as they were received, and added to the existing testimony of God. They forthwith became part of the sacred treasury of the church; and formed, not only as to the thoughts expressed in them, a portion of revealed truth, but also, as to the very terms employed, a kind of hallowed tongue, in which to give expression to such thoughts, when they might again present themselves for utterance. May we not appeal in support of this to experience? When one is really, and, in the proper sense, full of the Holy Ghost, do not his thoughts instinctively, as it were, run in scriptural channels, and clothe themselves, when he speaks, in the very language of inspiration? The more powerfully the Spirit works within, originating spiritual thoughts and feelings, the more readily do they always take this scriptural direction; as appears on the day of Pentecost itself, in the address of the apostle Peter, which is full of Old Testament quotations; and shortly after, when escaping from the hand of violence, and filled with the Holy Ghost, the apostles poured forth their hearts to God with one accord, in the very words that had been indited centuries before by the pen of David (Acts iv. 23–27). In like manner, the apostle Paul, who had the highest gifts of the Spirit, and spoke of the things of God "in the words which were taught by the Holy Ghost," ever makes the freest use of the earlier Scriptures, and sometimes, as when enjoining the duty of forgiveness, contents himself with reiterating the testimony of former times (Rom. xii. 19–21). And how often does the apostle Peter, throughout his first epistle, address to the New Testament church, as from himself, passages that were originally addressed by other servants of God to the church of the Old Testament? Yet such passages are as much the communications of the Holy Spirit on their second, as they were on their first appearance; for the purpose of God required, that a fresh utterance should be given to the sentiments they expressed, and the original form of expression was, on many accounts, the best that could be chosen.

Besides, there were ends of a more special kind to be served by the references and quotations from one prophet to another. For, these were like so many sign-marks along the line of ancient prophecy, indicating the relation of one portion to another—formal and specific authentications in the chain of God's testimony, connecting the earlier with the later, certifying the existence of the earlier, and confirming anew, or incidentally throwing light on its import. "The Old Testament prophets," says Caspari, "form a regular succession; they are members of an unbroken continuous chain; one perpetually reaches forth the hand to another. The later prophets had always either heard or read the prophecies of the earlier, and had these deeply impressed upon their minds. When, therefore, the Spirit of God came upon a prophet and irresistibly impelled him to prophesy (Amos iii. 8), it naturally happened, first, that here and there, sometimes more, sometimes less, he clothed what the Spirit imparted to him, in the words of one or other of the prophets, he had heard or read—the words of his prophetical fore-runner thus cleaving to his memory, and forming part of the materials of utterance of which the Spirit availed himself; and second, that the later prophet attached himself to the prophetical views of the earlier, and in the power of the prophetic Spirit, which descended on him from above and wrought in his soul, either confirmed them anew by a fresh promulgation, or expanded and completed them. For the most part, the coincidence in thought and expression, is found united in the prophets."[1]

Delitzsch, the friend and coadjutor of Caspari, has followed up this line of remark by similar observations in his introduction to the third chapter of the prophet Habakkuk—a chapter which is not less distinguished by the vein of originality that pervades it, than by the free use which is made in it of some of the earlier portions of Scripture, especially of Psalm lxxvii., "With the inspired penmen in general," he says, "and with the prophet in particular, simply from his being a living member of the spiritual body, there was formed an internal storehouse out of the substance of former revelations, which had entered into the very core of his spiritual life, and become amalgamated with it—revelations which

[1] Der Prophet Obadiah, Ausgelegt Von Carl Paul Caspari, pp. 21, 22.

sunk so deep into the memory and the heart of every pious Israelite, that he necessarily acted under their influence in the formation of his thoughts, and, when writing also, could not avoid making use of the older expressions, which already bore upon them a divine impress. Besides, the prophet could not otherwise be the organ and bearer of a divine revelation, than by sacrificing everything of a selfish kind, therefore all ambitious strivings after originality, that he might surrender himself to the operation of God; and this operation was partly of a *mediate* nature, through the work which had already been produced, and partly *immediate*, yet even then connecting itself closely with the existing word. The conformity of the new, which germinated in the mind of the prophet, with the old, which had been imported into his mind, was necessitated alone by the circumstance, that the revelation, in its *organic* development, could only present the aspect of something new, in so far as it took up the old, in order to confirm and still further unfold it, without the possibility, in the *process* of development, which proceeds from God Himself, the *Unchangeable*, of running into contrariety with what had preceded. This unison is the very seal of a divine revelation, as the work of one and the same Spirit operating in the workshops of many individuals."[1]

On the whole, then, this mutual inter-connection and dependence apparent in the prophetical writings was of importance, as an appropriate evidence and seal of the oneness of the pervading Spirit, of the brotherhood of the prophetical order in faith and love, of the advancing, yet ever-renewing light of the prophetical testimony, and, we may add, of the genuineness and authenticity of its several parts. The prophets were not rendered less human in their manner of thought and utterance, that they were supernaturally moved by the Holy Spirit; they thought as men, they spake as men; and the use they thus made successively of each others' writings, is a mark of verisimilitude on them *as*

[1] Der Prophet Habakkuk, Ausgelegt von F. Delitzsch, p. 118.

writings, a concealed attestation of their having been produced and published at the proper time, and a satisfactory indication as to the place they relatively and respectively occupied in the prophetic chain. It is an element that has most effectually withstood the rationalistic alchemy, and materially contributed to the defence of the integrity of the prophetical writings.

PART II.

APPLICATION OF PRINCIPLES TO PAST AND PROSPECTIVE FULFILMENTS OF PROPHECY.

CHAPTER I.

THE APOLOGETIC VALUE OF PROPHECY, OR ITS PLACE AND USE AS AN EVIDENCE FOR THE FACTS AND DOCTRINES OF SCRIPTURE.

THERE are three points that ought especially to be borne in mind, when prophecy is considered as an evidence, and brought to bear on the controversy we have to maintain with the assailants of the Bible. The first is, that as it is prophecy in its predictive character alone that is here made account of, this, it should be remembered, was only a branch, and not more than a subsidiary branch, of its revelations. We refer for the proof and grounds of the statement to the first chapter of the former part, and to the farther elucidations given respecting it in chapter third. But assuming the position now as a correct one, it were in itself wrong, and fitted to beget mistaken apprehensions on the subject, to conduct the argument from prophecy, as if the whole value of prophecy depended upon the number and clearness of its announcements of the future. This has been too often done in the past, and material injustice has in consequence been inflicted on the interests of revealed truth.

A second consideration, which was also brought out in the earlier part of our inquiries (chap. iii.), has respect to the more immediate design and function of prophecy. Its proper sphere is the church, rather than the world; and the primary end, for which its communications were given was to direct and comfort the children of faith, more especially in their seasons of greater darkness and perplexity. Of necessity, therefore, those who stand altogether without the region of faith, must be in an unfavourable position for appreciating, or even for distinctly understanding a large portion of the prophetical volume. It is only some of the broader features and more salient points of the subject, that can with any advantage be presented to them. We are obliged to act in the matter like persons who stand outside—looking, as from a distance, on the exterior of the sacred building, and pointing to such proportions and adjustments as are too conspicuous to be overlooked, or altogether denied; but are not in a condition to enter in, and take cognisance of the finer, the more profound, and far-reaching harmonies, which pervade the internal framework.

There is still another point, which must be taken into account, in itself, when duly considered, a source of great strength, but one that must also be attended with some disadvantage in conducting an argument with adversaries of the faith. In dealing with such persons, it is necessary, for the most part, to single out and press specific points, instead of surveying the matter in its proper compass and completeness. Now, the evidence of prophecy is essentially of a connected and cumulative nature. It does not consist so much in the verifications given to a few remarkable predictions, as in the establishment of an entire series, closely related to each other, and forming a united and comprehensive whole. This is peculiarly the case in respect to the prophecies, which relate to the person and kingdom of Messiah, which more than any others form a prolonged and connected series. Hence, to use the words of Bishop Hurd, "though the evidence be but small from the completion of any one prophecy, taken separately, the amount of the whole evidence, resulting from a great number of prophecies, all relative to the same design, may be considerable: like many scattered rays, which, though each be weak in itself, yet concentred into one point, shall form a strong light, and strike the sense very powerfully." [1]

Any one may see, on a moment's reflection, how great a difference this serial and connected character of Old Testament prophecy forms, in an argumentative respect, between it and the isolated, occasionally happy prognostications of uninspired men. The difference is such, as to secure for the argument founded on the fulfilment of Scriptural prophecy a conclusive force, if it is fully entered into and fairly dealt with; while, if looked at only in broken fragments, the distance cannot possibly appear so great as they would otherwise do between it and some of the more fortunate specimens of human augury. Even, however, with this disadvantage, the prophecies of Scripture will be found to have characteristics belonging to them, which such specimens fail to exhibit. The two most noted examples of the class, that have been brought, and in the present day are still brought, into competition with the predictions of the Bible, are taken from ancient Roman authors. One is the saying of a Roman augur, Vettius Valens, reported by Varro, in his eighteenth Book of Antiquities: If it was true, as historians related (si ita esset, ut traderent historici), that twelve vultures had appeared to Romulus at the founding of the city of Rome, then, since the Roman people had survived for 120 years, they would prolong their existence to 1200 years. And the other occurs in Seneca's Medea, where it is said, a time should come, when the ocean would relax the cords by which the world was then bound, and new regions of the earth come to be explored; when Thule (Shetland) would cease to be the remotest boundary of the known world. [2]

[1] "Sermons on Prophecy," p. 86.

[2] ———— Venient annis
Sæcula seris, quibus oceanus
Vincula rerum laxet, et ingens
Pateat tellus, Tiphysque novos
Detegat orbes; nec sit terris
Ultima Thule.

Now, in regard to both of these vaunted prophecies, there is no need with Hurd to press on the other side the serial and compact nature of the prophecies of Scripture. By doing so, indeed, we might place those of Scripture at a much greater and more conspicuous elevation above them. But, in truth, they cannot stand a comparison even with some of the earlier and less specific announcements of Scriptural prophecy. Bishop Horsley has tested that of Seneca with the prophecy of Noah, in respect to the relative fortunes of his posterity, and shown the immeasurable superiority of the patriarch's insight into the future above that displayed by the Roman sage. General and comprehensive as Noah's prediction is, it still comprises particulars which were capable of meeting as well with a marked contradiction, as with a distinct verification in the course of Providence, since it so expressly, and in perfect accordance with the results of history, ascribes to Shem's line the superiority in respect to the knowledge and worship of Jehovah; to Japhet's, the superiority in respect to extensive propagation and active energy; and to Ham's, the bad pre-eminence of degradation and servitude. It is easy to conceive how, in many respects, the course of events might have travestied this prospective distribution, instead of, as the issue has proved, strikingly verifying it. But, in regard to Seneca's augury, which has, no doubt, received a sort of fulfilment, it really predicts nothing but what might with confidence have been anticipated from the history of the past. There had already, within the period to which authentic tradition reached back, been a great enlargement of men's geographical knowledge; many discoveries had been made of new territories both by sea and land; and as it was certain that a vast extent of ocean still remained to be explored, nothing was more likely to occur to an imaginative mind than that in process of time further additions would yet be made to the ascertained boundaries of the habitable globe. But, beside this natural inference, all is vague and general. "Neither the parts of the world are specified from which expeditions of discovery should be fitted out, nor the quarters in which they should most succeed; or, if any intimation upon the latter article be couched in the mention of Shetland, as an island that should cease to be extreme, it is erroneous, as it points precisely to that quarter of the globe where discovery has ever been at a stand—where the ocean, to this hour, opposes his eternal barrier of impervious unnavigable ice."[1]

It fares still worse with the other prediction, the ancient oracle of Vettius. His prognostication from the number and appearance of the vultures, did not even profess to have more than a possibility for its foundation: "If it was so," he said, "as historians related." But every one knows now that, like other things respecting Romulus and Remus, the story about the vultures is not so properly the account which historians related as the legends which poets sung; it was altogether of a fabulous character, and the prediction hazarded on it could be nothing more than a fortunate guess. It appears, indeed, in the form of a calculation. If the Roman people have survived 120 years—that is, 12 times 10—then they shall do so ten times that again,—1200 years. But why this longer period? They certainly did survive so long; but we can see no probable grounds for the anticipation, none for that precise period any more than others that might be named.

We have, as we shall presently see, greatly more specific predictions in Scripture, than either of those heathen oracles —predictions which are not based upon any conjectural hypothesis, and far too discriminating to have been framed merely by shrewd inference and deduction from the history of the past. But were they less so than they really are, when taken individually, it is not to be forgotten that their immense number and connected order—as related to a great scheme, and pointing to a definite end—forms their peculiar distinction, and renders the argument deducible from them one of an exceedingly varied and cumulative nature. If it might be excepted against certain portions of the chain, that they did not afford conclusive evidence of supernatural foresight and

[1] Horsley's Works, I., p. 256.

Divine interposition, the whole surely cannot be thus excepted against. And, besides, even when taken in its full compass and connection, prophecy, it must be remembered, with its manifold accomplishments, is still but one branch of the Christian evidence. So far from having the whole weight to bear alone, there are several others equally important to be coupled with it—the miracles of the gospel, the originality of Christ's character and scheme, the sincere and self-sacrificing spirit of His apostles, the sublime morality of their teaching, with its profound adaptation to the wants and emotions of man's moral nature, and the blessed results it has accomplished in the world. All must be taken together; they are so many distinct but converging lines; and it is the combined force and operation of the whole, not the strength merely of a particular part, which must decide the claim of Scripture to be received as the authoritative revelation of God to men.

We must, however, quit these general considerations, and by a selection of particular examples show how the argument from prophecy may be most advantageously conducted. Dealing with the subject as it may be best fitted to tell upon the understanding and convictions of those who are enveloped in doubt or unbelief, our position should be chosen at a point where the ground is comparatively clear as to the main question, and no preliminary difficulties can be raised, or brooding suspicions entertained, regarding the possible occurrence of the events that fulfilled, before the utterance of the prophecies that foretold them. The interval between the prophecy and its fulfilment should be such as to leave no proper room to doubt that the one had been spoken and recorded before the other had come into operation. On this account many of the most explicit prophecies, whose deliverance and fulfilment are recorded in the same book, should be passed over in the first instance; as in the case of such, the adversary is ready with the answer, that he doubts the formal existence of the predictions till after the events themselves had taken place. We may, therefore, fix upon the period immediately subsequent to the Babylonish captivity, when the prophetical writings and the canon generally of the Old Testament had become complete—complete, we believe, in the strictest sense; but as some, not even avowed adversaries, are still disposed to except portions of Daniel, and to regard them as the productions of a still later period, however groundless the suspicion is, the consideration of such portions had better be postponed till others are disposed of.

SECTION I.

PROPHECIES ON THE STATES AND KINGDOMS WHICH CAME INTO CONTACT WITH ISRAEL.

Opening Old Testament Scripture, then, as it unquestionably stood at the period referred to, we would ask the person, on whom we seek to make some impression by the argument from prophecy, to note what is written there of the surrounding states and kingdoms, that either then stood, or had lately been standing, in an attitude of rivalry and opposition to the covenant-people. However it may have happened, the fact is palpable and notorious, that feelings of enmity existed, and proceedings of hostility had been carried on betwixt Israel and those heathen neighbours, not, however, without alternations of close intimacy and fraternal alliances, though on God's part expressly forbidden. Nor is the fact less palpable and notorious, that in the prophetic word a doom was pronounced against one and all of those surrounding states; and *that* although they respectively occupied very different positions in rank and power, and also inhabited very different territories. There were the smaller tribes of the Moabites, the Ammonites, and the Philistines; the bitterly inimical, and, even after the Babylonian era, still powerful Edomites; the enterprizing and flourishing community of Tyre, who had the maritime commerce of the world at their command, and whose ships frequented every harbour of the ancient world; Egypt with her hereditary renown, her natural and acquired resources, and still almost unsullied glory; and towering proudly above all, Babylon with her enormous walls and lofty battlements, her advantageous situation and treasures past reckoning, the seat, when the prophecies respecting her were uttered of a mighty empire, and though subject to the Medo-Persian sway at the time when the Jewish exiles returned to Judea, yet wanting little in appearance of her former magnificence, and not unlikely to assert again her independence, or become under her new masters the centre of as extensive and powerful a dominion as she had ever wielded. Such were the states and kingdoms, that surrounded the covenant-people, and against one and all of which, because of their ambitious rivalry or ungodly and spiteful opposition toward the kingdom which God had set up for the homage and blessing of the nations, prophecy uttered a doom of judgment. So far the doom was uniform —that all, as powers possessing or aspiring to dominion in the earth, should be brought down, and be made monuments of ruin. But, at the same time, there was considerable variety in the language employed; the predictions are by no means indiscriminate denunciations of coming evil; the form and extent of the evil announced varies, and with the evil there sometimes also intermingles the prospect of spiritual good. Thus, in the twenty-third chapter of Isaiah, after the most express intimation of the coming downfal of Tyre, it is added at ver. 18, that she should again recover from that first overthrow, and that "her merchandize and her hire should be holiness to the Lord;" and in chap. xix. 18–25, of the same prophet, a participation in spiritual blessings is distinctly promised in respect to Egypt and Assyria; the Lord was to smite and again to heal; Egypt and Assyria were to derive benefit from Israel; so that it might even come to be said, "Blessed be Egypt my people, and Assyria the work of my hands, and Israel mine inheritance." Yet with all this diversity, both as regards the measure of calamity in the threatened doom, and the prospect of spiritual good occasionally intermingling with the announcement of natural evil, it is declared with one voice by the ancient prophets respecting all those states and kingdoms, that their power and political existence should be utterly destroyed—they should, in that respect, become a desolation; but with a marked exception in the case of Egypt, which was merely to sink into irrecoverable meanness and degradation (Ezek. xxix. 15, etc.).

Now, looking at these prophetic utterances in this general light, and with respect to the more obvious results contemplated in them, as the import of the prophecies is plain, so the fulfilment of them is certain. There can scarcely be said to be any room for doubt either way. Nor was there any thing in the political aspect of the times, or in the natural position of affairs, which could in each case have warranted the prognostication of such striking results. It might, possibly, have been conjectured without any superhuman insight, that the lesser states, such as the Philistines, the Moabites, the Ammonites, should in process of time be extinguished by the great empires, which were then contending for the mastery of the world, or become merged into the wandering tribes of the desert. But what natural sagacity could have foreseen, that the Edomites, who continued comparatively strong and vigorous beyond the period that the prophecies respecting them were written, and who retained possession of their territory when Judea was laid waste, should yet become more desolate than their Jewish rivals, nay, should entirely cease to have a political existence, and should do so from their being swallowed up by the revived might and energy of Israel? This is the singular turn of affairs that was predicted as to the relative position of the two peoples: "Upon Mount Zion shall be deliverance, and there shall be holiness; and the house of Jacob shall possess their possessions. And the house of Jacob shall be a fire, and the house of Joseph a flame, and the house of Esau for stubble, and they shall kindle in them and devour them; and there shall not be any remaining of the house of Esau; for the Lord hath spoken it" (Ob. ver. 17, 18; Ez. xxv. 14). The meaning plainly is, that the Edomites should cease to be a separate kingdom; their name and memorial as such should perish; and as this was to come upon them specially on account of their vengeful hatred toward the children of Israel, so, to mark more distinctly the divine retribution, the Lord was to "lay his vengeance upon Edom by the hand of his people Israel;" other instruments of judgment might be employed, but this was to be the one that should actually effect the work of their national destruction. And so it was—though not till about a century and a-half before the Christian era. Instruments of desolation had begun to work at a much earlier period; for even Malachi could speak of their having been impoverished, and greatly decayed, though still existing as a separate people (chap. i. 3, 4); but in the time of the Maccabees, John Hyrcanus so completely subdued them, that he gave them the alternative of entirely abandoning their country (which then lay immediately to the south of Palestine, and even included part of ancient Judea), or submitting to the rite of circumcision, and conforming to the laws of Moses. They embraced the latter alternative, and so, as Josephus says, "They were henceforth no other than Jews."[1] Their national distinction was gone; their political existence, and their heritage had alike perished; and in such a manner as to render but the more conspicuous the nobler rank and destiny of Israel. Was there not here the manifest signature of the eye and the finger of Omniscience?

The case of Babylon is, if possible, a still more striking evidence. What merely human foresight could have descried the utter ruin and prostration of such a city? At the time the prophecies were written, she was in the noontide of her

[1] Antiq. xiii. 9. 1. Such also is the testimony of the grammarian Ammonius, as quoted by Prideaux, An. 129, "The Idumeans were not Jews from the beginning, but Phœnicians and Syrians; but being afterwards subdued by the Jews and compelled to be circumcised, and unite into one nation, and be subject to the same laws, they were called Jews." To the like effect also Dio. lib. xxxvi., "That country is also called Judea, and the people Jews; and this name is given also to as many others as embrace their religion, though of other nations."

glory; and her natural situation was such as might seem to betoken a perpetual continuance of prosperity. Even in the time of Herodotus, who visited the city and neighbourhood some generations after the prophecies were delivered, a full century after the first conquest of it by the Persians, there was everything to human appearance, that was calculated to secure for it a continued prosperity and greatness. The city was still the most populous and magnificent of the world, and might be said to have changed its masters, rather than its condition; for the Persian monarchs were wont to spend several months of the year in it. And the region in which it was situated, the province of Babylonia, was so exceedingly rich and fertile, that it supported the king of Persia, his army, and his whole establishment for four months of the year; in other words, it contributed one-third of the entire revenue of the kingdom. Yet the Spirit of prophecy, which guided the sacred penmen, perceived in the first blow that was struck by the victorious Persians, the infliction of a mortal wound; they declared it to be the commencement of a complete and total ruin. Centuries elapsed in the process, but the destined consummation travelled on. Against all present appearances, in spite of every natural advantage, and notwithstanding repeated efforts on a gigantic scale to turn back the tide of evil, the work of deterioration still proceeded. The civilization, commerce, wealth and dominion of the world took another direction, and Babylon continued to sink till nothing remained of all her glory but emptiness and desolation. Does not this again, we ask, bespeak the eye and finger of Omniscience?

The foresight displayed is scarcely less remarkable when we look to what was written of a nearer neighbour of Israel, the commercial and enterprising community of Tyre. That this wonderful state, the growth of centuries—grown till she had become sole mistress of the seas—should be destined to fall, should become a spoil to the nations, should even sink so low that her harbours would be forsaken, and she should become a place for the spreading of nets in the midst of the sea (Ezek. xxvi.)—this, especially when contrasted with the glorious things that were spoken of the little kingdom of Judah, by her side, was anything but what might on natural grounds have been expected. Her insular situation, itself a citadel of strength—her want of local territory, and comparatively small resident population, fitted, one might have thought, to exempt her from the cupidity and violence of ambitious conquerors—her peaceful and busy commerce, together with her numerous and flourishing colonies, each serving to unite her as by a bond of concord with the nations of the earth—all seemed to bespeak for her a prolonged existence, and, at least, to form a protection against the worst calamities. Yet here, also, the word of God stands fast. The thirst for conquest, first in Nebuchadnezzar, afterwards in Alexander the Great, could not brook the thought of such a state continuing independent, and holding treasures over which they had no control. The blow was once and again struck with fatal success; and, though centuries had to roll on before the judgment of Heaven ran its course, it did not fail to proceed. The commerce of the world found for itself other channels, and Tyre at length ceased, ceased for ever to hold a place among the communities of the earth.

But why should the same not have been predicted of Egypt? Why only a perpetual depression in the one case, and a total subversion in the other? Egypt was not, according to the delineations of prophecy, to become so thoroughly extinct in its national power and resources as Tyre or Babylon. It was not to be made perpetual desolations, but to be brought down from its supremacy, to lose its ancient prestige, to be humbled, and made to serve, and rendered base among the nations—which, indeed, as compared with what Egypt from of old had claimed to be, and still in a great degree was when the prophets wrote, indicated an entire revolution and change in the relative position of the earthly kingdoms. We need scarcely say that this also has happened. The land of the Pharaohs has never lost its fertility; its natural capacities, to this day, are great, though but imperfectly developed, but from the period of the Persian conquest, it has never regained its independence as a nation. Degradation and servility have been stamped upon its condition for more than twenty centuries; and, beyond all doubt, its ancient assumption of the highest place of honour, and pretentious rivalry with the kingdom of God, have irrecoverably gone.

Whichever way we look, therefore, among those ancient states and kingdoms that lay around the covenant-people, we see that the things written concerning them, in the prophecies of the Old Testament, hold good, alike in what was common to all the communities spoken of, and what was peculiar to some. And we should conceive it impossible for any one really open to conviction, carefully comparing this class of prophecies with their fulfilment, without having the impression forced on him that the prophets, in what they thus wrote, were supernaturally led by the Spirit of God. But there are persons, it is well to remember, who are not properly open to conviction, and who have preconceived notions, which tend effectually to prevent a fair and candid examination of the subject. In this position certainly are those who, on general grounds, deny the reality of all supernatural interference with the affairs of men; everything of this sort is against their "theory of providence," which makes account only of physical agencies and mechanical laws; and, therefore, prophecy, as implying a supernatural insight into the future, is concluded to be an impossibility. Persons of this philosophical creed, however, usually couple with their denial of the prophetical element, in the Scriptural sense, a kind of assertion of it in the natural. "Every department," they tell us, "of human knowledge and enterprise, has had its seers and prophets. What, in the first sense, was the Novum Organum of Bacon but a prophecy the most distinct, and which has been partially fulfilled in the present condition of science, and will, no doubt, be still further verified in its future fortunes? The deep political insight of Bonaparte enabled him to prophesy at St Helena the destruction of the old Bourbon dynasty, the succession of the Orleans branch, and the final establishment of a republic, events which have literally been accomplished before our eyes.[1] Entirely original minds are so rare in the world, occurring only here and there in the lapse of centuries, that the frivolous and unthinking portion of mankind is apt to regard all true insight into nature as a miraculous gift. Each succeeding age has beheld the fulfilment of the prophecies of Bacon, 'Man gradually establishing his reign in the interpretation of nature.'" And then we have the case of Columbus, "the Genoese sailor, whose soul was burdened with a material vision," which spurred him on by its internal promptings, till, in the face of gigantic difficulties, he fulfilled both it and the still older prophecy of Seneca; and not only Columbus, but Wickliffe also, and Luther, and Knox, were all, it turns out, seers, who, "in prophetic vision, saw the great futurity of Protestantism that was to shake the foundations of human faith throughout the civilised world."[2]

Such is Mr Foxton's view of the matter. Sagacity, shrewdness, philosophic culture, genius—these, one and all, though in different degrees, enable their possessors to rise higher and see farther than other men; and, in so far as they do so, the result is a prophecy! That is—for the explanation amounts to no more—a degree of discernment is obtained, to which the same general name is applied as that by which we designate the prophetic announcements of Scripture. For anything beyond this we deny the relevancy of the explanation. It does not touch the real points at issue, and as little accounts for the utterance of those definite and discriminating predictions regarding the countries around Judea, as it does for the creation of the world. Persons who can see no essential difference between the two cases must be held either as taking a merely superficial view of the subject, or as incapable, from their mental state, of reasoning soundly upon it. But, assuredly, they will need to produce other reasons than

[1] This was written in 1849, when there *was*, during a brief interval, a republic in France; but, alas! for its final establishment. Louis Napoleon soon dashed that chimera to the ground, and furnished a sad commentary on the deep insight displayed in his uncle's prophecy.

[2] Foxton's Popular Christianity, p. 117, sq.

those contained in the vague and general assertions of Mr Foxton, before they will be able to convince plain and unsophisticated minds that Hebrew prophets, living at such a time, and with so little to aid them of a scientific nature, could have succeeded otherwise than through supernatural guidance to give forth predictions relating to events so unlikely at the period, so far distant in time, and of so diversified a character.

Others of the same school with the writer just referred to, meet the argument drawn from such predictions by denying that they contained any definite and unambiguous announcement of coming events, or, that in so far as they did so, the predictions were as often falsified as confirmed by the event—therefore, only at best shrewd anticipations, or lucky hits. Such is the view more particularly dwelt on by Theodore Parker. The greater part of the prophecies were, according to his opinion, quite vague and indefinite. Some, however, were more precise; and of these he thinks there may have been some, though he does not condescend to specify any, which might be regarded, like some of the oracles delivered from the tripod of Delphi, "extraordinarily felicitous;" but he is quite sure there were others which proved false.[1] In the instances he alleges in proof of this statement, he shows no small degree of effrontery. The first is that of the seventy years' captivity predicted by Jeremiah, which he summarily pronounces to have failed, because the captivity was accomplished at three successive stages, and from neither of them does the period of the return make so much as seventy years. It would appear, therefore, that Theodore Parker is wiser than Daniel. He discovers a falsehood, where Daniel perceived a truth; or, as it will, perhaps, be more correct to put it, he is more hasty and superficial in his judgment, for Daniel, by careful search, found out the number of years which the prophecy required to run its course, while Mr Parker snatches at some shallow chronology—for which not so much as a single authority is given—and by the aid of it leaps to his desired conclusion.

[1] Discourse of Religion, p. 207.

It has been conclusively settled, by the most rigid examination, that the period of seventy years' desolation and captivity dates from the first deportation of the captive Jews (among whom was Daniel and his companions), about the year 608 or 609, before Christ; and the return took place about 536, making a period of full seventy years.

A second alleged failure is found, with the same easy and flippant superficiality, in Ezekiel's prophecies regarding Tyre—in one of which, chap. xxvi. 7, sq., he predicts the capture of the city by Nebuchadnezzar, while in another, chap. xxix. 17, sq., he represents Nebuchadnezzar as having served a great service against Tyre, but without getting any wages for it; on which account Egypt was to be given him for a prey. After the example of several German rationalists, Parker understands this latter prediction, as implying that Nebuchadnezzar had been obliged to raise the siege of Tyre, without being able to take the city; so that the second prophecy is held to be an undoubted evidence of the first having failed, or, rather of both being, what he calls, poetical odes, never intended to be taken literally. I have investigated this point, at some length, elsewhere;[1] and shall only state here, that the view is altogether groundless; that the second prophecy, which speaks of the want of recompense to the king of Babylon, by no means necessarily implies the defeat of his attempt to take the city, but only the comparative smallness of the treasure found in it; that there is, however, the strongest historical evidence, altogether independent of Scripture, of Tyre having, at this very time, sunk to a position of inferiority, from which she never recovered, and which can only be explained on the ground of her subjugation by Nebuchadnezzar. It is not, therefore, Ezekiel who is self-contradictory; but simply Theodore Parker, who in his anxiety and haste to find blemishes in Scripture, misinterprets Ezekiel, and misreads history.

These are the only specific cases, relating to Old Testament

[1] See Com. on Ezekiel in loco.

times, which are adduced by this reckless writer, to disparage the authority, and disprove the properly predictive character of Scriptural prophecy. They are really nothing to the purpose, and can only be characterized as arbitrary interpretations, built on false assumptions. On the other side, the argument founded on the remarkable fulfilments of prophecy, respecting the states and kingdoms around Judea, is never fairly looked at; nor is the slightest attempt made by him or Foxton, to show, how either shrewdness or sagacity, philosophy or genius, might have enabled the Hebrew prophets to see so far into the natural tendencies of things, as to be able, of themselves, to light upon such wonderful prognostications of the future. Having, therefore, no other rational explanation of the matter offered, and being able to conceive of none that appears deserving of being entertained, we must rest in the conclusion, that they were veritable prophecies, not coming by the will of Man, but spoken by those who were supernaturally enlightened and moved by the Holy Ghost. It is, however, a conclusion, which we could arrive at and rest in, only on such principles of interpretation as we previously laid down respecting the style and diction of prophecy; and if, with the extreme literalists, we were to insist on prophecy being understood and read like history, we should feel constrained to say, that the predictions we have been considering had been very imperfectly fulfilled.

Let us take Edom as an example. In some of our popular works on prophecy, which proceed on the principle of literalism, the prophecies concerning Edom are viewed as bearing respect merely to the land of Edom, as if it was the territory alone, and not rather the people who occupied it, which the prophecies respected, and then with this application given to them, they are applied in the most prosaic manner to the country, as it exists in the present day. A double error; for as the moral element in prophecy was always the main one, it is, in the first instance, the people that should be regarded as pointed at in the predictions, and the land only, in so far as its state might be a representation or emblem of the condition of the people. It seems, therefore, somewhat beside the purpose, to look to the Arabia Petræa of the present time, as of itself fulfilling what was spoken respecting Edom. For that region, it is known, had ceased to be the proper territory of the Edomites, two or three centuries before the Christian era. At the time of the Babylonish captivity, the Edomites began to move more upwards, spreading over the old country of the Moabites, and encroaching on the southern borders of the land of Judah; while, from the opposite quarter, the Nabatheans, a different race, pressed in from the south upon mount Seir, and became masters of the greater part of the old Edomite territory, including Petra, its rocky capital. The Grecian architecture which adorned Petra, sometime before, and for a considerable period after, the Christian era, and the ruins of which have been so often described, must have been the workmanship of the Nabatheans, not of the Edomites; for the latter had been supplanted by the Nabatheans, before the Grecian influence and taste had diffused itself in the East. Its subsequent desolations had, therefore, no direct relation to the Edom of Scripture; and if these desolations, which reach to the present day, are at all taken into account, it should only be as affording a collateral proof of the judgment that was to befal the children of Esau, and of their having signally failed to establish their ascendancy in the earth. But it is the desolations of an earlier period, and, above all, the utter extinction of Edom as a people, and *that* by the hand of Jacob, in which, as before remarked, the more direct and proper fulfiment of the predictions is to be sought. This, however, is but one error, and it is another, certainly not inferior, to seek in the present state of Arabia Petræa, for an exact and literal correspondence with the fervid, and in many respects figurative representations of prophecy respecting the doom of Edom. Such passages as those of Isa. xxxiv. 10, where it is said, "From generation to generation it shall lie waste, none shall pass through it for ever and ever," and of Ezek. xxxv. 7, "I will make Mount Seir most desolate, and cut off from it, him that passeth out, and him that returneth"—

such passages as these are quoted, and after appeals to the note of Volney, "This country has not been visited by any traveller," and the difficulties experienced by Burckhardt, by Irby and Mangles, and other travellers, in getting access to the region, the conclusion is drawn as certain, that "the prophecy must be literally understood and applied." Sometimes even the rage for literalism is carried to the ridiculous extent of palpably violating the very rule it seeks to establish; as when, in proof of minute prophetical fulfilment, the cases of Seetzen and Burckhardt are exhibited, as of men who "passed through the land," indeed, but did not live "to return." Strange verifications, surely, of a prediction, which foretold the cutting off of him that returned! Is the cutting off, which prevents men from returning, the literal accomplishment of a word, which speaks of cutting off such as *did* return? It were certainly a new species of literalism. And here lies the folly of dealing thus with such prophecies—they fail in our hands. Persons have, of late years, often passed and repassed through the Idumean territory, and scarcely a year elapses without its being visited by travellers, and fresh accounts coming forth of what they witnessed. Even particular localities, such as the ascent of Mount Hor, which the cupidity of the Arabs rendered difficult or impracticable to earlier travellers, are now found perfectly accessible. Mr Stanley and his party in 1852–53, appear to have met with no serious impediment in their course;[1] and the facilities are constantly on the increase. But in truth, there has never been a total cessation of persons going and returning; for the region has always been, to some extent, inhabited, and if not by European travellers, yet by Arab wanderers, it has, in every age, had its passing sojourners. The expression of the prophet Ezekiel was never meant to exclude this; it is merely a proverbial phrase for general desolation, and as such is used by another prophet, of the territory of the Israelites themselves (Isa. lx. 15). It intimated, that instead of being a powerful, flourishing, and prosperous

[1] See his interesting work, "Sinai and Palestine," p. 88-92.

community, with persons on all sides flocking to it, and returning from it, Edom was to be stricken with poverty and ruin: Edom, however, not simply, nor chiefly as a land, but as a people. This was what the prophecy foretold, and it has been amply verified—verified not the less that the "wadys are full of trees, and shrubs, and flowers, and the eastern and higher parts are extensively cultivated, and yield good crops."[1] Still, the Edom of prophecy—the Edom which was the enemy of God, and the rival of Israel—has perished for ever; all, in that respect, is an untrodden wilderness, a hopeless ruin; and *there*, the veracity of God's word finds its justification.

It is scarcely possible, one would imagine, for any person to read, with an unbiassed mind, the prophecies we have been more particularly considering, without perceiving that the poetical element enters largely into their composition, and that Edom often appears in them as the representative and head of a class. In the latter stages of the history of Israel, the Edomites surpassed all their enemies in keenness and intensity of malice; and hence they naturally came to be viewed by the spirit of prophecy as the personification of that godless malignity and pride, which would be satisfied with nothing short of the utter extermination of the cause of God—the heads and representatives of the whole army of the aliens, whose doom was to carry along with it the downfal and destruction of everything that opposed and exalted itself against the knowledge of God. This is manifestly the aspect presented of the matter in verse 15 of the prophecy of Obadiah; the fate of all the heathen is bound up with that of Edom; "For the day of the Lord is near upon all the heathen; as thou (viz., Edom) hast done, it shall be done unto thee, thy reward shall return upon thine own head"—that is, in Edom, the quintessence of heathenism, all heathendom was to receive, as it were, its death-blow. And at still greater length, and amid images of terrific grandeur, the same view is unfolded by Isaiah, in chapter xxxiv.; where all

[1] Robinson's Biblical Researches, *vol. ii.*, p. 552.

the nations of the earth are summoned together, because, it is said, "the Lord's indignation was upon them all;" while still, the fury to be poured out, was to discharge its violence, and in a manner rest, upon the land of Idumea. It is clear that the passage is throughout an ideal representation—clear from the very conjunction of all the heathen with Edom, and also from the peculiar boldness of the images employed—such as the dissolving of the host of heaven, the sword of the Lord bathing itself in heaven, the mountains melting with blood, the turning of the streams into pitch, and the dust into brimstone—which, like the ascription of corporeal organs and human passions to God, seem purposely intended to guard us against understanding the words in the grossly literal sense.[1] The ideal character of the representation still farther appears from the relation which Edom is represented as holding toward Israel, and which was such that the execution of judgment upon the one, was to be the era of deliverance, joy and blessing to the other—the era when the controversy of Zion should be settled, and everlasting prosperity be ushered in. So that the personification here employed respecting Edom is entirely of a piece with that which identifies Jacob or Abraham with the whole family of God, and connects the names of those patriarchs even with the final issues of the

[1] It is strange that the literalists do not perceive this; and that, while chiefly pressing the apologetic side of prophecy, they should not see how, by singling out some points as having been literally fulfilled, while others are left of which this cannot be alleged, they are surrendering the cause into the enemy's hands. It is but scraps of fulfilment which can thus be furnished out from the present state of Idumea; and an unbeliever may justly ask, when presented with them, where are the rest? There are ruined cities, it is true, and thorns and brambles, and wild creatures of the desert, where palaces once stood; but where is the carnage of all nations that was to precede these? where the burning pitch and brimstone? where the mountains melting with blood? and where, above all, the people themselves, who formed the very heart and centre of Isaiah's prophecy? We cannot speak of God's word being verified by halves; and of prophecies so interpreted, the adversary might justly say, they are made up of fortunate guesses alternating with palpable failures.

divine kingdom. (Gen. xxii. 18; Matt. viii. 11; Luke xvi. 22, etc.).

When stript of the mere form and drapery, in which it is clothed, the prophecy contained in the thirty-fourth and thirty-fifth chapters of Isaiah (for the two evidently form but one piece), is fraught with the following message: The enmity and opposition toward the Lord's cause and people, which the heathen nations in general, and Edom in particular, had evinced, shall be defeated of its end; not the nation that knows and keeps the truth, but the nations that reject and hate it, shall come to desolation; and as Edom might be fitly taken to represent the one, and Israel the other (precisely as of old in their progenitors, Esau and Jacob, the carnal and the spiritual seed had their representation), so the destroying judgment of heaven, on the one hand, is seen concentrating itself in Edom, while, on the other, its favour and blessing alight upon Zion, and thence diffuse all around the greatest joy and satisfaction. The prophecy, indeed, is a sort of recapitulation, and sums up in one glowing delineation, what had already been presented in several successive chapters. The prophet had gone over, one by one, all the tribes and kingdoms that had acted in a spirit of proud and envious rivalry toward the children of God's covenant, and in respect to each had declared, that their pride should be humbled, their glory tarnished, the very foundations of their dominion shaken and destroyed, while peace and prosperity should be the portion of Zion. And now gathering the whole into a common focus—bringing the contest to a single point, with the view of giving a more vivid and impressive exhibition of the issues that were pending, he represents the vials of divine wrath, as emptying themselves in a mighty torrent of desolation upon Edom, and securing as its happy result to the seed of blessing, a perpetual freedom from those who afflicted them, so that they should possess undisturbed their heritage of good, and be for ever replenished with favour from on high.

Such appears to be the natural import and bearing of this

prophecy; and that Edom is to be understood in this representative manner, and with reference more especially to the hostile attitude it had assumed toward Israel, seems further plain from other prophecies, which speak of a purpose of mercy in reserve for Edom, and for all the heathen, when the old relation should have been exchanged for another and better one. The prophet Amos (chap. ix. 11, 12), giving promise of a time when David's tabernacle should be raised up again, and its glory revived, mentions as the result, "that they (viz., those who belong in the proper sense to the house and kingdom of David), may possess the remainder of Edom, and of all the heathen over whom my name is called, saith the Lord of Hosts that doeth this." This clearly implies, that the Edom of prophecy, which was doomed to utter prostration and eternal ruin, is only the Edom of bitter and unrelenting hostility to the cause and people of God; that in so far as the children of Edom ceased from this, and entered into a friendly relation to the covenant of God, and submitted to the yoke of universal sovereignty committed to the house of David, instead of breaking it, as of old, from their necks, they should participate in the blessing, and have their interests merged in those of the people on whom God puts His name to do them good. A promise and prospect like this never can be made to harmonise with the result that is obtained from the predicted judgments upon Edom, as read by the strictly literal style of interpretation; for according to it, there should be no remnant to be possessed, no seed or place of blessing, as connected with Edom, but one appalling scene of sterility, desolation, and cursing. The demands of a prophetic harmony, as well as a due regard to the nature of the prophetic style, require that the revelations of judgment should be understood in the manner we have explained them.

SECTION II.

PROPHECIES RESPECTING THE JEWISH PEOPLE.

FROM the prophecies which respected the nations that surrounded Israel, we naturally pass to those which respected Israel itself. What prospects did the prophetic volume, as it certainly existed about the period of the return from Babylon, or shortly after, hold out in regard to the covenant-people? They were then undoubtedly in a very depressed and perilous condition; and, if judged merely by outward appearances and according to human calculations, they were not more likely to have a prolonged existence than the small states around them—immeasurably less likely to occupy a prominent place in the future history of the world, than Tyre or Egypt, Babylon or Persia. But the word of prophecy did not frame its anticipations by the outward aspect of things; and never did it speak in bolder terms and a more assured tone, of the future greatness and glory of the covenant-people, than when their political position had reached its lowest ebb. While it declared, that the Philistines were to cease from being a people—that the Moabites, the Ammonites, the Edomites, the wealth and power of Tyre, of Egypt, of Babylon, of the whole heathen world, were to pass away, it spoke in other language respecting the seed of Israel and the house of David—*they* were to rise and take root and flourish, when their rivals and oppressors had perished—were even to give laws to the world, and make the whole earth blessed in their blessing. There is scarcely one of the later prophets, by whom this high destiny of Israel is not disclosed, and in the larger prophetical books it occupies a most prominent place. Yet, when we look attentively into them, we find it is no indiscriminate assertion of future eminence and glory, not a resolute vindication of the highest rank for the Israelitish people at large, such as the fond yearnings of patriotism or the promptings of ambition might have put forth; but a variable and chequered prospect, in which the evil was strangely to intermingle with the good, and the greatest indignities and sufferings were somehow to be combined with the highest glory. In the latter half of Isaiah's prophecies these two themes constantly alternate with each other, in what is said of Israel's future. In an earlier prophecy also—the brief, but pregnant and comprehensive revelation of chap. vi.—it was distinctly foretold, that, on account of the prevailing hardness and corruption of the people's hearts, "men should be removed far away, and there should be a great forsaking in the midst of the land;" that even though there should be a remnant, a tenth, that should return, yet this also should be for consumption (or, being eaten); and for the same reason as of old, because sin should again obtain a footing in them; for it is added, that amid all troubles and consumptions, the holy seed should be the substance in them, a still existing conservative element. In like manner, in Daniel's prophecy regarding the coming of Messiah, toward the close of the seventy weeks, while the greatest results were then to be accomplished—"making reconciliation for iniquity, bringing in everlasting righteousness, sealing up the vision of prophecy, and anointing a holy of holies"—it is still said, that "desolations were appointed," insomuch that even "the city and the sanctuary were to be destroyed." So, again in Zechariah, chap. xiii. 8, 9, in immediate connection with the smiting of the shepherd of the sheep, there is predicted the cutting off of two-thirds of the people, and even the remaining third was to be "brought through the fire, and refined as silver is refined." In Malachi, the last of all the prophets, the aspect that is presented of Israel's future is in many respects dark and lowering; images of terror and alarm appear in it; it speaks of a day that should burn as an oven, consuming the wicked as stubble, of the Lord's presence being like a refiner's fire and a fuller's soap, of the land being possibly smitten with a curse;—while yet the salvation of the Lord was sure to come, and should bring with it power to tread down the wicked, and a heritage of blessing, which would excite the wonder of all nations.

Now, we have surely some right to demand of one, who, if disposed to doubt, is not determined to reject all proof of supernatural insight and direction, whether we have not in these diversified predictions the indication of a knowledge essentially divine? Here, again, it is not some loose and random utterances we have to deal with, such as either the forebodings of a gloomy imagination, or the excitement of a fervid and hopeful enthusiasm might call forth. There is not only foresight, but foresight of a most impartial and discriminating kind, capable alike of descrying the darker and the brighter aspects of the future, dwelling even with painful emphasis upon the coming evil and reiterating it; yet without ever losing sight of the coming good; and even when the clouds of present trouble gathered thickest, only proceeding with a clearer eye and a more assured step to reveal the glorious and blessed future that lay beyond. Most remarkably have both parts of the prospective outline been fulfilled. The subsequent history presents many a dark and troubled page to substantiate the vision of coming evil—corruptions within and calamities without, defections the most heinous, and chastisements the most severe; yet in the midst of all, and in spite of all, there came out a greatness and energy, an effulgence of light and life and glory, which strikingly contrasts with the comparative smallness of Israel's position, and the external meanness of their circumstances. The mightiest and most imposing of the surrounding kingdoms came to nought; but Israel still existed, and we may say, in the language of another (Dr Arnold), "Still exists unchanged. Still God's people in every land carry back their sympathies unbroken to the age of the first father of the faithful; the patriarchs and prophets are the spiritual ancestors of the apostles and ourselves; their prayers are ours, their cause was ours; for their God was ours [and the Messiah born of them is our light and salvation]. And if Israel after the flesh were to return to the Lord, what has she lost of her old identity? Place does not make a nation, but the sameness of sympathies. And in this respect there is nothing of Israel in the earliest times which would be dead to

Israel now. This can be said of no other nation upon earth; and thus has Israel endured, because she was, though imperfectly, the representative of the cause of that God, who alone endureth for ever."

It is enough here to look thus to the main features of the prophetic outline—those more prominent aspects of it, which cannot fail to impress themselves on any careful and unprejudiced reader of Old Testament prophecy, in connection with the past of Israelitish history. Its bearing upon the still remaining future is another point, and one that will call for separate and particular investigation. In the meantime, and as regards the plain import of a whole series of prophecies concerning Israel, it seems undeniable that most striking fulfilments have taken place of what no merely human eye could have foreseen, nor the shrewdest intellect anticipated.

SECTION III.

PROPHECIES RESPECTING THE MESSIAH.

THE portions of the prophetic testimony we have already considered, argue nothing directly for the truth of Christianity. They afford, we think, conclusive proof of the supernatural foresight of the persons who indited them; and so may be regarded as placing the seal of divine attestation on the writings of the Old Testament prophets. Unbelieving Jews, however, hold this in common with ourselves; while they reject Christ and the Scriptures of the New Testament, they appeal to the confirmation, which their own history and that of other nations mentioned in ancient prophecy yields of the divine direction, under which their prophets wrote. But the apologetic value of prophecy would be small, if it stopt there. By much the most important question now is, how it tells on the claims of Jesus of Nazareth to be the Messiah? For here we have to do with the main trunk of the prophetic tree, not simply with a few occasional branches. And accordingly it is here that the Scriptures of the New Testament lay the great stress of the argument from prophecy; "the spirit of prophecy," they declare, "is the testimony of Jesus;" and both Jesus Himself and His apostles made constant reference to the things written in the prophets, as what must be fulfilled in His person and work. Here, therefore, especially it is necessary to compare together prophecy and history.

We again conceive ourselves in the presence of one who doubts—doubts, perhaps, whether there were anything more in the prophecies of the Old Testament than certain indefinite longings after some distinguished guide and leader, or a series of guides and leaders, who might carry the nation to a high degree of glory; and whether anything written and verified in this respect was so peculiar as to exceed the limits of men's unaided powers. How should we proceed to deal with such a person? The difficulty is not where to find materials of proof, but which to select as best fitted to produce conviction on a mind that is likely to be affected only by the more palpable and obvious lines of resemblance. In such a case nothing more than fragments of the truth can be presented, as it will naturally appear to those who are conversant with the entire field. Yet even a fragmentary exhibition of the truth ought here to be sufficient, if rightly presented, to carry conviction to a mind that is not absolutely foreclosed against it. There is, in the first instance, the gradual contracting of the purpose of Heaven from a more general to a more specific object of hope and expectation, till it evidently centres in a person of singular gifts and endowments,—beginning with the woman's seed generally, though, as the nature of the case implied, and the course of Providence soon clearly determined, that seed only in the spiritual line; then confining itself to the seed of Abraham, still, of course in a spiritual line; then to the tribe of Judah, where it first distinctly assumes the personal form in the promise of a future Shiloh, or prince of peace; next, to the house of David, a family within the tribe of Judah, which is appointed to the high destiny of carrying out the provisions of the Abrahamic covenant, of bearing sway in the affairs of men, and diffusing among them the blessings of salvation; then, finally, to a son of that house, a definite child of promise, to be born of a virgin, and somehow mysteriously connected with the Godhead, so that divine names are freely applied to Him, and a divine work—the work of making reconciliation for iniquity, and, in the proper sense, redeeming a people whom He was to rule and bless, is associated with His appearance and mission.

Finding, thus, the proper personality and special destination of the Messiah distinctly marked in the prophecies of the Old Testament, we would, thereafter, point to the local circumstances and individual characteristics plainly ascribed to Him; the clear designation, for example, of the place of His birth, in Bethlehem-Ephratah, historically verified in a manner that effectually prevented the possibility of collusion; the mingled lowliness and majesty of His appearance, as of a rod from the stem of Jesse, and a branch, or tender suckling, from his roots; or, as one marred in his visage, and without either form or comeliness, yet, withal, a King, clothed with power and authority to subdue every form of evil, and bear the government on His shoulder, coming, like other kings, with a herald or forerunner, yet not coming in lordly state, but as one meek and lowly, riding on an ass; on the one side, having experience of the sorest trials and indignities, a man of sorrows and acquainted with grief; on the other, possessing every element of greatness, the elect of God, and the hope of the world; nay, more marvellous still, a priest as well as a king, and a priest that was himself to become an offering for sin, and give His life a ransom for many, while yet He should prolong His days, and out of the travail of His soul should have given to Him a seed and kingdom, in every respect worthy of His incomparable merits and successful mediation. What a singular combination of qualities and results! And yet how completely authenticated by the history! The heights and depths—the apparent anomalies and seeming incompatibilities, such as no human imagination of itself could have conceived, yet all most wonderfully meeting in the history of Jesus of Nazareth! If such a series of characteristics, traced out hundreds of years before the person appeared in whom they were to be exemplified, could have at once originated in human conjecture, and received, as they have done, the seal of Divine providence, then it may justly be affirmed, there are no certain landmarks between the human and the divine; the possible achievements of man have nothing essentially to distinguish them from the powers and operations of Godhead.

We might even carry the argument farther. As our Lord himself spake of things written concerning Him in Moses, as well as the prophets, that required to be fulfilled, so we might rise from the individual prophecies contained in the later writings of the Old Testament to the one great prophecy embodied in the law. We might say, to use the language of another, "Though you were to evacuate the Old Testament of every express miracle it records, though you were to convert the prophets into jugglers and the people into fools, and make our Elijahs and Isaiahs pretenders to power and conjecturers in knowledge, could you even so clear the Old Testament of wonders? You may deny the story of miracles, but can you deny the miracle of the story? Can you resolve the enormous difficulty of this history, these recorded habits, and, above all, this recorded religion? You deny, or, in confessing, you neutralise any typical import, any prospective atonement. Mark, then, the mysteries that emerge on your supposition. The whole spiritual system of the Hebrew Scriptures is made up of two elements, entwined with the most intricate closeness, yet absolutely opposite in character. You are, then, to answer how it was that every particular of a long and laborious system of minute, and often very repulsive, sacrificial observances is found united in the same volume with conceptions of God, that surpass, in their profound and internal spirituality, all that unassisted man has ever elsewhere imagined, nay, that all our modern refinement is unable to emulate. What miraculous mind was it that combined these singular contradictions? Where is there a *real* parallel to this mysterious inconsistency? Who is this strange Instructor, or series of instructors, that now portrays the form of the one everlasting essence, hid in the veil of attributes that are themselves unfathomable, and now issues the most minute and elaborate directions as to the proper mode and the tremendous obligation of slaughtering a yearling lamb; and this as the duty of him who would approach the eternal Spirit? Who is He that, at one moment, enounces the simplest, sublimest code of human duties in existence; at another, nay, in the same page, the same sentence, exhorts, with equal earnestness, to the equal necessity of drenching the earth with animal blood as the appointed path of human purification? Here, then, in the very texture of the Old Testament, and its polity, is a mystery greater than any you can escape by denying its predictive import. It is altogether impossible on any supposition but the one, the supposition which alone can elevate ceremonies to the dignity of moral obligations. Judaism, with a typical atonement, may be a miracle, or a chain of miracles; but Judaism without it is a greater miracle still."[1]

This train of thought, though more immediately directed to the establishment of the Divine character of the Mosaic writings, is equally applicable as an argument for the truth of Christ's pretensions. For a typical atonement—in other words, the concealed prophecy which was embodied in the sacrificial system of the Old Testament, this being what alone accounts for the system as it actually existed, the antitypical atonement of the gospel, or the accomplishment in Christ of a real propitiation for the sins of the world, and this as the grand end and object of His work on earth—shows a correspondence between the work of Christ as historically narrated in the gospels, and as pre-supposed and foreshadowed in the handwriting of Moses, which in both respects bespeaks the operation of a Divine hand. It does so all the more that

[1] Dr Archer Butler's Sermons, p. 192.

the correspondence is one which does not lie upon the surface, and which neither the friends nor the enemies of Jesus could be brought to understand, till the work itself was accomplished. But here, again, perhaps, it may be replied, that the argument derived from the fulfilment of prophecy, whether in its more concealed, or in its more direct and specific form, might have been sufficient to carry conviction, if there had been nothing to countervail it on the other side—if, in the same prophetical writings, there had not been other predictions which appear to have failed in their accomplishment. The predominating aspect under which prophecy spake of the expected Messiah was that of a King coming for the purpose of occupying the throne of David. But where were the signs of His royal state and dignity? Is it not a fact, to which the gospel-history itself bears ample witness, that His own disciples were disappointed in this respect; and up to the very eve of His departure—till, in short, they could not better themselves—clung to the hope that their Master should still set up an earthly kingdom? Is it not also a fact that many students of prophecy, in the present day, comparing what was predicted with what has been done, firmly maintain that Jesus has not yet got possession of the throne promised to Him, and cannot do so till He comes in glory to erect Jerusalem into the seat of His kingdom? There is no denying this latter allegation; and it cannot be too much regretted that the adversaries here have their quiver filled for them by the hands of friends. Could we bring the adversaries to the position of friends—could they be persuaded, on other grounds, to regard Jesus as the promised Messiah—it might matter comparatively little, whether they should consider the kingly rule and government now exercised by Christ as that designated of old by the name of David's throne and kingdom, or a provisional dominion in process of time to merge into the other. But it is another thing when the alleged want of the kingdom lies across the threshold, a stumbling-block to the acknowledgment of Jesus as the true Messiah, and it is urged as a reason for denying that prophecy met its proper fulfilment in Him. He was to come, it is said, as a King. As David's son and heir he was to be born in Bethlehem; to occupy David's throne, he was to be conceived of the virgin; and, in constantly allowing Himself to be addressed as the son of David, He plainly countenanced the idea that He was to have His throne in Zion. Did not the result, then, prove both Him and them to have been mistaken? Did it not evince that the ancient predictions, in one grand particular, failed of their proper end?

We unhesitatingly answer, No—though we should be at a loss to perceive, how such an answer could be given, on the strictly literal principle of interpretation—the principle, which holds that prophecy is nothing but history written beforehand; for if so, it must have adopted the style of history, and described every thing according to the naked appearance and reality. But the case becomes entirely different, if here, as elsewhere, the Spirit of prophecy gave intimation of what was to come, in language appropriate to an ecstatical condition, and, in doing so, served itself of known and existing forms to unfold corresponding, but nobler and better things to come. In that case, the representation *must* have been, to a large extent, figurative and symbolical—a representation of it after its nature, rather than the precise form it should assume. No more should it have been expected, that the Messiah was to be a king on the earthly model of David, than that he should be a prophet on the same level with Moses, or a priest after the imperfect type of those who presented their fleshly offerings on a brazen altar. No more, to prove Him the occupant of David's throne, was it necessary for Him to possess the outward forms and trappings of Jewish royalty, than to prove His people's personal union to Him, must they have the actual participation of His flesh and blood. Standing as to the constitution of His person, immeasurably above those ancient prototypes, he was, of necessity, higher also in the character of His work and kingdom; so that, when exhibited and promised under the form of the old, a relative agreement only, not an exact likeness is to be understood. That He was destined to occupy the throne and kingdom of David, meant simply, that He was, like David, to hold the place of a king over God's heritage, and to do, to the full, what David could do only in the most partial and imperfect manner—bring deliverance, safety, and blessing to the people of God. With the divine properties of the king, however, and the world-wide domain of His kingdom, all of necessity rose to a higher place; Immanuel's reign must be another thing than that of the son of Jesse—it must be spiritual, heavenly, eternal. A kingdom of an inferior description, if possessing more of a *formal* resemblance to David's, would have had less of *real* conformity to the word of promise; it could not have verified the prophecies; for it should have bespoken the absence of that Divine element, which lay at the foundation of all that Messiah was peculiarly to be and to do.

Thus, the objection against the fulfilment of prophecy in Christ, derived from his not having assumed the outward appearance of a Jewish monarch, falls to the ground. It proceeds on a merely superficial view of the connection between the old and the new in God's dispensations, and a consequent misapprehension of the import of the prophetic language, as growing out of, and founded upon, that connection. Follow it consistently out, and no landing-place can be found, short of the Christianized Judaism of popery. But take into account the whole circumstances of the case—make due allowance for the shadowy and imperfect state of things, under which the prophets lived and wrote—above all, give free scope to the higher elements, that, according to prophecy itself, were to develope themselves in Messiah's person and kingdom, and nothing will be found wanting of that real and substantial agreement, which we expect to subsist between the anticipations of prophecy and the facts of history. The more inward some of the lines of agreement are, they only serve to indicate a deeper and diviner harmony. Jesus of Nazareth needed no outward enthronement or local seat of government on earth, to constitute Him the possessor of David's kingdom, as He needed no physical anointing to consecrate Him priest for evermore, or material altar and temple for the due presentation of his acceptable service. Being the Son of the living God, and as Son, the heir of all things, He possessed, from the first, the powers of the kingdom; and *proved* that He possessed them, in every authoritative word He uttered, every work of deliverance He performed, every judgment He pronounced, every act of mercy and forgiveness He dispensed, and the resistless control He wielded over the elements of nature, and the realms of the dead. *These* were the signs of royalty He bore about with Him upon earth; and wonderful though they were—eclipsing, in real grandeur, all the glory of David and Solomon—they were still but the first heralds of His proper dignity, which David from afar descried when he saw Him, as his Lord, seated in peerless elevation at the Father's right hand, and on which He formally entered when He ascended up on high with the word, "All power is given unto me in heaven and on earth; and lo! I am with you alway even to the end of the world."

SECTION IV.

THE PROPHECIES RESPECTING THE DESTRUCTION OF JERUSALEM.

We have hitherto confined our attention to the prophecies of the Old Testament, and to that portion of these, which had scarcely, or not at all, entered on their fulfilment at the close of the Babylonish captivity; because it is in regard to such, that the conditions formerly specified as necessary to be borne in mind for handling successfully the argument from prophecy, most distinctly and obviously hold. It is only from the difficulty of rendering manifest, to a distrustful and doubting mind, the existence of those conditions in the case of some other prophecies, of some, especially in the writings of Daniel, where the particulars are most full, and the fulfilment in various parts the most striking, that we omit them in a consideration of the apologetic use of prophecy. Their use will be found rather in directing the views, and establishing the faith of those, who already believe in the Divine authority and inspiration of Scripture, than in overcoming the scruples of such as may still be lingering in the regions of unbelief. And from the close connection in form, partly also in substance, between the prophecies of Daniel, and the Revelation of St John, it is scarcely possible to enter on a particular examination of the one, without going first into a pretty full consideration of the other.

There is no reason, however, why the argument from prophecy should be altogether conducted with a reference to the predictions of the Old Testament. The Scriptures of the New Testament, in perfect accordance with the dispensation to which they belong, deal much less in specific announcements respecting the future, than those of the Old. But they are not absolutely devoid of such. There is one, in particular, which has also a point of contact with some of the Old Testament prophecies, and is but a detailed exhibition of what they more generally indicate—namely, our Lord's prediction regarding the destruction of Jerusalem. The prophecies of Isaiah (chap. vi.), and Daniel (chap. ix.), already referred to, gave no doubtful indication of troubles and desolations, which the spirit of apostacy was yet to bring upon Judah and Jerusalem, even after the people had regained a considerable degree of power and prosperity, nay, after the Messiah himself had come. Various prophecies also in Zechariah, especially those in chap. v., xii., xiii., evidently pointed in the same direction; in them the promise of Messiah and the prospect of good that was to be the characteristic of His times, was coupled with the mention of fearful calamities and floods of tribulation on account of sin. But it was our Lord, who first clearly announced the coming retribution, and described it as one, that was to bring along with it the most sweeping desolation, and as so near at hand, that the existing generation was to see it accomplished. The predictions of Christ, to this effect, were, no doubt, uttered not very long before the event, and it has sometimes been surmised, that the publication of the gospels, which contain the prophecy, may have been subsequent to the occurrence of the event. But the surmise is so destitute of all probability, that no candid and serious adversary can think of urging it. The very form of the prediction, in its most specific announcement, is against the supposition; since it is so much occupied with directions and warnings to the disciples how to conduct themselves in anticipation of the event; while the testimony of antiquity is quite uniform as to the priority of the prophecy. Uttered, then, at the time it purports to have been, that is, not less than forty years before the calamities it depicts—at a time when, in the political horizon, there was no appearance of any impending storm, and on simply natural grounds, there was no reason to apprehend extreme measures of any kind, it can be ascribed to nothing but Divine foresight on the part of Christ, that He should have so clearly descried, not only the approaching danger, but the overwhelming nature of the catastrophe, in which it was to terminate:—first, a strait siege of the city, then its surrender into the hands of the enemy, followed by its merciless destruction—its very temple laid in ruins, and its people scattered abroad, trodden down by the Gentiles; while, on the other hand, the gospel of His salvation, which they had despised and rejected, should spread far and wide, and everywhere take root in the earth. To foresee such results—results in many respects opposed to the intentions, and the general policy of the Romans, who were the chief instruments in effecting it—and with such a tone of assurance announce them so long beforehand, was not to speak in the manner of men; and no one, who looks calmly into the circumstances, can ever find an explanation that will be satisfactory to his own mind, by the help merely of some unusual degree of shrewdness on the part of Jesus, or of a certain peculiar combination of circumstances in Providence.

We refrain from entering farther into the details of the subject, which would carry us beside our present purpose. In another connection, the circumstances of Jerusalem's destruction will come again to be noticed in a subsequent chapter. And though the argument from New Testament prophecy admits of being strengthened by the consideration of what is written of Antichrist, and the great apostacy, yet we refrain also from taking up this topic in the present connection. The diversities of opinion now current even among Protestant and Evangelical divines on the precise import of the predictions bearing on that subject, have in great measure destroyed its apologetic value, and require for it in a work like the present, a separate treatment. Meanwhile, we trust, there is enough in the line of argument indicated, to show, that a most important and conclusive branch of evidence is yielded by prophecy in support of the great facts and doctrines of the Bible. We must say, however, in conclusion, that for a just appreciation of this evidence, and the capacity either of using or profiting by it aright, the careful study of the prophetic Scriptures, on sound principles of interpretation, is indispensable. Here also it is the patient and continued search, to which the choicest treasures are revealed. Could we only persuade those who have placed themselves in an antagonistic position, and contemplate the subject from a distance, to take up in a spirit of candid and earnest inquiry, so much as one or two portions of the prophetical Scriptures, and view them accurately on every side, we would expect more from the exercise, than from all argumentations of a more general kind; for though the circle embraced might be of limited extent, yet the deeper and more delicate lines of agreement it contains with the realities of the gospel, would be perceived, as well as those which are of a more palpable description. And in regard to those who would pursue the study, not for conviction, but for farther enlightenment in the knowledge, and a firmer establishment in the faith of the gospel, resort should be had, less to works devoted to an exposition of the argument from prophecy, than to the word of prophecy itself, and its exact interpretation. They should make themselves conversant more with exegetical, than with apologetical sources. And in proportion as their acquaintance with the divine word becomes more discriminating and comprehensive, they will also become more thoroughly satisfied respecting the coherence of its several parts, and be more sensible of the numberless points of coincidence, that exist between its predictions of things to come, and the subsequent events and issues of Providence.

CHAPTER II.

THE PROPHETICAL FUTURE OF THE JEWISH PEOPLE.

THE predictions noticed in the preceding chapter respecting the natural seed of Israel had respect only to the past fortunes of the people, and their existing condition. So far, there is a general agreement, both among Jews themselves, and among Christian interpreters, as to the import and fulfilment of the prophecies. But the matter assumes another aspect, when we turn from the past or present to the future. Here the greatest diversity prevails--not between Jews and Christians merely, but between one class of Christian interpreters and another. The Jews hold, and on *their* principles, indeed, consistently hold, that according to the prophecies of Old Testament Scripture, they shall, as a people, be gathered from their dispersions by the Messiah, and restored to their ancient territory—that there the temple shall again be built, and its worship set up anew, after the handwriting of Moses—and that, as thus established and presided over, they shall stand politically at the head of all the nations of the earth. Such, generally, is the Jewish expectation; and there are not wanting, especially in the present day, evangelical Christians, who entirely concur with the Jews in their interpretation of the prophecies, and confidently anticipate, not only a restoration of the Jewish people to the land of Palestine, but also a re-institution of the rites and services of the law, to be performed in a Christian spirit, and frequented by Christian worshippers from every region of the earth. A much larger portion, however, concur only in so far as the national restoration to Palestine is concerned, along with a certain pre-eminence in honour and Christian influence beyond what shall be possessed by any other people in Christendom. And another portion of Christian interpreters—also a very large one—deeming it impossible to divide, in the work of interpretation, between the national restoration of the Jewish people, and the re-establishment of their ancient polity and worship, reject the one as well as the other, and hold, that the proper meaning of the prophecies, in so far as they bear on the future of Israel, is to be made good simply by the conversion of the people to the Christian faith, and their participation in the privileges and hopes of the church of Christ.

Such, omitting all minor shades of difference, is the threefold view that prevails upon the subject, and which may be designated from the modes of interpretation on which they are respectively based, as the Jewish, the semi-Jewish, and the spiritualistic. In the Jewish, we, of course, include the first class of opinions maintained by Christian writers, not as intending thereby to disparage the Christianity of those who hold it, but because the view itself coincides in all its ostensible features with the distinctively Jewish one, and proceeds entirely upon the Jewish principle of prophetical interpretation. That principle is the strictly literal sense of prophecy, the principle which insists on reading prophecy simply as history written beforehand; and whatever has been urged in previous portions of this work against that style of interpretation, is applicable in its full force to this particular branch of the subject.[1] The principle of literalism is not espoused in this extreme form by those who hold what we have called the semi-Jewish opinion; they are prepared to apply to Christ and the church of the New Testament every prophecy that is so applied by the sacred writers, or may admit, on similar grounds, of such an application. They think, that in the language of prophecy, what is said of Zion and Jerusalem, or of David's throne and kingdom, has to a large extent already received its fulfilment in Christ, or is in the course of doing

[1] See particularly in Part I., Chap. v., Sec. i. and iii.

so; and that every prediction couched in the terms of the Old Testament shadows, must be regarded, in accordance with the spirit of the New Testament dispensation, as capable of receiving fulfilment only in a non-literal, or spiritual sense. But, at the same time, they are of opinion that many prophecies respecting the Jewish people neither require nor admit of any such modified application—prophecies which speak in so distinct, specific, and circumstantial a manner of the gathering of that people out of all their dispersions, and settling them again in their former haunts, with even more than their former glory, that it seems difficult, if not impossible to understand them otherwise than in the most obvious and natural import of the language. There are collateral considerations which appear in their judgment to strengthen the position which they occupy; but this aspect of the prophecies forms the proper basis of the view they entertain. So far, therefore, it also rests on the principle of literalism, though restrained within comparatively narrow limits, confined chiefly to what respects the land and people of the Jews. And the main point to be determined respecting it is, whether in the prophecies themselves, or in the mode of applying them in New Testament Scripture, there is ground for maintaining such a distinction as it draws between this particular subject and the others, with which it stands, in the prophetic volume, so intimately connected.

The class of interpreters, who adopt the spiritualistic view, conceive that there is no valid ground for the distinction referred to. Taking up their position on distinctively gospel principles, and contemplating all that is written in Old Testament Scripture of gospel times primarily in a New Testament light, they apply *uniformly* one and the same rule of interpretation to the prophecies, which bear on the future of the covenant-people. What it obliges them to hold in respect to the religion and the more distinguishing peculiarities of Israel, they feel constrained to hold also in respect to their land and polity. And in support of this view they are wont to adduce a number of particular passages, which in their plain and obvious aspect seem to abolish, along with other distinctions, those also of land and people, and to leave no room for any name or commonwealth in the kingdom of Christ, but that of the one body, formed out of all people and tribes and tongues, which is knit together by the bond of a living faith and a common participation in the blessings of Christ's redemption. It is not enough, however, to produce a series of passages possessing this import; for they are met by a counter-set of passages on the other side, and in looking at the subject as so presented, the mind is apt to be perplexed and bewildered by what seem so many cross lights and contradictory statements. The question can never be satisfactorily determined, by being viewed and discussed in so isolated a manner. It must be seen in the light, not of this particular Scripture or that, but of great fundamental principles—principles which may enable us to distinguish between Scripture and Scripture—between those parts of Scripture which relate to the *foundations* of God's kingdom, which fix and determine the *form* as well as the *substance* of things belonging to it, and those which, from being of a subsidiary nature, relate only to what may be fit or practicable within the setted landmarks. Unless some distinctions of this kind can be made good, there may be no end to the controversy on the field of argument; and it is with a view mainly to the establishment of such a result, that we propose now to conduct the investigation. Several incidental topics will be left unnoticed, in order the more fully to concentrate attention on what we deem to be the great and determining elements of the question.

I. With this end in view, we naturally turn our eye, in the first instance, to the direct teaching of our Lord and His apostles; for there, beyond all question, it is that we find the revelations, which are in the strictest sense fundamental as to all that is to distinguish the kingdom of God in New Testament times. What Moses was to the Old Testament church, Christ is to the New, though Himself as much higher than Moses, as the New is above the Old. And if the prophets under the Old Testament, from being in their position altogether inferior to Moses, and having only revelations by vision while he had them by direct and open intercourse, could introduce no alterations in the *principles* or even *forms* of things settled by him,—if the last of them wound up the whole prophetic testimony in its direct bearing upon those to whom it was delivered, by charging them to "remember the law of Moses, God's servant, which He commanded to him in Horeb for all Israel, with the statutes and judgments" (Mal. iv. 4):[1] —if the prophets of the Old Testament stood in this subordinate relationship to Moses, how much more must they have done so to Christ? They were charged with no commission to interfere with any thing, which the Mediator of the old covenant had ordained—to bring in no new rite, to establish no new relation—for even the kingly form of government was prospectively indicated and authorised by Moses; how much less, therefore, could any word have been given them, which was to have the effect of countervailing the principles, or modifying the constitution brought in by the unspeakably greater Mediator of the new covenant? Indeed, the consideration reaches farther than this; the conclusion derived from it holds, not merely as between the prophets of the Old Testament and Christ, but also between those prophets, and the apostles of Christ; for the least of the apostles was greater than John the Baptist, who again was greater than any of the prophets; and the communications by the apostles (for the most part) were also open and direct, not by vision. Here, therefore, in the teaching of Christ and His apostles, must be sought all the essential principles which go to determine the nature, the constitution, and form of Christ's kingdom; or, to use the words of a canon formerly enunciated, "Every thing which affects the condition and destiny of the New Testament church has its clearest determination in New Testament Scripture."[2] So that, where there is any doubt or uncertainty, it is by this later Scripture we are to interpret the prophecies of former times, not by the prophecies that we are to explicate or resolve the later and higher revelations.

[1] See Part I., Chap i. [2] See p. 153.

What, then, is the bearing and import of this teaching of our Lord and His apostles on the special subject before us? Is it such as to give us reason to expect a future restoration of the Jewish people, or a re-establishment of their old economy, as if something of importance for the church depended on it? Unquestionably, there is no explicit announcement to this effect in the whole range of the historical and epistolary writings of the New Testament. The infliction of divine judgment upon the mass of the Jewish people, was very distinctly proclaimed by our Lord Himself, with the destruction of their city and temple, and the scattering of the community at once from the kingdom of God, and from the land of their fathers. But in not so much as one passage does he unequivocally indicate for them a re-gathering to their paternal home, or a re-investment with their former relative distinctions and privileges; far less is there any statement to imply, that the temple-worship should be again set up as the common religious centre and resort of Christendom. And in these respects the disciples are of one mind with their Master; they are equally silent upon the topics referred to.

It is true, there are a few passages which are sometimes represented as by implication teaching those things; but still at the most it is only by implication; and the slightest consideration of them is enough to show, not necessarily or certainly even that. When our Lord, for example, spake of a coming time, when the twelve apostles should sit on thrones judging the twelve tribes of Israel (Matt. xix. 28), there is nothing whatever to indicate (even taking it quite literally) in what region it should be—under what form of religious worship—or even whether as collected into one body, or distributed through several localities. Nothing on such points is either affirmed or denied in the statement. Nor, again, when foretelling the coming overthrow and the long-continued degradation that was to follow, in the memorable words, "Jerusalem shall be trodden down of the Gentiles until the times of the Gentiles shall be fulfilled" (Luke xxi. 24), was any thing said of a return to the ancient home of Israel, and its ritual worship, not even of a restitution of the old nationality. Jerusalem is obviously to be understood not alone as a city, but as a city identified with, and representative of the Jewish people; and the word simply announces, that a bound was to be set to *its* down-treading on the part of the Gentiles—the ascendancy on the one side, and the degradation on the other, were to terminate; but in what manner, or to what extent, was left entirely undecided. Manifestly, the treading down might cease by the simple abolition of the outstanding distinctions between Jew and Gentile, and the coalescing of the two on a footing of fraternal love and equality, without any collective national re-union of all the seed of Israel (which but partially existed, indeed, when Jerusalem actually *was* trodden down), or any restoration of the old religious ascendancy and temple-worship. Nor yet, again, when in answer to the question of the disciples, "Wilt thou at this time restore again the kingdom to Israel?" our Lord said, "It is not for you to know the times and the seasons which the Father hath put in His own power," was any thing determined as to the points now under consideration. For supposing it to imply, that the kingdom was somehow and at some period to be restored, the question still remains, in what sense? To Israel in their natural relation merely to Abraham, or, as a spiritual seed? separate and alone, or merged with believers generally into the Church of God? in the land of Palestine, or diffused throughout the earth? On these points nothing whatever is indicated, while yet they involve the whole questions now at issue. It is nothing to say, that the disciples must have meant by Israel the natural seed and its political resuscitation; for through the whole of his earthly ministry, Jesus was ever using language, and language often far more explicit and direct than this, which they did not at the time understand. We have no more reason to affirm, that the sense in which *they* understood the words of Christ here was that also in which *he* employed them, than it was so when He spake of destroying the temple and raising it up in three days (John ii. 19); or, when pointing to his crucifixion, he said, "And I, if

I be lifted up, will draw all men unto me" (John xii. 32). It was the descent of the Spirit alone, which fitted them for entering properly into the meaning of any of our Lord's sayings; and the utter disappearance from their thoughts and language, after that event, of all reference to a national kingdom of Israel, separate from the Church of Christ, is quite sufficient to show how great a change their sentiments had undergone upon the subject.

This, however, is not all. It is not merely that in these fundamental teachings respecting the character and prospects of the Messiah's kingdom, there is the want of any formal and explicit announcement of either the national restoration of Israel to Palestine, or the re-establishment there, as in a religious centre, of a Jewish polity and worship; but that the want exists in connection with much that bore immediately upon the subject, and was fitted to call forth, or even to demand, some definite announcement regarding it, if such could have been made. Beside the careful reserve maintained by our Lord respecting it, on the occasions already referred to, when we turn to His parables, in which He indicated more concerning the future of His church and kingdom than He could do in His direct discourses, we find Him presenting almost every possible aspect of its coming fortunes and destiny, yet without once conveying an intimation that any of them were to turn upon the separate nationality or distinctive privileges of the natural Israel. In some of the parables He spoke plainly enough of their opposition to the spirit of His kingdom, and of the certainty of their losing their place in it, notwithstanding that they might be called the children of the kingdom (Matt. xxi. 28–46, xxii. 1–14; Luke xiii. 6–9, xv. 11–32, etc.); and in others He pointed to the corruptions which, in the course of time, should creep into the church, the troubles and difficulties it should have to contend with, the sure progress and enlargement it should continue to make, and the final issues of reward and condemnation, blessing and cursing, in which it should close (Matt. xiii. 24–50, xxv.; Luke xvi., xviii., etc.) But in not one of them is the least hint given of the prospective return of the Jewish people to a separate place and position in the kingdom; nor is the distinction ever drawn as one destined to exist and work for good, as between people and people, land and land, church and church. The kingdom always presents itself as a unity, alike in nature, privilege, and destiny for its real members, with the world at large for the field of its operations—divided only in so far as it was to be composed for a time of the false and the true, and to have its issues at last in evil as well as good. After Christ, the apostles touch the disputed territory on every side, but still with the same studied reserve. The Apostle Paul, who had every inducement, from his official calling and circumstances, to speak in the most conciliatory tone of his countrymen, and who does, in one of his epistles, treat at considerable length both of their general fall and of their future recovery (Rom. ix.–xi.), still utters not a word concerning their separate position, their local habitation, or their distinctive worship, as if in such respects they were to differ, when converted, from the other members of God's kingdom. On the contrary, he represents their return simply as a reconciliation with the one spiritual body, from which they are for a time cut off—an admission into the community, which, he plainly testifies, admits of no distinction between Jew and Gentile. With him the church in the future, as well as in the present—the church, through all its coming stages on to its consummation in glory, precisely as in the parables of Christ—is an organic unity, marred only by the false admixtures and the antichristian apostacy which were for a time to corrupt its simplicity. Nay, the Apostle Peter, the apostle pre-eminently of the circumcision, in all his discourses and epistles after the day of Pentecost, seems equally unconscious of any distinction awaiting the race of Israel in God's kingdom—none excepting that of being by privilege the first to receive, and by calling the most imperatively bound to spread abroad its blessings. This may be said to be the one theme of his first epistle, as addressed, more immediately, to believing Israelites scattered throughout the cities of Asia Minor. And in his recorded speeches on the day of Pentecost, and after it, how entirely does Christ's present reign, and his one kingdom of converted and saved men, take the place of what previously held such firm possession of his thoughts, the kingdom of Israel? The change is most remarkable. He appears, in the last interview with Jesus, along with the other disciples, making earnest inquiry about the restoration of the kingdom to Israel. But presently afterwards, when the Spirit has descended with his enlightening and elevating influences, he proclaims Christ as already "exalted to sit on the throne of David" (Acts ii. 30); or, as it is again expressed, anointed by God, according to the terms of the second Psalm, and now meeting the opposition of ungodly men, which was there predicted respecting the Lord's anointed King (chap. iv. 24–28). And when he points (as he does in chap. iii. 19–21) to the brighter future of the kingdom, he represents it as a future, which Israel, indeed, by their conversion and forgiveness, might do much to help forward, but which was by no means to be peculiarly connected with them—which, in its progress and consummation, was to bring not "the restoration of the kingdom to Israel" in the sense formerly imagined, but "the restitution of all things spoken of by all God's holy prophets since the world began," the one grand universal restoration to order and blessedness. The sphere of the apostle's vision has now immeasurably widened, and though in no respect to the prejudice of the natural Israel, yet to the indefinite expansion of their peculiar privileges, and the enlargement of the kingdom so as to embrace men of every nation, and the round circumference of the globe itself.[1]

Nor in the Apocalypse is there anything that can fairly be regarded as bearing a different import. It is true that in one passage there, in the sealing vision of chap. vii., the Israelites are mentioned, and twelve thousand from each tribe are represented as being marked with the seal of God. There is

[1] See Appendix H.

a class of interpreters who understand this of the literal Israel (including even Bengel in former times, and now Auberlen), and who regard the 144,000 thus made up as constituting the elect church from among the Jews, and the multitude without number from every nation, tribe, and tongue, in ver. 9, as the elect from among the Gentiles. This, however, is so utterly at variance with the whole style of the Apocalypse, and with the connection of this passage itself with what precedes and follows, that the opinion is rejected by many who in other respects adhere to the literal style of interpretation. If the natural Israel were really meant, then this portion of the book would form an exception to the general character of the Apocalypse, which ever represents New Testament relations and prospects under the imagery of those of Old Testament times. The temple and its courts afterwards mentioned, the city where our Lord was crucified, Sodom and Egypt, Jerusalem and Babylon, Mount Zion and Megiddo, the woman and the whore, are all used symbolically to indicate things and parties corresponding to what bore those names in earlier times; and it would be to mar the consistency of the apocalyptic style, and introduce the greatest arbitrariness into its interpretation, if the tribes of Israel were here to be taken in their natural sense. Nor would it accord with the symbolical import evidently attached to these 144,000. It is against all probability to suppose, on the hypothesis of the literal reading of the passage, that precisely 12,000 of elect ones were to be found in each of the tribes specified. And if that improbability could anyhow be got rid of, why should only twelve tribes have been specified, and not thirteen, the actual number of the tribes? Is it to be conceived that, while each one of those twelve should furnish 12,000, Dan, the tribe omitted, should furnish none? The very omission of this tribe, so as to leave the historical number, twelve, and the precise squaring of this number, so as to make the twelve times twelve, multiplied by a thousand, shows that it is not the meaning of the letter we have to deal with but the symbolical representation of a perfect and complete totality.

This appears, also, from the object of the sealing, which was to stamp, with the sure impress of Heaven, "the servants of the living God," the Lord's people generally, as being through the Divine protection safe from the desolations that were to sweep over "the earth and the sea." The sealed are manifestly the representatives of all whom Divine grace saves from the world-wide judgments contemplated in the vision; and hence quite naturally appear, during the process of the sealing, as made up of so many thousands taken from the tribes that historically composed the professing church. Not less naturally at the close of the process, when the act is completed, they present the aspect of a numberless multitude gathered from all lands. These reasons, drawn from the vision itself, which treats of the sealed company of Israelites, are still farther confirmed, and rendered altogether conclusive, by the subsequent reference that is made to the subject. In chap. xiv. the Lamb is seen standing on Mount Zion with 144,000, the same sealed company "having His name, and the name of His Father (so it should be read) written on their foreheads." These are described in terms that can only be understood of the elect generally, not of a mere fraction of the elect. It is said of them that they alone could sing the new song, and that they were virgins, faithful followers of the Lamb, redeemed from among men. They are, therefore, the saved; and appearing *as* representatives, forming an ideal number, and in a state of ideal perfection, they are also fitly called the first fruits unto God and the Lamb.

On every account, the conclusion seems inevitable, that the Israelites, in the sealing vision, must be understood symbolically, like all similar terms in the Apocalypse. And as this is the only occasion on which they are formally introduced into the vision of things to come, it remains certain, that the revelations given to St John, are in perfect accordance on this point with what appears generally in New Testament Scripture. As for the view of Hofmann, whom Ebrard, and some British writers, follow, that the woman in chap. xii., is simply the Jewish Church, and her seed that was to be driven into the wilderness, the Jewish people in their unbelieving and scattered condition, it is so palpably opposed to the whole spirit of the Book, and the general object of its prophetic revelations, that it needs no refutation.

It thus appears, that in the teaching of our Lord and his apostles, there is nothing to favour either the Jewish, or the semi-Jewish view of the prophetical future. Amid much incidentally bearing on the subject of Jewish prospects, there is still no distinct announcement of the national restoration and settlement of the Jewish people in Canaan, or of the re-institution of their temple-worship. There is nothing whatever said to indicate, that such events may be expected in the history of the Christian Church, or that any thing depends on them for the advancement and welfare of Christ's cause in the world. Christianity as exhibited and defined for all coming time by its great founders, acknowledges no such distinctions, and is silent as to any such prospects. And as the revelations that came by them, were for the church of the New Testament of a primal and fundamental character, it were to invert the natural order of things, and loosen the foundations of sound scriptural exposition, if Scriptures of an older, and from the first only of a subsidiary kind, should be alleged in support of an opposite conclusion. From the nature of things, they cannot be rightfully alleged. And the feeling of this, we have no doubt—however vaguely defined and imperfectly understood as to the principles on which it rested—the feeling, that the fundamental teaching of the New Testament was of the nature now described, and ought mainly to be regarded, was what led the Fathers with one voice (not excepting such as held the personal, millennial reign of Christ in Jerusalem), and all Christian writers, down to the seventeenth century, to reject as chimerical, the Jewish expectations, both of a territorial restoration, and of a revived Judaism.[1] The feeling itself was sound, though it could seldom, perhaps, have given a

[1] Conclusive proof of this may be seen, in a short compass, in the British and Foreign Evangelical Review for March 1855.

satisfactory explanation of the grounds, out of which it sprung, or made an enlightened defence of them.

It is true, that Christianity itself sprung out of Judaism, and that certain things belonging to it, may be, not explicitly stated and announced, but *presumed*, on account of the place they had in former revelations, and it has been alleged, that the obligation to observe the weekly Sabbath is of this description and the right to administer baptism to infants. These both rest chiefly upon grounds and principles definitely settled in the Old Testament Scriptures; and are, it is held, substantially on a footing with the supposed distinctions in the prophetic future between Jew and Gentile, or the return to a ceremonial worship. Our answer to this is very short. If the points now under discussion were really on a footing with the things referred to, they must have been presumed as continuously subsisting; they must have been held to be integral parts of Christianity as well as of Judaism, and opportunity must have been afforded to maintain them, at least in substance. But so far from this, they were authoritatively set aside, and an insuperable bar laid by God's providence in the way, even of their formal observance. If any thing could mark them as merely superficial and temporary distinctions, it was surely this. We hold it to be otherwise with the Sabbatical Institution, and the admission of children to a covenant-standing. These are no Jewish peculiarities or temporary expedients; they rest on primeval grounds of truth and duty, and enshrine principles, which are interwoven with the constitution of man, and were inwrought into the very foundations of the world's history.

II. This latter point, however, touches closely upon another, to which we now proceed. We refer to the typical character of the Levitical dispensation. And our position respecting it is, that as the Israelitish people, with their land and their religious institutions, were, in what distinctively belonged to them under the old covenant, of a typical nature, the whole together, in that particular aspect, has passed away—it has become merged in Christ and the gospel dispensation.

That this holds good in respect to the *religious institutions*, distinctively and peculiarly belonging to the old covenant, was, till quite recently, admitted by, at least, all evangelical Christians. The only party known in history to have disputed it, were the small and obscure Ebionite section of the early heretics, whom all credible historians represent as much more Jewish than Christian in their views. That men of evangelical sentiments, in other respects, should, in these latter times, have come to the same belief, maintaining the absolute perpetuity of the temple worship, and the certainty of its being again established for the benefit of all Christendom, we can only regard as one of those strange and bewildering meteors, that occasionally appear for a little in the theological heavens, and then pass away with the occasion that has produced them. The belief, we are persuaded, has gradually forced itself upon them, as an untoward, but necessary result of the false principle of prophetical literalism, to which the writers of this school had eagerly committed themselves, before they distinctly saw to what lengths it would conduct them. The anomalous position, which they now occupy, cannot possibly last. Consistency will oblige them, either to abandon their Judaism, or renounce their evangelism; for, as we said before, that the evidence for the historical Messiah cannot stand with their principle of prophetical literalism, so we say now, that the fair and grammatical exegesis of New Testament Scripture, can as little stand with the Judaistic hypothesis that has sprung from it. By the one result, the prophetical testimony to the Messiahship of Jesus is destroyed, and by the other the foundation is subverted of the Typology of Scripture.

The full proof of this can only be had by the establishment of a sound typological system, based on a close and comprehensive examination of the writings of both the Old and the New Testament. And as we have endeavoured to do that elsewhere (in the Typology of Scripture), it is the less necessary to say much upon the subject here. Indeed, with plain and unsophisticated minds, the matter admits of a very simple and direct solution. We might put it to any one of a free and candid spirit, if holding the Judaistic views now under consideration, he could have taken the part, which the apostle Paul did, in respect to circumcision and the law? Could he have resisted the introduction of these into the church as a matter of life and death? Could he have said, as Paul did to the Galatians, when he heard, not that they *abused*, but simply, that they *used* them—heard merely, that they "observed days, and months, and times, and years"—"O foolish Galatians, who hath bewitched you, that ye should not obey the truth? I am afraid of you, lest I have bestowed upon you labour in vain; Behold I, Paul, say unto you, that if ye be circumcised, Christ shall profit you nothing?" Or, could he have declared the proper subjects of the law, to have been placed by it in a state of bondage, or under a schoolmaster, from which, now that faith has come, they were set free? It is impossible—and a glance into the writings of those, whose views we are now discussing, brings us acquainted with quite another language. Hear, for example, Mr Birks, "They (the legal sacrifices and services connected with them), were taken away, from constituting any part of the true atonement for sin, which our Lord was coming to effect by the offering of his own body on the tree. As symbols or sacraments, pointing to something beyond, and far higher than themselves, and as adapted for an earthly stage of man's being, they were always acceptable, when offered in obedience to God's revealed will. But when adopted by others, to whom no such command had been given, or viewed as having inherent efficacy, they were denounced by the prophets as dishonourable to God, and unavailing to man; and the refusal to impose them upon Gentile converts, when the gospel was sent to them, was only a further and plainer testimony against the Jewish perversion of them, as in the days of Isaiah and Jeremiah, by pride and self-righteousness."[1] Did Rome itself ever produce a more palpable travesty of the import of Scripture? It might seem enough to rouse the shade of Luther

[1] Outlines of Unfulfilled Prophecy, p. 323.

from its repose. How differently did he write of the Judaizing spirit of the Galatians and apostles of Judaism? And Paul himself, did he simply *refuse to impose* the Jewish ritual of worship upon the Gentile converts? Or, when introduced, did he merely tell them, that it was only when coupled with pride and self-righteousness, the services became unavailing? but that as symbols or sacraments they were always acceptable? No such thing. It is the services themselves he condemns—because, in the very observance of them, where there was no bond of custom rendering it difficult to break them off, he descried the clear sign of an antichristian spirit; and the teaching which persuaded the Galatians to enter on their observance, he affirms to be "another gospel." The very existence of them anywhere, he terms a badge of servitude, and the things themselves are stigmatised as "beggarly elements." During the period appointed for them, they held the place only of temporary expedients—"shadows," but with Christ's coming, the "body" is present, and the shadows, as a matter of course, disappear. The whole system of carnal ordinances, he tells us in Hebrews, was abolished, not because of men's abuse of it, but because of its own *weakness and unprofitableness;* and he shows that they belonged to a priesthood and a covenant, which, according to Old Testament Scripture itself, were destined to be displaced, and now, he expressly declares, *were* displaced by the higher priesthood and the new covenant of Christ. In short, the question, as treated by the apostle, and as it should still be treated by us, is not, whether those carnal ordinances might not be observed by certain individuals under the gospel in a Christian spirit? But whether they were in themselves altogether good? And especially, whether they were adapted to the genius of Christianity, and properly fitted to nourish the Christian spirit? To this, the whole tenor of his remarks gives a decided negative, and we may say, an indignant rejection.

Such are the plain and broad features of the subject, as presented by the apostle to the Gentiles, which it is impossible to explain away, without subverting the very principles of a right interpretation of Scripture. But they by no means stand alone. Our Lord's declaration to the woman at Samaria, in which he said, "The hour cometh, when ye shall neither in this mountain, nor yet at Jerusalem, worship the Father; but the hour cometh, and now is, when the true worshipper shall worship the Father in spirit and in truth; for the Father seeketh such to worship Him;" this declaration contains the principle of the whole matter. For it intimates, that the distinction of places as to religion was on the eve of abolition, and that worship rendered at Jerusalem would be no more acceptable to God than that given in the most distant regions. But to say this, was to ring the knell of the ceremonial law, which necessarily fell with the exclusive honours of the one temple and the one altar at Jerusalem. It thenceforth ceased to be either binding or proper, though still it did not strictly die—but rather, like the chrysalis breaking its horny crust, and emerging into a higher form of life and beauty, was transfigured into Christ's form of doctrine, the new law of a spiritual Christianity. The same change was involved in the instructive fact connected with our Lord's death, when the veil of the temple was rent in twain; for this declared, as by an impressive sign from heaven, that the formal distinctions of the old economy were abolished at the very centre, and thenceforth should cease, even to the farthest extremities. From that moment, there was no longer, in the old sense, a sanctuary, and a holy of holies; the handwriting which had established such divisions till the time of reformation, was blotted out, the reformation itself having come; and the entire sacrificial system founded on it necessarily gave way. The change was still farther indicated in Christ's declaring, at His last passover, that He had greatly desired to eat it with his disciples, because now it was to be fulfilled in the kingdom of God (Luke xxii. 16): that is, the typical act it commemorated, was to be substantiated by the great redemption, whose commemorative rite must henceforth take the place of the former. Hence, in still farther explanation, the apostle Paul says, in 1 Cor. v. 7,

"For even Christ, our Passover, is sacrificed for us" (or, more exactly, For also *our* Passover, Christ, has been sacrificed), let us, therefore, keep the feast, not with old leaven, neither with the leaven of malice and wickedness, but with the unleavened bread of sincerity and truth." The meaning obviously is, that the Christian church now possesses, through participation in the death and grace of Christ, in the real and proper sense, what was only symbolically represented in the ancient passover and its accompanying feast. In another epistle also (Col. ii.), he expressly affirms, that the other most distinctive ordinance of the Old Testament, circumcision, has passed into Christian baptism; so that those who through the Spirit have been baptised into the spiritual body of Christ, are the circumcised in heart. And if, as the apostle in the same place announces, the handwriting of ordinances was in one mass, as in Christ's body, nailed to the cross and taken out of the way, there can be room for but one conclusion; for as many as look to that cross for salvation, the old ritual has for ever gone; and we may justly say of it with Luther, "Like Moses, it is dead and buried, and let no man know where its place is."

But what is thus said of the *religion* of the old covenant, as to its external form, is also said of the *people* on whom, in their elect and separate condition, it was imposed; they also in that condition possessed a typical character. As a chosen people, saved from outward bondage and corruption, and placed in covenant-relationship to God, they represented those who, when the true redemption came, should be delivered from all evil, and constituted members of God's everlasting kingdom. So long as that typical relation stood, the national distinction between Jew and Gentile necessarily continued—although, as the time for its abolition drew near, a certain approximation was made to its removal, by the dispersion of the Jews through the Roman empire, and the constant accessions made to them by proselytes from the Gentiles. The way was thus prepared, by Divine Providence, for the change from a typical to an anti-typical election—that is, from an elect seed, to an elect society; which began to take full effect as soon as the Christian church assumed an outstanding existence in the world. From that time we hear only of a precedence on the part of the Jew in the order of time—he stood nearest to the kingdom of God, and fitly had the first offer of its blessings; but he had no superiority in rank, privilege, or destiny. Again and again the apostle testifies, that in these respects, there was no difference; as in Rom. x. 12, "For there is no difference between the Jew and the Greek; for the same Lord over all, is rich unto all that call upon Him;" Gal. iii. 28, "There is neither Jew nor Greek, there is neither bond nor free, there is neither male nor female (these outward distinctions do not indeed cease, but they are nothing in a *religious* point of view), for ye are all one in Christ Jesus;" Col. iii. 11, "Where (*i.e.*, in Christ) there is neither Greek nor Jew, circumcision nor uncircumcision, barbarian, Scythian, bond nor free, but Christ is all, and in all." And in Eph. ii. 14, sq., where he speaks more formally of the constitution of the Christian church, "He is our peace, who hath made both one, and hath broken down the middle wall of partition; having abolished in his flesh the enmity, the law of commandments contained in ordinances; for to make in Himself of twain one new man, so making peace." Here, plainly, the ground of separation or enmity, the law of ordinances, is declared to have been removed by Christ, for Jew as well as Gentile; it was, henceforth, no more obligatory upon the one than upon the other; and should have ceased as soon as possible to be even observed, in order that the intended oneness of the Church might be effected, and converted Gentiles might feel that they were "no more strangers and foreigners, but fellow-citizens with the saints, and of the household of God." Hence, in token of this complete fusion of races, and the consequent merging of the type in the anti-type, believers in Christ, generally, are called Abraham's seed (Gal. iii. 29), Israelites (chap. vi. 16; Eph. ii. 12), comers unto Mount Zion (Heb. xii. 22), citizens of the free or heavenly Jerusalem (Gal. iv. 26), the circumcision (Phil. iii. 3).

It is to be added, that here also our Lord himself took the lead. He began to do so at a comparatively early period in his ministry, when on the occasion of the Centurion's remarkable faith, he exclaimed, "Verily, I say unto you, I have not found so great faith, no, not in Israel. And I say unto you, That many shall come from the east and west, and shall sit down with Abraham, and Isaac, and Jacob, in the kingdom of heaven; but the children of the kingdom shall be cast out into outer darkness" (Matt. viii. 11, 12). So again, when He was told of His mother and brethren desiring to speak with Him, "He answered and said unto him that told Him, Who is my mother? and who are my brethren? And He stretched forth His hand toward His disciples, and said, Behold my mother and my brethren! For whosoever shall do the will of My Father that is in heaven (or, as in Luke, hear the word of God, and do it), the same is my brother, and sister, and mother." Here, precisely as in the rending of the veil for the ceremonials of Judaism, the exclusive bond for the people was broken at the centre: Christ's very mother and brothers were to have no precedence over others, nor any distinctive position in His kingdom; spiritual relations alone should prevail there, and the one bond of connection with it for all alike, was to be the believing reception of the gospel and obedience to it. Finally, the command given the apostles to teach and baptise all nations, with no further difference than that they should begin at Jerusalem and the Jews, though they were not to rest, till they had reached the uttermost part of the earth, and preached the gospel to every creature—evidently implied the cessation of all outward national distinctions, as having any recognised place in the kingdom of Christ. So that the apostle Paul, in the explicit declarations we have quoted from his epistles, only carried out, and in a more concrete form expressed, the principle already embodied in our Lord's announcements.

So far, therefore, as regards Israel's typical character, their removed and isolated position is plainly at an end: all tribes and nations are on a footing as to the kingdom of God—members and fellow-citizens if they are believers in Christ, aliens if they are not. But admitting this, may not the natural Israel in some other respect have the prospect of a separate and peculiar standing in the church? It was not simply to be a type of the future election, that they were anciently separated from the nations, but also that they might possess the reality of a present interest in God's love and blessing, and do special service for Him in the world. Why may it not be so again? It may, certainly, and, we have no doubt it will, in some sense, and in so far as may consist with the fundamental principles and relations of God's spiritual kingdom. But it should be well considered how far, in respect to that, the history of the past itself may warrant us to carry our expectations. Beside the typical character of Israel, the only ground of distinction that belonged to them, at least as recognized by God, was their religious position; they were the nation that held the truth, and, as such, stood apart from the idolatrous nations of heathendom. But when that distinction virtually ceased to exist by the mass of the people abandoning the truth, and espousing the corruptions of heathenism, the Lord held the ground of separation to be abolished, and addressed and treated them as heathen (Isa. i. 1–10; Amos ix. 7, 8; Ezek. xvi., xxiii.). Or when it ceased on the other side by heathens renouncing their abominations, and entering into the bond of the covenant, the same abolition, though in a happier sense, took place as to any formal distinction. Never, indeed, was there any thing properly distinctive and peculiar to Israel as a people, apart from their standing in the knowledge and faith of God; whenever this ground of separation was removed on the one side or the other, the distinction itself disappeared; the natural seed of Israel no longer dwelt alone. And rightly. For their election of God to a separate place, viewed in respect to the time then present, was no act of favouritism; it was simply the appointed means to a great moral end; and when they were either no longer capable of reaching this, or no longer needed for doing so, it fell into abeyance.

Such was the state of matters viewed in respect to the past: And would it not be an anomaly of the strangest description, if now under the new dispensation, pre-eminent, especially for the freedom it has brought from outward restraints and adventitious distinctions, a kind of division were to be introduced, which had no existence even under the old? In the church itself of the Old Testament there was no recognized division; members of the stock of Israel formed its main trunk, and those who joined it from other tribes became merged in the common body; the separation was simply between this body and the heathen world. Shall it be otherwise now? In Christian times alone shall there be a recognized and abiding distinction *within* the church, between one portion of it and another? Even when the kingdoms of this world have become the kingdom of our God and of His Christ, shall the Jewish nation stand out and apart from the rest? Were it actually to do so, *it would not be a continuation or a renewal of the past, but the introduction of an entirely new principle into the Church of God.* When the kingdoms shall have attained to the condition mentioned, they will be relatively in the very position occupied of old by Israel itself—they will be one and all kingdoms holding the truth; and if converted Israelites were still to stand apart from and above them, it would not be the same thing that existed under the law, but something essentially different—something foreign even to Judaism; how much more, then, to Christianity?

The only just expectation respecting the position of the Jewish people in their converted state—that alone, which is warranted by the history of the past, or seems in accordance with the great principles of Christianity, is not that their singular and isolated place after they have entered the church, but that their entrance itself there, shall enliven and refresh her condition. The receiving of them, says the apostle, shall be "life from the dead." Cut off, as they have been and continue to be, for their impenitence and unbelief, they are, so to speak, in the condition of an amputated limb—lying in the bonds of death. And when animated anew by the breath of the Spirit, so as to become re-united with the living body of Christ, what else can the effect be, than that of sending a fresh impulse through every part and member of the body? How far this effect may be produced simultaneously or by successive stages, cannot be determined with certainty, and is of no moment as regards the general question. The apostle's language, in the eleventh chapter of the Romans, has been thought to imply, that the return of the Jews shall be in a kind of national capacity. It no more implies that, however, than our Lord's language respecting the calling of the Gentiles implies their simultaneous and national conversion, when he says in Matth. xxi. 43, "Therefore I say unto you, the kingdom of God shall be taken from you, and given to a nation bringing forth the fruit thereof." He spoke of the general result, in the comprehensive style of prophecy, as if the transference were to be begun and completed at once; while yet, we know from the history, it took place in the most gradual and successive manner. For anything we can tell, the reception of the Jews into the bosom of the church may also take place gradually, though it is spoken of as a single event. At the same time, from the close inter-connection that subsists among them, it is likely to be accomplished in a much briefer period, after the work of conversion has somewhat generally commenced, than in the case of the Gentiles. But long or short, we are assured, that it shall proceed till all Israel shall be saved; as on the other hand, also, we are assured, all the families of the earth shall be blessed. In that respect there is nothing properly peculiar to Israel; in both of the two ancient divisions of the human family, a universality was predicated in regard to salvation; there was first to be a blessed seed in the direct line from Abraham, and ultimately through them a blessed world. So that it makes nothing whatever for the future distinct nationality of Israel, that they are destined in their totality to salvation; for the nations of the earth generally are destined to the same. In respect to the one division as well as the other, the principle holds, that "the gifts and calling of God are without repentance," with no other difference, than that in the case of the natural Israel it has had in the past, as it may also have in the future, a more palpable exemplification. And if the present scattered, yet separately preserved condition of the Jews shall be found, as we may well conceive, to hasten forward the blessed consummation, shall there not be discovered a sufficient reason for the providence that has so kept them apart? Their preservation certainly has been wonderful, and we can scarcely doubt is destined in the issue to work out more signally God's great purpose of mercy for the world:—not, however, as by a distinct nationality (which need no more exist then than it does now), but rather as by a fresh infusion of life and energy through a thousand avenues into the church. Then shall "the remnant of Jacob be in the midst of many people as a dew from the Lord, as the showers upon the grass, that tarrieth not for man, nor waiteth for the sons of men."

But now, what we have affirmed first of the religion of the old covenant, then of the people, we must also affirm of the *inheritance*. This, not less than the other two, as formerly stated,[1] possessed a typical character in relation to gospel times: like them, it passed, when these entered, into something higher and better. And in tracing the connection between the new and the old things, Christ and his apostles make no difference between this and the two former particulars. Christ himself came into the world as the heir of an inheritance, but it was the inheritance of the earth, as given up to Him to be delivered from the bondage of evil, and ultimately glorified (Psalm ii.). Accordingly, one of the first benedictions he pronounced in his sermon on the Mount, was an assurance to His people of an interest in this large inheritance, "Blessed are the meek, for they shall inherit the earth." So, again, in the words he uttered in connection with the faith of the Centurion, the converts from every land are represented as sitting down with Abraham, Isaac, and Jacob, in the kingdom of God—sharing ultimately in their inheritance,

[1] See Part I., Chap. vi.

as they had already entered into their faith. In like manner, the apostle Paul speaks of believers in Christ, not only as children of Abraham, but also as heirs with him according to the promise (Gal. iii. 29)—having a joint-heritage, as well as a common standing with Abraham. He even designates Abraham "the heir of the world" (Rom. iv. 13)—which can only be explained by his identifying Canaan with what it typically represented, in the same way that Christ is called Abraham's seed (Gal. iii. 16), since in the immediate offspring the eye of faith contemplated the ultimate child of promise. In Hebrews xi. the patriarchs themselves are identified in their prospects of a future inheritance with believers in Christ; they are described as in their expectations overshooting the nearer possessions literally contained in the word of promise, and looking for the everlasting inheritance. And this inheritance, described by the apostle Peter as the destined portion alike of converted Jews and Gentiles (1 Peter i. 4), is also by him identified with the new heavens and the new earth, which the prophet Isaiah had held out in prospect to the church of the Old Testament, as the final resting-place from all their troubles (2 Peter iii. 13).

It appears, therefore, that the typical character which attached to the people and the religion of the old covenant, attached also to the inheritance—the land of Canaan; and that the transition to gospel times, is represented as effecting the same relative change in respect to this as to the others. It is true here, as of the people and of the religion, that the typical bearing was not the only one; immediate ends of an important kind were connected with the possession of the land, though they were never more than partially accomplished. But the typical bearing is the relation in which it stands to gospel times—a relation which it holds equally with the people, whose heritage it was, and the ceremonial worship they observed. How, indeed, could it have been otherwise? The land was, in a manner, the common basis of the people and the worship—the platform on which both stood, and in connection with which the whole of their religious observances, and their national history, might be said to move. To except this, therefore, from the typical territory, and withdraw it from the temporary things which were to pass to something higher and better in Christ, were to suppose an incongruity in the circumstances of ancient Israel, which we cannot conceive to have existed, and could only have led to inextricable confusion. Viewed in the light in which we have presented it, all is of a piece; a common principle pervades the relations of Old Testament times. The seed of Israel, as an elect people, placed under covenant with God, represented the company of an elect church, redeemed from the curse of sin, that they might live for ever in the favour and blessing of Heaven: and when the redemption came, the representation passed into the reality. In like manner, the religion of symbolical feasts and ordinances, which was imposed upon the people of the covenant, shadowed forth under various aspects the realities and consolations of the gospel; and when these were introduced, the other, as a matter of course, passed away—the type became merged in the antitype. So, once again, the inheritance which was given for a possession to the typical seed, and was to be a visible pledge of God's favour, so long as they fulfilled the obligations of the typical calling and worship, served for the time to image the final portion and destiny of the redeemed, and now, through the gospel, has been supplanted by the earnest and expectation of a world, the proper region of beautiful and blessed life. Here also the past links itself with the future, as the germ of a great and abiding reality, that was in due time to be developed. And precisely as Abraham was seen by inspired men perpetuating himself in the flock of Christ, and David in Christ Himself, so are Abraham's inheritance and David's kingdom to be regarded as having a prolonged and expanded existence in those of Christ and his people. There is the same principle in both. And, as a necessary result, the former relation of the Israelites to the land of Canaan affords no ground for expecting its re-occupation by them after their conversion to the faith of Christ, no more than for expecting, that the handwriting of ordinances shall then be restored, or the relations of the ancient world, generally, shall return to their old channels.

However viewed, therefore, the expectations of which we have been treating seem destitute of any solid foundation. They are to some extent at variance with the fundamental principles of the divine administration in general, and especially at variance with the spirit and genius of Christianity. The fulfilment of them would constitute, not an advance to a more perfect state of things, but a retrogression to what was essentially imperfect. The local temple, which formed the centre of the old religion, with its holy persons, and places, and seasons, bespoke in its very nature imperfection; since it implied, in respect to other persons, and places, and seasons, a relative commonness or pollution; so that the prophets themselves anticipated a time when it would be supplanted by something higher and better (Jer. iii. 17). The same kind of imperfection was inseparably connected with the idea of an elect people and a holy land; all lying beyond the hallowed circle, being necessarily regarded as either absolutely or relatively impure. Perfection can come only as this circle widens, and embraces the field of humanity in its compass. It properly began with the incarnation of Christ, the one complete, living temple of Godhead; and it grows as the Holy Spirit that is in Him finds for itself a home in the bosoms of believing men. Wherever such are, there also are living temples, surpassing in real glory the magnificent but lifeless fabric that stood upon the heights of Zion. And it is the grand aim of Christianity to increase and multiply these living temples of the Spirit, so that they may be found in every part of the habitable globe. Its tendency is not to centralise, but to diffuse abroad; not externally to communicate an impression of sanctity, by the mere touch of particular localities, and the observance of stated forms, but internally to sanctify men by the Spirit of holiness, and through them, as vessels of the Spirit, to sanctify all places and all times. The true ideal of Christianity is realised only in proportion as this regenerative process is accomplished;

and it were obviously a retrograde movement, if its free and expansive energies should be repressed by the local restraints of some particular region, or by having its more select agencies drawn from but a fragmentary section of the human family.

In what has hitherto been said, we have confined our attention, in the first instance, to the essential nature of Christianity, then to the typical character of Judaism, with scarcely any direct reference to the prophetical portions of Old Testament Scripture, beyond the terms of the Abrahamic covenant. It is to this, more especially, that the apostle Paul refers, when he treats of the future of the Jewish people in the epistle to the Romans. But neither in what he says regarding it, nor in the covenant itself, when rightly understood, is there anything to imply the restoration of the seed of Israel to a future and permanent possession of the land of Canaan. In reality it was never meant to secure in any sense, the possession of Canaan to more than a select portion of Abraham's seed; as the successive limitations made among his immediate offspring to the more peculiar blessings of the covenant clearly showed. It settled at length upon the children of Jacob, but only on the supposition (never more than partially verified) of their being collectively children of faith —for otherwise they could not have been entitled to any blessing.[1] And, as thus ultimately defined and fixed, it was in respect to the possession, no doubt, as well as other things, everlasting; not, however, as regards the *form*, but simply as regards the *substance* of its provisions. The form necessarily underwent a change with the coming of Christ, from whom everything in the future connected with God's kingdom takes its shape and character. He was Himself pre-eminently the Seed promised in the covenant; but, at the same time, unspeakably more than the seed primarily designated; it was now a seed embracing alike the Divine and human, and including as many as partake of the life of God. In correspondence with this, the possession becomes also unspeakably

[1] See Part I., Chap. iii.

more than the old land of Canaan—it embraces the whole extent of a recovered and renovated world. And wherever there is found a soul linked in vital union with Christ, there also are found the essential characteristics of Abraham's seed, and a title to Abraham's inheritance.

III. But we come now to glance at what are more strictly the prophetical parts of Scripture, and we here advance the proposition that they contain nothing which, taken according to the real nature and intent of prophecy, is at variance with the conclusions already arrived at. That they contain many passages which formally announce the re-establishment and perpetual existence of everything distinctively Jewish, admits of no doubt. But when read in accordance with the fundamental principles of prophetical interpretation, the true import is in perfect conformity with the views we have unfolded.

1. For, in the first place, by one of the most essential of these principles, the predictions of the future continually took the form and image of the present or the past.[1] Partly from the mode of revelation by vision, and partly from the necessary laws of the human mind, which the Spirit in His supernatural communications does not overbear, but leaves in free and unfettered exercise, there was no possibility of avoiding such a leaning upon history in the anticipations of prophecy. The new can only be conceived of under the aspect of the old; and by the aid of known relations the mind is obliged to feel its way to such as may belong to other states and conditions of existence. Of necessity, therefore, the form in such cases is always defective, and an accomplishment that should answer the description according to the letter would, in the nature of things, be impracticable. This holds as well of the New Testament delineations of our still undeveloped future, as of the Old Testament delineations of what has now become our present or past. Take, for example, some of our Lord's descriptions of the coming bliss and glory of His people.

[1] See p. 137, 150, sq.

Luke xii. 37, "Blessed are those servants, whom the Lord, when He cometh, shall find watching; verily I say unto you, that He shall gird Himself, and make them to sit down to meat, and will come forth to serve them;" xxii. 29, "And I appoint unto you a kingdom, as my Father hath appointed unto me; that ye may eat and drink at my table in my kingdom, and sit on thrones, judging the twelve tribes of Israel;" Rev. iii. 21, "To him that overcometh will I grant to sit with me in my throne, even as I also overcame, and am set down with my Father in His throne," etc. Of these and all similar descriptions of what is to come, no one needs to be told that they present only a shadowy representation drawn from known objects and relations upon earth, not the very form and image of the things hereafter to be realised. Understood otherwise, they would neither give assurance of the kind of felicity that is fitted to satisfy the desires of believers, nor would they be properly consistent with each other. And if such be the case with the prospective delineations of the gospel, how much more must it have been so with those which were given in the very age of shadows and symbols? Relatively, the people of those times were in the condition of children with respect to the better things to come, and these must either have been wrapt in absolute darkness to their view, or unfolded to them in a childish manner. In this form alone could they have formed any distinct idea of the coming future; and whatever imperfections may have cleaved to the form, it still was what alone could enable persons in their circumstances to obtain some apprehension of the reality.

Hence as the dispensations of God toward His people varied, and assumed in successive periods new aspects and relations, prophecy also changed the form of its representations. Instances have already been given of this (Part First, chap. iv.), and we glance here only at some of the general features. The patriarchal age was distinguished by the Lord's condescending to select, for the world's good, certain more peculiar instruments and channels of blessing, and prophecy then spake only of the way and manner in which the purpose to bless should be carried into effect. In the times of David and Solomon, when the kingdom, after many struggles, attained to a united and flourishing condition, the prophetic future assumed the aspect of a king contending and conquering—a kingdom in Israel bearing down all opposition, and gathering people of every name under its sway—and a blessed people, having their interests inseparably bound up with the person and fortunes of Him whom God had set upon the throne. But after the kingdom lost its unity, and the royal house of David was shorn of its glory, and the people themselves became peeled and scattered, then the spirit of prophecy, sighing amidst the mournful desolations, yet confident of the grace and glory still to be revealed, spake of this under the image of the removal of existing evils—of the reunion of Ephraim and Judah—of a reviving of the splendour of David's house—of the resuscitation even of David himself, to wield again the sceptre, in God's name, over a blessed heritage—and of the re-gathering of the scattered flock, to share in the peace and glory of His reign. How else could they have formed definite notions of the *nature* of the good in prospect? The existing evils must appear to be supplanted by the opposite good. Even the sorest of all their calamities, that which befel them at the overthrow of their beautiful city and temple, only served, in the hands of Ezekiel, for materials to picture out a restored community more perfect and glorious than the past, under the image of a temple and city, manifestly ideal in their whole structure and arrangements, yet admirably contrived to give assurance of a coming future that should totally eclipse the brightest era of the past. In Daniel a still further stage was reached in the development of the prophetic future, and, in accordance with his peculiar position, an altogether different form was given to it. Placed by Providence at a heathen court, it is from the midst of the worldly interest, not from that of the covenant people, that his prophetic outline of the future is given. It unfolds the relations between the kingdoms of this world and the kingdom of God, but contains nothing of the more internal relations growing out of the times of Abraham, or Jacob, or even David. And when he comes to designate the members of the Divine kingdom, the characteristics are drawn from the broadest ground. They are simply "the saints of the Most High;" and the kingdom itself, so far from being confined within the little bounds of Canaan, comprehends all people, and nations, and languages, under the whole Heaven.[1]

Taking, thus, the hue and aspect of the past—foretelling things to come, under the form and image of things which have already appeared—prophecy becomes comparatively simple as to its mode of interpretation and its leading results, if only (for there lies the chief difficulty) we can throw ourselves back to the position of those who disclosed it, and conceive of *their* relation to the future of the gospel dispensation, as we must do of our own relation to the still future dispensation of glory. Situated as the prophets generally were, it was quite natural, and, in a sense, necessary, that they should speak of the better things to come in language and imagery derived from such as were known and familiar to their minds, and especially that when disorder and confusion entered into the state of things previously settled, they should announce the recovery of what was lost, and the re-establishment on surer foundations of what had given way. This principle, in fact, pervades all their representations, and must be applied to one part as well as to another of the materials of which their representations are composed. The prophets themselves make no difference. They speak as distinctly, in some places, of a separate nationality for the covenant people, as in others of the healing of what was internally disordered; of the erection of the temple, and the joyful celebration of its worship, as of a restoration to the land of Canaan, and a re-built Jerusalem. It must ever appear arbitrary to separate between representations which are manifestly one in kind, and, if either intelligible or consistent, can only be found so by being based on a common principle. To hold by the form in one

[1] See Appendix I.

part, and let it go in another, is to introduce absolute confusion, and surrender the prophetic field to the caprice of individual feeling or the shifting currents of popular opinion. Indeed, on any other principle than that we have laid down, the prophetic testimony respecting the future of Israel would be of the most contradictory and discordant nature; for sometimes this future is exhibited under the form of a removal merely of the disorders that had crept into the old constitution of things, and at other times of the removal of this itself, on account of its inherent imperfections, in order that something better may take its place (Jer. xxxi. 31; Isa. lxv. 17, lxvi. 1–4; Haggai ii. 7). In one class of representations the nations are spoken of as going to Jerusalem to join in the restored feasts and ritual of Judaism (Isa. lxvi. 23; Zech. xiv.); in another, the distinctive peculiarities of Judaism and the temple service are described as no longer distinctive but everywhere diffused, as when Egypt and Assyria are placed on a footing as to covenant privileges with Israel (Isa. xix. 21–25); or, when the sacredness of the ark of the Lord is said to be shared in common by all Jerusalem (Jer. iii. 16, 17); or, when the most peculiar rites of the temple, such as the altar service, or the offering of incense, is connected with other countries, and even every region of the earth (Isa. xix. 19; Mal. i. 11). Ezekiel, writing when the heart of faith was prostrated by the fall of the house of God, seeks to reanimate it with the hope of a temple and a city incomparably more glorious and perfect than what had been lost; while John, living when the temple and all its forms were superseded, perceives no temple in the consummate glory of the New Jerusalem, with which his visions terminate. All, indeed, perfectly natural and intelligible, if they are understood to be merely the varying and imperfect forms under which men, guided by the Spirit of God, endeavoured to body forth, from their several points of view, the better future; but full only of discord and confusion, if their delineations are to be ruled by a prosaic literalism.

In this also, we have a satisfactory answer to the demand,

that is often made for the same kind of events in the prophetic future of Israel, as have appeared in their past history. Both, it is alleged, must be on the same level, equally outward and palpable in the one case, as in the other. If so, then the future in God's kingdom must itself be on the same level with the past; there must be no rise, no progressive development; Christianity must move in the same sphere with Judaism; the history of Providence, instead of ever advancing forward, must turn back to its old channels, and its movements in that direction must even have been more clearly descried by ancient seers, in the dusky twilight, than by apostles and prophets in the bright noon-day of the gospel. To affirm such conclusions, is to place the word of God in antagonism to nature and reason, and to set one part of its revelations in antithesis to another. For the prophecies that were to have their fulfilment in the gospel history itself, lying, so to speak, on the boundary-line between the old and the new in God's dispensations —for such prophecies, a considerable degree of correspondence in the very form, might justly be expected between the terms of the prediction and the manner of its accomplishment—as is often, though not uniformly found to be the case in the recorded fulfilments of the gospels. But when the work of Christ was finished, a higher class of relations entered; the Divine administration rose greatly beyond its former level; and, in so far as prophecy pointed to what should thereafter take place, we should no more expect to see it fulfilled after the precise letter of its announcements, than we should expect the fruit of genius in mature years, to retain the exact type of its early promise.

2. Another essential principle in prophetical interpretation, is the primary and pre-eminent regard, that is ever had in it to the moral element. This appears particularly in two ways. It appears, first, in those predictions which refer to different nations and people, by pointing more especially to the persons or communities composing them, the real subjects of moral treatment, rather than to the territories they occupied. It appears, again, in the conditional character of those predic-

tions, which contain promises of good things to come—these always implying a corresponding spiritual condition on the part of those in whom they are to be fulfilled, and a failure or modification, according to the nature of that condition.[1] Now, it is absolutely impossible to carry out this principle in the interpretation of many of those prophecies, which refer to the future of the Jewish people. For, in these prophecies, Israel does not stand alone, but in connection with the surrounding nations, who represented, in different degrees, the ungodliness and enmity of the world, as Israel was called to represent the truth and holiness of God. But in the light, in which those nations were contemplated in prophecy, they are gone; as distinct and separate communities, maintaining an ambitious rivalry with the covenant-people, they are utterly extinguished; their very existence is numbered among the things that were. How, then, can the prophecies, which speak of either Israel's restoration to the land of Canaan, or their forming in that land the religious centre of a blessed world, be fulfilled according to the letter? It is not the naked fact respecting Israel, of which the prophecies speak, but of this as imbedded amid relations derived from their old historical position. Their return, for example, to their ancient possessions, is described as being made, sometimes with the help, and sometimes to the confusion and overthrow of those, who formerly afflicted them: "They shall fly upon the shoulders of the Philistines toward the west; they shall spoil them of the east together; they shall lay their hand upon Edom and Moab, and the children of Ammon shall obey them" (Isa. xi. 14); "And this man (Messiah) shall be our peace, when the Assyrian shall come into our land: and when He shall tread in our palaces, then shall we raise against Him, seven shepherds and eight principal men" (Micah v. 5); "In that day will I raise up the tabernacle of David that is fallen, and close up the breaches thereof; and I will raise up his ruins, and I will build it as in the days of old; that they may possess the remnant of Edom" (Amos

[1] See Part I., Chap. iv.

ix. 11, 12). To the same class belong also such passages as Zech. xiv. 16–19, and Isa. xix. 23–25, referred to under the last head; for the Egypt and Assyria spoken of as one with Israel, is manifestly not the mere territories, but the people or kingdoms that had their seat of empire there; these it is who are represented as undergoing, at last, an entire change of relationship toward Israel, laying aside their hostility and joining her in brotherly communion. But the people mentioned in all these passages, have disappeared from the stage of history; and neither the restoration itself of Israel, nor the events growing out of it, can be understood according to the letter of the description; in that sense, considerable portions of the prophetic Scriptures can have no proper fulfilment. And why, then, should *any* be supposed to have? Why not understand these also, like the others, as prophetic delineations written in the language and imagery supplied by history? It is undeniable, as we have already shown,[1] that prophecies were sometimes written thus, even such as found their fulfilment under the old dispensation; and it is in accordance with the nature of things to suppose, that what was *occasionally* done in predictions relating to Old Testament times, would be *constantly* done in those which foretold the better things of the New. For, in the one case, it might have been dispensed with, but in the other, it could not; here there was no alternative—the prophets were obliged to avail themselves of the former things to depict those that were to come.

The prominence given in prophecy to the moral element in the other respect mentioned, confirms, still farther, this result. For, the prophecies now under consideration, are all of the nature of promises of good things to Israel; and these God invariably hung, to a certain extent, upon the spiritual condition of the subjects of them; and the determinate thing in them was not the precise mode and measure of the accomplishment, but rather, the purpose of God to do good to His people, and to what extent they might look for his blessing.

[1] See p. 160.

But the proper result was continually marred by their short-comings and sins; and some, even of the most explicit prophecies of this description, referring to the return of Israel from their first dispersion, and their future prosperity in the land—prophecies that should have been fulfilled before the coming of Christ, had never more than a very partial fulfilment. The prediction in Jer. xxiv. 5–7, may be specified as an example, since the Lord there says of the portion of the Jews, that had been carried captive to Babylon, as contradistinguished from the other portion that still remained in Judea, that he would "bring them back to their land, and would build them, and not pull them down, and plant them and not pluck them up." There are various prophecies of a like nature in Zechariah—as at chap. i. 16, ii. 4, where, after the captivity had in part returned, the Lord declared, that he had "returned to Jerusalem with mercies," that it should be "inhabited as towns without walls for the multitude of men and cattle therein," that He would Himself be "a wall of fire round about, and the glory in the midst." So again, in chap. viii. he renews the declaration, that he "was returned unto Zion, and would dwell in the midst of Jerusalem; and Jerusalem should be called a city of truth, and the mountain of the Lord of Hosts, the holy mountain." That these and other predictions of a like kind, intimated what the Lord was ready to do for the people, and what should have been found in the immediate future, seems quite plain; but the want of a proper sanctification on their part rendered the full accomplishment impossible; as in other cases, so also here, the natural had to bend to the moral—the promised good could only be so far realized as the people were prepared and fitted to receive it. In other words, it was not the natural Israel merely as such, but these as the seed of God, the church, to whom the promises were made; and the natural element in the thing promised, necessarily had its amount as well as form determined by Israel's relation to the church, and God's dispensations toward her. Even in legal times, it never was more than a secondary point, whether Canaan was to be the home of the seed of Jacob; what alone gave it importance, was its selection as the chosen theatre of the one acceptable worship, the religious centre of the world. And when no longer needed for this, what should we expect, but that the natural element in the prophecies referred to, should fall yet more into abeyance, and the moral, which has to do with spiritual realities and abiding relations, alone become prominent?

We may say, therefore, in regard to the entire class of prophecies, to which the above examples belong, that from their very nature their fulfilment, according to the letter and form, could not be expected to be more than partial; but as to the substance it becomes complete, though only when the form has passed away. During the time that the temple and Jerusalem stood, and formed the centre of the divine kingdom and worship, the predictions, which were of the nature of promises, received a measure of fulfilment in the case of the true covenant-people to whom alone they properly referred. But from the moment that Christ was glorified, as the temple and Jerusalem lost their original character—as the Jerusalem and the temple, which thenceforth constituted the real habitation of God and the seat of worship, rose heavenwards with its Divine Head (Gal. iv. 26, Rev. xxi. 2), it is in connection with that higher region that we are to look for what yet remains to be fulfilled of the predictions. So long as God's dwelling-place needed to have an outward and local position upon earth, it continued, according to the word of promise, to have it. He did, as he said, encamp round about it, drew towards it from every quarter his sincere and faithful worshippers, and rendered it a fountain of holiness and peace to the children of the covenant. And when Christ personally appeared, and brought in redemption, not for the sins of Israel alone, but for those of the whole world, while he did not take from his people a centre-place of meeting and fellowship with God, he yet shifted its position; he raised it from earth to heaven; and instead of saying, "You shall find me here," or "Go to meet me there," he said, "Lo, I am with you always, even to the end of the world, and to the uttermost bounds of the earth."

So that Zion, considered in its higher and moral sense, as the seat of the divine government, is always a holy mountain, and Jerusalem, viewed as the centre of true worship and hallowed influences, abides still, and in higher perfection than before. Beyond the reach of violence or corruption, it cannot be removed or pluckt up for ever; and the word stands fast, which assured the covenant people of a perpetual residence of God in the midst of them, a home of safety and a fountain of blessing.

3. Another, and quite essential principle of prophetical interpretation, as of every species of writing which is accordant with truth, is that the mode of understanding its declarations must involve nothing absolutely incredible, or contrary to the nature of things. By things of this description we do not mean what may be designated natural impossibilities; for the whole work of grace, like the birth of Isaac and of Christ, is of that sort; it is above nature, and in such a sense contrary to it, that if the laws and forces of nature alone were to operate, it might justly be pronounced impossible. To the heart of faith such things are not incredible, because it takes into account the supernatural grace of God, which does what nature is alike incompetent and unwilling to do, by bringing to its aid a truly divine energy. But there are limits even to the operations of grace, and of the power of God generally. There are things of a providential kind, which we may say God cannot do, as we say, in respect to his moral character, that he cannot lie. And no interpretation of the prophecies can be sound, which, when fairly and consistently applied, would involve the belief of such things being brought to pass.

Now some things of this description, in our opinion, have already been specified under this general head, as flowing from that style of interpreting the prophecies, against which we contend. Such are the self-contradictory statements, which on this literal style are found in them (noticed at p. 94, sq.), since both parts cannot be literally verified; and such, also those, which presuppose the existence of states and communities, that have altogether ceased to exist. These are spoken of, not in the general sense of lands or countries, but of corporate societies and distinct races, standing in a known and definite relation to the covenant-people. In this respect the old condition of things referred to in the prophecies is gone; and gone irretrievably. But there are other things of the same nature mentioned of the covenant-people themselves. Thus the prophecy in Zech. xii., which is commonly pressed as one of the clearest proofs of the permanently separate condition and restoration of the Jews in the latter days, implies the existence of the old organization also as to families; the family of David is represented as mourning apart, and the families of Nathan, of Levi, and of Shimei. In other prophecies of a like nature, the priests and Levites are mentioned apart, even the children of Zadok, as contradistinguished from the other priestly families, and every tribe in its own order (Isa. lxvi. 21; Mal. iii. 3; Ezek. xliv. 15, xlviii.). But all such internal distinctions have long since perished; the course of divine providence has been such as to sweep them entirely away. And from the very nature of the case, such distinctions, when once lost, can never be recalled; the revival of them would involve, not the resuscitation of an old, but the creation of a new state of things. So long as any prophecies were depending for their fulfilment on the separate existence of tribes and families in Israel, the distinction betwixt them *was* preserved; and so also were the genealogical records, which were needed to attest the fulfilment. These prophecies terminated in the Son of Mary, the branch of the house of David, and the lion of the tribe of Judah; but with him this, and all other old things ceased—a new era, independent of such outward and formal differences, began. Hence, we find the apostle discharging all from giving heed to endless genealogies, as no longer of any avail in the Church of God; and the providence of God shortly after sealed the word by scattering their genealogies to the winds, and fusing together in one undistinguishable, inextricable mass, the surviving remnants of the Jewish family. Now, prophecy is not to be verified by halves; it is either wholly true, in the sense in which it ought to be understood, or it is a failure. And since God's providence has rendered the fulfilment of the parts referred to manifestly impossible on the literal principle of interpretation, it affords conclusive evidence, that on this principle such prophecies are misread. In what it calls men to believe, it does violence to their reason; and it commits the word of God to expectations, which never can be properly realized.

The ground on which these remarks are made, holds also in regard to other predictions; for example, to that of Zech. xiv. 16, which speaks of all nations going up to worship every year at Jerusalem, and to keep the feast of tabernacles; to that of Isa. lxvi. 23, which affirms the same respecting the new moons and even the Sabbaths; to that of Ezekiel, chap. xl.–xlviii., which sketches a temple and city and a new distribution of the land, which by no conceivable adjustments can be brought within the bounds of the possible. It was never intended to be so; its aim was to unfold by means of the old external symbols and relations, freshly arranged and expanded, certain great truths and elevating prospects (as we have shewn in our Commentary on that part of Ezekiel); and similar ends were aimed at in all the other prophecies of a like description. By being so viewed, it is true, they are rendered less specific in their meaning, and we can derive little information from them regarding the precise arrangements and forms of things in the latter periods of the Christian dispensation. But then, it never was the design of prophecy to give us such information; this is the province of history, not of prophecy. It is the part of the latter to inculcate great principles, to lay open the springs of God's moral government, to awaken earnest longings and expectations regarding the good in prospect for the people of God, and indicate the greater lines and more marked characteristics of those spiritual movements, on which the destinies of the church and the world are to turn. These are its leading objects; but for subordinate details of providential arrangements, we have no warrant to look to it, unless it be in exceptional cases, such as times of peculiar darkness or great emergency.

4. We shall refer only further—not to an additional principle of prophetical interpretation, strictly so called—but to a particular prophecy—for the purpose of giving what we conceive its true interpretation. We have already done so, indeed, in another place (the "Typology of Scripture," vol. i., p. 416), but must present it anew here, on account of the bearing of the passage on the subject before us. It is the prophecy in Isa. lix. 20, 21, which, as applied in the eleventh chapter of the epistle to the Romans, has been supposed incapable of explanation, excepting on grounds that necessarily involve at least the restoration of the Jewish people. "And so," says the apostle—that is, after the fulness of the Gentiles has come in, and the blindness is again removed from Israel, "all Israel shall be saved: as it is written, There shall come out of Zion the deliverer, and shall turn away ungodliness from Jacob; for this is my covenant unto them, when I shall take away their sins." One not of the least difficulties connected with this passage is the change which the apostle makes on the words of the original. In the prophet, it is *to* Zion that the Redeemer was to come, not *out of* it; and He was to come, not to turn away ungodliness from Jacob, but "to those that turn from transgression in Jacob." Such deviations from the words and scope of the original have appeared to some so material, that they regard the apostle here, not so properly interpreting an old prediction, as uttering a prediction of his own, clothed as nearly as possible in the familiar language of an ancient prophecy. A manifestly untenable view; for how could we, in that case, have vindicated the apostle from the want of godly simplicity, using, as he must then have done, his accustomed formula for prophetical quotations ("As it is written") only to disguise and recommend an announcement properly his own?

We repudiate any such solution of the difficulty, which would represent the apostle as sailing under false colours. Nor can we regard the alterations as the result of accident or forgetfulness. They can only have sprung from design; and we take the right explanation to be this :—The apostle gives the substantial import of the prophecy in Isaiah, but in accordance with his design gives it also a more special direction, and one that pointed to the kind of fulfilment it must now be expected in that direction to receive. According to the prophet, the Redeemer was to come *to* or *for* Zion—somehow in its behalf, and in the behalf also of penitent souls in it—those turning from transgression. So, indeed, he had done already, in the most literal and exact manner; and the small remnant who turned from transgression, recognised him, and hailed his coming. But the apostle is here looking beyond these; he is looking to the posterity of Jacob, generally, for whom, in this and other similar predictions, he descries a purpose of mercy still in reserve. For, while he strenuously contends, that the promise of a seed of blessing to Abraham, through the line of Jacob, was not *confined* to the natural offspring, he explicitly declares this to have been always included—not the whole, certainly, yet an elect portion out of it. At that very time, when so many were rejected, there was, he tells us, such an elect portion; and there must still continue to be so, "for the gifts and calling of God are without repentance;" that is, God having connected a blessing with Abraham and his seed in perpetuity, he could never recal it again; there should never cease to be *some* in whom that blessing was realised. But, besides, there must here also be a fulness: the first fruits of blessing gave assurance of a coming harvest. The fulness of the Gentiles itself is a pledge of it; for if there was to be a fulness of these coming in to inherit the blessing, because of the purpose of God to bless the families of the earth in Abraham and his seed, how much more must there be such a fulness in the seed itself? The overflowings of the stream could not possibly reach farther than the direct channel. But then, this fulness, in the case of the natural Israel, was not to be (as they themselves imagined, and as many along with them still imagine) separate and apart; as if by providing some dispensation of grace or external position for them individually. Of this, the apostle gives no intimation whatever. Nay, on purpose, we believe, to exclude that very idea, he gives the more special turn to the prophecy, so as to make it *out of* Zion that the Redeemer was to come, and with the view of turning away ungodliness *from* those in Jacob. For, the old literal Zion, in the apostle's view, was now gone. Its whole framework was presently to be laid in ruins; and the only Zion, in connection with which the Redeemer could henceforth come, was that Zion in which he now dwells, which is the same with the heavenly Jerusalem, the church of the New Testament. He must come *out of* it, at the same time that He comes *to* or *for* it, in behalf of the natural seed of Jacob. And this is all one with saying, that these could now only attain to blessing in connection with the Christian church; or, as the apostle himself puts it, could only obtain mercy through *their* mercy—namely, by the reflux of that mercy which, issuing from Israel, has gone forth upon the Gentiles, and has been bearing in their fulness. It is one salvation, one blessing for both parties alike, which Israel had the honour to bring in, and was the first to receive; but which they shall be among the last to receive fully.

Thus explained, both the prophecy itself, and the apostle's use of it, are in perfect accordance with his principles of interpretation elsewhere, and with those we have endeavoured to establish. And it holds out the amplest encouragement in respect to the good yet in store for the natural Israel. It holds out none, indeed, in respect to the fond hope of a literal re-establishment of their ancient polity. It rather tends to discourage any such expectation; for the Zion, in connection with which it tells us the Messiah is to come, is the one in which He at present dwells—the Zion of the New Testament church; *to* which he can no longer come, except at the same time by coming *out of* it. Let those, therefore, who already dwell with him in this Zion, go forth in his name, and deal in faith and love with these members of the stock of Israel. Let them feel that in such evangelistic work, the presence and power of the Lord are pledged to be with them; and let them do it in the sure conviction and hope that the conversion of Jew and Gentile shall happily react on each other, till the promised fulness on both sides is attained. For this important work, and the animating prospects connected with it, they have sure ground to go upon; but for local changes and external relationships, they have none; and it is no part of the design of prophecy to lead the Christian church either to wait for such, or to work for them.

CHAPTER III.

THE PROPHETICAL FUTURE OF THE CHURCH AND KINGDOM OF CHRIST.

UNDER this general head may be comprised all that requires to be said, in an elementary treatise like the present, on what the prophecies unfold respecting other topics connected with the Christian dispensation. These topics all stand related in some manner to the condition and destinies of Christ's church and kingdom. They are presented, however, under different aspects and relations; and it is impossible to arrive at any satisfactory knowledge of the general purport of what is written, without either going through the prophecies in order and giving a regular exposition of their contents, or endeavouring to exhibit, in connection with a few leading points, the light they collectively throw on the tendencies and results of gospel times. Either way it were scarcely possible to avoid a certain degree of complexity and repetition, as both the prophecies themselves, and the subjects of which they treat, frequently run into each other. But by being viewed in a definite order and connection, there will be found less of repetition than might otherwise be possible, and there will also be secured a more distinct continuity and progression of thought. We, therefore, adopt this latter method, and, in following it, shall take the latitude that is indispensable to a proper investigation of the subject—not confining our survey to what may still with some confidence be reckoned the prophetical future of the gospel dispensation, but embracing also what might be regarded as future from the era of its commencement.

SECTION I.

THE CHURCH AND KINGDOM OF CHRIST IN THEIR RELATION TO THE KINGDOMS OF THIS WORLD.

THE prophecies which relate to this subject are, in one sense, of great variety and compass, but in another of comparatively limited extent. They are the one or the other, according as we have respect to prophecies of a general, or to prophecies of a specific and determinate nature. Those of the former class begin with the times of David, when the great promise of blessing, originally given to Abraham, first assumed a distinctly personal shape, and became linked with the expectation of one in David's line, on whom the hopes and destinies of the world were to depend. In the series of predictions originating in this covenant with David, and unfolding its prolific import, whatever other topics are introduced the kingly character of the expected Messiah always holds a prominent place; and not only that, but also the sure and final ascendancy of His kingdom over all the rival powers and kingdoms of the world. His right to rule in the affairs of men was to be alike absolute and universal; and however resisted for a time, and left apparently to struggle for existence, the destination of this king was to be that of one "conquering and to conquer," till everything was subdued, and all became subject to His hand. There is not one of the more properly Messianic Psalms in which this progress and result are not exhibited, though some dwell more particularly on one style and aspect of the history, some on another. And such also is the character of those predictions scattered through the prophetical books, which, on the ground of the promise made to David, point to the future establishment of Christ's church and kingdom. In general, they begin by exhibiting an inherent contrariety in spirit between the things pertaining to this Divine kingdom, and those of the world—the one being of God, therefore holy, just, merciful, and blessed; the others of the earth, and partaking, in consequence, of its selfishness, carnality, and corruption. Then, as the natural result of this inherent contrariety, the mutual antipathy and death-like struggle for the mastery is depicted, and that with infinite fulness and diversity—the kings of the earth, with all whose characters bear the earthly impress, appear combining together, taking counsel, and, with consummate malice and energy, striving to crush the person and arrest the progress of the heaven-appointed King. But all in vain. It is not He but they who suffer in the conflict; He goes on like a resistless hero, lifting up the head, while they fall under the arrows which He sends forth in the cause of truth and righteousness; so that but one of two alternatives is before them, either to yield themselves to His sway, or to perish under the stroke of His indignation. And, finally, in the last lines and issues of the prospective delineation, the cause and kingdom of Messiah become everywhere triumphant. The kings of the earth, in so far as they have not fallen under His wrath, are seen walking in His light, and doing homage to Him; their kingdoms have become, in a manner, *His* kingdoms; all the ends of the world turn to the Lord, and the families of the nations worship before Him—throughout the earth "one Lord, and His name One."

Now, in respect to the substance of these prophecies, only a comparatively small portion of them can be said to belong to what is still the future of the Christian church—that, namely, which relates to the absolute completeness and universality of the kingdom of Christ. The other and larger, as well as more circumstantial parts of them, which describe the mutual antipathy and struggle, the rise of the personal Messiah and His cause from small beginnings, and in the face of the most violent and long-continued opposition, till the greater part of the old civilized world owned His supremacy, and many kings, nominally at least, did homage to His name:—

All these belong to the past; their fulfilment is legibly inscribed in the records of the world's history. And in regard to what still remains to be accomplished, though we cannot but see in the present state of the world, and even of the professing church, many great and discouraging obstacles in the way of success, yet when viewed in the light of what has already been achieved, they cannot with certainty be pronounced insurmountable to Christian effort and resources. The small mustard-seed *has* sprung up into a lofty tree; and whatever hindrances there may be tending to impede farther progress, and prevent ultimate success, they are of the same kind with those over which the truth has in a considerable degree prevailed, and which no one has a right to say it cannot wholly overcome. Besides, who can tell what special providences may be in store to favour the advancement of truth and righteousness? How many changes and revolutions, even of a civil and literary kind, may arise fitted to strike at the root of prevailing errors and superstitions, and prepare the way for the triumph of the cross? Above all, as living Christianity spreads, and the feeling grows among enlightened and earnest minds, that the highest well-being of the world is bound up with the diffusion of the gospel, what seasons of refreshing, in aid of their exertions, may not be sent from the presence of the Lord? In such considerations there is enough to make the contemplated issue probable, even without any great departure from the regular course of events; and that it shall somehow take place is the united testimony of all the predictions referred to. Christ shall reign till His enemies have become His footstool, and shall cause the knowledge of the Lord to cover the earth as the waters cover the sea. The word of prophecy can never reach its full accomplishment till this result is attained.

But while the result is very distinctly and frequently announced in this class of predictions, nothing very particular is intimated in them as to the relation of Messiah's kingdom to the kingdoms of the world individually. These kingdoms are viewed in the general, as all alike opposed to the character and claims of Messiah, and alike also destined to submit or be destroyed. It is not doubtfully indicated of some of them, that, in process of time, they would renounce their hostile for a friendly position, and help forward the cause they at first sought to withstand: as when David speaks of "princes coming out of Egypt, and Ethiopia stretching out her hands to God" (Ps. lxviii. 31), and when Isaiah makes promise to the church, of kings being her nursing-fathers, and queens her nursing-mothers, of the forces of the Gentiles coming to her, and kings ministering to her (chap. xlix. 23, lx. 10, 11)—with many more of a like kind. Such passages plainly imply, that while the struggle was still pending between the cause of Christ and the powers of the world, while the people of God were still in need of help for the conflict in which they had to engage, different nations with their rulers, would successively give in their adherence, and contribute their aid to the final result. But in what way, or to what extent this might be expected to take place, we can learn nothing from such general predictions.

We turn, therefore, to the other and more specific class of prophecies, which, as we said, are comparatively limited in number. Indeed, they are peculiar to Daniel and the Apocalypse; and in these, again, are so related to each other, that those of Daniel, form the foundation of what is written in the Apocalypse; the latter simply resuming the subject, as it had been left by Daniel, and prosecuting it farther into detail. We shall, therefore, glance first at the prophetic outline which is exhibited in Daniel, and then consider the subsequent and related visions of the Apocalypse. The view, presented in both respects, must necessarily be brief and confined to the more leading features.

I. The prophecies in Daniel, which have respect to Messiah's kingdom in its relation to the kingdoms of the world, are those contained in chap. ii. and vii.—the one containing Nebuchadnezzar's vision of the great composite image, with the interpretation of it by Daniel, and the other, the vision and dream, given to Daniel himself respecting the five monarchies. That the two visions relate to the same subject, and differ only in presenting it under diverse aspects, can admit of no doubt. The diversity also (as previously noticed, p. 110), has its foundation in nature, and is in perfect accordance with the relative position of the parties, through whom the visions were given. It is the external aspect of the matter that is presented in the vision of Nebuchadnezzar, while the internal is brought out in that of Daniel. The heathen king sees such a symbol of the kingdoms of this world and of the kingdom of Christ, as was adapted to the carnal eye, which has a capacity for apprehending the *appearances* rather than the *realities* of things. The man of God, however, has an eye that looks beyond the surface; he must see things as they really are; and so, the vision presented to him, while it may be said to follow in the same track, and cover the same field with the other, lays open the actual nature of the different kingdoms—the minuter shades of difference in the worldly kingdoms themselves, and their collective and fundamental difference from the kingdom of Christ.

1. This contrariety, however, and those differences are not entirely overlooked in the vision of Nebuchadnezzar; they are indicated there also—but only on the external side, and from the point of view, in which it was natural for the Chaldean monarch to contemplate them. It is in this light that the various materials of a natural kind in his vision are to be considered. They are symbols—but not of the relative worth and greatness of the several kingdoms respectively; for then the fourth kingdom, imaged by the iron, must have been inferior to those which preceded it, and the fifth, the Divine kingdom, having only a stone for its emblem, still again inferior to it. Nor, for the same reason, could the progressive descent in the value of the materials be intended to mark a progression in the world's degeneracy and rooted opposition to the work and kingdom of God.[1] These are not the points of

[1] This idea is taken up by Auberlen (p. 200-6), who, at some length, seeks to make out, that the materials of the image symbolize a twofold

comparison which come here into notice, or which would have been proper for such an occasion. The person, to whose mind the image was presented, was the representative of a grand, though, for him, intensely carnal and selfish idea—that, namely, of having the whole world reduced under a single head, and fused together into one mighty empire. He was not content, like those who had preceded him in the field of ambitious rivalry or conquest, with strengthening the foundations of his dominion at home, or increasing his power and resources by subjugating foreign countries to his sway. His ambition towered higher; he sought to be himself the one lord of the earth, and to have his kingdom like the gigantic tree that afterwards imaged it, "reaching unto heaven, and the sight thereof unto the end of the earth," It was, indeed, the idea of a Divine kingdom among men—but, as attempted to be realized by the Chaldean monarch, a vain and presumptuous parody of the idea, not a proper realization. This, however, it must be remembered, is the point of view, from which the whole vision is to be contemplated; and by a reference to this, must the properties of the different materials be taken into account. In themselves, therefore, and as component parts of the image, they are symbols of the apparent relative fitness of those successive monarchies to fulfil the destiny at which they severally aspired, of becoming, in the proper sense, universal kingdoms.

Let us see how admirably they do it. In the first place, as standing at the top of the list, and representing the idea in all its freshness and majesty, Nebuchadnezzar and his dynasty are fitly represented by the head of gold. Then, comes the

progression—that of a growing civilization and culture (indicated mainly by the brass and iron), and along therewith a growing contrariety to the truth and holiness of God. In this he forgets the last material mentioned, which, though not a part of the image, still belongs to the vision, and belongs to a lower territory in nature than the iron. If the qualities of the other things are to be made account of, in the manner he suggests, the stone also must be included. But it is only from Nebuchadnezzar's point of view, that the whole is to be considered and each element interpreted.

Medo-Persian, physically, indeed, stronger at the time of its appearance, than the monarchy it supplanted, yet inferior (as it is expressly called, verse 39), in respect to the main point under consideration; because in its very foundation it was of a divided nature; formed by the junction of two races who differed considerably in their religion and other characteristics; and never properly cohering together in its several parts, nor presided over by heads fitted to consolidate its interests: therefore not less fitly represented by the secondary metal of silver, and by the breast and arms of the image—in which not compact unity, but rather doubleness and division are prominently exhibited. Brass is remarkable for its pliancy, for the fine polish of which it is susceptible, and the brilliant glitter it emits. As such, therefore, nothing could more appropriately symbolize the third great kingdom, which began with the splendid achievements of Alexander, and carried in its train the high intellectual culture of Greece. But withal, it betokened little durability or consolidating strength; and the part of the image that was formed of this material, the belly and the thighs, gave indication of a loose, disjointed, heterogeneous state of things, that could not hold well or long together. How exactly emblematic throughout of an empire which aimed at universal sovereignty, and seemed as if, by a few brilliant efforts, it should succeed in the enterprise, but which fell asunder at the death of its founder, and became henceforth, the prey of intestine divisions! Where it failed, however, the gigantic Roman empire, which comes next upon the stage, particularly excelled, and far outstript all its predecessors. The slow and steady growth of ages, Rome struck her roots deep, wherever she obtained a footing, and left the impress of her sovereign will, and of her imperial laws and institutions on every region of the ancient civilised world. "The arms of the republic," says Gibbon, as if writing the interpretation of this part of the vision, "sometimes vanquished in battle, always victorious in war, advanced with rapid strides to the Euphrates, the Danube, the Rhine, and the ocean; and the images of gold and silver or brass, that might serve to represent the nations and their kings, were successively broken by the *iron* monarchy of Rome." Yet, while it could break and beat down every thing opposed to it in the existing powers and dominions of the earth, while it grew and prospered till it had become co-extensive with the known world, it could not secure for itself the eternity, which it so ambitiously aimed at. There was in it, indeed, the strength of the iron; but the legs of the image, which were composed of that material, themselves indicated division—a division strikingly exemplified by the partition of the empire into the two sections of the East and West; and still farther, when, as symbolized by the toes and the feet, part of iron and part of clay, the irruptions of barbaric hosts entirely broke up its unity, and with the introduction of fresh races upon the theatre of the world, brought in also new elements into its social arrangements and civil institutions.

Thus as regards the component parts and the various distribution of the great image in this vision, every thing finds its striking verification in the annals of history. Indeed, the verification is so striking, and the parallel so exact in all its parts, that we cannot but discern the impress of the same Divine hand in both; the very conception and distribution of such a symbolical image was as manifestly from God, as the successive rise and the varied characteristics and fortunes of the gigantic empires, which fulfilled its prophetic import. Nor does the correspondence fail, it becomes, if possible, still more wonderful, when we look at the aspect presented of the last, the only truly universal, and everlasting kingdom in the world. It is from this point of view, that the subject is still to be contemplated; as thus only can we see the fitness of the material chosen to represent the divine kingdom. A stone is, indeed, a poor emblem of such a kingdom, if viewed with respect to the proper nature of the kingdom, and the high objects it is designed to accomplish—the one gross, earthly, rigid, dead; the other spiritual and heavenly, all instinct with life and blessing, and with pliant energy adapting itself to every relation and circumstance of being. But in the particular respect now under consideration, in the fitness and destination of this kingdom to supplant the other kingdoms, and attain to the universality and permanence of dominion, which they vainly strove to possess, what better emblem could be found than that of a stone! Massy, firm, compact in structure, crushing in the dust the looser and softer materials with which it comes in contact, and itself, not only retaining its original unity, but growing into a huge mountain, and filling the whole earth with its vastness! Here at last was the sublime idea of the Chaldean monarch realized; but realized in a very different way from that in which his fond ambition was prompting him to attempt it. Existing altogether apart from the image, which symbolized the kingdoms of the world, this stone evidently pointed to a kingdom entirely different in its origin and nature from theirs: a stone, not graven like the other by art or man's device, but cut out from the unhewn rock, and cut without hands—how expressive of a kingdom formed by the immediate operation of the Great Architect of nature! and, as such, partaking of the irresistible might and the endless duration of its Divine Author! Every thing, therefore, gives way before it; it destroys in its progress whatever is contrary to it, and itself at length possesses and fills all.

It remains to be asked, how much of this prophetical outline belongs to the past, and how much to the future? The question has been variously answered, according to the different views entertained by writers on prophecy, respecting the character and prospects of Messiah's kingdom. But, looking simply to the language of the symbolical prediction, there are, it will be perceived, two points in which the description appears indefinite—the one is as to the precise time, when this divine kingdom, represented by the stone, should make its appearance; and the other, the precise manner, in which its establishment should actively press on the other kingdoms, and cause their annihilation. In regard to the first of these points, it is merely said, that "in the days of these kings shall the God of Heaven set up a kingdom, which shall never be destroyed" (ver. 44). By the "days of these kings" have sometimes been understood the latter stages of the fourth monarchy, when it became subdivided into many separate states. But, while this rent and broken condition is plainly referred to in the vision, it is not described as being distinguished by separate kings or kingdoms; and, therefore, the only reference to which the days of the kings can legitimately apply, is the collective period of the kings or kingdoms symbolized by the image. The language is purposely indefinite. It does not indicate at what particular time, or even under what precise dynasty, the kingdom represented by the stone should begin to develop itself on the theatre of the world—though, from being mentioned the last in order, and from the fourth worldly kingdom being the one, with which alone it appears coming into collision, the natural inference obviously is, that the commencement of the heavenly kingdom is to be assigned to the fourth or last form of the earthly one. The whole of these successive monarchies of the world are taken together, as but different phases of the same worldly principle; in a somewhat different form the old always lived again in the new; so that the image which represents the entire series, appears still standing in its completeness—the several successive kingdoms, which it symbolized were to the last ideally present; but, from the nature of the case, they could only be so as seen in that, which was more immediately represented by the legs and feet of the image. Even here, however, there is an indefiniteness; for, while the stone is spoken of as pressing with irresistible force upon the image first when the history had reached to what is symbolized by the feet, it is not said that the stone then for the first time appeared. On the contrary, before the stone smote the image, we must think of it as taking form in the world; it must be viewed as coming into substantive existence, as being cut out, before it began to act aggressively; the rather so, as it is not the simple appearance of this divine kingdom, and its universal establishment, that is the subject of the vision, but its growth from small beginnings onward to complete and ultimate success. The moment of the bruising, therefore, is not necessarily, nor even probably the moment of the actual formation of the stone; and a period seems to lie there of indefinite length—the period of the rise and early progress of Christianity, when, by an agency altogether its own, and holding directly of God, it gradually advanced to a distinct organization, and a form, in which it could act extraneously upon the affairs and destinies of the world.

The other point mentioned had respect to the manner in which the establishment of Messiah's kingdom was to tell on the worldly kingdoms. This is described in the action of the stone, as that of bruising the image, so as to render its component elements, the iron, the clay, the brass, the silver, and the gold, like the chaff of the summer threshing-floors, which the wind carries away. A sublime image truly of their evanescent nature, as compared with that which destroyed them, and of their utter disappearance from the face of the world! But if we ask, in what respect, or by what kind of operation was this work of demolition to be wrought, nothing definite is indicated; nor, indeed, could it be from the nature of the representation; for it is only (as we have repeatedly stated) the *external* aspect of the matter that is here presented to the view—the appearances and effects of things alone are described. So far as these are concerned, we are distinctly informed that the whole of the magnificent image, which engrossed the vision of Nebuchadnezzar—or, in plain terms, that a world-embracing monarchy, such as he contemplated, presided over by one human will, and directed for the glory of its earthly head, in every shape and form, which it might assume, was doomed to perpetual destruction. And that, not as a thing of itself dying out, but as a thing put out, and for ever abolished by the establishment and the progress of that divine kingdom, to which alone the real universality and the absolute right of governing upon earth was to belong. This, it is well to be noted, though it is too commonly overlooked, is the only kind of abolition spoken of in the vision; it is not the subversion of constitutional government, and the dissolution of earthly states and kingdoms (a subject not brought into consideration here), but simply the extinction of those ambitious monarchies, which grasped at the dominion of the world, and the causing them to disappear for ever by the establishment of a higher kingdom, in which the idea they sought to embody was to be, and alone could be realized. Has, then, the introduction of Christ's kingdom wrought such an effect? We answer, unhesitatingly, that it has. And if we are asked how? we reply, in the only way, in which such gigantic and self-deifying schemes could be effectually abolished—by rendering men familiar with divine realities, with elevating principles, with heavenly aims and prospects. It has spread through humanity a regenerating leaven—the sense of God's redeeming love to man; and by the wondrous acts of mercy and gifts of grace, therewith connected, has diffused far and wide the feeling of the brotherhood of man, yea, and breathed the spirit of a new life into the history and aspirations of the world. It has thus, even with the manifold imperfections that have attended its working and progress on earth, for ever antiquated the idea of a universal monarchy, in its old and grosser sense; and shewn this to be alone possible in the hands of Him, who as at once God and man, Lord of heaven and earth, combines in his person the qualities, and holds at command the gifts, necessary to the establishment of such an empire. Since the diffusion of Christianity, the only thing in a wrong direction, that has properly aimed at, or has ever seemed in any measure to possess, the character of a world-embracing dominion, is the parodying by corrupt doctrine and a false usurpation of this divine kingdom itself. But that is an essentially different matter from the old world monarchies, and falling within the domain of spiritual things, is brought out, as we shall see, in another connection.

2. So much, then, for the first great prophecy of Daniel on the point before us—the relation of Christ's church and kingdom to the kingdoms of the world. Like those previously noticed, it speaks chiefly of the past, so far as anything definite and particular is concerned; but points also to

the future; inasmuch as it declares the absolute universality of Messiah's authority and rule among men, His unlimited and everlasting sway. This is yet far from having been established: while the stone has broken in pieces the image, which sought to pre-occupy the entire ground, it has not yet itself grown so as to fill the whole earth. Let us turn, then, to the other prophecy in Daniel—the vision and dream recorded in the seventh chapter—and see if any further insight is furnished on the subject. Here, as already noticed, it is the internal aspect of the kingdoms to which prominence is given—their respective characteristics and differences, first in regard to each other, and then in regard to the kingdom of Christ.[1] Viewed as a whole, the worldly kingdoms have their representation in so many wild beasts, because in them the beastly principle was predominant—that is, the earthly, sensual, grovelling tendency, with all its selfishness of working and its debasing results. In Nebuchadnezzar's personal history, the man's heart was taken away, and a beast's heart for a season given him (Dan. iv. 16)—as a judicial sign and token from the hand of God, that by living, as he had been doing, for the gratification of his own selfish desires, and for having all made subservient to his own grovelling ambition, he was acting the beastly, rather than the human part. And, accordingly, when the man's heart returns to him, with the wisdom to use it aright, his eye at once turns heavenwards, he rises above self and the world, and acknowledges his dependence on the power and goodness of the Most High, who does, as he expressed it, according to His will among the armies of heaven, and the inhabitants of the earth. We can have no doubt, therefore, as to what is meant by beastly

[1] We take it for granted, that the succession of kingdoms in this case is the same as in the other, and that the attempts of some modern Germans, followed by Moses Stuart, either to divide between the Median and Persian kingdoms, or to take Alexander's kingdom for the third, and that of his successors for the fourth, with its ten subdivided kings or kingdoms, have palpably failed. They have been thoroughly refuted by Hofmann, Hengstenberg, and latterly by Auberlen.

natures being chosen to represent the successive worldly monarchies: it intimates, that they were to be so many personifications of earthliness—all pervaded and governed by the same prone, ungodly, carnal, and self-deifying spirit. In fitting accordance with such a common character, they are also represented as having a common origin: they appear rising together out of the sea, at the moment of its being driven and agitated by the winds of heaven; in other words, they spring from beneath, from the lap and bosom of earth; nor from this in its better moods, as it exists in seasons of peaceful repose, but when moved by violent commotions, heaving and agitated by the fierce passions and tumultuous elements raised by sin. What real good could come, or what lasting creations proceed, from such a mode of generation?

In respect to the characteristic differences among the several worldly kingdoms, it is unnecessary to say much. Under the emblem of a lion with eagle's wings, which were afterwards plucked, itself also placed in a standing and erect posture upon the earth, no longer slavishly directed to this, but having a man's heart given it to look upward, we have a representation of the Babylonian empire, as exemplified in its head: first, its lion-like majesty and strength, combined with the winged speed of its march to conquest and dominion, and its soaring sublimity of spirit; then, the checks and arrests laid upon it, rendering farther enlargement impossible; and, finally, the humbling providences, which forced on it a sense of the power and sovereignty of God, and with the loss of dominion brought reason again to the ascendant. Then, by means of a beast like a bear, raising itself on one side, with three ribs in its teeth, and a command given it to devour much flesh, we have an image of the Medo-Persian kingdom—in its general thirst for blood and conquest (comp. Hosea xiii. 7, 8, with Isa. xiii. 15–18; Jer. li. 20–24), its notorious disregard and lavish expenditure of human life, its originally composite character, as if one side were dissimilar to the other, and by the strength of one chiefly (the Median) it was to arise for the work of conquest, with the three-fold direction in which it was to have its appetite in this respect satiated.[1] The panther or leopard comes next, with four wings of a fowl, as for flying, and also four heads; one living creature, yet with a fourfold partition in the very seat of life and motion, and having dominion given to it: a strange compound, but strikingly expressive of the Grecian monarchy, which, in its movements, like the leopard, was remarkable for the quickness and rapidity of its spring, as also for cunning and dexterity in seizing its prey (Hab. i. 8; Jer. v. 6), and which, after having astonished the world by its elastic energy and wonderful feats of prowess, in the person of its founder, split into four dominions, which survived till a much greater than they overspread the field. This greater empire, the greatest of all in its aspirations after worldly dominion, and the most extensive and lasting in its ascendancy, the Roman, is most aptly represented by a nameless monster, "dreadful and terrible, and strong exceedingly, devouring and breaking in pieces, and stamping the residue with its feet, and diverse from all the beasts that were before it." This was, unquestionably, the characteristic of the Roman power in the days of its vigour and conquest. For, though it was a part of Rome's policy, to treat the nations she conquered with many marks of respect and kindness, to leave especially their religion and social manners untouched, and to fill them with sentiments of veneration and attachment to the "eternal city;" yet the whole aim of her administration was directed to the purpose of moulding every province and state of the world into one vast empire, and consequently to destroy and obliterate every sign of national independence—to merge the individual in the universal. The other kingdoms that preceded her, were comparatively rapid and hasty in their formation; they neither possessed nor displayed anything like the skill and pains put forth by Rome, through a succession of ages, with

[1] Compare chap. viii. 4, where the ram representing the Medo-Persian empire, is described as pushing westward, northward, and southward—Babylon, Lydia, and Egypt, being perhaps more immediately intended.

the view of smoothing down national peculiarities, and compacting them into one huge system of universal government. All the more remarkable, too, on her part, that the whole was done, not, as in the case of the rest, for the aggrandisement of one man or family, but from a systematic and hereditary love of rule in a city and people; so that the name of Rome became itself a kind of magic influence, and the gigantic sway connected with it, formed the nearest approach that could be made, in a mere earthly government, to a kingdom of spiritual influences, and living dependence on an invisible Head. It was still, however, far from this, and in spirit and tendency as diverse from it, as in other respects from the worldly kingdoms that preceded it.

Strong as this empire was, compact in its organization, and spirit-like in its power and influence, it contained, like everything earthly, the elements of dissolution and decay. This was indicated in the former vision by the legs of the image, the feet of iron and clay, and the toes of the feet. And here it is brought out by means of ten horns, which were seen on the beast, and which are afterwards explained as the kings (meaning thereby kingdoms,) which were to arise out of the fourth empire. By arising out of it must be meant, that they were to be historically connected with it, and to be in a sense its continuation; as there can be no doubt that the various kingdoms, which sprung up after the irruptions of the barbarians into the Roman empire, had much in common with Rome, while in policy and character they were diverse from it; they still had her laws, her language and literature, her institutions and customs, for the basis of theirs.[1] There was, however, too much of the new to admit of a proper amalgamation with the old—as was intimated in the vision of the image, by the mixing of clay with the iron, and the attempts at union by intermarriages and compacts, "mingling themselves with the seed of men," yet not cleaving one to another. But this, and everything, indeed, of an individual kind,

[1] For some remarks on the number ten, see the concluding portion of Section 3 of this Chapter.

respecting the ten kingdoms, is here passed over, as in haste, in order to concentrate attention on that peculiar kingdom, diverse from all the others, which was symbolized by the little horn, which came up among the others, and which is represented as not only plucking up three of these others, but also as taking such a part against the kingdom and people of God, and exercising withal such an influence over the rest, that it drew on the judgment of the whole. Nothing whatever is said of this extraordinary power in the former vision; for it manifestly comes within the domain of the church, and is much more a spiritual than a civil and earthly dominion; so that it did not properly fall within the range of Nebuchadnezzar's view, which, with strict propriety in adhering to the natural as the basis of the supernatural, was confined to the outward and temporal aspect of things. On this account, also, we refrain from here adverting more particularly to what is said of this horn or kingdom, as, we think, there can be no reasonable doubt, that it is to be identified with the antichrist, and will, therefore, fall to be considered under our next division.

But it is in connection with the wickedness practised through the instrumentality of this power, and the judgment to be inflicted upon it, and all its abettors, that the fifth, the Divine, and alone universal and everlasting kingdom, is here introduced. On this occasion it appears, not in its rise and progress, but in its strength and glory, and for the execution, more immediately, of the work of judgment. First, the Ancient of days, as He is called, v. 9, the Eternal God, is represented as appearing, on account of the heaven-daring spirit manifested by the power in question, and the evils it was occasioning among men, and, with thrones of judgment set, and streams of fire issuing from before Him, as well as myriads of attending spirits, proceeding to reckon with, and condemn to deserved punishment, the offending parties. These—that is to say, the wicked power itself, and the other powers or horns which were led to take part with it in the evil—are spoken of as being consigned to a common funeral-pile;

while the rest of the beasts had only their dominion taken away, and their lives prolonged for a season and time. The same apparent anomaly occurs here as in the vision of the second chapter. All the symbolical characters appear to the last as existing together on the stage; while, from the description given of them, they are not contemporaneous but successive powers, each rising on the ruins of its predecessor, so that, historically, all the preceding ones must have been gone ere the last rose to the ascendant. The reason, however, of admitting such an anomaly, and of conceiving of the other powers as still existing, was merely to bring out more distinctly the moral truth involved in this part of the delineation. Those earlier forms of the worldly power, while all rooted in sin and essentially ungodly, were yet far inferior in guilt and wickedness to the last, especially as represented by the little horn, with its outrageous blasphemies, and disastrous influence in the church, and violent persecutions against the saints of God. Therefore, when the time for judgment comes, this last must appear first—the stroke of vengeance must alight directly, and with its heaviest retributions, upon the power which has done most to provoke its inflictions; and bad as the fate was of the others, having lost in the taking away of their dominion all that they contended for, it seemed mild as compared with the doom now appointed to the consummate offender. *There*, pre-eminently, the carcase appeared; and *there* the eagles must primarily be found gathered together.

It is evident, then, that this part of the vision is framed with a view to one great object—to render prominent the moral element in the history of God's dispensations. The delineation of the worldly side of the picture is carried on continuously (as very commonly in prophecy) till it reach its culminating point; the iniquity of the worldly power, in its last and most aggravated phase, grows till it becomes full; and then the righteous kingdom, with its Divine head, comes forth to condemn and cast out the evil. It were quite a mistake, however, on this account, to suppose that the kingdom of God had no existence in the world till this terminating part of the process; and would evince as great a misunderstanding of the proper import in one respect as it had been in another, to suppose the continued existence of the three first kingdoms as actual powers in the world, down to the time that the judgment is represented as taking effect upon the last of them. It is, throughout, an ideal representation, formed so as to exhibit, in the most effective manner, the real tendencies and final issues of things; and, as a natural consequence, matters are compressed into a single act which might be the product of ages, and events appear in close juxta-position, which, in actual history, might stand ever so far apart. So was it, for example, in Isaiah's vision of the doom of Babylon (chap. xiii.), and Ezekiel's vision of the destruction of Tyre (chap. xxvi. 7, sq., xxviii.); the work which it was to take centuries to accomplish, is presented as a thing devised and executed at once. We are not, therefore, to suppose here that because the doom of the worldly power is represented in a similar manner, that it is to fall by a single stroke; or that the kingdom, through which the consummating act is to be inflicted, then for the first time enters upon the stage of history. Indeed, the reverse is manifest, from the dream-part of the vision given in explanation of that which was seen. In the vision itself the prophet saw thrones set (so it should be rendered at ver. 9; not cast down, but set or placed down) for kingly persons being seated upon, in order to pronounce judgment, implying that the judgment was not to be the act simply of the Eternal, nor the inflicted doom to proceed straight from the bolt of Omnipotence. But who were those assessors in judgment? By whom was it that the powers of evil were to be judged and cast out? By looking to the explanations in ver. 19–27, we learn that they are not the angels, as has too commonly been supposed (these are never represented as judging, always only as ministering spirits), but the saints of the Most High, the same saints who, along with the Son of Man, are to possess the kingdom. It is to them that the work of judgment on the worldly power is committed (ver. 21); it is they who sit in judgment, and take away his dominion, and consume and destroy it to the end, and, in turn, receive the kingdom for an everlasting possession, of which the other has been dispossessed (ver. 26, 27). But whence should these saints have come? How have they attained to such numbers, and such authority and power? Not, we may be sure, of a sudden, or by any miraculous intervention of Providence. They can be none other than the members of the kingdom, which has been in existence since the Lord came from heaven to found it by His incarnation and blood. And their appearing here in such numbers, and with such judicial authority and power, merely indicates that the kingdom to which they belong has at length acquired the mastery; the cause of righteousness and truth, with which it is associated, has become triumphant; and the interest opposed to these vanishes from the field, as smitten with irrecoverable perdition. So long as that interest appeared to prevail and prosper, it seemed as if God's rectitude slumbered; and men were disposed to sigh with the Psalmist, Oh! that He would awake to the judgment, that He would establish the just! But when the reverse takes place, when the cause of wickedness goes down, they are equally ready to feel and to say, Thou satest in the throne, judging right; Thou hast destroyed the wicked (Ps. vii. ix.).

II. These views of the vision before us are fully borne out by the representations given in the Apocalypse. Indeed, the whole drama in that mysterious book, from chap. iv. onwards, may be said to be a simple expansion of this part of Daniel's vision, by following it out into detail. There, in the opening vision, we have presented to our view the Ancient of Days on the throne, with the Son of Man (as the Lamb) in the midst of it, and round about the central throne four-and-twenty other thrones (so it should be, not *seats*), for the four-and-twenty crowned elders, the representatives of Christ's royal priesthood, or entire membership of a redeemed church. The scene is, in truth, an ideal representation (precisely as in Daniel) of the Lord, and His assessors in judgment, the saints, whom He exalts to sit with Him on His throne, and destines to possess with Him the kingdom. These appear together in the attitude of dealing judicially with the ungodly world, and preparing the way for the final occupation of the inheritance. Hence thunders, and lightnings, and voices proceed from the midst of them (ver. 5), the awful signs of coming wrath; and the seven-sealed book is opened, which contains in successive stages the world's doom and the church's victory; and scene after scene follows, with sounding of trumpets and pouring out of vials, during which the same action is constantly proceeding to its proper issue. The whole ends, as here, with the utter destruction of the beast, and with the saints living and reigning with Christ upon the earth; in other words, possessing the kingdom. So that, were it otherwise doubtful, the scheme and arrangement of the Apocalypse would make it certain and manifest that the brief and vivid representation of Daniel in reality covers an extensive field of operations; that it embraces the general progress, as well as the final result of Christ's cause upon earth, and includes the main substance of the Book of Revelation. Only, while Daniel, for the reasons already stated, points more directly to the close of the action, St John unfolds the numerous stages by which it was to be reached, the many windings and evolutions in the work of judgment upon the world, till judgment is brought forth into victory.[1]

In this general outline of the scenery and action of the Apocalypse a fair idea is conveyed both of the common agreement and the characteristic differences, which pervade the representations of the two Apocalyptists. They are precisely such as might have been expected from the one theme they had to handle, and the different positions they occupied in relation to it. Where the one merely gives a result, as seeing everything from afar, the other, speaking from a nearer point of view, gives us a process, with many attending characteristics alike of its nature and of its issue. While the look of Daniel

[1] Compare what is said in Part I., Chap. v., Sec. 4, near the beginning.

into the future, also, is inward, as compared with that of Nebuchadnezzar, it is, as might have been expected, far inferior in depth and inwardness, especially as regards the affairs of the Divine kingdom, to that of the Evangelist. On the other hand, the worldly kingdoms, amid which Daniel was standing, and which were then only beginning to run their ungodly career, occupy a place in his visions, which they no longer possess in John's; here it is the last only, and the last chiefly in the latter stages of its history, that is particularly dwelt upon, as it was with this alone now, that the people of God had to do. We shall, therefore, present in a few leading points what is peculiar in the representations of the Apocalypse on the subject before us, and shall notice, as we proceed, the relation (whether of correspondence or diversity), in which they stand to those of Daniel. Occasion also will be taken to draw attention to some features in the latter, which have, as yet, not been more than cursorily referred to.

1. We notice first the representation that is given in the Apocalypse of the worldly power. In Daniel this appeared under a succession of beasts, each symbolizing a new and somewhat different form of the great monarchies of the world. But now it appears simply as a beast (chap. xiii.), a beast, however, that had the same origin with those of Daniel, like them rising out of the sea, and a composite creature, uniting together the several forms of the three first in Daniel (the lion, the bear, and the leopard), and possessing also the ten horns, which were seen in the fourth. These points of coincidence with the vision of Daniel, plainly indicate a fundamental agreement, and, at the same time, such a difference as is obtained by the compression of a diversity into a unity. The beast of the Apocalypse, accordingly, is the worldly power, not in its several parts or successive forms of manifestation, but in its totality. Having already passed through its earlier phases, and reached its last regular form, it is naturally represented as one, or rather, as a composite whole, possessing still all that it ever had of a beastly, grovelling, God-opposing character, combining them together in its present visible realization.

There is no essential difference in this from the view given in Daniel; for there also, as we have had occasion to notice, both the four beasts, and the several parts of the image, were represented as at once successive, and in a sense also co-existing. The seven heads in the beast of the Apocalypse, present more of an apparent dissimilarity, and may seem at variance with the notion of an essential oneness between it and the monarchical symbols in Daniel. For these were only four, corresponding to the number of kingdoms, in which the general idea exhibited in them was attempted to be realized. How, then, if referring substantially to the same thing, should John have seen seven heads upon the beast—heads with crowns, consequently denoting so many kingdoms? The main reason, no doubt, must be sought in the reality, which the symbol represents, and which must somehow have been contemplated in a sevenfold aspect by the Evangelist. He afterwards tells us in chap. xvii. 9 (for, we hold it as a settled point, that the beast there discoursed of, is identical with the one here), that "the seven heads are seven mountains"—which may certainly have some reference to the seven-hilled city of Rome, where the beast then had the seat of his dominion; but it cannot possibly rest there, or have that for its chief reference; since in a description otherwise entirely symbolical, the term "mountains" cannot be taken in a merely literal sense, nor without respect to its usual emblematical import of states or kingdoms. We have no doubt, however, that it does carry, in the first instance, an allusion to the seven hills of Rome. But to prevent our resting in this literal sense—to lead us rather to regard those Roman hills as themselves the symbols of something higher, a kind of natural indication of the concentrated worldliness of Rome, as in a manner combining in her dominion all the phases of the worldly power, it is immediately added, "and they are (not "and there are"), seven kings"—meaning thereby, so many kingdoms, according to the uniform import of the word in this connection. There is, therefore, a double reference; and hence it is introduced with the saying "Here is the mind which hath wisdom," to intimate that there is something peculiar and enigmatical in what follows—and that it contained, if rightly understood, an important key for the understanding and application of this part of the vision.[1]

Still, with this explanation of the language, the question recurs, why should the worldly power have appeared to the Evangelist in a sevenfold aspect? To suppose that it has respect to seven forms of government that successively appeared in the Roman commonwealth, from its commencement, is entirely arbitrary and fanciful. Any changes of a merely political kind, Rome might have undergone, and before it came into contact with the church, are of no moment as regards the subject of this prophecy; they mark for it no epochs, and lie altogether outside the territory on which it moves. It treats of the worldly power only in its relation to the kingdom of God, and of that in a collective respect, as it has existed and manifested itself throughout history. The sevenfoldness ascribed to it, therefore, must be, not seven forms of government in one state, but seven different states or forms of dominion, in which the worldly spirit, in its self-idolatrous and God-dishonouring form, successively embodied itself. And these the Evangelist finds by simply taking a wider range of view than Daniel, as he was naturally called to do, and contemplating the matter in its whole historical compass. Thus surveyed, the number seven readily occurred by adding to the four of Daniel, first, the Egyptian and Assyrian kingdoms, which preceded, and which as regards their own character and their relation to the Divine kingdom, were essentially one with the others; then the new and divided state at the close into which the dissolved

[1] There is a precisely similar use of the literal as symbolical of the figurative in the description of the whore, which, with reference to the historical Babylon appeared sitting on many waters (ver. 1)—so Babylon of old did, having near and around her, the streams and canals of the Euphrates, one of the great sources of her fertility and wealth—but, like Rome's seven hills, in respect to the seven kingdoms, so the waters of ancient Babylon are explained of "the peoples, and multitudes, and nations, and tongues," (ver. 15).

Roman empire fell. As it was of these chiefly that the Evangelist was called to treat, and as they were to hold, in some respects, a very different relation to the kingdom of God, from that of heathen Rome, they quite naturally came to be represented as an additional head of the beast. Indeed, Daniel himself gave a sort of occasion for their being so regarded, by representing them under the emblem of clay, which did not properly assort with the iron of ancient Rome; in one respect, they belonged to it, but not in another. In what respects their relation was to differ, will appear in the sequel; but, meanwhile, as it was one leading object of the prophecy of this book to exhibit the difference, and to reveal the peculiar part those kingdoms were to play in the history of God's church, the state of things they were to introduce might well be entitled to rank as a new and final phase of the worldly power.[1]

In the realities of the subject, we thus find a solid ground for this part of the symbolical representation. But an additional ground may also be noticed, in the connection exhibited between the beast, or worldly power, and the devil. This also is one of the points of difference between the Apocalypse and Daniel, one of the indications it gives of a deeper insight into

[1] It was Hofmann, we believe, who, in more recent times, suggested this mode of interpreting the seven heads of the Apocalyptic beast, though by leaving out Egypt, and dividing between the Greek empire generally, and Antiochus, he arranged the matter somewhat differently. But it is in reality the ancient interpretation, the same substantially, which is given in the oldest connected commentary on the Revelation—that of Andreas of Cæsarea, who lived about the end of the fifth century. He also began with Assyria, and made the Median as well as the Persian monarchy a separate kingdom. These, however, are differences only as to detail; the fundamental idea is the same; and we refer to the antiquity of the interpretation, as a proof, that it is really one not very far to seek. It is the tendency of Protestant interpreters, in later times, to find Rome, heathen and papal, everywhere in the Apocalypse, which has given currency to the idea of seven Romish forms of government, being indicated by the number—an idea wholly arbitrary and incapable of yielding satisfaction.

the spiritual world, since it lays open, in respect to the movements of evil upon the earth, the mighty, though invisible influence of Satan. The outward manifestations of the worldly power are here but the signs of Satan's working; and, as in the history of the fall, when he identified himself with the serpent, so here the beast is at once the image and the instrument of Satan. As the one, therefore, appeared under the form of a great dragon, with seven heads and ten horns (chap. xii. 3), so must the other, that is to reflect his nature and exercise his power. And seven is peculiarly the sacred number; as such it is constantly recurring in the book of Revelation, and is used as an emblem of the Spirit of God, in His active operations in the church ("the seven spirits of God," chap. i. 4, iv. 5, v. 6). Hence, it is the number which Satan may be supposed to affect, especially in those operations in which he tries to deceive and corrupt the church of God. In those he ever seeks to parody and imitate the work of God's Spirit. We, therefore, think (with Auberlen, p. 270), that some respect may be had to this consideration in the use here made of the number seven. But we are not disposed to lay much stress on it, and regard the other reason stated as undoubtedly the chief one.

2. We turn now from the apocalyptic representation of the adverse or worldly power, to that of the church and kingdom of God. Here, also, while we have a fundamental agreement with the visions of Daniel, we have important and characteristic shades of difference. Indeed, we may say, it is the kingdom only, and not what we more properly understand by the church, that has any representation in the two visions of Daniel. He speaks simply of the kingdom that was to supplant the worldly monarchies, and obtain the everlasting and universal dominion they aspired after. And we must attend for a little to the form, under which he presents it, as this not only contrasts in a striking manner with the representation given of the other kingdom, but also lays the foundation of the more special language used in the Apocalypse, and in other parts of the New Testament. The other kingdoms have their emblematic representation in so many wild beasts, be-

cause they were to be in their pervading spirit and operations more beastly than human. But when the divine kingdom appears on the field, the form that represents it is one "like a son of man," and "coming with the clouds of heaven." Though the form is simply human, there is evidently connected with it a superhuman elevation. For it comes, not like the base representatives of mere earthly rule, from beneath, but from above, and riding in the peculiar chariot of Deity, the clouds of heaven; and it might seem but the fair conclusion that here also the form was indicative of a higher nature than outwardly appeared—that the human likeness, to be properly human, required to be associated with the divine. It is, therefore, to give but a poor and partial exposition of the subject, to say, that it meant the Messiah "would be a human, not an angelical, or any other kind of being; for, in the oriental idiom, *Son of man* and *man* are equivalent."[1] Let it be so, the question remains, why should the head and representative of this kingdom alone have been exhibited in the form of a man, while all the others, who really *were* men, should have been symbolized by so many beasts? And why, having the likeness of a man, should he have been represented as coming, not like the others, from below, as cast up by the waves of a raging and tumultuous sea, but descending from the lofty elevation and serener atmosphere of a higher world? Why such marked differences if the *human* alone was all that the expression, with its attendant circumstances, was designed to exhibit? It is true, that the form here, as in the other cases, was not simply personal, but emblematic; indeed, it might not (for aught that could have been certainly gathered from the vision itself) have been personal at all; it might merely have been intended to represent symbolically the nature of this kingdom, which God was going to erect, as contradistinguished from the rest. In that respect, it denoted, that while in them the merely animal powers and sensibilities should come into play, terror and physical force should prevail,

[1] Dr Campbell in his Dissertations on the Gospels.

all downward and grovelling tendencies should rise to the ascendant, in this divine kingdom the nature of man should attain to its true dignity, and, re-united to the life of God, the moral elements of its being should be brought into proper exercise, and a softening, humanizing influence be diffused through the entire domain. But then, who could be the instrument of setting up such a kingdom? Like all the others, this kingdom must have a head, from whose spirit and character the whole was to take its impress, and one, in whom personally, and through whom instrumentally, the true ideal of humanity was at length to be realized. Was this work, so different from what man had hitherto achieved, an undertaking for man alone to effect? Unquestionably not; and hence, in the vision, the human form representing at once the head and nature of the kingdom, appears as the denizen of a higher sphere, and the personal associate of Godhead. It indicated that the ideal should remain an ideal still, so far from being realized, continually outraged and trodden under foot by the ascendancy of the baser elements in nature, till the human should be interpenetrated by the divine, and God should in very deed dwell with men upon the earth. Every thing, therefore, is in its proper place and character:—As the devil had from the first assumed the beastly form in the serpent, whose nature it is to crawl upon the dust, so now in the Son of Man, God was to appear in the form of man, to raise all above the beastly, and conform it to the spiritual and divine.

Such seems the fair and natural explanation of the epithet, "Son of Man," as originally and prospectively used in the vision of Daniel. And it is fully confirmed by one of the first recorded appropriations of it by our Lord. This occurred in the course of his conversation with Nicodemus, when he said, "And no man hath ascended up to heaven, but he that came down from heaven, the Son of Man, who is in heaven" (John iii. 13). It sounds like a contradiction, and might, at least, have seemed an unintelligible enigma, but for the vision in Daniel, to which it manifestly refers, and which fully justifies and explains its meaning. No man, it is thus found to declare, who simply *is* a man, fallen and degenerate, as mankind now are, ever has ascended to heaven; his progress is all in the contrary direction—not upwards to heaven, but downwards to earth and hell. The Son of man, however, in whom the idea of humanity was to be realized, in whom it is found according to its original type and destination, as the living image of God,—He belongs to the heavenly; *that* is His proper region; and when he appears (as he now does) on earth, it is because in what properly constitutes his being and character, He has come from above. This thought, too, it should be observed, respecting the head of the kingdom of God, was most fitly introduced in connection with a discourse on the necessity of regeneration from above, in order to admission into the kingdom. The head of the kingdom, the realized ideal of humanity, is Himself from above; He is emphatically "the new man," "the Lord from heaven;" and so, all who hold of Him, and are to participate in the rights and blessings of His kingdom, must be *made* new; their humanity must be regenerated after the pattern of His, and by virtue of the divine power with which He is replenished. Thus only can there be a proper correspondence between the head and the members; and thus only can the earth be filled and possessed, according to the promise, by a kingdom of saints, in room of the corrupt and brutalizing powers, which have so long held possession of the field.

In the same way is to be explained another application of the term, which, from overlooking the reference made in it to the original prophecy, has very commonly had a mistaken or inadequate sense put on it. The passage is in John v. 27, where our Lord speaks of Himself as having received authority from the Father to execute judgment upon men, "because He is the Son of Man." Taken by itself the passage contains a seeming incongruity. But connect the assertion with the prophecy of Daniel—regard it as indicating the divine-human (perfectly human, because, at the same time, really divine) person and character of Messiah, through whom the everlasting kingdom of righteousness was to be brought in, and by whom, along with his elect people, the powers of evil were to be adjudged and cast out; and then the meaning and reason of the statement become obvious. He now announced Himself as the new man, to whom was to be "put in subjection the world to come," and who, therefore, held at his command both the regenerating grace necessary to establish the good, and the judicial power and authority commissioned to expel the incorrigibly evil. Nor can there be any reasonable doubt, that it was mainly on this account He so commonly designated Himself in His public discourses by the title of the Son of Man, rather than any other. He would thereby lead men to regard Him as the type of what humanity should be, and as come on purpose to found the kingdom in which, according to ancient prophecy, it was to be generally exemplified. And, doubtless, also, it was a reference to the same prophecy which led to the so frequent designation of the kingdom of Messiah as that of "the kingdom of heaven." The expression, like that of the Son of Man, was taken from Daniel; and was employed rather than "the kingdom of David," because more directly pointing to the divine and spiritual character of the kingdom, and thereby fitted to correct the mistaken notions of the Jews respecting the Messiah's reign. But as Son of Man applied personally and emphatically to Jesus, was all one with Son of David, so what in accordance with some prophecies was called the kingdom of God or of heaven, can be no other than that elsewhere identified with the throne of David.

Turning now to the Book of Revelation, we find the whole of its representations regarding the affairs of the New Testament church based upon the same views. The book speaks throughout of the kingdom and coming of Christ. And in the opening vision, which presents us with an ideal delineation of Him, from whom all its revelations came, his appearance is described (precisely as in Daniel) to be that of a "Son of man," while the great theme of the revelations is to make known, how, as such, he was to proceed in bringing into subjection "the world to come." We have thus at the outset a clear indication of the close relationship between the Apocalypse, and the visions of Daniel. When viewed in this connection, also, the Book itself is seen to be of a piece—made up of two equally necessary, and though different, by no means heterogeneous parts. The symbolical description of Christ's person at the beginning, and the addresses to the seven churches, unfold the nature of the kingdom, over which as Son of Man he presides, and shew how far the idea had begun to be realized, how far it had failed in a series of particular churches. This portion is in reality the foundation of all that follows, and supplies the standard by which its other descriptions are to be ruled; for it brings fully and distinctly out the mind of Christ on such important topics as these—what kind of persons he would recognize as "the saints," who were to possess with him the kingdom—in what manner they were called to make good their title to the character—what seductive influences and threatening dangers should strive to hinder them from attaining it—what prospects of bliss and glory awaited them, if they did attain it; what condemnation and judgments, if they failed. It is by what is written on these points in the direct addresses, that we are to interpret what is afterwards symbolically written concerning the church: we have here the criteria for determining what is such in the estimation of her Divine Head, and for discerning between the true and the false.

Then, in regard to the other and prospective part of the book, we find a striking divergence in the form of the representation from that of Daniel, but one that naturally arose from the different and more advanced position of the Evangelist, and necessary as a cover, under which to present the more minute and varied aspects of the future, that were now to be unfolded. Standing at a point so far removed from the Messiah's kingdom, Daniel could only have revelations given him of its general character and destinies. Even the form under which it was imaged to his view, was symbolical rather than personal—symbolical of the whole in the first instance, and only by inference admitting of personal application to an individual. But now that that ideal form had become embodied in a glorious personality, that the foundations of the kingdom also had actually been laid, and matters were in a train for reaching the destined consummation, it became necessary in some way to distinguish between the head and the members of the church, as also between the church in a militant and imperfect condition, and the church prepared for her final inheritance. This is done without any essential, but only by a relative, change in the symbol: the *human form* is retained for the new prospective delineation of the church, but the *female*, not the *manly*, type of the human. Taken complexly, the human still makes up the representation of the kingdom, but as the kingdom now falls into two parts, so does the symbol, which represents it: Christ, the Son of Man, the male son (ὑιον ἀῤῥενα, Rev. xii. 5), as He is called, to denote the perfection of his manly nature, and the church the woman; the one the antithesis to the dragon, and the other to the beast. For this division there was even from early times a Scriptural foundation. The relation of God to Israel began under Moses to be spoken of in terms borrowed from married life (Ex. xxxiv. 15, 16; Num. xiv. 33); and in many of the prophets it is formally compared to this relation—God is the husband, and Israel the wife (Isa. l. 1, liv. 1; Jer. ii. 2, 20; Ezek. xvi., xxiii.; Hosea i. iii.). The forty-fifth Psalm, also, and the Song of Solomon, are extended representations of the same idea. And it meets us again from time to time in the pages of the New Testament; in the words of John the Baptist (John iii. 29), and in various parabolical statements of our Lord (Matt. ix. 15, xxii. 1, xxv.), followed by others of the apostle Paul (2 Cor. xi. 2; Eph. v. 25–32). But in these latter passages, Christ, being as truly divine as He is human, occupies the place formerly ascribed generally to God; and now also the prevailing form is that of the bridegroom on the one side, and of the bride on the other; as if the union could not properly be consummated, so long as the church is in so inferior a condition, compared with her Divine Head, and must stand over till she has become complete in number and perfect in holiness. Most appropriately, therefore, the Evangelist, whose peculiar calling it was to disclose the existing imperfections of the church, the seductions with which she was to be but too successfully plied, and the many trials and humiliations through which she must pass on her way to glory, presents her under the aspect of a woman—a woman espoused, but not yet married—while militant and incomplete, the Lamb's bride, but at last, when the troubles of time are over, and its corruptions done away, the Lamb's wife, sharing with Him in all the blessings and honours of the kingdom.

We should note, however, how careful the apocalyptist is, before he exposes the perils and defections of the church, with their sad and fearful issues, to exhibit ideally the church's perfection; he first of all unfolds what she is in calling, what she should ever aim to be in character, and what in the consummation she is destined to be in the reality. We have this description at the beginning of chap. xii. There she appears as a woman in heaven—in the same blissful and elevated region with her Divine Head; for *there* her citizenship lies, as well as His (Phil. iii. 20). Not only so, but her condition is in full accordance with her place, she is clothed with the sun—the grand luminary of heaven, and the uniform emblem of a truly divine and celestial glory, as contrasted with the darkness and corruption of the world. Ideally, therefore, the church has heaven's light and glory for her own—according to Isa., chap. lx. 1, "Arise, shine, for thy light is come, and the glory of the Lord hath risen on thee." And as a natural consequence, she stands nobly superior to the corrupt attractions of what is reckoned glorious on earth; she feels that she is called to higher and better things. Hence she appears, not only clothed with the sun, but having also the moon under her feet—the comparatively little orb, which has, indeed, a measure of light and glory, but such only as is derived from the earth, and which altogether belongs to the earthly sphere—fit emblem of the riches, the culture, and the honours of the flesh, which all perish with the using. These the true church keeps beneath her feet; they are not her real glory, or her proper portions. Finally, her head is emblazoned with a crown of twelve stars—emblems of her proper representatives, the twelve apostles—emblems of them and those they represented, as called to shine and rule with Christ. *Their* position, also, is in the heavenly sphere; they are, one and all, by their Christian calling, bearers and dispensers of the light of heaven; placed aloft, and endowed with their respective gifts, that they may exhibit the mind and truth of God to those who are sitting in darkness and corruption. What a lofty idea! Would that the church had from the first kept it stedfastly before her eye, and striven with unflagging zeal to have it realised! How innocuously should the darts of the adversary then have fallen upon her, and from what sloughs of corruption, and seas of blood, should she have been preserved! And would she but do it yet! For, the moral pestilence still wastes within her borders, and the work of judgment for apostacy is far from having run its course. But in this we are anticipating what belongs to another department.

3. We turn, then, to a third point, the last we shall advert to in connection with this branch of the subject—the representation given in the apocalypse of the relation of the spiritual to the worldly power, or of the kingdom of Christ to the kingdom of the prince of this world.

Proceeding on the deeper insight he has obtained into the spiritual region, and the more detailed aspect which it thence became necessary to present of spiritual things, the apostle here divides between the church and her Divine Head. He gives, first, in the case of the latter, a compressed view of the nature and issue of the conflict, as carried on in the entirely spiritual sphere, of which that afterwards to be carried on through the church, on the visible theatre of the world, was to be, on the whole, though not without many grievous backslidings and partial failures, a reflex. The representation in this first part has necessarily a retrospective, as well as a prospective, aspect—a circumstance not unusual in visions, which require to connect the past with the future, in order to give a comprehensive view of the reality (for example, in Daniel's visions of the image and the beasts, and St John's account of the seven-headed beast). The appearance of the head of the kingdom is sketched from its commencement. As he was to be born of a woman, and through her made under the law, so the church is represented as a woman (personally exemplified, of course, in Mary), travailing and in pain to be delivered of what was at once her great burden and her great hope—the long-expected man-child. But while she is in this position, the dragon (who is simply the devil, in his relation to the powers of this world, Ps. lxxiv. 13; Ezek. xxix. 3; and personified for the time in Herod) stands ready to devour—his chance of success being now suspended upon the destruction of this child of hope, and his whole energy in consequence directed to the accomplishment of the object. How likely, to human view, that he should succeed! He, on the one side, being possessed of such enormous power, that seven crowned heads are needed to represent his might on earth, and in heaven the third part of the stars are carried off by the sweep of his tail (*i.e.*, a large proportion, like a third, of the world's *spiritual* lights and rulers, corrupted and destroyed by his influence); while, on the other, all that appears is a feeble and helpless child, seemingly an easy prey to the devourer! But the destiny of this child is to rule all nations with a rod of iron—to rule them so as to break their hostility, and bring them into subjection to God. And the destiny must be fulfilled; for it is of God. Therefore, the power and malice of the adversary are defeated; the child, having escaped the dangers, and triumphed over all the difficulties that encompassed it in the earthly sphere, is caught up into the heavenly sphere, and seated in the very throne of God. And now, in this higher sphere, everything is reversed; with the rise of the Son of Man, on the ground of His perfected redemption, to be the Head of all principality and power in the heavenly places, the fall of the prince of darkness follows as its proper counterpart. He is, therefore, cast down from the higher region of power—the conflict having been fought and won against him, in regard to its fundamental principles—and he is reduced to the position of a mere earthly head; so that all he can even appear to do of evil, is in respect to the body of Christ, the church, during her continuance among the relations of sense and time.

This is, of course, to be understood as an ideal representation, like the rest of the vision, though resting on a historical basis. It seems, therefore, entirely out of place here (with various writers, both British and Continental), to draw from this passage, in conjunction with some others of a like nature, the conclusion that, up to the time of Christ's ascension, Satan was allowed to mingle freely with the angelic hosts, while afterwards that liberty was withdrawn. Nor is there any better foundation for the idea expressed by some, that the transition of Satan, from heaven to earth, indicated an enlargement of his influence and operations in the affairs of men. The reverse is plainly meant; as, throughout the prophetical Scriptures, the symbolical action of falling, or being cast down from heaven, always denotes a loss of power and authority. It is Satan's downfal, therefore, which must here be understood, necessarily bringing with it a restraint to his operations, not the giving of an additional licence or effect to them. If an increase in any respect might be thought of, it could only be in the greater bitterness and guile which he would endeavour to infuse into his policy, on account of the defeat he had sustained on the high places of the field. In respect to this, he is said to have come down, "having great wrath." And when our Lord declared, even while on earth, that by reason of the mighty power He exercised, and the work of perfect righteousness and mercy He was performing, "He saw Satan fall like lightning from heaven," and that "the prince of the world was judged and cast out" (Luke x. 18; John xii. 31), he plainly teaches, that what is to be understood, and the whole that is to be understood, by such language, is this capital abridgement of power and dominion. We say the whole, for, if taken more literally, the different passages would manifestly run counter to each other—what in one place is described as the result of Christ's ascension, being, in the others, represented as taking place before it.[1] Understood figuratively, the casting down of Satan might be connected with different periods, as the result it indicated had successive stages. But, in a comprehensive ideal delineation, it was most fitly connected with our Lord's ascension to the right hand of power and glory, as this formal elevation on the one side necessarily inferred a corresponding depression on the other. It is with Christ's personal work and history, therefore, according to the natural import and bearing of the passage, that the statement should here be connected, and not with the age of Constantine. And since the question has been thus settled as between the respective heads of the two kingdoms, how certainly must a like result follow to all connected with them? What occasion can there be any more for despondency or doubt as to the issue, if there be but the eye of faith to discern the Divine Redeemer enthroned within the vail, having all angels, principalities, and powers, made subject to Him?[2]

But, now, this sure foundation being laid in the heavenly sphere, and the triumph on the side of good secured once for all, personally, by the Redeemer, the apocalyptist proceeds to set forth the progress and issues of the conflict in that lower sphere, which was still open to the adversary, in the history of the church in the world. Here the comparative advantage of the adversary is indicated in the very symbol

[1] It is perfectly gratuitous to represent our Lord's statement in Luke x. 18 (as some do; for example, Mr Birks in his Outlines, p. 99), as spoken prophetically; it is plainly spoken of what was at the time proceeding. And, though the figure is different, the idea is the same in Col. ii. 15, where the triumphing over principalities and powers is connected with the death of Christ.

[2] We have taken no special notice of the conflict in the heavenly places being, in chap. xii. 7, 8, ascribed to Michael and his angels; holding it to have been virtually settled by Ode (De Angelis, p. 1032, sq.), Vitringa, Hengstenberg, etc. on the passage, that Michael is but another name for Christ—a name given Him in special connection with this great conflict to indicate the certainty of His success, grounded on His divine nature, for it means, Who is like God?

used to represent the object of his malice and guile—the woman, humanity in its weaker division, over whom he so fatally triumphed at the commencement of the world's history. Some allusion is, doubtless, made to the circumstances of the fall in this part of the representation; but the mystical drama that follows has rather for its historical basis the relations of Israel under the old covenant, and the manifold experiences and transactions through which they passed. For the evil as well as for the good, the materials of the representation are found there. It is with the exhibition of the good that the story begins and also ends. It discloses what should pertain to the true church (the chaste and faithful spouse) in her preservation from the assaults of the destroyer, her trials, her victories, and final deliverance and glory; but much of the intermediate portion is taken up with the other and darker side of the picture—the history of the false church (the adulterous mother of abominations), her apostacy and corruption, deserved and irrecoverable doom. It is, however, with the former and better portion alone of the prospective delineations that we have at present to do, as the things written of the other belong to what properly lies outside the Christian church, though nominally within—the antichristian apostacy—and will fall to be considered under our next division.

The church, then, as represented by the woman, the true spiritual mother of children, when pressed with the dangers raised against her, flies into the wilderness—that is, into such a hiding-place as might be found in some secure and silent retreat,—a flight that had its first historical exemplification in the temporary withdrawal of Mary, and the infant Jesus, to Egypt, to escape the persecution of Herod. This original withdrawal was the sure prelude of many similar expedients that should need to be resorted to in the future. And, accordingly, no sooner did the members of the church become large enough to attract the public notice of the world, than they were scattered abroad, reviled, buffeted, driven from the public walks of society, and glad often to find an asylum in what were comparatively the dens and caves of the earth. Speaking generally, however, her place of retreat might be regarded as what is called in Ezekiel (chap. xx.), "the wilderness of the peoples"—the moral deserts of the earth—in the first instance, Rome and the other cities of heathendom, which were the world's deserts as compared with the land of Judea, where Christianity had its birth, and afterwards, when the earlier places of refuge had themselves become theatres of danger or bloodshed for the followers of Jesus, the more obscure and unenlightened parts of the empire. Such places of retreat from the world's thoroughfares were to be to the true church in Christian times much what the wilderness of old was to Israel, refuges of safety at once from outward violence and from moral pollution; and with evident allusion to this, it is said that the place was prepared for her by God, and that the wings of a great eagle were given to bear her to it (chap. xii. 6, 14, comp. with Ex. xix. 1–4; Deut. xxxii. 11). In former times, the Lord had borne His people, as on eagle's wings, away from the violence, oppression, and contaminating influence of Egypt, to a place of safety, and of wholesome discipline in the wilderness; and the same was to be done also in the case of the Christian church. The old was substantially to recur again. In spite of all the efforts of the adversary to strangle her in her birth, she should be preserved, and nourished, as with food from heaven, for a certain space, the mystical period of 1260 days.[1] The adversary, however, follows her into her wilderness-retreat. He "sends out of his mouth a flood after her, that he might cause her to be carried away by the flood" (ver. 15). This flood is an emblem, not of things in the spiritual sphere, such as corrupt doctrines, or false teachers, for these cannot, according to the symbolical import of the dragon, be the direct and proper emanations of *his* mouth, but of the vast hordes, the teeming and fluctuating masses, which the prince of darkness raises up and influences to effect his purposes of mischief (compare chap. xvii. 15 with Ps. cxxiv. 4; Jer. xlvi. 8; Isa. viii. 8,

[1] See, on this number, Sec. 3, at the close.

etc.) These never assumed more of a flood-like appearance, or were employed with a more hostile design, than in those ages, when the irruptions, especially of the Germanic tribes, convulsed the whole fabric of society, and threatened to bring back a state of universal barbarism. Had such a result actually ensued, the cause of genuine Christianity had inevitably been lost, for it can only maintain its ground, and diffuse its regenerating influence with proper effect in an orderly and peaceful state of things. But the Lord again restrained the violence of the storm. He made "the earth to help the woman," *earth* being taken symbolically for a designation of the world in its more settled aspect, as the *sea* for its heaving and tumultuous conditions. The meaning, therefore, is, that what is firm and solid in the constitution of the world set bounds to its more restless and wayward elements, so that the wild chaos of disorder, which for a time prevailed, again took shape, and the several states of modern Christendom came gradually into being. During this phase, therefore, of her connection with the world, the church was to be, and, by the evidence of history actually was, both oppressed and protected, now evil-treated, and again screened and saved from the destruction meditated against her, through the instrumentality of the powers and kingdoms of the earth.

But another phase of evil commenced when this was over. The cessation of the world-floods by no means exhausted the malice and resources of the tempter. "The dragon (it is said, ver. 17) was wroth with the woman, and went to make war with the remnant of her seed, which keep the commandments of God, and have the testimony of Jesus Christ." The words too plainly indicate that the dragon had not altogether failed in his object by the troubles and disorders he had already raised against the church. At the beginning of the conflict, it was said generally of her members, that "they overcame him by the blood of the Lamb, and by the word of their testimony" (ver. 11). But now the *remnant* only of the woman's seed are spoken of as keeping God's commandments and the testimony of Jesus. The war needs to be continued only against a portion of the seed, a faithful remnant, implying that another, and, indeed, a larger portion had already been won over to the cause of the enemy, and were virtually on the dragon's side. The great apostacy, in short, was to have begun, and even made much progress, before the dark epoch, marked by the upbreaking of the old Roman empire, had run its course. How truly the history here also coincides with and verifies the prophetic outline needs no proof to intelligent Christians.

The descriptions that follow in several succeeding chapters, may be regarded as an expansion of the announcement contained in this last verse of chap. xii.; they give a symbolical representation of the kind of war waged by the beast against the woman, the unflinching resistance given to it on the part of the true seed, the honour and glory they, in consequence, received from God, and the judgments sent down to avenge their cause, and punish the apostacy and wickedness of that other portion of her seed, who were to take part with the adversary. It is here, that the seven-headed beast rises first into view; for it was only now, that the church was to come into conflict with those later operations of the worldly power, which it was the more especial design of the Apocalypse to unfold. But as the conflict had, in reality, begun before that, and was even coeval with the birth of the New Testament Church, therefore, the representation is here also in part retrospective; as is evident from the seven heads which embrace the whole of the successive phases of the worldly power, and perhaps, also from the period assigned (chap. xiii. 5), to his dominion, forty and two months, or 1260 days, the very same period, during which the church was to be in the wilderness (chap. xii. 6). But the sojourn of the church there, as we have said, was the immediate result of what took place on our Lord's ascension, and embraces, not merely what ensued after the dragon sent forth the flood, or multitudinous hosts after her into the wilderness, but the whole of her trials and contendings there. If this number, therefore, is not entirely symbolical, and even if symbolical but not arbitrarily used, its employment here must be regarded as indicating the past, as well as the future, ascendancy of the worldly power in respect to the church. But it is the future that is more particularly depicted—the actings of the worldly power after it had begun to assume its last head. And here, first of all, the striking peculiarity is mentioned, that one of its heads appeared to be as it were wounded to death (ver. 3). This we take (with Auberlen), to mean, that a change, in regard to the worldly power's ostensible relation to the church (for in that respect alone is it represented under the aspect of a beast), was to take place; in one of the forms of its manifestation it was not, indeed, to be actually and properly killed, but to appear *as if it were wounded to death: i. e.*, to drop for a season its wonted appearance of hostility to the cause and kingdom of God—to cease, for a time, to act as a beast; which it could only do by assuming either a truly religious, or a professedly religious character. Now something that precisely answers to this change did take place about the period in the church's history, to which the symbolical delineation refers—the period, when the sixth head of the beast tended towards the seventh and last, when the Empire began to totter to its fall, and fresh races strove to form themselves into new states and dynasties. It seemed then, as if the beast had received a deadly wound; for in the last stages of the old Roman empire, and in the formative epoch of the new states, the beast apparently passed into the woman, through the formal reception of Christianity by the ruling powers. The beast then, as is stated in the corresponding passage in chap. xvii. 8, 11, "was not, and yet was;" for the deadly wound was presently healed; the old spirit of contrariety to the mind of God, and conformity to the flesh and the world, soon returned though under another form, and as a kind of Christianized paganism. Nay, and to mark the character of this modern heathenism, its more subtle, demon-possessed, artfully-contrived nature, the beast is said to come now, not as formerly from the sea, but "from the abyss:" as if in a state of closer union with the power and cunning of the adversary. So that the work of self-deification began to proceed anew (chap. xiii. 4, "They worshipped the beast, saying, who is like unto the beast?"), and the blaspheming of God (viz., by the usurpation of Divine prerogatives), and the war against the saints. It is even said respecting the latter (ver. 7), that it was given him to overcome them; the reverse of what had been testified regarding the early part of the conflict, when it was said (chap. xii. 11), that *they* overcame *him* by the blood of the Lamb and by the word of their testimony. Now, on the other hand, *he* overcomes *them*—which, of course, implies, that they renounced their confidence in the blood of the Lamb, and played false with the word of their testimony. They did so, not by utterly casting off the profession of the faith—for then they would simply have belonged to the worldly power itself; but by falling in with the secularized Christianity, which that power had espoused; by ceasing, in short, to be the proper bride of the Lamb, and becoming (as is fully represented in chap. xvii.), the whore borne up by the beast. As in the world before the flood, and in Israel before the captivity, the church was to join hands with the world, and assuming an essentially worldly position, was to set itself against the real interests of God's kingdom, while still professing to have them at heart.

Such was to be the result of this new phase of the worldly power—what was to come from the healing of the wound of the beast; a new, and master-stroke of Satanic policy. The dragon would no longer openly devour the woman, which had ceased any longer to be possible; but by bringing her into subjection to his own power, would rather, through her instrumentality, carry on his purposes of mischief. And the plot has wonderful success; in this new form, the beast is found to have even more than recovered what he had lost by the wound. For now it is said, "power was given him over all kindreds, and tongues and nations, and all that dwell upon the earth shall worship him whose names are not written in the book of life of the Lamb slain from the foundation of the world" (ver. 7, 8). An all but universal dominion! in struggling and holding out against which, it is immediately intimated, the faith and patience of the saints were to have their grand trial (ver. 10). And we have no doubt, with reference to the same, the apparent anomaly in chap. xvii. 11, is to be explained, where we read, "And the beast that was and is not, even he (or, he also), is the eighth (viz. kingdom), and is of the seven, and goeth into perdition." So great was the power and success to be gained by the change of policy, and especially by the Lamb-like beast which was to come to his aid, that the last head of the beast has the appearance of more than a mere head; it is like the beast itself in its entireness, a concentrated form of the whole, and so less properly the seventh as originally formed out of the ten horns into which the Roman empire fell, than an eighth, though it was still of the seven, because it sprung out of them, and was in reality a prolongation of their complex being. Not only was the clay of Daniel's vision to take a distinct form; but the clay itself, as with plastic powers, and by the reception of certain Christian elements, was to undergo a transformation, such as should give it a new and more formidable character.

If in this part of the representation we find a characteristic difference between the Apocalypse and the vision of Daniel, it becomes still more marked in what immediately follows. St John not only saw farther than Daniel into the changes, which the worldly power in its later stages was to undergo, but he also had a revelation given him of an ally, which that power was ultimately to obtain, and of which no trace is to be found in the earlier and more compressed predictions of Daniel. This ally is described under the symbol of a second beast coming up out of the earth, having two horns like a lamb, but speaking as a dragon (xiii. 11). The rest of the description refers to the doings of the power symbolized by this image; but it is by the image itself that the essential nature of the power is to be determined, and the relation in which it was to stand to the other powers mentioned in the vision. Now, as it is a fundamental principle in the interpretation of prophetical symbols, that there must be uniformity of meaning ascribed to them in the things wherein they agree, there are certain points in the description given above, which from their coincidence with things going before, leave little room to doubt as to the proper character of this power. The first is the *name*—a beast; which proves it to be entirely of a worldly character—like a beast looking downwards to the earth, having the world for its god. Throughout the visions both of Daniel and the Apocalypse, the beasts are symbols of what belongs to the earthly and human, as contradistinguished from the divine and heavenly sphere. The several beasts in Daniel denote simply human governments, or the worldly power in its successive phases (as is done also by the other beast in the Apocalypse with its many heads and horns); and when a power rising up among them, and aspiring to something higher, laying claim (though unjustly) to the spiritual and divine, had to be indicated, it is described as so far differing from the others, that it had eyes like those of a man. Here, however, there is no such appearance; the form is altogether beastly, and consequently the power represented by it, only human and worldly. A second point is its *origin;* it came up out of the earth—from beneath, not from above; and so, like the first beast, was to be entirely terrene in its character. It differed, however, in this respect, that it appeared to spring not from the sea—image of the world in its heaving, disordered, and tumultuous state—but from the solid earth; that is, the world in a state of settled order and fitness for civilization. Terrene, therefore, as this power was going to be, it was yet to possess earthly elements of a higher kind than the other—properties more refined, and distinctive of humanity in its advanced and orderly condition. Thirdly, it had *horns like a lamb*—horns, the symbol of power, but the horns of a lamb, among beasts the emblem of what is gentle, harmless, and engaging:—and, therefore, disposed to exercise the power, not in deeds of violence or with overawing displays of majesty and force, but by methods of a suasive kind, and suited to a peaceful and settled state of things. Perhaps, something even more specific is indicated—a studied imitation of *the* lamb with seven horns, formerly mentioned (chap. v. 6), an affectation of Christ-like virtues, or a striving after the lamb-like qualities, which appear in their highest perfection in Christ. We can scarcely doubt, indeed, that this more specific reference was intended. But, lastly, notwithstanding this lamb-like appearance in regard to the *form* which this power was to assume for its exercise, the spirit directing and animating it was to be widely different: "He spake *as a dragon*." It was to be by *speech* that the beast was to give indication of what it was, and by the character of its speech it was to be found in the strictest sense from beneath, an instrument of Satan, not of God; earthly, sensual, devilish.

There can be no certainty in the interpretation of symbols, if these traits do not determine the power here described to be simply a power of this world—not spiritual or ecclesiastical, which necessarily infers either a real or an assumed connection with the divine, but one both actually and ostensibly holding of the world. It has been, we think, the great error of writers in this country, to give too little heed to such fundamental and decisive characteristics in the appearance of the symbol, and to make account rather of dependent and subsidiary points. They have hence commonly adopted the opinion of its being an ecclesiastical power, and have sought to identify it with the priesthood of Rome. Indeed, this opinion very naturally grew out of a previous misapprehension—the identification of the first beast with the papal sovereignty of Rome; and there are not wanting things in the description now before us, which admit of being readily applied to the Romish priesthood—if only a proper foundation existed for such an application. But it is there precisely that the fanciful and groundless nature of the opinion discovers itself. And the more fundamental and strictly exegetical treatment, which the subject has received on the Continent, has led to the general adoption (among others by Hofmann, Hengstenberg, Auberlen) of what seems to us the correct view (though Gaussen and Ebrard still hold to the other). According to this view, the power here symbolized is that of worldly wisdom, comprehending every thing in learning, science, and art, which human nature of itself in its civilized state can attain to—the worldly power in its more refined and spirit-like elements, *its* prophetical or priestly class. There can be no doubt, that it is the same power, which in three subsequent passages (chap. xvi. 13, xix. 20, xx. 10) is called expressly "the false prophet;" so that, as was already indicated by the power of *speech* ascribed to it, it belongs to the intellectual and moral, not to the physical or political sphere. But the marked separation in those passages between this false prophet and the whore, or the corrupt church, and the equally marked intimacy of connection between the false prophet and the beast, point to the conclusion we have otherwise arrived at, of its having to do with prophecy, not in the ecclesiastical, but in the worldly sense. The things which concern the whore, as forming a class by themselves, have a distinct representation; though nearly connected with the beast, and for a time serving herself of this, she still is judged and destroyed apart. But the false prophet never appears separate from the beast; he comes upon the stage as the mere servant and tool of the latter, and the two both work together, and perish in the same condemnation. They are alike, therefore, in origin, in character, in aim, and in destiny; an embodiment, only in different respects, of the sensual, grovelling, ungodly spirit of the world.

This second lamb-horned beast, then, is a personified representation of the world's *gnosis*—"the gnosis, falsely so called," of the apostle Paul; and hence the power professing and exercising it, is emphatically *the false prophet*. False—not because always or necessarily propounding things in themselves untrue, but because actuated by a wrong spirit in its investigations and pursuits—cultivating the talents, studying the works, plying the higher avocations of nature in a state of practical divorce from God and the interests of salvation, as if those were alone sufficient to bless the soul, and render the world a scene of satisfaction and delight. The teachings of such a spirit of prophecy are false, even when setting forth what is in itself true, because they ignore the existence, or belie the testimony, of what is emphatically *the truth*. Yet a formal opposition to this truth, though it might certainly be expected in part to characterise the operations of this power, is what it should rather, by the description given of it, seek to avoid. The lamb-like horns imply as much—indicating that the power in question would strive to conceal its base origin and character, and even work upwards to a resemblance of that, which has its true embodiment in the Divine Author of Christianity. The same thing is also implied in the note given of the relative period of its manifestation; the period, namely, of the last times of the worldly power: "He exerciseth," it is said, ver. 12, "all the power of the first beast before him, and causeth the earth, and them that dwell therein (all the worldly-minded) to worship the first beast, whose deadly wound was healed." If the deadly wound of the beast be, as formerly represented, the professed reception of Christianity by the ruling powers of the world, by which they went, or seemed as if they went over to the side of Christ; and if the healing of that wound be their return to an essentially ungodly state, a kind of Christianised Paganism, then this second beast's appearing in connection with the healed condition of the other, presents it to our view as a power more especially of the latter days, attaining to strength when the world itself had attained to the likeness of a formal Christianity. It was only then, indeed, and by reason of this very connection with the Christian name, that the wisdom and learning of the world *could* come to be peculiarly dangerous to the people of Christ, and be apt to supplant the truth that is in Him. In its old, and avowedly Pagan form, it was too palpably antagonistic in its nature to possess much of this character; and hence the philosophic class in ancient times, either stood entirely aloof from Christianity, or hatched abortive schemes of doctrine, which met with the strong and stedfast reprobation of the church. But matters have presented another aspect, since the kingdoms of the world came to assume somewhat of the Christian type. Since then, a comparatively sober, refined, and softened spirit, has been widely diffused. The prophets of the world have in many respects caught the reflection of that, which is from above; and the literature, art, and science, which they have been giving to the world, not only render many a formal homage to Christianity, but partake much, also, of the elevating influence which has flowed from it.

Yet with all this change to the better in the world's prophets, they are the world's still—breathing its spirit, working for its interests, and out of regard to its ends and objects, evacuating or setting aside the more essential truths of the gospel. The speech is ever such as befits the dragon's mouth; and the grand tendency of its teaching, of its discoveries and inventions, is to lead men to worship the beast—to make a god of this present world. It even teaches them that dwell on the earth, as St John most characteristically described it beforehand, "that they should make an image to the beast, which had the wound by a sword, and did live. And he had power to give life unto the image of the beast, that the image of the beast should both speak, and cause that as many as should not worship the image of the beast should be killed," etc. (ver. 14, 15). The image here spoken of, which was undoubtedly suggested by the image of the Roman emperors, "denotes," as Auberlen has excellently interpreted, "the deification of the world, and the worldly power. And the false prophet's breathing living breath into this image, with much felicity describes, how the false teaching has skill to give to the foolish idolatry of the creature's deification, a kind of spiritual, reasonable, philosophical impress: the worldly spirit, with its revelations, is this dead and now again life-breathing idol deity, before which the whole world does homage. It is (he means in its actual tendencies and final outgoings) the new heathenism, sinking down again to the deification of nature and humanity; and it is impossible to predict what foolish and beastly forms it may yet assume." The extraordinary workings ascribed to this power in the prosecution of its aim, which are designated miracles, and in which it is even said to call down fire from heaven, point to its great achievements in nature, and also to its lofty pretensions, seeming to rival those of the real witnesses of God's truth, and the faithful expounders of His will to men (chap. xi. 5). Nothing in heaven or earth should appear to be above the reach of its inquiries, and the skill of its hand. And the exclusion from merchandise, the assignation even to death (by which must be understood, not literal, but social or political death, *civil* martyrdom, for in this sense only could death with any propriety be ascribed to the speech of a prophet), which it should have power to appoint to as many as would not worship the beast, disclose the extreme eagerness, and the wonderful success, with which this last and highest form of the worldly spirit should drive after its object. The saying, that "the world loves its own," should receive through it, the most striking exemplification; and those, who were not of the world, and held by the faith of Christ, would be disliked, shoved into corners, maligned, and vilified. Who that is but moderately acquainted with the history of modern Christendom, or has any discernment of the signs of the times, can fail to perceive how much the tendency of the world's culture is in this direction! how little it commonly sets by the interests of salvation! nay, how jealously it eyes such as give these their proper place! And rising, as it continually does, in its achievements and consciousness of power, growing incessantly in its command over the elements of nature, and the materials of earthly comfort and enjoyment, who can but fear that its future progress may be marked by times yet more perilous than hitherto, and more audaciously opposed to the claims and spirit of the gospel! It would only require an intensifying of powers already in extensive operation, and a quite conceivable development of the world's culture, to make the unswerving profession of Christianity, and the carrying out of its heavenly spirit into the various relations of life, a matter of constant sacrifice, and of virtual exclusion from all the more prominent positions of worldly life.

So far we can without material difficulty find our way to the import and application of this part of the Apocalyptic vision. On the number of the beast, and of his name, we refrain from making any remark at present; as, indeed, we have little more to offer than an analogical probability, which may be better noticed, in connection with other numbers, at the close of Section III. The result, however, as regards the church's relation to the power and kingdoms of the world, is sufficiently humiliating as to the past, and not without some anxious forebodings in respect to the future. The last, and in some sense Christianised form of the beast, has already proved, in accordance with the view presented beforehand in the Apocalypse, a more dangerous and formidable opponent to the cause of God than it was in its earlier and more palpably antichristian manifestations. And what is afterwards said of this beast itself, in chap. xvii. 14–17, xix. 11, sq. (of which particular notice will be taken in the next section), together with what is here said of his ally, the false prophet, seems plainly to indicate, that the warfare of the church with this dragon-like power, is far from being ended, and, probably, in some of its aspects, has not yet reached its climax. It may be doubted whether there be any just foundation for the idea entertained by some, and among others by the writer recently quoted (Auberlen), that days of active and violent persecution still await the church, and that only by the suffering of blood she must expect to win her latest, as she did her earlier, victories. In so far as this apprehension is based on the description of the false prophet, it seems to be without any just foundation; as it is against the proper nature of the symbol to connect it with acts of external violence and corporeal infliction. The conflict in its later stages is more likely to occupy itself with the higher region of thought and feeling, and to be primarily a war of opinion, though it may also carry in its train certain political and social disturbances. The tactics of the adversary may henceforth be expected to grow in subtlety and refinement. The more Satan succeeds in transforming himself into an angel of light, the more he can lead his servants to exchange obsolete notions and brute force for weapons more accordant with the views of cultivated minds, and less directly opposed to the nature of the gospel, the more disastrous is likely to be their effect in impeding the progress and thinning the ranks of genuine Christianity.

But however that may be, the issue of the struggle is not doubtful. The same inspired pen, which has so wonderfully traced its general character and progress unfolds in the most distinct manner the triumph of the kingdom of Christ, and the irretrievable ruin, both of the beast and the false prophet. We reserve what is written on this point for the next section, where we must consider the judgment of Babylon, which is so intimately connected with that of the other two, that they can with no propriety be examined apart. But the most cursory glance into the representations which follow, is enough to satisfy us, that if the seer of Patmos was a watchman of the night, he was also a herald of the approaching morn, and that, amid all the combinations of malice and guile, which were to be arrayed against the church of God, he foresaw the higher elements of power were still to be with her. Nay, no sooner has he described the appearance and proceedings of the lamb-like beast, than he points attention to the real Lamb on Mount Zion, with his noble army of 144,000 tried and faithful followers (chap. xiv.). By these are represented the truly effective forces, powers, and agencies, mightier by far than those which were symbolized by the beast and false prophet. And by means of them, changes are accomplished, and processes of judgment carried forward, which terminate only with the final overthrow of the adversary, and the exaltation of a pure and faithful church to the possession of the inheritance.

SECTION II.

THE PROPHETICAL FUTURE OF THE CHURCH AND KINGDOM OF CHRIST, IN THEIR RELATION TO THE CHARACTER, WORKING, AND FATE, OF THE ANTICHRISTIAN APOSTACY.

WHEN the church or kingdom of Christ, and the kingdoms of this world, are viewed in their original character and relative positions, the connection between them, as we have seen, is one simply of antagonism. They meet on the stage of the world's history, but only to conflict with each other, not to coalesce, or to merge their respective properties in a state of things common to both. The relation, therefore, when so considered, is necessarily of an external nature. It is that of kingdoms moving in different spheres, animated by a different spirit, and embracing not only different but conflicting interests, so that the progress and triumph of the one inevitably carries along with it the conquest and subversion of the other. But there is also another and more internal relationship, of which we have already had occasion to notice several intimations in prophecy, and which was to arise from an unnatural coalition between the two parties—or, rather, between the apparent, not the real, power on the one side, and the antagonistic power on the other. The kingdom of God, like its Divine Author, cannot change in respect to its essential elements, or cease to be opposed to the powers which are Satanic in their origin, and bestial in their character. But it might *appear* to do so, after it had obtained a distinct organization, and assumed an outstanding position in the world. It might, in the hands of its ostensible representatives and agents, renounce its opposition, and become more or less identified with the operations of the worldly power. Nor was it from the first by any means unlikely that such a result should take place, for Satan's policy has always been to corrupt what is of God, when he has failed to destroy it. And situated as the church of Christ is in the world—beleaguered, on every hand, by the powers of evil—within, liable to be drawn aside by the remains of indwelling sin—and without, alternately pressed by the violence and the blandishments of those in power—it was not to be wondered at if the world should make encroachments upon the church, and the adversary should find for himself an interest and an agency under the very banner of heaven.

The prophecies of Daniel, which, in Old Testament Scripture, contained the most distinct and varied perspective of the more public relations of Christian times, did not fail also to exhibit this feature of the distant future. As might have been expected, no indication is given of it in the vision of Nebuchadnezzar, which, in accordance with its general character, presents merely an external aspect of the different monarchies; and as regards the relation of Messiah's kingdom to the others, gives prominence only to its prevailing might, absolute universality, and endless continuance. But it is otherwise in respect to the vision of the seventh chapter, which was communicated to Daniel himself. Under the last worldly monarchy, in the times of which the kingdom of heaven was to begin to lay claim to the world, a representation is given of a remarkable change that was to take place in the former, by which it was to a certain extent to throw off its bestial appearance, and become assimilated to that of the divine kingdom, though still retaining its essential contrariety to it. Before, however, looking at this representation, we may glance at another in the subsequent visions of Daniel, which is so far related to it, that the things it describes formed the nearest approach to a typical exhibition of the more distant future to be found in ancient times. Generally speaking, the kingdoms of the world, with which the covenant-people came into contact, aimed only at an external supremacy and control over them; they did not interfere with the internal affairs of the religious polity of Israel, or set their hearts on establishing a conformity between it and the religions of heathendom. But in the periods intervening between the return from Babylon, and the coming of Messiah, the worldly power was to quit its outward position and force its way within. It was, in one remarkable instance, to lay its hand upon the very life and spirit of the theocratic constitution of Israel, with the view of bringing this into formal agreement with the state of things in its own territory. And both because it was to form a somewhat singular turn in the affairs of the old covenant, and to afford the nearest parallel these were to present to the most singular and perilous evolution in the future history of Christ's kingdom, a very prominent exhibition was given of it in the later visions of Daniel. We meet with it first in chap. viii., in the vision of the ram and the he-goat, which are explained to mean, the one the kingdom of the Medes and Persians, the other the kingdom of Greece. Then, after quickly passing over the subjugation of the former kingdom, by the latter—the rapid conquests of the Grecian kingdom, and its division, on the death of its founder, into four smaller monarchies, a power is described as going to rise up out of one of these, symbolized by a little horn, which was to wax great and do extraordinary things, especially toward what is called the pleasant land or the land of beauty. By this is undoubtedly meant the land of Canaan (compare Ezek. xx. 6, 15); and of the operations of this power there it is said, ver. 10–12, "And it waxed great to the host of heaven, and it cast down of the host and of the stars to the ground, and stamped upon them. And he magnified himself even to the prince of the host; and by him the daily (or continual, viz., burnt-offering) was taken away, and the place of his sanctuary was cast down. And the host (so it should be rendered) was given (viz., to him) along with the daily sacrifice, because of transgression, and the truth was cast down to the ground; and it (viz., the horn) practised and prospered." The *host* in this last verse must be the same as in ver. 10, 11; it must be the Lord's host, the covenant-people, considered in their ideal character, as possessed of a theocratic constitution, and forming, amid the heathen kingdoms of this world, a kind of heavenly constellation. Notwithstanding this elevated position, however, violence was to be done to it by the bold and aspiring power represented under the little horn: it was to suffer a humiliating prostration, though, as is presently explained in ver. 13, 14, only for a comparatively brief season. And in regard to the reason of this dreadful reverse and temporary invasion of the worldly power on the Divine order and prerogatives, it is said in the explanatory verses toward the end of the chapter, that it was to take place "when transgressors should have come to the full;" that while his power should be mighty, yet it should "not be by his own power," plainly meaning that the iniquity harboured and practised among the covenant-people was what should call forth the visitation, and that the power which was to work so disastrously was really lent by God for the occasion as an instrument of vengeance. And, again, in chap. xi., where the operations of the same power are chiefly detailed, the king in question is not only described as having "indignation against the holy covenant," but also as "having intelligence with them that forsake it" (ver. 30), and "corrupting by flatteries such as do wickedly against the covenant" (ver. 32); while the design of the whole, on the part of God, is "to try them, and purge them, and make them white" (ver. 35).

It is evident, by a comparison of all the passages bearing on the subject, that the period referred to was to be one of deep backsliding and apostacy among the covenant-people, and that this was to be taken advantage of by the worldly power, then in immediate contact with them, for the purpose of breaking up the commonwealth of Israel, and reducing it internally to a level with the states of heathendom. Such certainly was the occasion and aim of the proceedings carried on against the people of Israel by Antiochus Epiphanes, as described in the books of Maccabees. The origin of the whole is ascribed to a Hellenizing party in Israel, who introduced the Grecian culture and games, and thought that strength and safety were to be acquired by assimilating their manners and customs to those of their more polished neighbours (1 Mac. i. 11–15, 43–53; 2 Mac. iv. 7–20). This spirit of defection had invaded also the priesthood; so that some of the priests even assumed Grecian names, and the office of high-priest was made matter of merchandise. It was the world in its baser forms entering into the sanctuary of God; and in Antiochus, a fitting representative of the world, it reached a climax of presumption and wickedness. He is, beyond doubt, the power, that in connection with the Grecian monarchy, was to act so lawless and violent a part against the covenant. It is hard to say what precisely was the object of this man in many of his proceedings; for they not unfrequently resembled more the doings of a madman, than those of a reasonable being; on which account the epithet *Epimanes* (the mad), was often substituted for *Epiphanes* (the illustrious). But from his applying to himself on some of his coins the epithet of *Theos* (God), and on the reverse of others, exhibiting the likeness of Jupiter, taken in connection with the general character of his reign, it would seem, that he identified himself with the Olympian Jupiter, and thought himself justified in resorting to any measures for the purpose of establishing the worship of this deity, and along with it his own absolute supremacy. He prosecuted this design also among the Jews; and in the course of his operations succeeded, not only in inflicting the most revolting cruelties, but also in polluting, through the instrumentality of the Hellenizing party, the altar and temple at Jerusalem with the foulest abominations. "He did according to his will, and exalted himself, and magnified himself above every god, and spoke marvellous things against the God of gods, and prospered till the indignation was accomplished" (Dan. xi. 36). It was, therefore, quite a peculiar relation which the worldly power held for a season, in the person of this Antiochus, to the kingdom of God in Israel. It occupies essentially the same relative place in the third worldly kingdom, that antichrist was to do in the fourth, and has hence been generally designated the typical antichrist. There is the more reason for viewing it thus, as in some of the descriptions of antichrist in New Testament Scripture, in that especially of 2 Thess. ii. 4, sq., the very words are used, in which Antiochus and his outrageous proceedings are described by Daniel. But of this occasion will be found to speak afterwards.

We revert, then, to the description of a similar kind, though pointing to a later period, which is found in the seventh chapter of Daniel (ver. 8, 20, 21, 24, 25). The period is that of the latter stages of the fourth kingdom, subsequent to the tenfold division into which it was to fall; and so the power described must be posterior to the Christian era; it must be not the typical, but the real antichrist. This power is described, precisely as the other, under the emblem of a horn—at first a little horn; but presently waxing great, so as to pluck up by the roots three of the horns out of which it sprang; and differing also from the others, nay approximating in appearance to the kingdom, which was from above, since it had eyes like the eyes of a man, and a mouth speaking great things (ver. 8). How far, however, the reality was from corresponding with this appearance, how much similarity of form (as might naturally have been suspected from the manner of its origin), was assumed as a cloak to mask the most intense contrariety of spirit, was plainly brought to light in the explanation given in the subsequent parts of the vision. There we find, that this horn or power was to be entirely of the same spirit with those, among which it should come up, and was to form, indeed, the concentration of all the enmity and ungodliness by which they were, in common, characterised. While he was to be diverse from them in having eyes like a man's, his look was to be more stout than his fellows, and he was to make war with the saints and prevail against them (ver. 20, 21). "He shall be diverse from the first," it is added, ver. 24, 26, "and he shall subdue three kings. And he shall speak words against the Most High, and shall wear out the saints of the Most High, and think to change times and laws; and they shall be given into his hand until a time, and times, and the dividing of time. But the judgment shall sit, and they shall take away his dominion to consume and to destroy it unto the end."

In this description much is purposely left vague and mysterious; but there are a few points which admit of being clearly determined from it. 1. It is first distinctly intimated, that the power of which it speaks, the last offspring and development of the fourth worldly monarchy, was to be distinguished by many of the higher qualities of earthly goodness; by human-like culture and adornment. The eyes as of a man bespeak this; for the spirit of life and intelligence is in the eye; and if the eyes had been *altogether* those of a man, then the power symbolized would, in spirit, have realized the proper ideal of humanity—it would have been the Divine kingdom itself. But since the eyes were not actually man's, but only *like* those of a man, it indicates an approach merely to the true pattern—such a resemblance as fallen human nature by the cultivation of its own powers, and the skilful use of its means and opportunities might of itself accomplish. So that in respect to art and science, general culture and refinement, and the various elements of social order and enjoyment, this last development of the earthly power should constitute an advance upon those which preceded it. Nay, considering that before its full formation, at least, if not as the very condition of its existence, the truly Divine kingdom, represented by Him who had the proper being, as well as likeness of a Son of man, must have begun to diffuse itself in the world, it was but natural to infer, that the human-like power would avail itself of many elements presented to its hand by this higher kingdom, and through these work up the appearance of things to a closer resemblance of the true pattern. The more it could take into its system of the *forms* of the Divine, the more would its aim be accomplished of looking *like* this. And the mouth speaking great things, or making high claims and pretensions, seems not doubtfully to indicate, that such would be the case; for, after the introduction of those things, which were to constitute the proper greatness and well-being of humanity, no power could well arrogate to itself the title, or possess the appearance of the truly human, without assimilating to itself much that bore this loftier impress. The higher qualities, therefore, which were to distinguish this singular power, must have derived something from the heavenly, as well as the earthly, so as to form a peculiar compound of flesh and spirit. 2. On the other hand, there comes plainly out, as a second point in the description, the intense worldliness, and God-opposing character of this power; it was to have still the essential spirit of the beast, and that in a state of the greatest virulence and energy. This appears, first of all from the manner of its origination and growth—springing up simply as a fresh horn of the beast, and with such vitality as to pluck up by the roots, three of the existing horns. Worldliness in full life and vigour is evidently the least that can be understood by such a symbolical representation—the earthly, sensual, self-idolizing spirit in its ripeness. But the same thing appears also from the actions ascribed to this power; making war with the saints and prevailing against them, even wearing them out by the keenness and constancy of its opposition, and, in the highest spirit of self-deification, speaking words against the Most High, and changing times and laws. Such things plainly bespeak, not only an unabated, but even an increased contrariety to the mind and will of God; the higher culture, and the nearer approach in appearance to the Divine kingdom, which this power was to assume, should but serve, as it were, to whet its appetite and inflame its zeal against the real interests of that kingdom. But the very circumstance of its having assumed something of an apparent resemblance to the higher power, and by dint of cultivation and art, changed the original beast-like form into a kind of human aspect, necessarily implied the adoption of a different sort of policy in the prosecution of its ungodly measures, from what had been practised in the earlier stages of its history. If the old spirit of opposition to God and divine things was to be continued, and become more intense than ever, it could no longer be in the rough and undisguised form of heathenish antagonism to the claims of Jehovah and the higher interests of men; the circumstances of its condition would manifestly oblige this power to keep up the appearance of a regard to these, while the reality was maintained of a deadly and inveterate opposition.

So far one might easily go in reading the interpretation of this part of Daniel's outline of the distant future. And the certainty of an ultimate failure of the objects aimed at by the worldly power in this last form of its existence—of the downfal of the power itself, and the rise, in spite of its malice and persecution, of the saints of the Most High to the place of power and dominion; these also are points so clearly unfolded, that there is no need for dwelling particularly upon them. But with so much that is plain in the vision, there is much also that is left in darkness and uncertainty, especially in regard to the probable period in the church's history, when this mysterious power should arise, and the manner and degree in which it should seek to cultivate the human aspect of the divine kingdom, and thereby prove itself to be diverse from the more grovelling worldly kingdoms that preceded it. On such points as these it had been premature to give any specific information in the time of Daniel; and in so far as they might be prophetically given, it is only in the Scriptures of the New Testament that we can be warranted to look for them. To these, therefore, we now turn; and though it is only the visions of the Apocalypse which properly resume and fill up the symbolical perspective of Daniel, yet it is necessary in the first instance to refer to certain direct intimations of the coming evil, which are found in the earlier portions of New Testament Scripture. For thus only can we gather with certainty and precision the light which is furnished to the Christian church respecting the last and most dangerous form of the worldly power.

1. We naturally look first to the discourses of our Lord; but as these were chiefly intended to lay the foundations, as to doctrine and duty, of the Christian church, and unfold the calling and prospects of her real members, they contain com-

paratively little that bears on our present subject. Not unfrequently they point, though in a quite general way, to the difficulties and dangers through which his genuine followers should have to pass, the violence and oppression they should have to meet, and the corruptions and counterfeits that should rise up in the midst of them and continue till the time of the end. Such, in particular, are the parables of the tares and the wheat, the labourers in the vineyard, and the importunate widow. Almost the only information of a more specific kind contained in our Lord's discourses regarding the usurpation of the world upon the church, is to be found in what he says of the false pretenders to divine light and power, and the dangerous ascendancy they were to acquire. A warning on this head had been thrown out in the sermon on the Mount: "Beware of false prophets, which come to you in sheeps' clothing, but inwardly they are ravening wolves" (Matt. vii. 15). But it is repeated, and more pointedly pressed in the discourse respecting the last times in Matt. xxiv.; first at ver. 11, "and many false prophets shall arise and deceive many;" and again at ver. 24, "There shall arise false Christs and false prophets, and shall show great signs and wonders; insomuch that if it were possible they shall deceive the very elect." From the connection in which the words are spoken, there can be no doubt, that they taught the disciples to look for the appearance of such characters among the signs of the approaching downfal of the old Jewish constitution; and from the relation which this bore to the time of the end, in the more general sense, we are warranted to expect, that the sign would repeat itself in the latter stages of the world's history. Both points, however, are so much more fully brought out by the apostles of our Lord in their addresses and epistles, that we pass at once to what proceeded from them.

2. Here it is not unimportant, at the outset, to notice a historical passage, which serves to throw some light on the import of one of the terms used by our Lord. In Acts xiii. 6, the Jew, Barjesus, who was with Sergius Paulus, the proconsul of Cyprus, and who there withstood the preaching of

the gospel, and sought to turn him from the faith, is called a false prophet (ψευδοπροφήτης). And in still farther explanation of his real character, he is called Elymas the magos—two words, indeed, of the same import, only the one Aramaic (or Arabic) and the other Greek—Greek, at least by adoption, though originally Persian. Elymas (from âlim, wise), and magos both alike denote the man of wisdom in the Eastern sense; that is, a person addicted to the study of philosophy, and furnished with the skill of secret lore. It did not necessarily convey the sinister meaning of our magician or sorcerer, but comprehended also the better wisdom of that higher learning, which was the common pursuit of eastern sages. In apostolic times, however, this learning had become so much identified with astrology and the magic arts, that too often, as evidently in the case of this Barjesus, the persons who professed it were mere soothsayers and sorcerers. Prophets of this low and reprobate description swarmed in the countries around Judea; and notwithstanding the strong denunciations in the law against all magical arts and false divinations, they were found also in great numbers among the Jews. It was, indeed, one of the crying sins of the times, a proof of great hardness of heart and depravation of manners; and there can be no doubt that the wonders wrought by Jesus and His disciples, would, with a certain class of minds, give a fresh impulse to the evil. Such a singular manifestation of the true wisdom, with its attendant power, could not fail to produce a general fermentation and a craving very favourable for the display of the false; and as our Lord foretold, so it happened, that many false prophets arose, and deceived many.

The account we have in Josephus of the last crimes and troubles of Judea, serves also to show, how large a part prophetical delusions played in that fearful tragedy. But the spirit of error did not work altogether without the territory of the church: it was always striving to press inwards. The apostle John even speaks of great numbers having been misled by it. "Beloved," he says, "believe not every spirit, but try the spirits, whether they are of God: because many false prophets are gone out into the world" (1 John iv. 1). He does not precisely say, that they had proceeded from within the Christian community; but it is clear from what follows, that he had chiefly in view the false teaching, which had begun to appear partly within, and partly, also, on the outskirts of the church. For, he presently states, that those spirits are not of God, which do not confess Christ to have come in the flesh, and that such also are of the spirit of antichrist that was to come. So that, according to this apostle, false prophets, unsound teachers, and antichrist, belonged to the same category, and were but different forms or operations of the same spirit. Indeed, as regards the Christian church, the false prophesying warned against, could have found no great scope for its exercise excepting in the form of teaching untrue or corrupt doctrines. Hence, it was the prevalence of false teachers (ψευδοδιδάσκαλοι) in New Testament times, corresponding to false prophets in the Old, of which the apostle Peter so earnestly admonished believers in his Second Epistle (chap. ii.), and whose disastrous influence he so strikingly portrays. It was of the same, also, that St Paul spake in his address to the elders of the church of Ephesus, when he announced it as certain, that after his departure "men should arise from among themselves, speaking perverse things, to draw away disciples after them; that grievous wolves also should enter in among them, not sparing the flock" (Acts xx. 29, 30); and many parts of his epistles bear evidence to the same apprehensions and foresight of evil pressing upon his mind. The only question, therefore, is, how far, or in what respects this false prophesying or corrupt teaching in the church coincided with the false Christs and the spirit of antichrist also predicted to arise?

It was Jesus alone who foretold the appearance of false Christs. By such can only be understood false pretenders to the name and character of Messiah. Precisely as false prophets are those who laid claim to gifts they did not really possess; false Christs must denote such as would assume to be what Jesus of Nazareth alone was. In the strict sense, therefore, *false* Christs could only arise outside the Christian church, and among those who had rejected the *true;* and in so far as they did so, they verified the word of Christ, "I am come in my Father's name, and ye received me not; if another should come in his own name, him ye will receive" (John v. 43). The most noted example of the kind, as well as the earliest, was the case of Barchochbas (the son of a star), as he chose to designate himself, with reference to the prophecy of Balaam, and who drew multitudes after him to destruction. False hopes and pretensions, however, of a similar kind have been ever renewing themselves among the Jews, though circumstances have not admitted of their reaching such an imposing magnitude, and entailing such a common disaster.

But we cannot altogether limit our Lord's declaration respecting false Christs to such merely Jewish pretenders, especially as it was a declaration made for the special instruction and warning of His own disciples, and for them the danger of being seduced by persons of that description must have been comparatively little. We are rather to conceive that in this as well as in other things noted in His discourse of the latter times, He wished them to regard the immediate future as but the beginning of a remoter end—a beginning that should in substance be often repeating itself, though the particular form might undergo many alterations. It matters little, any one may perceive, whether men might or might not call themselves by the name of Christ, and openly set up a rival claim to the faith of mankind. If they should assume to be, or to do what by exclusive right and appointment belongs to Him, they then become, if not in name, at least in reality, false Christs. Should any one undertake to give a revelation of divine things higher than that communicated by Christ, and different from His—to propound essentially other terms to the favour and blessing of heaven than those which proceed on the foundation of His perfect atonement—or to conduct the world to its destined consummation in light and blessedness otherwise than through the acknowledgment of His name and the obedience of His gospel—such an one would as really act the part of a false Christ as if he openly disallowed the claims of Jesus, and challenged to himself what rightly belongs to the Son of God. Hegesippus, therefore (in Eusebius' Eccl. Hist. IV. 22), had perfect right to include, among the false Christs predicted by our Lord, the early heresiarchs and their followers—the Simonians, Marcionists, Valentinians, Basilidians, etc.—"from whom," he says, "sprung the false Christs, and false prophets, and false apostles, who divided the unity of the church by the introduction of corrupt doctrines against God, and against His church." While, in the teaching of such parties, a certain deference was paid to Christ, and some elements of the truth of His gospel were embraced in their views, yet in the general aim and tendency of these views they undoubtedly sought to supersede Christ and contravene the spirit of his gospel. And the same substantially may be said of not a few persons and systems of later times—such as Mahomet, and the advocates in every age of nature's sufficiency to reach for itself a position of acceptance with God, and of honour in His kingdom. These, in reality, disown the claims of Jesus, and set themselves up in His room as the guides and saviours of the world. And we cannot fail to perceive an indication of the varied forms such characters should assume, and the many different quarters whence they might be expected to arise, in the warning of our Lord respecting them, "If they shall say unto you, Behold, he is in the desert, go not forth; behold, he is in the secret chambers, believe it not."

It is Christ alone, however, as we have said, who speaks of false Christs. Elsewhere, we read of antichrists, or the antichrist, and have various descriptions given us of the corrupt and pestilential power which the term denotes. What, then, precisely does it denote? Does it imply that the power or party indicated by it should, in some form or another, arrogate Christ's peculiar office and work, or does it simply express a spirit of contrariety and opposition to His doctrine or kingdom? Nothing, in this respect, can be gathered with certainty from the word itself, for the preposition (ἀντι), which is here used in composition with Christ, alike expresses formal opposition to an object, and the supplanting of it by taking its place; and there is a series of compounds, in which the one idea, and a series in which the other idea, is embodied.[1] It is only, therefore, by the usage of the word, and the comparison of parallel passages, that we can determine in what specific sense it is to be understood, and what kind of contrariety to the truth of Christ it was meant to designate. The first passage in St John's Epistle, by whom alone the word is used, stands literally thus: "Little children, it is the last hour (or season); and as ye heard that the antichrist cometh, even now many have become antichrists (ἀντίχριστοι πολλοὶ γεγόνασιν), whence we know it is the last hour" (chap. ii. 18). Here there is no precise definition of what the term antichrist imports, but the assertion chiefly of a fact, that the idea involved in it had already passed into a reality, and that in a variety of persons. This, however, is itself of considerable moment, especially as it conveys the information that while the name is used in the singular, as of an individual, it was not intended to denote the same kind of strict and exclusive personality as the Christ. Even in the apostolic age John finds the name of antichrist applicable to many individuals. And this, also, may so far help us to a knowledge of the idea, since, while there were numbers in that age who sought within the church to corrupt the doctrine of Christ, and without it to disown and resist His authority, we have yet no reason to suppose that there were more than a very few who distinctly claimed the title of Christ, and presumed to place themselves in Messiah's room. The next passage occurs very shortly after the one just noticed, and may be regarded as supplementary to it; it is in the 22d verse. The apostle had stated that no lie is of the truth; and he then continues, "Who is the liar? (ὁ ψεύστης, the liar by pre-eminence) but

[1] For example, in ἀντιλογία, ἀντίθεσις, ἀντίβιος, ἀντικείμενος, the relation of formal opposition; and in ἀνθυπατός, ἀντιβασιλεύς, ἀντίλυτρον, that of taking the place of, substitution.

he who denieth that Jesus is the Christ. This is the antichrist, who denieth (or, denying) the Father and the Son." Here it is the denial of the truth concerning Christ, not the formal supplanting of Christ by an impious usurpation of His office, to which the name antichrist is applied. Yet it could not be intended to denote every sort of denial of the truth, for this would have been to identify antichristianism with heathenism, and Judaism, and unbelief generally, which was certainly not the meaning of the apostle. The denial of the truth by the antichrist was made in a peculiar manner—not as from a directly hostile and antagonistic position, but under the cover of a Christian name, and with more or less of a friendly aspect. While it was denied that Jesus was the Christ, in the proper sense of the term, Jesus was by no means reckoned an impostor; His name was still assumed, and His place held to be one of distinguished honour. That this was the case is evident not only from the distinctive name applied to the form of evil in question, but also from what is said (in ver. 18, 19) of the origination of the antichrists. "Many," says the apostle, "have become antichrists;" they were not so originally, but by a downward progress had ended in becoming such. And, still further, "They went out from us, but were not of us;" that is, they had belonged to the Christian community, but showed, by the course of defection they now pursued, that they had not formed a part of its living membership, nor had really imbibed the Spirit of the gospel. When, therefore, the apostle says in the verse already quoted, that those whom He designated antichrists denied Jesus to be the Christ; and when, in another verse (chap. iv. 3), he says, "Every spirit that confesseth not Jesus Christ come (ἐληλυθότα) in the flesh, is not of God; and this is that spirit of antichrist whereof ye have heard that it should come (literally cometh), and now already is it in the world;" and, still again, when he says in his Second Epistle, ver. 7, "For many deceivers have entered into the world, who confess not Jesus Christ coming in flesh (ἐρχόμενον ἐν σαρκί); this is the deceiver and the antichrist." In all these passages it can only be of a virtual denial of the truth that the apostle speaks. He plainly means such a depravation of the truth, or abstraction of its essential elements, as turned it into a lie. And when farther he represents the falsehood as circling around the person of Jesus, and disowning Him as having come in the flesh, we can scarcely entertain a doubt that he refers to certain forms of the great gnostic heresy—to such as held, indeed, by the name of Jesus, but conceived of Him as only some kind of shadowy emanation of the Divine virtue, not a personal incarnation of the Eternal Word. Only by taking up a position, and announcing a doctrine of this sort, could the persons referred to have proved peculiarly dangerous to the church—so dangerous as to deserve being called, collectively and emphatically, *the Deceiver*—the embodiment, in a manner of the old serpent. In an avowed resistance to the claims of Jesus, or a total apostacy from the faith of His gospel, there should necessarily have been little room for the arts of deception, and no very pressing danger to the true members of the church.

We arrive, then, at the conclusion, that in St John's use of the term *antichrist*, there is an unmistakeable reference to the early heretics, as forming at least one exemplification of its idea. Such, also, was the impression derived from the apostle's statements generally by the Fathers; they understood him to speak of the heretics of the time, under the antichrists who had already appeared. For example, Cyprian, when writing of heretics, Ep. lxxiii. 13, and referring to 1 John iv. 3, asks, "how can they do spiritual and divine things, who were enemies of God, and whose breast the spirit of antichrist has possessed." On the same passage, Œcumenius says, "He declares antichrist to be already in the world, not corporeally, but by means of those who prepare the way for his coming; of which sort are false apostles, false prophets, and heretics." So Damascenus, l. iv., orth. fid. 27, "Every one, who does not confess the Son of God, and that God has come in the flesh, and is perfect God, and was made perfect man, still remaining God, is antichrist." And

Augustine, in the third Tractatus on 1 John, in answer to the question, whom did the apostle call antichrists? though he extends the term to comprehend every one who is contrary to Christ, and is not a true member of His body, yet he places in the first rank, as most directly meant, "all heretics and schismatics." It is plain, indeed, that the existing antichrists of John, the abettors and exponents of the ψεύδος, or lie, under a Christian profession, the deniers of what is emphatically the truth, belonged to the very same class with the grievous wolves and false brethren of Paul, of whom he so solemnly forewarned the Ephesian elders, and of whom also he wrote in his Epistles to Timothy (1st Ep. iv. 1, 2d Ep. iii. 1), as persons who should depart from the faith, teach many heretical doctrines, and bring in upon the church perilous times. John, writing at a later period, and referring to what then existed, calls attention to the development of that spirit, of which Paul perceived the germ, and described the future growth. The one announced the evil as coming, the other declared it had already come; reminding believers also of their having previously heard (with reference, doubtless, to the prophetic utterances of Paul), that it was to come. So that the *antichrists* of John are found to coincide with one aspect of our Lord's *false Christs;* they were those who, without renouncing the name of Christians, or without any open disparagement of Jesus, forsook the simplicity of the faith in Him, and turned His truth into a lie. In so far, they might be said to supplant Him, as to follow *them* was to desert Christ; yet, from the circumstances of the case, there could be no direct antagonism to Jesus, or distinct unfurling of the banner of revolt.[1]

[1] This seems so clearly implied in the apostle's statements, that we cannot but feel surprised how Mr Trench, in his "New Testament Synonyms," p. 120, should regard those statements as implying, that resistance to, and defiance of, Christ, is the essential mark of antichrist. Defiance of Christ necessarily involves avowed and palpable opposition, which is the part, not of deceivers, and of teachers who had corrupted the truth by a lie of their own, but of open enemies and unbelievers. We

Assuming this, however, the question still remains, whether we are to regard the idea of the antichrist as exhausted in those heretical corrupters of the gospel in the apostolic age, and their successors in future times; or should rather view them as the types and forerunners of some huge system of God-opposing error, or of some grand personification of impiety and wickedness to be exhibited before the appearing of Christ? It was thought from comparatively early times, that the mention so emphatically of *the antichrist*, bespoke something of a more concentrated and personally antagonistic character, than the many antichrists, which were spoken of as being already in the world. The Fathers generally were of opinion, that those were but preliminary exemplifications of some far greater embodiment of the antichristian spirit, and commonly thought of a monarch (like Antiochus) of heaven-daring impiety, and unscrupulous disregard of everything sacred and divine, who, after pursuing a course of appalling wickedness and violence, should be destroyed by the personal manifestation of Christ in glory. This view, however, was founded, not simply, nor even chiefly, upon the passages above referred to in the Epistles of John, but (along with what is written in the Apocalypse) on the words of St Paul, in 2 Thess. ii. 3–10. Amid many crude speculations and conflicting views upon this passage, none of them doubted, as Augustine states (De Civ. Dei xx. 19), that it referred to antichrist, who was understood to be indicated by "the man of sin," and "the son of perdition." And beyond all question the evil portrayed here is essentially of the same character as that spoken of in the passages already considered, only with the characteristic traits more darkly drawn, and the whole mystery of iniquity more fully exhibited. As in the other passages, the antichristian spirit was identified with a departing from the faith, and a corrupting of the truth, of

agree with him, however, that, as used in John's writings, the term antichrist does not imply an assumption of Christ's title and offices—not, at least, excepting in the modified sense already stated, of propounding what was virtually subversive of Christ's authority and work.

the gospel; so here the coming evil is designated emphatically *the apostacy* (ἡ ἀποστασία, ver. 3); by which we can only think of a notable falling away from the faith and purity of the gospel; so that the evil was to have both its root and its development in connection with the church's degeneracy. Nor was the commencement of the evil in this case any more than in the other, to be far distant. Even at the comparatively early period when the apostle wrote, it had begun to work, and in his ordinary ministrations he had forewarned the disciples concerning it (ver. 5, 7); plainly implying, that it was to have its rise in a spiritual and growing defection within the Christian church. Then, as the term *antichrist* evidently denoted some kind of antithesis in doctrine and practice to Christ, a certain use of Christ's name, with a spirit and design entirely opposed to Christ's cause; so in the passage before us, the power personified and described, is designated the opposer (ὁ ἀντικείμενος, ver. 4), one who sets himself against God, and arrogates the highest prerogatives and honours. Yet, with such impious self-deification in *fact*, there was to be nothing like an open defiance and contempt of all religious propriety in *form;* for this same power is represented as developing itself by "a mystery of iniquity"—such a complex and subtle operation of the worst principles and designs, as might be carried on under the fairest and most hypocritical pretences; and by "signs and lying wonders, and all deceivableness of unrighteousness," beguiling those who should fall under its influence, to become the victims of a "strong delusion," and to "believe a lie"—viz., to believe that which should have to their view the *semblance* of the truth, but in *reality* should be its opposite. Not only so, but the temple of God is represented as the theatre of this impious, artful, and wicked ascendancy (ver. 4); and in respect to the Christian church, the apostle Paul knows of no temple but that church itself, nor can any other be understood here, as even Augustine did not fail to perceive.[1] It is the only kind

[1] He states, indeed, as a possible alternative, the ruins of the old

of temple usurpation in Christian times, which can be conceived of as affecting the expectations and interests of the church generally, and that alone, also, which might justly be represented as a grand consummation of the workings of iniquity within the Christian community. So that, as a whole, the description of the apostle presents to our view some sort of mysterious and astounding combination of good and evil, formally differing from either heathenism or infidelity—a gathering up and assorting together of certain elements in Christianity for the purpose of accomplishing, by the most subtle devices and cunning stratagems, the overthrow and subversion of Christian truth and life. It is, therefore, but the full growth and final development of St John's idea of the antichrist.

Of the descriptions generally of the coming evil in New Testament Scripture, and especially of this fuller description in the epistle to the Thessalonians, nothing (it appears to us), can be more certain on exegetical grounds, than that they cannot be made to harmonize with the Romish opinion—which Hengstenberg and others in the Protestant church have been seeking to revive—the opinion that would find the evil realized in the power and influence exerted in early times by Rome, in its heathen state, against the cause and church of Christ. In such an application of what is written, we miss all the more distinctive features of the delineation. If it might be said of the heathen power in those times, that it did attempt to press into the church or temple of God, and usurp religious homage there, the attempt, as is well known, did not succeed; nor

temple at Jerusalem, but evidently leans to the idea of the church being intended; and adds, "Unde nonnulli, non ipsum principem, sed universum quodammodo corpus ejus, it est, ad eum pertinentem hominum multitudinem, simul cum ipso suo principe hoc loco intelligi antichristum volunt: rectiusque putant etiam Latine dici, sicut in Græco est, non, *in templo Dei;* sed *in templum Dei sedeat,* tanquam ipse sit templum Dei, quod est Ecclesia" (De Civ. Dei, xx. 19)—understanding by the temple the church, and by the power usurping it the corrupt body that was to compose so large a part of the church.

did it even assume the appearance of an actual sitting, or enthroning one's self there (as the words import), for the purpose of displacing the true God and Saviour from their proper supremacy. In the operations of that power also we perceive nothing that could fitly be designated "a mystery of iniquity"—the iniquity being that rather of palpable opposition and overbearing violence—in its aim transparent to every one, who knew the gospel of the grace of God, and involving, if yielded to, the conscious renunciation of Christ. As to the signs, and lying wonders, and deceivableness of unrighteousness, and strong delusions which the apostle mentions among the means and characteristic indications of the dreaded power, there is scarcely even the shadow of them to be found in the controversy which ancient heathenism waged with Christianity. On every account, therefore, this view is to be rejected; failing, as it does, to establish the necessary correspondence between the leading features of the description and the supposed realization in providence.

Another view, however, has of late been rising into notice, which, if well founded, would also save the Romish apostacy from any proper share in the predicted evil; and which, we cannot but fear, if not originated, has at least been somewhat encouraged and fostered by that softened light, which the mediæval and antiquarian tendencies of the present age have served to throw around Romanism. The view we refer to would make the full and proper development of the antichrist, an essentially different thing from any such depravation of the truth, as is to be found in the Papacy, a greatly more blasphemous usurpation, and one that can only be reached by a pantheistic deification of human nature. So Olshausen, who says, on the passage in Thessalonians, "The self-deification of the Roman emperors appears as modesty by the side of that of antichrist; for the Cæsars did not elevate themselves *above* the other gods, they only wanted to have a place *beside* them, as representatives of the genius of the Roman people. Antichrist, on the contrary, wants to be the only true God, who suffers none beside Him; what Christ demands for Himself in truth, he, in the excess of his presumption, claims for himself in falsehood." Then, as to the way in which he should do this, it is said, "Antichrist will not," as Chrysostom correctly remarks, "promote idolatry, but seduce men from the true God, as also from all idols, and set himself up as the only object of adoration. This remarkable idea, that sin in antichrist issues in a downright self-deification, discloses to us the inmost nature of evil, which consists in selfishness. In antichrist, all love, all capability of sacrifice and self-denial, shows itself entirely submerged in the making of the I all in all, which then also insists on being acknowledged by all men, as the centre of all power, wisdom, and glory." The proper antichrist, therefore, according to Olshausen, must be a person—one who shall be himself the mystery of iniquity, as Christ is the mystery of godliness, a kind of embodiment or incarnation of Satan. He can regard all the past manifestations and workings of evil, only as serving to indicate what it may possibly be, but by no means realising the idea; and he conceives, it may one day start forth in the person of one, who shall combine in his character, the elements of infidelity and superstition, which are so visibly striving for the mastery over mankind. Some individual may be cast up by the fermentation that is going forward, who shall concentrate around himself all the Satanic tendencies in their greatest power and energy, and come forth at last in impious rivalry of Christ, as the incarnate son of the devil. Mr Trench appears substantially to adopt this view, though he expresses himself more briefly and also more vaguely on the subject. With him the antichrist is "one who shall not pay so much homage to God's word as to assert the fulfilment in himself, for he shall deny that word altogether; hating even erroneous worship, because it is worship at all; hating much more the church's worship in spirit and in truth; who on the destruction of every religion, every acknowledgment that man is submitted to higher powers than his own, shall seek to establish his throne; and for God's great truth 'God is man,' to substitute his own lie, 'man is God.'" (Synonyms, p. 120).

It is certainly not to be denied, that there are tendencies in operation at the present time, fitted, in some degree, to suggest the thought of such a possible incarnation of the ungodly and atheistic principle; though nothing has yet occurred which can be said to have brought it within the bounds of the probable. But, at all events, it is an aspect of the matter derived greatly more from the apprehended results of those tendencies themselves, than from a simple and unbiassed interpretation of the passages of Scripture under consideration. Such an antichrist as that now depicted, the impersonation of unblushing wickedness and atheism, has every thing against it, which has been already urged against the view, that would identify the description with the enmity and persecutions of heathen Rome. Instead of seating itself in the temple of the Christian church as its own, and arrogating there the supreme place, that antichristian power could only rise on the ruins of the temple. And whatever audacity or foolhardiness there might be in the assumptions and proceedings of such a power, one cannot, by any stretch of imagination, conceive, how, with such flagrant impiety in its front, it could present to God's people the appearance of a *mystery* of iniquity, and be accompanied with signs and wonders and deceitful workings, destined to prevail over all who had not received the truth in the love of it. Conscience and the Bible must cease to be what they now are, cease at least to possess the mutual force and respondency they have been wont to exercise, ere so godless a power could rise to the ascendant in Christendom. It may even be said, the religious susceptibilities of men, in the false direction as well as the true, would need to have sustained a paralysis alike unprecedented and incredible. And besides, the historical connection would be broken, which the passages, bearing on the antichristian apostacy, plainly establish between the present and the future. In what already was, the apostles descried the germ, the incipient workings of what was hereafter more fully to develope itself; while the antichrist now suggested to our apprehensions, if it should ever attain to a substantive existence, would stand in no proper affinity to the false doctrine and corruptions of the apostolic age. It would be a moral phenomenon altogether novel.

The tendency, we believe, on the part of evangelical writers, to fall into such mistaken views of the antichrist, has arisen in good measure from isolating too much some parts of the apostle's description (particularly 2 Thess. ii. 3, 4), and overlooking as well the agreements, as the necessary differences, between the ultimate and the typical antichrist. The part of the description more immediately referred to, consists almost entirely of Daniel's words and imagery; and when the two are viewed in their proper relations, considerable light is thrown on the import of the later revelation. In the first place, it holds alike of both, that the opposing and blaspheming power was to have its root and the occasion of its manifestation within the professing church. Even in the case of Antiochus, though he stood outside, yet the party whom he represented, and through whom alone he obtained the power and the opportunity to practise his enormities, had their place within; he merely gave a head to the evil that had been working in Israel, and brought it forth into full efflorescence. So also in the apostle's description all is connected with the rise and progress of iniquity in the church; viewed complexly it is "the apostacy," beginning in men's failure to receive the truth in love, and having pleasure in unrighteousness; so that the revelation of what is called emphatically "the wicked," or "the man of sin," can be nothing but the growth of the internal corruption to its proper magnitude—assuming, as it were, its head and crown. The distinctive characteristics, therefore, must have been the same throughout. Then, in regard to the more offensive part of these characteristics, the one power also was the prototype of the other; and in neither case is absolute atheism or utter irreligiousness meant to be ascribed to it. It was said of Antiochus, the typical antichrist, that he should do according to his will, should exalt himself, should magnify himself above every god, and speak marvellous things against the God of gods; though we know, that he did all as a professed and zealous religionist. His course is described, after the common manner of prophecy, not by its *formal*, but by its *real* character; so that his fiery zeal for Jupiter is resolved into its true source—his own arbitrary self-will and frenzied devotion to the false religion and corrupt manners of Greece, which only sought for itself a cover in an affected regard for the honour of a particular god. He really magnified himself above every god, because in the service of heathenism he did what was contrary to the genius of heathenism itself, as well as outrageously dishonouring to the God of heaven. And it is undoubtedly in the same way, that St Paul's application of those terms to the New Testament antichrist ought to be understood; they should be held descriptive of its real, rather than its formal character. The self-exaltation of this power above all that is called God or worshipped, so far from excluding a show of religion, might rather be expected to involve this as its necessary condition—the direct and naked exhibition of such a spirit being, from the nature of things, fitted to provoke indignation and ensure defeat. The more lofty and towering its pretensions, the more indispensable should it find a religious pretext to carry them out. And hence the scene of its operations is expressly laid in the temple of God, as something essentially significant of their nature: "So that as God he sits"—not simply "and he does sit," as a distinct part of his proceedings, or an aggravation of their impious character, but of necessity he takes this course, in order to make good his self-exalting projects: "So that, as God he sits in the temple of God, showing himself that he is God." In short, *the church was the requisite sphere for such a power developing itself;* in this alone could it reach the height of presumption and God-dishonouring worldliness it aspires after; and consequently, the opposition to God and assumption of divine prerogatives must be virtual only, and not formal or professed; there must needs be the show of religion, as well as the setting up of a standard, and the encouragement of practices, that are opposed to the spirit of the Bible.[1] Then, thirdly, con-

[1] See Appendix K.

sidering the change which Christianity has introduced, and the differences subsisting between Old and New Testament times, while substantially the same acts are ascribed to the typical and the antitypical antichrist, the manner of their accomplishment must be understood to have not only allowed, but required some diversity. This is common to relations generally between Old and New Testament times. In the one, both the religion and the history partook much of the local, the outward, and the individual: while in the other, it is the inward, the general, the diffusive, which chiefly predominate; and hence things which might, while the old relations stood, have been transacted in a particular spot, or embodied in a single individual, must now, though occupying relatively the same place, be quite otherwise carried into execution. Since the Christian church, which is confined to no land or region, has taken the place of the ancient temple, and is called by its name, no individual could do in it precisely what was done by Antiochus at Jerusalem. The corresponding power, which is described as that of an individual, because it was to be informed and animated by one spirit, could admit of being so described, only by being viewed collectively; in reality, it could no more, than the temple it was to usurp, and in great part also occupy, be simply local and personal. And, indeed, even in former times, Antiochus was rather the exponent and representative of an evil, that had spread far and wide in Israel, than an independent power; but much more must this be the case with what should correspond to it in Christian times. So that, as antichrist was shown even in the apostolic age to be a collective designation, such terms as "the wicked," "the man of sin," "the son of perdition," must have been intended to bear a like extent of meaning. They all point back to the vision of Daniel, in which the divine kingdom had its representation in one like a Son of Man; and indicate, that this apostate power would strive to imitate the man-like appearance of the other—would *profess* to be what it *really* was; but so far from being, like it, the image of the spiritual and divine, should be rather the impersonation of the sensual and the devilish. It would be a son, indeed, but like Judas, a son of perdition; a manly rather than a beastly form, but one gathering up and garnishing with a deceitful show the worse elements of man's fallen condition, and so, incurring the doom of the heaviest condemnation.[1]

On the whole, then, the conclusion which forces itself upon our minds from a full and impartial consideration of the apostolic testimony, is that the antichristian apostacy cannot be identified either with the heathenism of ancient Rome, or with any conceivable form of infidelity or atheism yet to be developed. The conditions of the prophetical enigma are not satisfied by either of these views. So much for the *negative* side of the question. And in regard to the *positive*, if we may not say (as, indeed, we by no means think it can in truth be said) that in Romanism and the papacy the anticipated evil has found its *only* realization; yet we cannot for a moment doubt, that it is there we are to look for the most complete, systematic, and palpable embodiment of its grand characteristics. *There*, we perceive, as nowhere else, either to the same extent, or with the same firm determination of purpose, a mass of errors and abuses "grafted on the Christian faith, in opposition to, and in outrage of, its genius and its commands, and taking a bold possession of the Christian church." We see "the doctrines of celibacy, and of a ritual abstinence from meats, against the whole spirit of the gospel, set up in the church by an authority claiming to have universal obedience; a man of sin exalting himself in the temple of God, and openly challenging rights of faith and honour due to God; advanc-

[1] In saying that we do not reject the notion of Langé, as quoted by Auberlen, p. 307, of Auberlen himself, and many others, that "as every phase of mind has its more prominent representatives and directors, so the different aspects of antichristianism appear blooming in individual antichrists;" but we are of opinion, that it is pressing an Old Testament analogy too far, and overlooking the diversity of circumstances introduced by the gospel, when it is announced as at once an historical and a Scriptural result, that "these individual antichrists shall one day reach their close in an evil genius far outstripping all predecessors." We see no proper ground for such an expectation.

ing himself by signs and lying wonders, and turning his pretended miracles to the disproof and discredit of some of the chief doctrines or precepts of Christianity; and this system of ambition and falsehood succeeding, established with the deluded conviction of men still holding the profession of Christianity."[1] All this meets so remarkably the conditions of St Paul's prophecy, and in its history and growth also from the apostolic age so strikingly accords with the warnings given of its gradual and stealthy approach, that, wherever else the antichrist may exist, they must be strangely biassed, who do not discern its likeness in the Romish apostacy. We may the rather rest in the certainty of this conclusion, as it is matter of historical certainty, that ages before the Reformation, and, indeed, all through the long conflict that was ever renewing itself on the part of kings and men of faith against Rome, the Pope was often denounced as the antichrist, and man of sin. But it is one thing to find a great and palpable realization of the idea there, and another thing to hold, that it is the only realization to be found in the past or the future. And if Romanists have made void the testimony of Scripture in rejecting the one application, we fear Protestants have too often grievously narrowed it by excluding every other. Of this, however, we shall have a fitter occasion to speak, when we have examined that remaining portion of New Testament Scripture, which treats of the same subject, and in a way peculiarly its own. We refer, of course, to the Apocalypse.

3. In turning to this last division of the New Testament writings, we find no use made of the more peculiar part of the phraseology we have recently been considering. The terms "antichrist," "man of sin," "son of perdition," or "apostacy," are never met with—though there is no want of terms and representations, which coincide with them in meaning. In the first part of the book, which describes the things that *were* in connection with the seven churches of Asia, and through

[1] Davison's Discourses on Prophecy, p. 448.

them presents us with the Lord's idea of a true church, we are furnished with many proofs of an already begun apostacy, and see a prevailing tendency towards the forms of evil, the antichristian spirit of error and corruption, of which we have been discoursing. In almost every one of the churches addressed, there appears an intermingling of the false with the true; Satan already had something of his own in them. And in some the evil had assumed the precise form of a mystery of iniquity, or a course of deep and deadly defection, under the guise of lofty pretensions, and a crafty ensnaring policy. Not only do we read of an Ephesus, where the first love was lost, of a Sardis, where little more than a name to live continued to exist, and a Laodicea, where fleshly ease and self-confidence generally prevailed, but we have also a Pergamos, and a Thyatira, where false prophets or teachers, designated Nicolaitans and followers of Balaam, plied their arts of seduction, seeking with their false gnosis to draw men away from the true; and the false prophetess Jezebel (whether an individual, or, as may rather be supposed, an influential party) through whom the community were being enticed to spiritual whoredom, or led to couple with the profession of the faith a heathenish looseness and carnality of spirit. In these disclosures respecting the existing state of things, we have presented to our view, as already in active operation, the antichristian spirit—the mixture of false doctrine with true, of corruption in practice with swelling words of profession—of the world, in short, with the church, which constitutes the distinguishing peculiarity of Paul's apostacy, and John's antichrist. And so essential was it, according to the mind of Christ, to the condition and calling of the church, for her to resist and stand free from the elements of corruption, which were thus striving to press in upon her from the world, that the Lord, throughout the whole of these epistles, threatens with the sorest judgments such as might yield to the pernicious influence, and declares His purpose to recognise now as His real people, and hereafter reward with the honours of His kingdom, none but those who should overcome, and hold fast the purity and stedfastness of their allegiance to him. All besides were of the wicked one, and not of Christ; deceitful workers and children of perdition, not temples of the Spirit, and heirs of glory.

Now, in these representations of the things which *were*, we have a key to the general object and meaning of the symbolical revelation given in the remainder of the book of the things which were *to come*. In respect to the church at large, and its coming fortunes, we have there exhibited the same tendencies, conflicts, and results. We see the church, by reason of her connection with Christ, destined to conquer and reign, but meanwhile greatly marred by the darkness and corruption which was to press in upon her from the world. In consequence of this, she is by the visitation of God chastened and purged; in her worst part judged and tormented by having her sin turned into her punishment; calamities and woes are brought upon her in manifold succession from that world which she sinfully coveted and embraced; until the work of purification being accomplished, and a church in holy beauty being prepared for the glories of the Lamb, the full and proper union between her and her Divine Head is consummated, and the mystery of God concerning His work on earth finished amid songs of triumph and scenes of ineffable delight. In the evolution of this singular and complicated symbolical history, the anticipated degeneracy of the church, and the formation in her of a vast antichristian power of the kind already described, is continually implied, and sometimes more, sometimes less explicitly alluded to; but there are two portions more particularly, in which it is distinctly and formally represented.

The first of these is introduced at chap. xi., in connection with the sixth trumpet, and is presented under the image that had been previously used by the apostle Paul (2 Thess. ii. 4), that of the temple of God. "There was given me," it is said, "a reed like unto a rod: and the angel stood, saying, Rise and measure the temple of God, and the altar, and them that worship therein. But the court which is without the temple leave out, and measure it not; for it is given unto the Gentiles; and the holy city shall they tread under foot forty and two months." We can regard this remarkable passage in no other light, than as an expansion of St Paul's description, indicating more particularly how the antichristian power was to sit in the temple of God, and the relation in which it should stand to the true church. Romish writers, and latterly, also some Protestants, have laboured hard to impose the same interpretation upon this, as upon the passage in the Thessalonians, and to understand by the two parties described, the Christian church, on the one side, and on the other, the opposing and persecuting power of heathen Rome. But the attempt must ever appear fruitless to those who understand the symbolical language of Scripture, and would give it a consistent and unbiassed application. The words manifestly delineate, not merely two different and opposing parties, but two classes of worshippers—parties alike professing to belong to the same visible temple of God, though one of them alone really and properly abiding in it. This latter class are those who are symbolized by what was to be measured, as that which had its appointment of God, and was under His careful guardianship—"the temple of God, and the altar, and them that worship therein." They are, in a word, God's living temple—his "spiritual house," or "holy priesthood," whose duty and calling it is to "offer up spiritual sacrifices acceptable to God by Jesus Christ." The other portion, though also, in a sense, belonging to the same sacred building, only lying outside the strictly sacred territory, was to be left unmeasured, as wanting the right connection with God, and a real interest in His faithful keeping. It is called "the court without the temple," and is represented as "being given to the Gentiles," with reference to the uncircumcised condition of those, who of old, worshipped in such a court, and, without doubt, to indicate the uncircumcised, or really unsanctified state, of those whom it imaged, however holy they might externally seem. That they were to have, more or less, the *semblance* of this, their position in the temple-court clearly denotes; but that it was to be only a semblance, that it was to want the reality of divine grace and life, the merely external, essentially heathenish or worldly nature of the position, not less clearly demonstrates. The characters indicated, therefore, were of necessity to form a church party, but the false as contra-distinguished from the true—the world in the church; and so, coinciding in character with the apostacy of Paul, and the spirit of antichrist in the epistles of John. And when it is said of this corrupt party, that they should "tread the holy city under foot forty and two months," we are plainly informed, that they were, notwithstanding the false position they occupied, to have the ascendancy in the professing church of God; nay, and should trample on and oppress those who alone rightfully belonged to it. The "holy city" is but another name for the church, the true members of which have their names written, as it were, among the living in Jerusalem; and to tread down this city is, in other words, to rule with proud domination over the sincere people of God, and treat them with persecuting violence. The period during which this unnatural state of things was to last is described by the mystical term of "forty and two months," which, whether it may be capable or not of being definitely determined, must have been meant to comprehend a period of some continuance. For, in another place, it denotes the time during which the church was to be in the wilderness (chap. xii. 6), that is, in a tried, humbled, and afflicted condition; a state, into which she *began* to enter, shortly after the Lord's ascension to the heavenly places, and out of which she is only to come to possess with him the inheritance. Here also it embraces the whole time between the rise of the corrupt and apostate party in the church, and their complete overthrow, which takes place at the sounding of the seventh trumpet, when the kingdoms of this world are declared to have become the kingdom of our Lord and His Christ (ver. 15). During this time the real church is represented as occupying chiefly a witnessing condition. Precluded from outwardly ruling in the things of God, she can only deliver a testimony—and is, therefore, symbolized by two witnesses, the legal number for such a purpose; implying that God would still continue a succession of faithful persons, adequate, though but barely adequate, it may be, to such a purpose. And as the testimony they should utter was that of God's own word, it could not be without effect; the protest it delivered against reigning error and corruption, and in behalf of the truth of Christ, must make itself heard, like the testimony of old on the tables of the covenant, alike in the ear of Heaven and in the consciences of men. It is on this word, which is the expression of God's mind and will, that all blessing and cursing is found to turn; by it the windows of heaven are shut or opened, and life and death (spiritually) are administered among men (ver. 5, 6). No wonder, therefore, that the ungodly dominant party, who are said to have their dwelling upon the earth (ver. 10), because they belonged entirely to the earthly sphere, should seek to stop the mouths of those who had such a testimony to deliver, and even proceed to the last extremities against them, by utterly silencing them, or, as it is called, putting them to death, killing them as witnesses. To make it more apparent, how, and by whom this should be effected, it is said to take place "in the great city, which spiritually is called Sodom and Egypt, where also our Lord was crucified;" that is, it was to be done by an apostate church that had formally joined hands with the world, as when the Jewish church combined with Pilate and Herod to destroy Jesus, and had become like the most reprobate portions of the world itself. But still it does not succeed in its object; the tormenting testimony cannot so be quenched; it revives again, all the louder and more impressive in its utterances for the violence that has been done to it; the old saying is anew verified, that the blood of the saints is the seed of the church; and thus, by striving unto blood, and holding fast the word of her testimony, the cause represented by her faithful children grows and prospers—after suffering, and through it they rise, like their Divine head, to the higher region of power and influence, until at length the system of antichristian error they opposed falls under the doom of heaven, and the world in the church comes to be exchanged for the church in the world.

Such briefly, and without reference to explicit times or periods (of which we may afterwards speak), is the tenor and import of this first symbolical representation in the Apocalypse of an apostatizing and corrupt, as contra-distinguished from the true church. So closely does it join itself to earlier revelations upon the subject, especially to the passage in the second epistle to the Thessalonians, that it seems much like the turning of what had been there written into a parable, or presenting it in the form of a symbolical narrative—only with less regard, than in St Paul's description, to the means by which the antichristian usurpation was to be effected, more to the manner in which it should be met and overcome by the remnant of a faithful church. And it should be well noted in respect to this latter point, which is here, for the first time, distinctly exhibited, that no mention is made of any instrumentality on the part of the church, or in behalf of the cause of righteousness, but the unswerving and devoted use of the testimony of God's word. The operation and effects of this are described (in accordance with the general character of the vision), under material imagery, such as the power of the witnesses in opening and shutting up heaven, fire going out of their mouth, and latterly the occurrence of an earthquake, shaking, to its foundations, the corrupt city, and partly destroying, partly leading to the conversion of its inhabitants. But all these are manifestly images, not of agencies employed, but rather of effects produced, by the one grand agency of a living church, plying the mighty weapon of God's testimony. As the result of her doing this, undoubtedly, many external and even political changes must ensue, such as cannot but carry the aspect of woes and judgments to the apostate and worldly power. But the primary and fundamental result—that also which carries all else in its train, is the success of the testimony itself; it is this alone which can secure a moral victory, and, in such a case, nothing but a moral victory can be either adequate or permanent; it, and nothing else, lays the axe to the root of the tree, and cuts it down for ever. Apart from this, outward calamities or temporal judgments, at most effect but the removal of a few branches.

The other formal representation given of this subject in the Apocalypse is founded upon a different image; upon the Church's relation to Christ as His bride or spouse. It was especially for the purpose (as noticed in last section), of obtaining a symbolical foundation for unfolding the false and unfaithful part, which so large a portion of the professing church was to play in the future, that the symbolical representations of St John, while coinciding so much with those of Daniel, split here into the two parts of humanity, what in the former case had been preserved in its unity. With John as well as with Daniel, the Divine kingdom as a whole, in its ideal grandeur and perfection, has its representation in one, who had the appearance of a Son of man, and that irradiated with a brightness and glory altogether divine. But since this representation had been embodied, before the writing of the Apocalypse, in a living personality, and the idea involved in it was there realized in all its completeness, it became necessary, when tracing out the perspective of the church's history amid the imperfections of a present life, and the defections of an unfaithful and apostate spirit, to divide between the head and the members. This was done by choosing the female side of humanity for the symbol of the church, viewed in connection with the bonds, obligations, and prospects of the marriage vow. The real church, therefore, is the woman clothed with the sun—the chaste virgin without spot or wrinkle, pure and glorious, therefore fit to be the Lamb's wife, and to share with Him in the blessings and honours of His kingdom. But there is another woman, a harlot, who stands related to the true church precisely as an unfaithful and profligate spouse to one of unshaken probity and worth: not, therefore, a simply unrighteous and wicked party, but such a party with a Christian profession; a church degenerate, faithless, sunk in the mire of worldliness and sin. Such, precisely, is the sense in which this symbol is employed in Old Testament prophecy; and in designating the false and corrupt church a harlot, or mother of abominations, St John only followed a precedent, that had been given in a multitude of prophetical passages (Isa. lvii. 3–5; Jer. ii., iii.; Ezek. xvi., xxiii.; Hos. i., ii., etc.). *There* the terms adulteress, harlot, or whore, with scarcely an exception, denote the backslidden and apostate community of Israel. Our Lord also makes a similar use of the image (Matth. xii. 39, xvi. 4; Mark viii. 38). And in the earlier part of the Apocalypse, the incipient evil in this respect, the declension that had begun in certain churches, by falling into the corrupt ways and practices of the world, is characterized as whoredom and the committing of fornication (chap. ii. 14, 20, 22); as, on the other hand, the true and faithful church is afterwards represented as a company, who retained their virgin-purity (chap. xiv. 4), while immediately in contrast to them, the faithless portion is brought into view as the great whore (ver. 8). So that both the general usage in prophecy, and the usage in particular portions of this book, can leave no reasonable ground to doubt as to the sense meant to be conveyed by the figurative expression.[1]

This view is also confirmed by the descriptive signature emblazoned on the forehead of this mystical woman: "Upon her forehead was a name written, mystery, Babylon the great, the mother of harlots and abominations of the earth." The designation of Babylon points to the essentially heathen, un-

[1] It is marvellous, and can only be accounted for by the perverting bias of a false hypothesis, how, in the face of this whole stream of prophetical usage, Hengstenberg (following the Catholic, and a few continental Protestant writers), should understand by the whore merely the worldly Romish state, and by her fornication the arts with which she drew the nations of the earth under her sway. For any appearance of support to this view, he can only refer to the two passages, Isa. xxiii. 15-18; Nah. iii. 4, where the figure is used similarly of Tyre and Nineveh. But two such isolated passages can be of no force in determining the usage in a book, which, as to its language, is an echo of that of prophecy in general. But were it otherwise doubtful, the connection in this book itself, between the whore and the woman, renders it certain that the former can only denote a corruption of what is denoted by the latter.

godly character of the power represented, and its hostile relation to the true church of God; with the further indication (which is more expressly brought out in ver. 18), that it was to have a seat and concentration of influence in a modern city (that, namely, of Rome) similar to what the Chaldean monarchy once had in Babylon. If this, however, had stood alone, we should only have had presented to us the antichristian and worldly character of the power, without anything to imply that it had become such by a process of declension and apostacy. But a single word, and that the very first in the inscription, proclaims this; it intimates that the really Babylonish character of the power was so far from being the ostensible one, that a spiritual discernment should be needed to perceive it. The term *mystery*, in the quite uniform usage of Scripture, denotes something which lies beyond the ken of the merely natural apprehension, and is revealed only to such as have the mind and Spirit of God. So it is used frequently by the apostle Paul (Rom. xvi. 25; 1 Cor. ii. 7–10; Eph. iii. 3, 5; 1 Cor. xv. 51); and by St John himself, first at the commencement of this book, chap. i. 20, where the explanation of the seven candlesticks and the seven stars is called a mystery, because disclosing in connection with them something greater and deeper than the bodily eye perceived; and again at chap. x. 7, where the work of God's providence towards the church and the world is styled a mystery, plainly from its containing so much that lay above and beyond the reach of the natural understanding, and which could only be learned by special revelation from above. Now, there had been no mystery in this sense, had the power here referred to been merely a worldly kingdom, opposing and persecuting the church of God, and as such called Babylon from its resemblance to the old heathen power of that name; the commonest understanding might have perceived the meaning and the propriety of the designation. But there *was* a mystery in the strictest sense, if the power so designated professed to be the very reverse of what the designation implied; if by a spirit of degeneracy and unfaithfulness it had, while still retaining its claim to spirituality, sunk into a condition of the grossest earthliness and corruption. In that case there would be needed the wisdom that comes from above, the hidden wisdom of God's Spirit, to look through the external appearance, and discern the real state and character underneath. To call this power, therefore, in connection with the appellation Babylon, a mystery, was quite of a piece with calling Jerusalem in our Lord's time, and in after times the corrupt and apostate church *spiritually*, Sodom and Egypt (chap. xi. 8): it denoted a character the reverse to the spiritual mind that it should seem to the carnal. And when along with this indication of a reality contrary to the appearance and profession, we find coupled the epithet of "mother of harlots and abominations," the evidence is complete, that a degenerate power of the worst description, a false, apostate, corrupt and worldly church, must have been the kind of power represented in the image.

Very striking, also, and still farther confirmatory of what has been said, is the manner in which the image is introduced, and the place and appearance ascribed to it. The evangelist represents himself, as carried in the spirit, for the purpose of beholding this sight, into a wilderness (ver. 3). Had it been the worldly dominant monarchy of Rome, which was to be exhibited in vision, this had certainly been a strange place to be taken to see it; the marts of commerce or the lofty mountains would have been the more fitting scenes. But it perfectly accords with the view we have given of the subject, and is no doubtful link of connection between the present representation and a former one. The prophet had left the true church, as symbolized by the woman that was clothed with the sun, in the wilderness, whither she had fled for safety, and whither, also, she was followed by the dragon with his flood-like hordes. We already saw, in what is said at chap. xii. 17, of a *remnant* only of her seed being said to keep the commandments of God and the testimony of Jesus, evidence of a certain success having been won by the adversary in the efforts he was thus going to put forth against her. And now, when the prophet is again borne in the Spirit to a wilderness, instead of seeing *the* woman he had seen in such a place before, he beholds *a* woman, indeed (there is no article), but one so unlike the former, that the name only remained: one so far from being all radiant with celestial brightness and glory, like the other, that she was immersed in the foulness and degradation of earth; sitting on a scarlet-coloured beast, and herself arrayed in purple and scarlet colour, decked with gold and precious stones and pearls—the best, no doubt, of a worldly attire, but still all of the earth, earthy. While the woman is so different, the beast is the same as before—the same seven-headed, ten-horned monster, full of a spirit of blasphemy (ver. 3, comp. with chap. xiii. 1); in plain terms, the worldly antichristian power in its last great embodiment; so that a woman sitting on this, must be a church sunk down to the world's level, and having no higher place than that of leaning on worldly confidences, and to a certain extent directing and ruling in the worldly sphere. But of necessity she could only do this by entering into the beast's hostility to the kingdom of God, and warring with the real members of that kingdom, who should hold the faith and testimony of Jesus. Hence the woman appeared also "drunk with the blood of the saints, and with the blood of the martyrs of Jesus" (ver. 6). This explains why the prophet wondered at the spectacle, even with a great admiration! Had it been merely a heathen power, or one that stood altogether apart from the things of God's kingdom which he saw thus represented before him, there had been no great reason for astonishment; the ungodliness, corruption, and persecuting violence exhibited were precisely what might have been expected. But such a transformation—a power spiritual in its origin, and claiming by its appearance still to possess a spiritual character—for such a power to have sunk so low, and come to act so atrocious a part, might well awake the most profound astonishment. It was the same thing substantially, but with far greater aggravations, which, in Old Testament times, led the prophets to call both upon heaven and earth to express amazement as at an unheard-of enormity (Isa. i. 2; Jer. ii. 10, xvii. 13).

The result, then, which must here be arrived at is manifest; every essential feature in the symbolical delineation forces on us the conclusion, that it is a fallen and degenerate church which is delineated—a power claiming the character, but opposed to the spirit and interests of the real church—worldly, temporising, persecuting. Nor only so; but it was to be also a power most extensive in its dominion, and preponderating in its influence; for the woman appeared sitting on many waters, which are explained to mean "peoples and multitudes, and nations and tongues" (ver. 15); so that she should seem to want little of a complete universality. It is the great apostacy of St Paul come to its perfection, the antichrist in its full development, and well-nigh in total possession of the earth which is the inheritance of Christ and his church. It is itself the church become worldly, promising to those who imbibe its spirit a crown without a cross, a pathway to glory without suffering in the flesh and ceasing from sin; presenting to them, not the Lord's cup of manifold temptations and resistance unto blood against sin; but the golden cup of fleshly indulgence and foul abominations (ver. 4); not operating as the light of the world and making itself felt throughout the earth as a preserving salt, but, on the contrary, corrupting it by the teaching of false doctrines, the sanctification of abuses, and the hatred and scorn exhibited toward the faith and purity of the saints (xix. 2). If it is asked, where such a church is to be found? we cannot hesitate to reply, In that church, which in the nature and extent of its power and influence became in the course of a few generations after the apostle's time the city in another form which reigned over the kings of the earth (chap. xvii. 18)—in the church pre-eminently of Papal Rome. For there it is that the essential elements of the antichristian apostacy, worldliness of spirit, corruption of doctrine, licentiousness of manners, hatred and oppression of the truth, have had, not as by stealth, or in spite of a better faith, but formally and on principle their great and most systematic operation: there, that the queen-like elevation of Babylonish pride and security has been most conspicuously manifested: there, in a word, that the more distinctive characteristics of the Apocalyptic whore have found their most complete and palpable exemplification. When inquisition is made for the blood of saints and for those who have the mark of the beast, there can be no doubt, among such as know the mind of God, that they will be found in the communion of Rome.

But while we thus hold the charge to be applicable to the Romish church, primarily and peculiarly, we by no means think it should be laid there, as it too commonly is, exclusively. The Eastern church, which does not differ essentially from that of Rome, must also be included; and much, too, that is to be found under the name of Protestantism. This Book of the Revelation of Jesus Christ, like the book of God's revelation generally, is pregnant with great principles of good and evil, which were to find their application far and wide in the coming future; and no more in regard to the antichrist, than to Christ Himself, is it to be said, Lo, here he is, or, Lo there, as if he were to be confined within some local territory, or pent up in the forms of an external worship. God is no respecter of persons, nor a creator of artificial distinctions. Wherever the symptoms of an antichristian spirit, or of a grovelling and worldly condition, discover themselves in the church, there, we say with our Lord, in a like case, the carcase is, and there, also, the eagles shall be gathered together. The assurances which are sometimes held out to the Protestants of this land and America, of safety from the doom of antichrist—because, forsooth, "we never formed, or do not now form, a street of the mystical Babylon," or because we never actually "shed the blood of the martyrs"—sound to our ears very much like the flattering unction of those of old, who deemed that, as they had not themselves killed the prophets, so they should not inherit the condemnation of them who did, or of those who sheltered themselves under the thought of being Abraham's seed, as enough to screen them from the judgments denounced against their sins. Our Lord showed himself to be of a different mind when he charged the one class with being children of the devil, and the other with being in danger of the accumulated retribution due for all the righteous blood that had been shed in bygone generations of the world; and of like mind also were the ancient prophets, who so often identified the condition and doom of Israel with those of the heathen (Ezek. xvi.; Amos ix. 7, 8, etc.) In the realities of the world's history, as in the visions of the Divine seer, there are two, and only two, kinds of Christianity—the false and the true, the worldly and the spiritual. The one is found in those who, in their state and character, correspond essentially with the symbol of the woman clothed with the sun, with the moon beneath her feet, or, which is all one, possess what is commended in the seven Asiatic churches; the other is found in the merely outer court worshippers, who have not the faith that overcomes the world, whose citizenship is not in heaven, who mind earthly things. All who are not of the Lamb's wife, and related to the New Jerusalem, are necessarily of Babylon, and must share in her inheritance of evil.

On this point there is much truth in the following remarks of a writer, to whom we have often already had occasion to refer, and which we the rather quote, as they exhibit an aspect of the matter too much overlooked by writers in this country:—"The whore is at bottom as old as the woman, just as the visible and the invisible church have scarcely ever been absolutely identical. There was a time for Israel of first betrothed love, of which Jeremiah speaks (chap. ii. 2, 3), the time of the departure from Egypt, and the beginning of their sojourn in the wilderness. So, too, was there a time of first love for the Christian church, the apostolic age, especially in its earlier periods, which are also represented in Rev. xi. 8, xii. 6, 14, as those of Egypt, and of the entrance into the wilderness. But the whorish way very soon began. Israel, as a people, was, in general, inconstant; and the small company of genuine believing Israelites, the woman, was at all times only as the kernel concealed in the shell. This is indicated in the Apocalypse itself, since it exhibits the whore as sitting upon all the seven worldly kingdoms, thereby extending the idea embodied in her, as it does also that of the woman, to the times of the Old Testament. The prophets describe at large, in particular Ezekiel, in chap. xvi., xxiii., how shamefully Israel committed fornication with the worldly kingdoms, Egypt, Assyria, Babylon. The same story is resumed in the New Testament. In Rev. xii. a representation is given of the first period of Christianity, when apostate Israel had become the whore, and the young Christian community was the woman—that time of first love among Christians, when the church, as a whole, stood so faithful to her Lord. But whorish ways soon pressed in upon the Christian church herself, so that the general aspect this presents, as seen in chap. xvii., no longer looks like the woman, but the whore, the great Babylon, in which the people of the Lord (equivalent to the woman), were concealed (xviii. 4). We are met here by a fundamental view of the Bible, which is of importance for a right understanding of all prophecy and history. God has granted to humanity at large, for its development, the two essential communal institutions of state and church—the latter in a twofold form, as it first existed in Old Testament times, with people and state bound together, then in the New Testament with a spirit of liberty. State and church are noble gifts of God, the one a gift of nature, a creation gift; the other a special gift of grace, the offspring of revelation. But these divine ordinances reach their proper end only in the case of a small number of men. Taken generally, they are deformed and desecrated by sin. States fall away to the manner of the beast, churches to that of the whore. Still, however, they continue to exist under the Divine forbearance till their purpose is fulfilled; and under the protection of the state, under the superintendence of the church, under the pressure even of their mal-administration, an elect people, the chaste and faithful spouse of Christ, are gathered. For this kernel the beast and whore serve as a shell, as a scaffolding for the true temple. And when the kernel has fully grown, when the building is finished, then shall the shell fall off, and the scaffolding be dashed in pieces;

and every one who does not belong to the temple must have his doom among the rubbish that is to be destroyed. So will it be found then, when the judgment alights upon Babylon, and the word is heard, Go ye out of her, my people. And so was it when the judgment fell upon the people of the old covenant, from among the ruins of Israel and Jerusalem came forth the young Christian community. . . . This absolute separation, which the Holy One is to make, between light and darkness, between the kingdom of God and the world, between the woman and the beast, appears strange to us, especially in the present age. Hence do we find it so hard to understand the Apocalypse. The key to it (according to chap. v. 9) is the cross, through which the world is crucified to us, and we to the world. The fundamental error, however, in our Christian theory and practice, is the mingling together of God's kingdom and the world, which the Holy Scriptures stigmatise as whoredom. We, therefore, cannot understand the Divine zeal against it. We want the clear, spiritual discernment for the sins of the church and of Christians—we want it for our own sins. Hence we think the thunder-words of chap. xvii. and xviii. cannot be for the church, they must be meant for worldly states. Ah! had we but the eye with which prophets, apostles, and Jesus himself, the friend of sinners, looked upon the church of their times! The Pharisees were, confessedly, not so very bad a people; they had, in their own way, a zeal for divine things. And yet with what terrible severity does the Lord rebuke them! The prophets lived, in great part, under good kings, such as Hezekiah and Josiah; and yet what powerful calls to repentance, and threatenings of judgment, do we hear from their lips! The seductive and heretical teachers, with whom the apostles had to do, were far from being of so dangerous and fundamentally erroneous a kind as those of the present day; and yet with what words do Paul and John, Peter and Jude, testify against them! Sin is, in God's eye, a much viler thing than it is in man's. But its character is vilest in those on whom God has bestowed His grace, who possess and know

God's word, and are called to serve Him. The driving after the world in the church is the most worldly and the most profane. Therefore, in its descriptions of Babylon, the Apocalypse combines the main features, not only of Israel's sins, but those also of the heathen, as they are found in the prophets. Therefore it pursues at greater length, the representation, of the whore's abominations and judgment, than of the beast's. Therefore is the whole section, which begins with chap. xvii., presented under the aspect of the judgment of the great whore. Therefore, finally, is there even in heaven a quite peculiar joy over her fall more than over that of the beast (xviii. 20, xix. 5)."[1]

We pass now to this fall itself—the judgment to be executed on the apostate and worldly church. Here it is necessary to mark the order of the issues described, the succession, as well as the connection, of God's dealings with the guilty parties. These are altogether three, the beast, the false prophet, and the whore; all of them so many wicked parodies and usurpations of the divine in Christ, and his true church. And they are all so far connected together that they have one and the same worldly foundation, one and the same carnal interest at heart; so that it is not possible to conceive of a complete destruction of one of them, which should not involve also the destruction of the others. Yet in the representation given of the final issues respecting them, there is a marked prominence and priority in the case of the false church. Let us mark the successive stages of the process, as seen in vision by the prophet. First, after it has been said, that the kings or kingdoms into which the Roman monarchy was to fall, and which were to constitute the seventh phase of the beastly power, should have given their power and strength to the beast, it is intimated in what is plainly a general announcement (xvii. 14), that "they shall make war with the Lamb, and the Lamb shall overcome them; for He is Lord of lords, and King of

[1] Auberlen der Prophet Daniel und die Offenbarung Johannis. Page 287, sq.

kings; and they that are with Him are called, and chosen, and faithful." This brief statement covers, we may say, the whole of what follows, to the end of chap. xix.; for it is only with the close of this chapter that we have the victory of the Lamb over the kings and the beast, brought to an absolute termination. The whole, therefore, of the intervening part must be regarded merely as the filling up of the picture, briefly sketched in the verse above quoted; it presents in detail the process of overcoming the adverse powers. Then, secondly, in this vanquishing process, the whore is the party that occupies both the first and the most conspicuous place. It is said, at chap. xvii. 16, "And the ten horns which thou sawest upon the beast, shall hate the whore, and shall make her desolate and naked, and shall eat her flesh and burn her with fire. For God put it into their hearts to do His mind, and to do one mind (so it literally is), and to give their kingdom unto the beast, until the words of God shall be fulfilled." There was to be a certain unity of sentiment and action among the kingdoms, after they had passed through the stage of a temporary conversion (when the beast seemed as if it were killed), which should show itself in their giving their kingdom to the beast, or exhibiting in their general principles and behaviour much of the beastly nature. And they should do this till the words of God should be fulfilled—but only, it is implied, till then; and when the divine purpose required it, they should turn their mind against the whore, and utterly abolish her existence. The remarkable thing here is, that it is not said they changed their relation to the beast, while they so entirely changed it to the whore: the destruction of the false and apostate church, which had played into the hands of the godless, worldly power, and leant for support on this, as this again on that, is represented as taking place by itself, while still the conflict between the kingdoms and Christ, if begun, was by no means concluded. Lastly, after the description of Babylon's downfal, or the infliction of judgment and ruin on the false church, and the shouts of triumph raised over her in heaven and earth (detailed at length in chap.

xviii. and xix. 1–6) comes an account of the prosecution of the war with the kings or kingdoms of the earth. In this representation, the scene is transferred from earth to heaven; for it concerns Christ and the true church, who all along, as to position and character, vital power and influence, have been contemplated as belonging to the heavenly sphere, in contrast to the inhabiters of the earth, who belong to the beast and his agencies. The Divine King of Zion, therefore, who in this heavenly sphere has the direction of all the power and the instrumentalities connected with it, appears foremost in the field—he goes forth in battle array, with many crowns on his head (the symbol of complete and universal sovereignty), and in the character of the word of God, with the sharp sword (that, namely, of the word) going out of his mouth. The name and weapon alike proclaim him to be a spiritual warrior, who was to prevail through that word of truth, which is the grand instrument and manifestation of him as the Personal Word. But he does not go thus alone; the armies of heaven follow him on their white horses, clothed in fine linen, white and clean; in other words, the representatives of the true church, spoken of a little before, as the Lamb's bride, arrayed in fine linen, which is the righteousness of the saints (xix. 8); and the same, doubtless, that were mentioned in chap. xvii. 14, as the called, chosen, and faithful band that appeared with Christ as the leader of victory. It is not Christ directly, therefore, but Christ in and through His faithful church, by whom this battle was to be waged, and the victory won. His personal appearance to the eye of the prophet no more necessitates His visible intermingling in the actual conflict, than His opening the seven-sealed book bespoke his personal manifestation among men, to announce or perform the things it contained; or than the appearance of an angel flying through heaven with the everlasting gospel (in chap. xiv. 6) necessarily implied the outward spectacle of such an apparition. What was seen here by the evangelist in the heavenly sphere, like everything else of a like kind in this book, was but a representation in vision of what was actually to take place in the earthly sphere,—a representation of it as going to be accomplished by virtue of a power, and through means of an instrumentality, that hold not of earth, but of heaven—that belong truly and properly to God. It informs us that a living and faithful church, sustained by the presence, and replenished with the power and spirit of Jesus, shall rise to the ascendant as the false and apostate church goes down. With the Lord upon her side giving effect to her spiritual armoury and her work of righteousness, the powers of darkness and corruption shall be driven away; and the beast and the false prophet, with all their misguided followers, shall share substantially the same fate with Babylon; that is, their interest shall perish, and the saints shall enter on their millennial reign of blessedness and peace, holding undisturbed possession of the inheritance which they have at length vindicated from the serpent's brood, and converted into a habitation of righteousness.

We have said, that there is nothing here necessarily implying the visible and personal manifestation of Christ upon the earth. But neither, of course, is it absolutely excluded. Whether he shall actually appear for the decision of this conflict must depend upon the general question whether the Divine economy shall then have reached such a stage of advancement as will render such an appearance fit and proper. It rather belongs, therefore, to the subject of our last section, where we shall have to treat of the kingdom of Christ, in relation to His own second coming, and the nature of the millennium. The questions, which here more immediately call for consideration have respect to the *kind* of judgment to be executed upon the doomed parties, and the manner of its execution. What, precisely, is its nature? Is it simply the conversion of the world to right thoughts and feelings respecting the things of God? Or is it something of a more outward and fleshly character? And, whether the one or the other, how should the judgment upon the whore come to be represented as done by the kingdoms, while these kingdoms still appear to be in opposition to Christ, and to be subdued by Him only at a later period?

To refer to the latter point first, we think it would be a hasty, and perhaps false conclusion from the place given to the judgment upon Babylon, were we to infer (as is very commonly done by writers in this country, also by Auberlen), that Popery and other forms of a corrupt Christianity are certainly to be repudiated by the kingdoms of the world before the work of conversion has made much progress amongst them, and that a considerable interval may elapse, possibly for the church a very trying and perilous interval, between the doom of the false church, and the doom of the worldly power itself, or the destruction of the beast and the false prophet. It may be so; on such a point we would not speak with confidence. It certainly is not a new thing in the history of God's dealings, for the world, even in its unconverted state, to be made the instrument of punishing and humbling to the dust a corrupt and apostate church. Such was signally the case at three great epochs of the past--when Assyria acted as the rod of God's anger in scattering backsliding Israel, when Babylon led captive the people of Judah, and when in the last and worst stage of Jewish impenitence and guilt, the Romans took away their place and nation. In accordance with a great principle in the Divine government the Lord in these, as in many similar cases, made the people's sin their punishment; the staff on which they unrighteously leaned pierced their hand; the same world through which the old serpent beguiled them into unfaithfulness to God, turned against them with the fury and might of an Apollyon. And in one sense, we have no doubt, the same principle will ever be exemplified anew, in so far as the same course is pursued. But there may be different modes of accomplishing it; and it may not be necessary, that the world, when employed in the work of retribution, should always remain in precisely the same state as it was, when used as an instrument and occasion of sin. This must depend on circumstances; and manifestly the circumstances in respect to the church's relation to the world at the period of the ancient judgments referred to, differed very materially from those which belong to the carnal and apostate church of modern times. In the one case the two parties stood formally apart from each other, and the relation, however close, was still only political and outward; in the other there is an actual amalgamation, the church having in its degeneracy given itself to the service of the world, and the world in its several kingdoms identified itself with the church. So that from the very nature of the case the execution of a work of judgment now upon the church by the world must involve much more than a mere change of external relationship; it must imply a revolution in the world's own sentiments on the subject of religion; since what, in this respect, it embraced before, it is now to hate and repudiate. Here, again, it is necessary, not to look merely into the agreements between Old and New Testament things, but to take account also of the differences; and especially to bear in mind, how very greatly more every thing in connection with the affairs of God's kingdom has come to assume an inward and diffusive character, than it formerly possessed. It is also to be borne in mind, that in the pictorial delineations of prophecy, the moral element often discovers itself, even in the mode of representation adopted; and that to give prominence to this, the place of priority in judgment is sometimes assigned to the party which has been the worst in guilt, though it may not actually be the one that has first to fall. Thus, in the vision of Nebuchadnezzar, the great stone is represented as smiting the image first upon the toes, and proceeding upwards till the whole was crushed to atoms, the head last; although, in the reality, the order was the reverse; and the last is placed first in the vision, merely because it seemed ripest for destruction, and stood most prominent in the eye of the mind. These considerations ought to be taken into account here, not as of themselves disproving the notion of a priority in point of time in the world's execution of judgment upon Babylon, before it is itself either judged or converted; but as showing the necessity of cautious and careful inquiry in determining the probable sequence of such events.

Indeed, it might seem to accord best with the nature of the case, viewed in respect to its singular complexity and inter-connected relationships, that no precise order should be marked out definitely beforehand, as necessary or certain in every case to be followed. Amid the prevailing unity, there could not fail to be a manifold diversity in the degrees of apostacy and guilt adhering, at different times and places, to the false church; and there naturally would be a corresponding diversity in the way and manner in which the destined judgment should take effect. History, too, confirms the impression; for it shows, in the partial judgments already executed upon the apostacy, a very considerable diversity, both in respect to the relative time, and the precise manner of its accomplishment. In many communities at the Reformation, it was through a process of enlightenment and conversion, that the world was brought to hate the whore, and shake itself free from her abominations. But in the France of last century, this work of hatred and judgment was carried on, while the kingdom gave its strength and power even more than ever to the beast; it had light enough from its own oracles to repudiate a false Christianity, but none to receive and cherish the true; and so, we cannot doubt, would it be with many papal regions of the present day, if circumstances should allow them to embody their opinions in action. In Spain and Italy it is much more the worldly power of the kingdoms, than the false church in them, which has hitherto been smitten with judgment. Such ascertained diversities in the past, may readily be supposed to extend into the future; and if so, then sometimes the worldliness and corruption of the church, sometimes those of the kingdoms shall appear to be the first to be judged and cast out. But, in truth, from the connection subsisting between the two, a complete work of judgment cannot be conceived to take place, without both being alike involved in it. Any priority that may be practicable, can belong only to the beginning, not to the consummation of the process. On the one side, the existence of the whore implies the existence of the beast, or the ungodly state of the world; and, on the other, so long as the beast has a horn left, human nature being what it is, the whore will find means somehow to hang by it.

Accordingly, in the Apocalyptic representation, nothing of a very definite kind in this respect is indicated. While the judgment upon Babylon has a fearful prominence assigned to it, and is brought to a close before the war against the kings of the earth, as identified with the beast and the false prophet, is particularly related, still the notice of this war has so far the precedence given to it, that it is cursorily mentioned, even before the kings are said to have turned against the whore (chap. xvii. 14). It may, therefore, be supposed to have, at least, commenced, and made some progress before the period of Babylon's destruction. At the same time, if the war itself is essentially a spiritual one—if its grand characteristic and object is to stand in overcoming their hostility to the cause of Christ, and bringing them from the service and interest of Satan to those of the living God—if this is the nature of the conflict indicated, and the victory to be won, then, in the very nature of things, the doom of Babylon, that is, the general hatred and repudiation of a false and corrupt Christianity, must always, more or less, precede the subversion of the worldly spirit itself. All experience testifies, how much easier it is to detect and abhor hypocrisy, than heartily to embrace the truth—to abjure the pretensions of a false religion, than to become dead to the world, and alive to the interests of God's spiritual kingdom. In the social as well as the personal sphere, there will naturally be some interval between the two—not unfrequently a very considerable one, and one attended with struggles and dangers peculiar to itself. Nor, when the general course of events, and the particular tendencies of the present age are duly considered—especially when it is reflected what advances the world is making in science, literature and philosophy, how, in every department, the knowledge connected with its own earth-sprung culture is growing, and rising continually nearer in its assimilation to the Divine; can it be deemed otherwise than probable, that light may very generally be diffused, sufficient to beget a hatred of Popery, and the false forms of Christianity, while the idolatry of self and the world holds its place as before, or even waxes bolder for a time in its pretensions. In the negative part of the process, profane science and learning may do the part they have often done already; they may expose and reject the falsehood, corruption, and hypocrisy, which enter into the religion of an apostate and spurious Christianity, and thereby prepare the way for its formal abolition. But higher elements will assuredly be required to complete the process. Worldly negations can never wholly uproot what has so many grounds of support in the constitution of society, and the condition of the human heart. And only the reception of that divine truth, which reunites the soul to God, and effectually expels the world from the heart, will be sufficient to work the final extirpation of the antichrist. So that the judgment of the whore can only in part precede that of the beast and the false prophet, or of the world itself in its self-exalting and God-opposing tendencies. They have been too closely united in their lives to be in their deaths far divided.

But *is* the war, with its final issues on the side of Christ's cause and kingdom, of the kind referred to? Is this great conflict to be carried on and decided mainly by the use of spiritual weapons, and not rather (as is very commonly conceived) by some obtrusive and overwhelming displays of divine power and glory? Is it not by the compulsion of resistless might, rather than by moral suasion, that the evil is to be driven out, and the field won for the saints? To answer such questions, we must call in the aid of collateral considerations, as there is nothing in the representation of St John, which can fairly be regarded as absolutely decisive on the subject. He distinctly enough intimates, that the judgment of one of the obnoxious parties—the repudiation and downfal of Babylon—certainly one grand object and result of the war, is to be mainly accomplished by the instrumentality of the kingdoms, which had formerly given her their homage; by a change of mind on their part, or a healthier tone of thought and feeling, the judgment written is to be enforced. And if so much thus, one naturally asks, why not more? why not the whole? Yet, possibly, it might be wrong to extend the inference so far, as the means capable to a large extent of subverting the false, might fail in establishing the true; while they may go far to procure the fall of a corrupt church, they yet may come short of reforming an ungodly world. But there are not wanting considerations to show, that the spiritual element is chiefly to prevail in the matter, and that all else can be little more than incidental and subsidiary.

First of all, the very nature of the conflict points in this direction. It is a conflict with the error and hypocrisy, the selfishness and corruption of the world; and these are to be driven from the souls of men, and cast into the bottomless abyss, not by any mechanical process, or external emanations even of divine glory, but by the truth of Christ established in the heart and conscience. "This is the victory that overcometh the world, even our faith"—the only victory that is real and enduring. Then, secondly, the victory achieved by Christ himself, and the judgment executed by Him directly upon the adversary, was entirely of this description; it was obtained exclusively by the manifestation of the truth of God, and, in doing and suffering, fulfilling His righteous will. Now, in the progress and issues of the divine kingdom, every thing takes its impress and direction from the personal Saviour; and the conflict which is to be waged by the church in the world, in so far as it is properly maintained, is but the reflex of that, in which Christ has himself engaged and overcome. It would be to quit the higher field for a lower, and make the spiritual give way to the carnal, were the church to be indebted for *her* success chiefly to the application of external force or physical suffering. She triumphs far more nobly, and executes judgment greatly more thorough and complete, when, by the aid of spiritual appliances, she causes the truth to be felt in its proper force and magnitude. So is it also in nature: "The light in its silent, beneficent operations, is far mightier than the lightning, notwithstanding the roar that follows it." It was the weak element in the conquests won, and the judgments wrought upon the ungodliness of the world through Israel of old, that they had in them so much of what was merely outward, so little of the Spirit's internal power of conviction to penetrate the heart, and slay its enmity to God in the root. And it is only by having what was then comparatively wanted—by the beneficent operation of the Spirit of truth and holiness in the church and through her instrumentality, not by calling down fire from heaven, or shewing wonders from the deep, that the effectual overthrow may be expected of the adversary's dominion in the world. Thirdly, there is the remarkable circumstance mentioned in chap. xiv. 6–8, of the appearance of an angel (emblem, beyond doubt, of the church in her active ministrations) speeding his way with the gospel among all nations, and calling on them to fear and worship God—and this as the immediate precursor of Babylon's doom, carrying in its train the downfal of the great apostacy. For immediately on that being done, the cry is reported to have been heard, that Babylon was fallen. What can this action import, but that the church was to look for the driving back of the evil that oppressed her, not to any miraculous interposition in her behalf, but to the revival of that testimony, which had been so shamefully abandoned in the apostacy, and the virtue of that blood, which had been so much buried out of sight? She must grasp anew, and with fresh energy display the old banner of the faith, that was delivered to the saints, and in God's name make war with all the powers of darkness and the forms of corruption. Were there but faith for this among the people of God—faith to realize, that the title to the inheritance is already won for them, and that it is their calling and destiny to make it good against all opposition, who can tell what results might be accomplished! what spring-times of life and blessing might yet burst forth upon the world!

That in the circumstances in which the world is placed with so many powers of evil working in it, and forms of corruption established on every side, the struggle may be long and arduous, is only what may be expected. And there may also be expected in its progress many interminglings of external judgment; political convulsions, desolating wars and tumults, which the fermentings of opinion and the operation of the truth themselves will naturally tend to bring on; and besides these, perhaps, also pestilences, famines, fearful troubles, and disturbances in nature, to discomfit the worshippers of nature, and drive them to seek for other means and resources than it can supply. Nay, it is far from improbable, that before the world is cured of the distempers that rage in it, and brought heartily to embrace and carry out the principles of the gospel of Christ, times of uproar and distress may have to be appointed for it, such as have not been witnessed in the past; such times as are spoken of by our Lord, when all things shall seem pregnant with evil and involved in gloom—when it shall be as if the sun were darkened, and the moon did not give her light, and the stars did fall from heaven, and the powers of the heavens were shaken. We need not be at all surprised, if such a time should come in the course of this great conflict; and especially, when it is drawing toward its close, and the adversary knows that his time is short. Though the battle by that time may have been in great part won, yet he may not quit his hold without more fiercely than ever rending his victim. And how but amid great agitations and convulsive movements, can the basis be laid of a new and permanently good order of things? The turmoil, however, shall not last; the days of evil shall be shortened; and whatever there may be connected with them of external appliances, whether in the higher or the lower sphere, can only come to second and enforce the grand agency of a living church with her armour of righteousness and the Spirit of grace making it effectual. May we not appeal for confirmation to the history of the past? What great deliverance has ever been wrought for the kingdom of God apart from this spiritual agency? What did even our Lord's personal appearance and astounding miracles effect, compared with the showers of grace and blessing that came down at Pentecost, and after it? Or compare the spiritual work of the Reformation with the outburst of the French Revolution. Viewed in an external aspect, this last event, no doubt, with its convulsive throes and fiery ebullitions, its merciless retributions for abused power, its confiscations of church property, and summary proceedings against a corrupt clergy, and a superstitious worship, had most the appearance of the execution of a work of judgment on apostate Rome:—And yet how little ultimately did it effect compared with the other? The Reformation struck less violently, but it struck far more powerfully; it was a blow at the root. The secret of its strength lay in resorting so little to physical force, and so much to divine truth and principle. It was distinguished only for the free and copious use made in it of the instrumentality heralded by the angelic precursor of Babylon's fall—the preaching of the everlasting gospel. On this account pre-eminently it proved a season of refreshment to the world, scattered everywhere the seeds of faith and love, undermined the strongholds of error and corruption, and breathed a healthier tone through the whole framework of society. This, therefore, is the kind of work, refreshing times like these are the operations, on which more especially the issue of the conflict is to turn: for them the long-suffering of God waits, suspending, that they may proceed, the time for the final executions of judgment; for them the risen Saviour continues to abide within the veil, that He may dispense of the Spirit's fulness of life and blessing, to help forward the cause of the world's regeneration. And for the church, in any of her members or branches, to stand aloof from such operations—to neglect the word of God and prayer, to allow abuses to remain unrectified, to lay down her testimony against prevailing corruptions, to leave unoccupied any available channel, at home or abroad, for shedding forth the light of the gospel, and advancing the interests of righteousness—for the church so to act, in the hope that the work, which might and should be done *by* her, shall somehow be done *for* her by an outward and judicial display of divine power, were but to prove herself unworthy of her calling, and to continue in sin, not that grace, but (still worse) that iniquity first, and then judgment may abound.

SECTION III.

SUPPLEMENTARY: CONTAINING AN OUTLINE OF THE GENERAL PLAN OF THE APOCALYPSE, FROM CHAP. V. TO THE CLOSE OF CHAP. XIX., WITH REFERENCE MORE ESPECIALLY TO THE DISTINCTIVE CHARACTER AND RELATIVE ORDER OF THE THREE GREAT SERIES OF THE SEALS, THE TRUMPETS, AND THE VIALS.

1. The parts of the Apocalypse more particularly referred to in the two preceding sections, are those which indicate generally the character and relations, the dangers, struggles, and triumphs of the church, from the planting of Christianity to the introduction of the Millennium. They are comprised mainly in the chapters which reach from the beginning of the eleventh to the close of the nineteenth. But there are other things also in these chapters, the actions especially of the vials, in part also of the trumpets, and the times and seasons mentioned, of which no special notice has yet been taken. Before proceeding, therefore, to the consideration of the topics embraced in the three concluding chapters of the Apocalypse, we propose to attempt a brief synopsis and explanation of the Apocalyptic scheme, as contained in chap. v. to xix.; which may be missed by those who are disinclined to enter into such an investigation. Our main object in it will be to arrive at the *proper reading of the symbols themselves, and their mutual relation to each other*, as therein must be sought the key to the structural arrangement and general design of the whole scheme, and the ground of its more particular application to specific movements or results in Divine Providence.

2. The first thing that presents itself to our notice is the account given in chap. v. of the seven-sealed book, remarkable

not only for the number of its seals, but also for the marvellous difficulty connected with the opening of them. After the challenge had been thrown out to the wide universe for any one to attempt it, no one, it is said, was found capable of undertaking the task, but the Lion of the tribe of Judah, and the Root of David. It is clear from this, that by the opening of the book, something more must have been meant than the mere disclosure of its contents; it must have involved, besides, the personal appropriation of these, with a view to their actual accomplishment. Nothing else could have created so gigantic a difficulty. It is clear, also, from the designation of Christ on the occasion, as the Lion of the tribe of Judah, and the Root of David, that the book must have borne respect to a work of war and conquest—a work in which heroic energy and lion-like strength should require to be put forth, and that too for the purpose of vindicating the peculiar honour and blessing secured in covenant to the house of David. What, then, was this? No other than the universal possession and sovereignty of the earth, the right to reign over it, to its uttermost bounds, in the name of the Lord (Gen. xlix. 9, 10; Num. xxiv. 9; Ps. ii., xxii., etc.). The book, therefore, with which none but this royal personage could intermeddle, was, in other words, the book of the inheritance—laying open the way by which the possession must be made good. And it was a sealed book—seven times sealed —not only because there were to be successive stages in the course, such as might fitly be distributed into that number, but because the course itself was to be a hidden one—not patent to men's view, nor one they could beforehand have anticipated, but a complicated mystery, lying under the secrecy of a sevenfold seal. Hence, as if to explain where peculiarly the mystery lay, it is in the character, not of a lion-like hero, or royal personage, but "of a lamb as it had been slain," that Christ is seen approaching to take the book, and enter on the task of disclosing and fulfilling its burden. The songs of praise, also, that are presently afterwards ascribed to Him by the redeemed, celebrate His worth and goodness, especially on this account, that He had "redeemed them by His blood;" and they declared Him to be worthy to take the book, and open the seals thereof, because of His having been slain, and redeemed to Himself a people, whom He has made kings and priests unto God. When they farther add, "And we shall reign on the earth," they point, not only to the expected realisation of their hopes, but also to the assurance, which the action with the book had brought in respect to that expectation; they now see the end desired and looked for, clearly in prospect. Plainly, therefore, the mystery of this book is the mystery of Christ's cross and crown: all that is wonderful and arduous in the working out of His claim to the conquest and dominion of the earth, has its explanation in the difficulty of getting men, within the professing church and without, to receive the doctrine of a crucified Redeemer, as the foundation of all blessing, and to carry out the spirit of humble, holy, self-sacrificing, and devoted love which it breathes. To bring this doctrine and this spirit to the ascendant in the affairs of men, is the mystery and the burden of the seven-sealed book.

3. Though it is our object rather to explain the symbolical structure and meaning of the prophecy before us, than to discuss the topics which it embraces, yet we pause here for a moment to state, that the sealed book having such a purport as we have now stated, there necessarily arise two great aims to be prosecuted in the sequel. There must be first the gathering out and preparing of a people, on the ground of the doctrine of the cross; and then the preparing of the earth for their inheritance, by the dispossessing of the powers of evil, who resist or corrupt the doctrine, that it may become an abode of righteousness. In the typical relations of ancient Israel, we see precisely the same twofold aim prosecuted. An elect people had in the first instance to be found; found both in sufficient numbers to occupy the destined inheritance, and in such a moral condition as might in some measure fit them for accomplishing the ends designed by its occupation. This itself required a long period of preparation, during which alternately trial and blessing, judgment and mercy, now the

oppression and again the protection of the world, were brought into play. And when, through the operation of such varied and conflicting forces, the result, as regards the people, had been in good part attained, then followed the prosecution of the other branch of the divine scheme—the occupation of the inheritance by judging and dispossessing the adversaries. The same, substantially, in both respects, falls to be done now by Christ, in connection with his redeemed people—only with the usual differences that distinguish the relations of the antitype from those of the type. All has now to be conducted on an immensely larger scale, and in the sphere more immediately of spiritual realities rather than of sensible transactions —by means, also, of the Word and Spirit of truth, not of fleshly weapons and political arrangements. What in the earlier line of things was done but imperfectly, with defection and failure adhering to the last, and marring the completeness of the work, must now, by reason of the higher agency employed, and the more advanced stage that has been reached in the divine economy, be perfectly realised; the result must be one altogether worthy of Him who conducts it to its destined completion; it must provide both a people thoroughly prepared for the inheritance, and an inheritance completely won and beautified for their possession. But such a result will inevitably require a most complicated machinery of operations to effect it; and the history may well be expected to be marvellous, both for the good and the evil, the processes of judgment as well as of mercy, with which it is sure to be intermingled.

4. To return, however, to our more proper business. From the very nature and objects of the sealed book, it would seem that its symbolical contents must cover the entire field of the future militant condition of the church, and reach down to the time when the mystery of God shall be finished by the instalment of the church with regal power and glory, in the possession of the inheritance. Such being the case, any other prophetic symbols, or series of prophetic symbols, that follow, must stand to it in the relation of synchronal, not of continua-

tive and posterior developments. To this conclusion, also, the analogy of other portions of prophetic Scripture points. It is a general characteristic in the structure of prophecy, that of its delineations in any particular line or class of relations, each picture stands complete in itself. In that specific direction the prophetic outline is conducted to a close. Many of our Lord's parables are striking exemplifications of this—those, for example, of the sower, of the wheat and tares, of the talents, of the ten virgins, since they, one and all, present the divine kingdom under so many distinct images or aspects, and, in connection with these, disclose its progressive advancement and final issues.[1] The Messianic Psalms—in particular, Ps. ii., xxii., xlv., lxxii., cx.—are formed after the same pattern; and so are many predictions in the greater prophets, such as Isa. ii. 1–5, xi. 1–9, xlix., liii.; Ezek. iv., xvi., xxxiv. But the visions in Daniel make the nearest approach in form to those of the Apocalypse; and there we find the characteristic in question very strongly marked. In Daniel the prospective history of God's kingdom, in its relation to the world, and its own varied fortunes, is presented under the aspect of a twofold series of symbols—first, that of the composite image, and the stone cut from the mountain; then that of the different beasts out of the sea, and one like a Son of Man from

[1] Hence the impropriety, too often exhibited by writers on prophecy, of taking up the representation in a particular parable, and pressing it to the uttermost, as if it contained the whole. This is to do violence to the principle on which they are constructed, and inevitably leads to the giving of undue prominence to individual traits, and making the instruction in one parable clash with that of another. Thus the parable of the tares and the wheat represents the divine kingdom as continuing to the end more or less intermingled with corrupt principles and false members; while in the parable of the leaven the divine element appears fermenting and working on till the whole sphere participates in the renovating change. Two different aspects, but perfectly consistent, if the parts in which they differ are not isolated and unduly pressed, but viewed the one as the complement of the other. By the first we learn that the evil shall never be wholly extirpated (though it may be indefinitely diminished) till the final consummation; by the second, that the good shall not cease to diffuse itself till it has become co-extensive with humanity.

heaven. And each of these delineations covers the same space—continues the history, in its own specific line, to a close; so that they are necessarily synchronal, not successive, in their relation to each other. But, along with these, there are supplementary revelations, one of them also exhibiting a most important aspect of the affairs of the kingdom, entirely omitted in the two former visions—that, namely, in chap. ix., which has respect to the first appearance of Messiah, and His expiatory death. Others do not introduce anything entirely excluded from the first pair, but only present, more in detail, particular traits of the symbolic picture contained in them. Of this class are the visions in chap. viii. and xi. The analogies, therefore, furnished by other portions of the prophetic field, are of such a nature as to confirm the expectation that the seal series in this book shall form a complete whole in itself; and that any other series, or individual representations, which may follow, shall be either wholly, or in part, synchronal—that is, they shall either, under some new aspect, conduct the history of the divine kingdom over the same ground, or bring more fully and particularly into view certain definite portions of the territory. It is the latter, perhaps, that we might chiefly expect to find; as in connected prophecies, like those of this book, it is usual not so much to give diverse exhibitions of the same totality, as rather to supplement what may already have been comprehensively, though somewhat briefly, unfolded, by the introduction of more specific representations.

5. We turn, then, to the three great series of symbols, for the purpose, in the first instance, of ascertaining whether what has now been suggested seems to be the case. In doing so, we look simply at the symbolic representations themselves, and take them in their broader aspect—as such representations ought always to be taken[1]—in order to learn if any traces are to be found in them of synchronal order and connection. Now, the first series, that of the seals, certainly has the ap-

[1] See p. 138.

pearance of forming by itself an entire and comprehensive whole. It commences with the representation of one going forth in the attitude of a warrior, conquering and to conquer, and it ends with the show of a complete and universal subjugation. Under the sixth seal the whole world appears in the last throes of trouble and confusion; nature, in all its departments, is trembling and convulsed; the mountains flit away like shadows; men, of every rank and degree, rush in dismay from the presence of Him whom they had formerly despised, and seek a hiding-place from "the wrath of the Lamb." And, when the next and final seal opens, all is silence. The struggle of conflict is over, the noise and tumult of war have ceased, and the whole field lies prostrate before the one sovereign and undisputed Lord. Taken by itself, therefore, the delineation is complete. It leaves much, indeed, that might be added as to the manner in which the process of resistance and defeat went on, and how the respective parties stood when the struggle came to a close. Yet one does not see how there could be any farther continuation in the same line of things; so far as concerns mere conflict and victory, the end has been reached.[1] In collateral directions, however, there was evi-

[1] We are simply, it must be remembered, endeavouring to read the language and import of the symbols, not attempting to find for them any specific application. But the mere description implies, that we regard the sixth seal as having some other and higher reference than that which would confine it to the age of Constantine. What then took place was a very mingled good, and rather altered the political relations of Christianity, than tended materially to aid it in securing such a triumph, as it is the more peculiar object of the Apocalypse to predict and help forward. To say nothing of the masses of heathenism which stood side by side with the formal Christianity of the empire, not only in Constantine's time, but for centuries afterwards, let any one compare, with the light furnished by late researches into church history, the Christianity of the 4th and 5th centuries with that depicted in the second and third chapters of this book, and ask seriously, whether in the eye of the apocalyptist, the comparatively superficial change which marked the age of Constantine could have, in any adequate degree, substantiated the magnificent imagery of the sixth seal. It is impossible that such a change could have exhibited more than the faintest shadow of what is there delineated.

dently not only room, but much need also, for supplementary revelations; for in the abrupt and stately march of those seals everything appears in the mass. Classes of objects or events are described, but nothing is indicated respecting the more particular relations of the church and the world. And at one remarkable stage of the proceedings an appearance presents itself which manifestly implies much that is untold, and, from its very nature, seems to call for more detailed representations. It occurs in the action of the fifth seal, where were "seen under the altar the souls of them that were slain for the word of God, and for the testimony which they held"—whence it appears that a fierce and bloody persecution of the true church had preceded, or was then in progress, while yet nothing had been expressly related of that description under the earlier seals. Turning, however, to chap. xi. 7, we find an indication given of it in what is written of the faithful witnesses, whom the beast from the bottomless pit was to overcome and kill. But this forms part of the transactions belonging to the sixth trumpet, which may, therefore, be regarded as probably synchronizing with the events of the fifth seal, and one or more of the preceding. We find it again at chap. xii. 11, in what is said of the violence of the dragon after the ascension of Christ. He persecuted to the death the followers of Christ, who, even in death, overcame him by the blood of the Lamb, and the word of their testimony. Still, again, it appears at chap. xiii. 7, in the transactions ascribed to the beast after the healing of his wound—that is, in the last great phase of his manifestation, when, in conjunction with the whore, he made war with the saints, and shed their blood (compare chap. xvii. 6). At different stages and periods, then, there was to be this suffering unto death for the testimony of Jesus; and as the victims are spoken of quite generally under the fifth seal, as they appear simply as the class who had so suffered already, or were yet to suffer, there can be no propriety in understanding the description of any portion less than the whole. We must hold the accounts in the later visions to contain the particulars which make up the collective representation given in the fifth seal, so that this seal and the fifth trumpet, in part, at least, must lie alongside each other. The seventh trumpet also, which, after great manifestations of wrath, and turning of things upside down, issues in the proclamation of the kingdom or dominion of the world having become our Lord and His Christ's, plainly coincides with the closing action of the seals. It brings matters to a termination in *its* peculiar line of things, and with a precisely similar result. The dominion of the world becoming Christ's, in the one line, corresponds to the disappearance, in the other, of all power and authority opposed to Christ's, and the establishment of utter silence and prostration before Him.

6. The connection between the series of the trumpets and that of the vials, is of a still more palpable and pervading kind, and has many more points of contact, than those noticed between the seals and subsequent visions. The two series, indeed, run throughout so closely parallel in regard to the objects and operations described in them, that it is scarcely possible to believe they can relate to two disparate and consecutive lines of procedure. The first trumpet has for its scene of action the *earth*, on which it represents fire and hail mingled with blood being cast; and, in like manner, the first vial is poured upon the *earth*, causing a noisome and grievous sore to those that dwell on it. The second trumpet turns the *sea* into blood; the second vial is poured into the *sea*, and it becomes as the blood of a dead man. The third trumpet brings the visitation of the star wormwood upon the *rivers and fountains of waters*, and renders them deadly; the third vial is poured upon the *rivers and fountains of waters*, and they become blood. When the fourth trumpet sounds, the *sun* is smitten to the extent of a third part, as also the moon and the stars; the fourth vial is poured upon the *sun*, and he scorches men with fire. At the sound of the fifth trumpet the *bottomless pit* is opened, and hordes of scorpion-locusts issue forth with most destructive power; the fifth vial is poured upon the *seat of the beast*—which is but another name for the bottomless

pit, as it was from thence he ascended after his wound was healed (chap. xi. 7, xvii. 8), and the reference here is undoubtedly to a period subsequent to that. The sounding of the sixth trumpet looses the four angels in *the great river Euphrates,* who presently send forth their armed myriads, riding on horses with breastplates of fire, with heads like lions, and fire, smoke, and brimstone going out of their mouths; the sixth vial is also poured upon *the great river Euphrates,* so that its water was dried up, and the way of the kings of the East was prepared, and unclean beasts, the spirits of devils, issued out of the mouth of the dragon, and of the beast, and of the false prophet. Finally, with the sound of the seventh trumpet *great voices in heaven are heard,* for the day of God's wrath is come, the final retributions of good and evil are to be awarded, and the sovereignty of the world passes into the hands of Christ; so, when the last vial is poured into the air, *a great voice comes out of the temple of heaven,* from the throne, saying, "It is done;" for the day of recompense has arrived, and great Babylon comes in remembrance before God. It is surely against all reasonable probability, to suppose that these two lines of symbolic representation, touching at so many points, alike in their commencement, their progress, and their termination, can relate to dispensations of Providence wholly unconnected, and to periods of time separated from each other by the lapse of ages. It is immeasurably more probable, that they are but different aspects of substantially the same course of procedure—different merely from the parties subjected to it, being contemplated in somewhat different relations. Nor would it be possible, if two entire series of symbolical delineations, following so nearly in the same track, were yet to point to events quite remote and diverse, to vindicate such delineations from the charge of arbitrariness and indetermination.

On the whole, therefore, we deem it morally certain, from a simple comparison of the prophetical visions before us, apart altogether from any specific sense or application that may be given to them, that each is in itself complete, and in the particular province it occupies, leaves nothing more to be done. They cannot, therefore, refer to consecutive periods in the history of God's dispensations, the next always beginning where the previous one ends; but must be viewed as indicating parallel, though, in some respects, diverse operations. Both alike end with "a great earthquake" (chap. vi. 12, xi. 19, xvi. 18), which shakes every thing to its foundations, and prepares the way for a new and better order of things. Let us then look at each series separately, that by a consideration of the symbols themselves, and the actions respectively connected with them, we may (if possible) learn the distinctive nature of each, and their relative place and object in the Divine dispensations. We shall find, that by this closer survey, other parallelisms will discover themselves than those yet noticed.

7. The first series, that of the seals, contains (as has been already stated), a representation of the unfolding, not theoretically merely, but practically also, the actual progression of the Lord's mysterious work of conquest, whereby the earth becomes his possession. It is mysterious, because of the character in which He addresses Himself to the work, as a Lamb that had been slain, or the crucified Redeemer; and from the peculiar manner in which He proceeds to make good His title to the possession. The opening of the first seal presents the proper claimant, the only party that has the right and destiny to the dominion of the world—namely Christ, and His body the church. They have their representation in a warrior on a white horse, having a crown given him, in token of universal sovereignty, and "going forth conquering and that he might conquer" (ἵνα νικήσῃ)—*i. e.*, for the very purpose of conquering, and with the certainty that he should do so. And had there been upon earth any thing like the same feeling which prevails in the heavenly places—had men been everywhere disposed and ready to count the Lamb worthy to receive power, and riches, and wisdom, and strength, and honour, and glory, righteousness and peace had been diffused around, and the world had become a field of blessing. But a different state of mind is found to prevail; the worldly

power in all its dominant forms of authority and influence, refuses to own the right as exhibited by the representations of Jesus, and feels, as if without having aught to do with Him, it could secure for itself peaceable and blessed possession of the worldly domain. It must, therefore, be taught the contrary; and so, at the opening of the next three seals there come forth successively three riders of a very different stamp from the first. A rider appears first on a red horse, having power given him to take away peace from the earth, and cause men to kill one another; then one on a black horse with a pair of balances in his hand, as in the stinting times of scarcity, when the blighted earth has yielded but a partial increase, and every thing has to be carefully measured and weighed; finally comes a rider on a pale or wan horse, with death for his rider, and hell for his pursuivant, laying all waste around him by the most terrible instruments of destruction :—All of them, how unlike in character and opposite in working to the gentle Lamb of God, with His benignant sceptre of love and peace! They are so many emblems of the world's powers—natural, social, and political—turned against itself, preying upon its own bowels, and showing how little it is able to control the elements of evil, or to protect its votaries from the most repeated and sweeping desolations. Its history, so long as the claims of Jesus were rejected, and the principles of His gospel contravened, was to be marked by perpetual returns of war, famine, pestilence, and whatever is fraught with calamitous results to those who live only in the worldly sphere; and these not coming as at random, but in consequence of men's sinful repudiation of the doctrine of the cross. On this account not only are the seals successively opened by the Lamb Himself, as if sending those destructive forces forth upon their mission, but at the opening of each of them, one of the four living creatures cried, *Come* (ἔρχου). The voice was a call to the rider to proceed on his errand; and was most fitly uttered in turn by those living creatures, who, in their composite forms, represented the whole living creaturehood of earth, and preeminently man (whose structure predominated in their appearance), in his state of ideal perfection.[1] These, the highest representatives of the world, and the nearest to the throne, call successively upon each of the powers symbolized by the riders to come and do the work assigned them:—first, the right royal Rider with His kingdom of righteousness, and peace and joy in the Holy Ghost; and then, because of the disregard and opposition manifested toward Him, the riders who symbolized the disastrous influences of war, scarcity, tumult, and sweeping desolation. For the earth still is the Lord's, and it cannot be a theatre of blessing, but must be ever and anon turning its powers and resources into instruments of chastisement against its inhabitants, while they refuse to do homage to its rightful Lord.[2]

8. There are no more riders heralded by the call to come; for the four sufficiently represent all the powers that were to be in visible and active operation during the pending history. But the opening of the fifth seal discloses another power, one not belonging to the visible sphere, and not regarded by the world, but still mighty and powerful, because entering the ear of God: the cry, namely, of his own elect—not the cry of their prayers merely, but the cry of their blood, which had been shed, for the word of God and for the testimony which they held. It discloses by implication, rather than by direct discourse, the history of the real church in the world, the true followers of the Lamb, who, like Him, are meek and suffering, using no weapons of violence, but simply holding by the word and testimony they had received from Him, and for its sake loving not their lives unto the death. In such the Lamb

[1] See Typology of Scripture, vol. i., p. 221, sq.

[2] The proper design and import of the call of the living creatures at the opening of the first four seals, has been greatly obscured by the false reading, come and see (ἔρχου καὶ βλέπε), as if it had been a call to the Apocalyptist or others, to behold what was going to appear. On the contrary, it is a call to the symbolical horse and rider, as is evident from the corresponding expression used in regard to the two first: "and he came forth" (ἐξῆλθε), as if in coming upon the stage, he had but answered the previous call. The correct reading is restored in the latest and best editions.

and His cause had their proper representatives; and now the cry of their blood ascends to the highest heavens, and demands the recompense that was meet upon the world, which had so wickedly shed it—a cry that *must* be heard by Him who loveth righteousness and hateth iniquity. It began, indeed, to be heard before it was finally answered—so that a period must elapse from the time it seemed to be listened to, till the whole company of faithful witnesses and martyrs had completed their testimony, and the world's iniquity had become full. In other words, the same work of testifying and suffering for the truth of Jesus was to go on, longer than the church herself thought and expected it should—not, however, because the Lord was indifferent to the evil, but because the efficacious means of testifying and suffering must be plied till the divine forbearance with the world is exhausted, and the proper time of recompenses for evil has come. That time, however, must assuredly come; and so, without any thing farther being indicated as to the operations of the church, the next seal exhibits the cause of the Lamb triumphant, by the world giving way, as it were, beneath the feet of those who had hitherto held possession of it, all its foundations getting for them out of course, and filling them with overwhelming dread and dismay. They at length find the Lamb whom they had despised too mighty for them. But lest the members of the church, being themselves in the world, and liable to share in its calamities, should also feel appalled by the prospect of such things going to come on the world, the episode in chap. vii. of the sealing vision is introduced, which represents an 144,000, a perfect number, symbol of a complete church, as sealed for God, and thereafter glorified in the heavenly places; and that before even the winds were allowed to blow upon the earth to hurt it: not, therefore, pointing so much to the future, as to the past, showing how even from the very commencement of the tribulations, which were to come on the world, and of which every seal but the first had only disclosed successive stages, the Lord had His eye on His own people, and would both keep them in perfect security, and conduct them to final bliss. It is impossible, we think, by any fair or natural interpretation of the scenes described, to understand this sealing vision otherwise than of past and present times—of what was to take place in reference to the troubles, which had been long in progress, and should reach their culmination during the sixth seal. By these unquestionably the earth was to be hurt, with all that naturally belonged to it, nay, brought to utter shame and confusion. And then, the work on both sides being finished—the number of the elect being made up, and the resistance of an ungodly world effectually subverted and overthrown, the seventh seal discloses the state of thorough subjugation and repose that should ensue—all keeping silence before the Lord, as now everywhere acknowledged governor among the nations.

As previously remarked, the representation in this first series is a general one; the wonderful march of Providence and the prospective history of the world are exhibited only in their grand outlines: Christianity is there as a whole, the church as a whole, and so also the world in its deeds of evil, its instruments of mischief, its judgment and doom. It must ever appear arbitrary to limit to single epochs or particular individuals what has purposely been left indefinite in these respects on the sacred page. Nor can it by any possibility be done so as to produce general confidence and satisfaction. For anything of a more special nature, we must look to subsequent revelations.

9. The next series by the very symbol employed to characterize them—the trumpet—bespeaks an active and stirring agency; for the trumpet was peculiarly the instrument of warlike preparation; its loud shrill sound was the immediate call to battle; and employed here, in connection with the great struggle, which was to be carried on by the Lamb of God, as the head of the divine kingdom, with the powers and kingdoms of this world, it must be regarded as the Lord's war-note, proclaiming successively that another and another instrumentality was to be employed by Him for the purpose of bringing the world under Him. The things indicated, there-

fore, by the trumpets, should not have formally the character of judgments executed upon doomed and incorrigible offenders, who were reserved only unto wrath. They should rather be of the nature of mixed dealings—on the one hand chastisements on account of sin, which should form so many calls on men to repentance, and on the other, revelations of mercy to lead them from sin to salvation. It is by this combined twofold instrumentality, that the Lord always strives to overcome, or in effect does overcome the obstinacy and wickedness of men. And when we look both to the beginning and to the close of the series, plain indications discover themselves, that they were to be of the character, and designed for the purpose now stated. They are preceded by the action of an angel at the golden altar offering much incense, with (*i.e.* carrying with it, embodying) the prayers of all saints; and the smoke of the incense with these prayers, it is said, ascended up before God out of the angel's hand. This denotes their acceptance with God; they came up as a sweet memorial, which He could not fail to regard; and the actions that follow are the answer that He gives to them. But "the prayers of all saints" are the united cry of the Lord's people, His royal priesthood, not for the destruction, but for the salvation of the world; for judgment, indeed, in so far as that might be necessary to hold in check the power of the adversary, and bring home to men's bosoms the knowledge and conviction of sin; but still, in the midst of this, and through this for mercy, that the way of peace and blessing may be found. Then, when we look to the end, we hear as the termination and result of the whole, the joyful announcement pealed forth, "The kingdom of the world has become the kingdom of our Lord and of His Christ"—a result, which shews the gracious design that must have pervaded the entire series, and which could only have been reached by such a combination of severity and goodness as we have described. Bent on overcoming the world, by subduing its sinfulness, and bringing it into the obedience of His truth, the Lord comes forth as a man of war; the successive trumpet-notes herald the different means and agencies He employs in the conflict; and partly moved by fear, but partly, also, and much more drawn by the word of grace and truth, the hearts of men yield, and the field is at length won from the grasp of the enemy.

Such appears to be the general character and aim of this series of symbols, very fitly following on the former, as tending to show how the conquest more generally unfolded there, was to be wrought out and brought to a successful issue. And a glance at the particulars confirms this view. The series is divided in the vision itself into a four and a three. The four so far stand by themselves, and coincide with each other, that the things indicated by them are of the nature of inflictions on the outward territory of nature; as a whole they travel the round of that territory, and turn it in all its departments into the occasion of trouble and calamity to those who cleave to it as their portion. First, the *earth* itself is visited, not by fertilizing showers, but by hail and fire mingled with blood; so that a third part of the trees and grass are burnt up. Then, the *sea* is to the same extent turned into blood by a burning mountain being cast into it; whereby a third part of the creatures in it, and the vessels sailing on its bosom, were destroyed. Next the *rivers and fountains of waters* by the star wormwood are, to the extent also of a third, rendered so bitter, that many died of them. Lastly, the higher region of nature is visited, and again in a third part the sun, moon, and stars, are so smitten, that for a third part of the time both by day and by night there was only darkness. All the departments of nature, or rather what might correspond to these in the political and social sphere, were thus to be successively visited, and rendered instruments of affliction and trouble. Yet still with a marked reserve, as if only for chastisement and warning; in each case only the third part was affected, as a proof how loath God was to proceed to extremities—how he restrained even while he afflicted—and by the very character of his rebukes discovered his unwillingness to destroy, his desire that men should repent and live.

By such means, however, no effectual result is accomplished;

though the world is stricken in all its sources of natural sufficiency, multitudes still cling to it as a portion, and for its sake continue to disown Christ, and reject the gospel of his salvation. Therefore, other and more effectual measures must be brought into operation; and these are represented by the three last, the woe-trumpets, as they are called. It must be remembered, however, in what respect it is they are so called; it is merely because of their power to bring to an end the beastly, grovelling, God-opposing character of the world; to pour confusion and ruin on the worldly interest, as such, that the interest of truth and righteousness might take its place. It is said, therefore, at the commencement of these trumpets, "Woe to the inhabiters of the earth," on account of them; by the inhabiters of the earth being meant those whose proper home and portion was there, such as entirely belonged to it, the earthly-minded, and hence aliens from that church, the true members of which have their names written in heaven, who are contemplated as ideally with the Lord in Zion. The woes to the persons described, therefore, were woes merely in respect to their earthly-mindedness and devotion to the world; but instruments and occasions of blessing, if they would but see in them the chastening hand of God, and abandon the worse for the better part. Now, of the three woes, the first is described as the action of a fallen star—fallen from heaven to earth—emblem of a degenerate power, an angel of light, become one of darkness; and as such sent on the bad errand of opening the bottomless pit, and letting out, amid the smoke of hell, a horde of scorpion-locusts, whose commission was not to touch the herbs and trees of the field, but to torment men, all such as had not the seal of God in their foreheads—the men simply of the earth. These locusts, the direct emanation of the world of darkness, were also in their personal characteristics a strange compound of the beastly and the human (shaped like horses, yet with faces like men, and crowned, as if kings of their kind), of the soft and the savage (the hair of women, and the teeth of lions), of the courageous and the vicious (rustling as with chariots and breastplates of iron, yet stinging as with tails of scorpions). What an image of the emissaries of Satan, who, sometimes with high pretensions and king-like authority, sometimes with winning gentleness, and again with bold effrontery, teach the doctrines of devils—doctrines which tend to make men the slaves of corruption and lust, to bind them up in strong delusion to believe a lie; and so, in reality, amid all professions and appearances to the contrary, acting a beastly, savage, and vicious part, and involving their followers in many sore and grievous troubles! Apollyon, the destroyer, is their king; for it is his interests they serve, to the cruel bondage and manifold miseries of men. Though confined to no particular age, yet undoubtedly they had their most exact representation, and their largest embodiment, in those corrupters of the Christian doctrine, who gradually brought on the murky atmosphere of the dark ages, and formed into shape the great apostacy which converted the new Jerusalem into Babylon, and entailed numberless evils upon Christendom. Hence also, as having its grand impersonation in an apostate and degenerate church, the work is ascribed to a fallen star.

The next woe-trumpet, the sixth in the whole series, presents us with a phenomenon in its earlier part, somewhat similar in kind, and in some respects even more threatening and formidable than that which preceded. The scene here is laid in the Euphrates, which implies that Babylon, which stood on the Euphrates, and from which the Euphrates derives all its symbolical value and significance, has anew sprung into being. Euphrates by itself is nothing in Scripture, no more than any other river, excepting as "the great river" (here emphatically so called) on which Babylon stood, and which ministered so much to the wealth and security of the city; it is hence so far identified with Babylon, as to share with it in symbolical applications. This mention of Euphrates, also, and by implication of Babylon, confirms what has been said of the preceding symbol; as it plainly betokens that corrupting influences had been at work, and had even formed a new Babylonish power. And now when the call is given, under the sixth trumpet, to loose the four angels that had been bound in the great river Euphrates, and when, as the result of this loosing, myriads of horsemen rush forth, and come with such destructive energy, that the third part of men are represented as killed by them, a power must be indicated which, as to its origin, was very closely connected with the Babylon understood, was even one grand source of its strength and prosperity, but which now was to turn with prodigious force and destroying might against it. The very waters that nourished her were to become her plague and her destruction. And what these were, we learn from chap. xvii. 15, "The waters which thou sawest, where the whore (Babylon) sitteth, are peoples, and multitudes, and nations, and tongues,"—in other words, the kingdoms of the world, represented by the beast, on which the whore was seen sitting, because on their carnal power and influence she leant for support. So that this Euphrates-host of warriors are instruments of mischief issuing, as it were, from her very bowels, from the ground of worldliness and corruption on which she stands, and making her the object of their hatred and rapacious violence. It is the same thing substantially that is meant in chap. xvii. 16, by the kingdoms turning to hate the whore, so as "to make her desolate and naked, to eat her flesh, and burn her with fire." And hence, as having such an origin, and working for such a purpose, the army here mentioned was of the most singular and anomalous description; it is an army of horses rather than of horsemen, for the horses are said to have heads like lions, sending forth from their mouths fire, smoke, and brimstone, whereby the third part of men were killed; and not only so, but tails also like serpents, with which they still farther do hurt. In short, it is the devil's agents, turned by the judgment of heaven against the devil's own interest; a beast-like instrumentality, full only of rapacity and violence, Satanic guile and wickedness, assailing and subverting that which, though chiefly of Satan, had still too many elements in it of a better kind to suit the taste of the more outrageous and heaven-daring spirit that was to characterise the last times. It comprehends, therefore, the ultimate proceedings both of the beast, and of the false prophet—the world's power and wisdom applied, as they in part have been, and will yet more fully be, with determined and ruthless vengeance to put away from them the corrupt and worldly religion, the Babylon that had usurped and lorded it over them.[1] And that such was the character of the party more especially to be visited by this unscrupulous and vengeful instrumentality, is rendered still more clear by the description given of the results (ix. 20, 21), "And the rest of the men, which were not killed by these plagues, yet repented not of the works of their hands, that they should not worship devils, and idols of gold and silver, and brass and stone, and of wood, which neither can see nor hear, nor walk; neither repented they of their murders, nor of their sorceries, nor of their fornication, nor of their thefts." The sins of which they did not repent, and for which, therefore, the chastisement of heaven had been sent, formed precisely that kind of revived heathenism, that trafficking in the idolatry and abominations of the world, which, with the name of Christianity, constitute the Babylon of the Apocalypse. So that in this part of the sixth trumpet we manifestly have a representation of the severity to be employed in the latter days against the modern Babylon, for the purpose of chastising her guilt, and delivering the world from her abominations. And the severity was to be inflicted in its worst form by means of the worldly powers, which it had been her policy to embrace, and use for her own carnal and selfish purposes.

10. But this was not the only agency to be employed in con-

[1] Hengstenberg thinks the angels must be good ones, most strangely; for were ever good angels represented before as being *bound?* Or did they ever head such a serpent-like and hellish agency? Good angels could only be understood, if they had been employed to keep back the agency till a certain time; but this is not the idea; it is that they had been prepared to send it forth; and to do so "for *the* hour, and day, and month, and year"—so it should be read—it means that when the precise time should come for such a visitation, the proper agency should be found ready.

nection with the sixth trumpet. Beside severity, there was also to be mercy, as there was indeed a purpose of mercy running through the whole of this series; only now, when the final issues are approaching, it is more fully and distinctly exhibited. It might have seemed, from such a long and dreadful succession of afflictive dealings, as if severity and judgment alone were to prevail during this series of symbolical actions—precisely as during the former series it might have seemed, up till the sealing vision of the sixth seal, that the Lord's own people were to have no defence and security above others. Here, therefore, under the sixth trumpet, as there under the sixth seal, a long and precious episode is introduced, which should have formed, as in the other case, a separate chapter, but which is thrown into chap. x. and xi. 1–13. Like the sealing vision, it is of a regressive as well as prospective character; and is intended to exhibit the better agency which all along had been in operation, in connection with the severer measures employed, and which was necessary to carry out the design of these by leading men to repentance. The one was like the law, intended, by its awful utterances and deadly wounds, to penetrate with a humbling sense of guilt and danger; while the other, the gospel, with its gentle and persuasive voice, entreated men to arise and flee from the wrath to come. The representation of this better agency is introduced by the appearance of a mighty angel (who, by what follows, can be understood to be no other than Christ), with a cloud and rainbow about His head, the symbol of mercy after judgment; indicating that, notwithstanding the floods of wrath which He had been making to pass over the world, He still had a purpose of grace, and that His design was not to destroy but to save. His whole appearance and manner denote great determination of purpose, and irresistible might, in carrying His design into execution. To show what the design was, He plants His right foot upon the sea, and His left upon the earth, to indicate His sovereign right in respect to both, and His firm resolve to put that right into execution. He farther, by a solemn oath, declares, that, viewed in respect to the stage of operations marked by the sixth trumpet, the time should not be long for having the whole carried into execution. He swore that "time should no longer be (*i.e.*, there should be no farther delay), but in the days of the voice of the seventh angel, when He shall begin to sound, the mystery of God should be finished." And then follows the instrumentality more especially to be employed for the accomplishment of the intended result. This is the little book given to John to eat, a symbolical action to denote that the contents of that book must be received into the heart and soul of those whom John represented, the confessors and witnesses of the truth,—as only by being so received on their part, and then proclaimed before "peoples, and nations, and tongues, and kings," could the end in view be attained. The book is called little, much for the same reason that faith, even in its mightiest operations, is compared to a grain of mustard-seed, because it *is* little and insignificant in the estimation of the world, and in the eye of sense, as compared with the gigantic and obtrusive forces it has to contend with, and the vast results it must achieve. It is simply the gospel of the grace of God, which becomes, in respect to those who cordially embrace and own it, the word of their testimony. This is the one grand weapon of the Lamb, the sword that goeth out of His mouth to bring the people under Him, or else consign them to destruction as finally impenitent. This, believingly received, and confessed and handled by a faithful church, is the chosen instrumentality by which the tide of evil in the world is to be turned, and the inheritance rescued from the power of the adversary. After the brief indication of the weapon and the instrumentality comes the vision of the measurement of the temple, and the history of the witnesses, retrospectively connecting the past with the present, showing how the character of God's temple or church had been outwardly transformed—how that which *apparently* was such, and had become dominant, was really the reverse, an essentially heathen or worldly party under a godly name and profession—how this spiritual Egypt, or Babylon, had sought to corrupt the truth, and trample under foot those that believed and proclaimed it—how they had even, for a time, utterly suppressed the open testimony of the faithful, and violently made away with them—but how the Lord, notwithstanding, stood by His servants, gave testimony to the word of His grace, and, at last, rendered it so mighty and powerful that the respective parties altogether changed places, the faithful witnesses being exalted to heaven, the place of power and influence; while the proud and persecuting city (Babylon) falls as by an earthquake, multitudes of her people are slain, and the rest are affrighted and give glory to the God of heaven. We only indicate here the train of thought, as the subject has been formally discussed in the preceding section. But it should be noted how different the result now is from what it was at the close of the more judicial parts of the process. By these many were left who did not repent of their sins and evil deeds (chap. ix. 20, 21); but now that the instrumentality of life and blessing is brought distinctly into view, the work of repentance is accomplished; the terror produced by the severer measures disposes men to embrace the mercy offered in the gospel, and embodied in the testimony of the witnesses; the remnant, even in Babylon, believe and are saved. And then comes the end; not, indeed, without many heavings and agitations, convulsions of various kinds, caused by the truth of God rising to the ascendant. But still it comes; and when the seventh trumpet sounds amid those complicated disturbances, it is only that the joyful announcement may be proclaimed, "The kingdom of the world has become the kingdom of our Lord and of his Christ; and He shall reign for ever and ever."

Thus it appears that the series of the trumpets constitute a clear and decided advance upon that of the seals. They exhibit the train of causes and effects by which the marvellous results unfolded in the seals were to be brought about; the twofold kind of agencies by which the Lamb and His followers should at length come to change places with the world—viz., the rod of chastisement and the word of reconciliation;

afflictive providences and retributory judgments, on the one hand, and, on the other, the gospel of salvation, unflinchingly and perseveringly proclaimed by a chosen band of witnesses till it should become everywhere triumphant. In this way the cause that went forth at the first to conquer does conquer, and secures for itself a universal dominion. But one point still remains to be cleared. It has come out in the course of this last series that, in the work of conquest to be achieved, it was not simply the world in its original and palpably heathenish form, which had to be brought into subjection. A professedly religious, though really intensely worldly and antichristian domination, had come into the field, and, indeed, so extensively occupied at last that field, that it is with this latterly the struggle appeared to be more especially conducted. Whence, then, this extraordinary change? How did such a worldly Christianity rise into being; and what precise measures were to be adopted in respect to it?

11. Now, it is chiefly to provide an answer to these questions, which most naturally present themselves, that the visions reaching from the close of chap. xi., to that of chap. xix., eight whole chapters, have been introduced. This portion occupies so large a space because it more directly concerned the church's dangers and difficulties, and was required to put her fully on her guard against the coming evil, or to leave her inexcusable, if she became involved in it. Like the visions already noticed, it embraces an extensive range, and, as we have previously had occasion to show, points back to the past, as well as onwards to the future, in order to show how the evil originally sprung up, and how it was to develope itself till it reached the gigantic magnitude and formidable character it ultimately assumed. This is done more particularly in chap. xii. and xiii., where the matter is represented in connection both with the personal spite and malice of the tempter, on account of the victory gained over him by Christ; and with the beast, or worldly power, in its varied forms and manifestations, more especially in the times following the general spread of Christianity, after the deadly wound caused by this

gospel had again been healed. Out of the healing of the wound came Babylon, which consists of an unnatural conjunction of the church and the world, the church having thereby become essentially antichristian; and because of the greatness of the guilt, and the heaviness of the doom, incurred by such a degeneracy, it has a very large and prominent place given to it in the prophecy. In chap. xiii. we are told how the introduction of Christianity led the worldly power to assume a form corresponding to the altered state of affairs; and the success following its altered policy implied, that the church, to a large extent, had sacrificed its character, and joined hands with the world. Accordingly, in the next chapter, chap. xiv., the true church, as contra-distinguished from the false, is brought prominently into view. The apostle sees an elect and faithful company with the Lamb on Mount Zion; while he hears, and, for the first time, hears the name of Babylon proclaimed as the object of divine wrath, and as destined to fall by the preaching of the everlasting gospel (ver. 6–8). At the same time, to show the essential agreement of the power designated Babylon, with that previously represented by the beast and his image, the wrath of God is also proclaimed (ver. 9–11) against all who receive the mark of the beast and worship his image—that is, against all who surrender themselves to the lusts and interests of a present evil world, though they may gild it over by a Christian name. For all such, it is declared, the fiery indignation and final judgments of God are reserved; while, in marked contrast, is brought out (ver. 12, 13), the safe and everlastingly blessed condition of those who, crucifying the flesh through the Spirit, renouncing the world for the better part, keep the commandments of God and the faith of Jesus. Then follow an entire series of visions, each containing representations of God's judicial proceedings and closing acts toward those adherents of earthliness and sin. The first is a quite general one (chap. xiv. 14–20), and appears under the image of a vine to be reaped and trodden, an image similarly used in Old Testament prophecy (Isa. lxiii.). It is called the vine "of the earth"—

earth's own spontaneous production—and so a fitting representation of those who had nothing about them savouring of a higher world, but were children of corruption. No distinction, therefore, is here made between one class of doomed sinners and another; they are considered in the mass; and being, without distinction, lovers of a corrupt and perishing world, they are regarded as growing together till they become ripe for judgment, when they become the heirs of a common destruction.

12. The next series, however, is of a more specific kind; it consists of the seven vials; and has somewhat of the same relation to the trumpets, that the trumpets had to the seals. The trumpets, as we have shown, disclose God's dealings with the world in order to bring it to repentance, and the faith of Christ; they are, therefore, of a mixed character, and partake alike of chastisement and mercy. But the world is here contemplated simply in its guilt; not its natural guilt merely, but that far deeper and more aggravated guilt which it had incurred by rejecting the salvation of Christ, and even turning his scheme of grace and truth into a huge Babel of falsehood and corruption. The dealings here, therefore, are strictly judicial; they bring out the severe aspect of God's character, and end only with the utter destruction of the party against which they are directed. That party, precisely, as in the case of the trumpets, is the sinful world at large, but viewed with a more especial reference to its condition after the introduction and general spread of Christianity, and still more after the formation of the Babylonish counterfeit. Hence, the general subject being the same, as in the case of the trumpets, though contemplated and dealt with in a somewhat different aspect, the one series runs so uniformly alongside the other, and does not so properly represent a diverse and separate order of things, as the dark, the judicial, the simply punitive character and operation of the same things.

In accordance with this character and design, the distinctive symbol here used is that of the vial, a round cup or goblet, into which ingredients of a deleterious kind are supposed to be put, that they might be poured out upon the subjects of vengeance. The action of pouring out in this sense, and sometimes also with the mention of a cup from which the contents were to be poured, is frequently used in Old Testament prophecy (Ps. lxxv. 8, lxxix. 6; Jer. x. 25, etc.); it denotes the full, resistless, overwhelming energy with which the visitation of evil should come. The vials here are hence called vials "full of the wrath of God;" and are represented as belonging to the seven angels who have "the seven last plagues; for in them is filled up the wrath of God:" not that the things here represented were absolutely posterior to all that had gone before, but that they belonged to the procedure of God in its terminal processes of judgment upon the guilty world—processes that should not run out till the worldly, God-opposing interest of the adversary was effectually put down, and all its adherents were scattered to the winds. As being the last actions of this description, God's judicial proceedings against the worldly power in its ultimate forms of manifestation, the heavenly inhabitants are represented as singing in contemplation of them "the song of Moses and the Lamb," coupling together the victory to be won over the last, with that won over the first great embodiment of the anti-righteous worldly power; spanning, in their notes of triumph, the whole field of struggle and conquest. And finally, the work of judgment to be executed is represented as emphatically a work of holiness, by the seven angels appearing to come out of "the temple of the tabernacle of the testimony"—that is, out of the temple, which contained the tabernacle of the testimony; in other words, they came forth as representatives of that holy law of God, which was called the testimony of the tabernacle, because it testified against all unrighteousness of men, and called for Divine judgment against it.

Looking now individually at the vials, the first four have formally the same immediate objects, and perform exactly the same round as the trumpets: first the earth is smitten, then the sea, then the rivers and fountains of waters, and last of all the sun. There is this difference however, that here, in accordance with the strictly penal character of the series, the effects appear more extensively and directly hurtful, and are also more explicitly connected with the sins which called them forth. Instead of only the third part of the objects immediately affected being mentioned, it is the effect upon men themselves, which is brought specially into notice, whose sin and punishment are expressly linked together. In the first case a grievous and noisome sore falls upon the men who have the mark of the beast and worship his image; in the second the sea becomes blood and every soul in it dies; in the third, when the rivers and fountains have been made blood, the Lord is praised as righteous in His judgments, because He had given those blood to drink, who had shed the blood of His saints; and in the fourth, power was given the sun to scorch men with fire, on account, as is plainly implied, of their still daring and growing wickedness, which was such, that they even blasphemed His name, while suffering under the direful visitation. It is manifestly impossible to understand such things literally; they never could be meant to be so taken. But the general sense is obvious; the men whose souls clave to the dust, who, in spite of all that the Lord had done to reclaim them to Himself, continued to reject or corrupt His truth, that they might live on in conformity to the flesh and the world, should find the whole circle of worldly powers and influences, so far from keeping a covenant of peace with them, often turned into instruments of evil: So that from the world in its more settled state (the earth), distressing sores should come upon them; from its heaving agitations and troubles (the sea), violence and bloodshed; even from its more refreshing and gladdening influences (the streams and the sun), tormenting and pestiferous effects, which they should be powerless to resist. Such things ever and anon occurring, and as might be supposed, at certain periods occurring in more marked and dreadful visitations, would tell how far the world, in its antichristian and ungodly portion, was from having gained by its contrariety to God; how little it could do to avert the deadliest evils from its followers; and how much it lay under the frown and chastisement of an angry God. The vexations and disorders coming on it while under antichristian rule, and on this very account coming on it, must be ever rendering it a valley of Achor to those who perversely cling to and worship it.

13. These, however, are only the more general forms of divine judgment (though, if the world perseveres in guilt, and high-minded opposition to the truth, it is by no means improbable they may find more specific and marked exemplifications than have yet been given them); the more peculiar and decisive ones are exhibited in the three last vials. The fifth was poured upon the seat of the beast, which (as before observed under the fifth trumpet) is all one with the bottomless pit. It is not said here what came forth from it, for that had been fully described under the fifth trumpet; but as the result of the smoke and the scorpion-locusts which issued forth, the kingdom of the beast, it is said, was filled with darkness, and men gnawed their tongues for pain, and went on blaspheming the God of heaven: involved in darkness and misery, and yet cleaving to their idols and abominations! in their stricken and miserable condition manifestly lying under the rebuke of God, and yet continuing in the things which dishonoured and provoked Him! Of this the comfortless, ignorant, deluded, and enslaved state of Papal kingdoms generally, during the night of the dark ages, formed the most extensive and striking exemplification. The next vial is poured upon the great river Euphrates, and the result is, that the water thereof is dried up, that the way of the kings of the East might be prepared. The waters of the Euphrates, as already noticed, were the source of Babylon's riches and security; she relied on these to the last, when the judgment of heaven was overhanging her—fatally relied on them; for by diverting their course, and drying up their wonted channel, the Medes and Persians entered and took possession of the city. These Medes and Persians were actually the kings of the East, coming, as they did, from the country east of Babylon, and coming with such royal might and plenitude of re-

sources, that the proud mistress of the nations fell an easy prey into their hands. Here, however, the epithet, "Kings of the East," precisely as Euphrates and Babylon, is used symbolically to denote powers and influences of a kind, that in their relation to the mystical Babylon, should correspond with those of the Medes and Persians to the literal. They are none other than the dreadful Satanic agency, symbolized under the sixth trumpet by the myriads of horsemen, whose horses had tails like serpents, and sent forth fire, smoke and brimstone, from their mouths. Another, but not less appalling representation is given of them here, under the "three unclean spirits like frogs," which the prophet saw coming "out of the mouth of the dragon, and out of the mouth of the beast, and out of the mouth of the false prophet." They are farther described as "the spirits of devils (demons), working miracles, which go forth unto the kings of the earth and of the whole world, to gather them to the battle of that great day of God Almighty." The description here, as well as in the parallel passage, points to the last, the most wreckless, antichristian, and blasphemous manifestations of the beast and the false prophet, when impregnated to the full with the spirit of Satan, and acting as his agents in the final effort he makes against the kingdom of God. It is on this account, that the evil spirits, likened to frogs from their low, unclean, and loathsome character, appear as coming out of the mouth, first of all of the dragon, being, so to speak, direct emanations of the prince of darkness, and ready to give vent to his foul blasphemies, and intense malice against the truth. They proceed also from the mouths of the beast and the false prophet, because the power and wisdom of the world supply the immediate instruments—the wonder-working skill, the lofty achievements in art and science, the daring speculations, lawless doctrines, resolute energy and might—by which the work is to be carried forward. Babylon, or the corrupt and apostate church, is not mentioned as having directly to do with the issuing forth of these moral plagues; for they belong to a stage beyond hers, and are to have their great use in tearing up her foundations and overthrowing her confidences. It is through this agency of evil that the kingdoms come to hate the whore; or in the symbolical language of this vision, that the waters of the great river Euphrates (the multitudes and peoples), on which Babylon sat, and to which she looked for her security and strength, are dried up—nay, are made to send forth against her hosts of adverse forces, which shall do to her substantially what the kings of the East, the Medes and Persians, Babylon's own tributaries, did to the ancient city. Had these relations been perceived, and the real character of the conflict been understood, there would have been little difficulty in understanding the remaining feature in the description; in which it is said, that the conflicting hosts were to be gathered together for a final decision in a place called in the Hebrew tongue Armageddon. It is another allusion to the history and relations of Old Testament times, and indicates, that the Old was virtually to return again. Armageddon is simply the hill of Megiddo; and in sacred history the neighbourhood of Megiddo is celebrated for a very memorable and mournful event, the overthrow of Josiah's army, and his own death by the host of Egypt (2 Kings xxiii. 29, 30)—the discomfiture of the professing church of God by the profane worldly power. The reason was, that though Josiah was a good man, the church itself had become a Babylon; corruption of every kind continued to nestle in it; the prophets were at the time uttering in the strongest terms their denunciations and threatenings against it; and not only was the step taken by Josiah a false one, betokening too superficial views of the evil within, and the difficulties to be contended against without, but the event proved that the world was now the stronger party, and was used as God's instrument to rebuke a corrupt church, and warn her of her approaching downfal. *There*, therefore, was the type of the mighty and portentous future now under consideration: the great battle of Armageddon is to be on the grand scale, what the old battle of Megiddo was on the small one: the world, as animated by the spirit of darkness, is to rise up with such fresh might, and to bring into the field such potent and effective instruments of its own, that the false church shall be unable any longer to control, powerless to cope with it: Babylon shall be worsted. Hence the propriety and importance of the call in ver. 15, uttered immediately before the final conflict: "Behold, I come as a thief: Blessed is he that watcheth, and keepeth his garments, lest he walk naked, and they see his shame." It virtually points to the case of Josiah, and warns against its imitation in the future. The corrupt and antichristian church *must* go down—the world *shall* prevail against it. Let all, therefore, who would be found on the Lord's side, and avoid a shameful exposure, take heed how they have to do with it; let them see, that they occupy the right position, and stand only in the truth and purity of the gospel.

Thus the whole of this part of the vision receives a quite natural explanation; the peculiar references to ancient history couched under the terms "Euphrates," "Kings of the East," and "Armageddon," are found to be most appropriately and consistently applied; and the numberless arbitrary and far-fetched interpretations, which have been employed regarding them, are no longer needed.[1] All, then, is seen in the action

[1] It is unnecessary to refer particularly to these interpretations. Among the most current are those, which take Euphrates as a name for the Turkish empire, "Kings of the East" for the Jews, and Armageddon for some great political struggle in the Levant (latterly, the Crimea) or in Italy. All merely external and political affairs, which are foreign to the great theme of the Apocalypse! Euphrates, too, taken literally in the midst of symbols! and kings of the East coined for the occasion as an epithet of the Jews! Such confusion and arbitrariness needs no refutation; it is our reproach, that interpretations embodying them could ever have been listened to. Less fanciful, in regard to Megiddo, but far from satisfactory, is the explanation offered by Mr Stanley in his recent volume on Sinai and Palestine, p. 330; where, on account of the natural position of Megiddo, as forming a convenient and suitable arena for conflicts between the people of Palestine and the surrounding nations, it is supposed to have been selected "as the battle-field of the world, and passed, through its adoption into the language of the Apocalypse, into a universal proverb." It is possible enough many battles may have been fought on Megiddo, or in its immediate neighbourhood; but there is only one re-

of this vial approaching to the final consummation; the last forms of ungodliness are in full operation, and the false church is vainly struggling against them; her old ground is sinking under her feet. And then with the pouring forth of the seventh vial the closing stage commences: the controversy both in respect to the false church and the world is brought to an ultimate decision, and first on the one, then on the other, the desolating judgment of heaven alights. This last vial is represented as being poured into the air—not from any real or supposed connection between the air and evil spirits, but with reference to the air as the region, on which the earth immediately depends—the region from which in peaceful times descend the genial and blissful influences of nature, but the region, also, when things are out of course, which is charged with the deadliest elements, and gives birth to the most desolating effects. Hence voices, thunders, lightnings, and a great earthquake are the immediate results, which follow the pouring out of this vial: all of them belonging to the region of the air, and the symbols of the mightiest changes and fearful catastrophes in the moral world. They indicate, that the judgments of God upon the ungodliness of the world and the apostacy of the church, have at length run their course; "it is done" respecting these forms of evil; the cities of the nations fall, that is, they are destroyed in their character as strongholds of error and wickedness; and great Babylon comes in remembrance before God to give to her the cup of the wine of the fierceness of His wrath. All, in short, undergoes a revolution; and the antichristian spirit, which had so long wrought in the world, and so deeply rooted itself in the kingdoms of the earth, is judged and cast out.

corded, that had any peculiar moral bearing on the affairs of the old covenant—the one, namely, in which Josiah fell before the might of Egypt. And as it is the moral, not simply the natural aspect of things, on which the use of such historical circumstances in the Apocalypse proceeds, we should have no hesitation how to explain the allusion before us. It is only by viewing the matter in the light we have presented it, that the precise place also, as well as the nature, of the allusion can be understood.

14. After this comes, another and more specific series, representing the guilt and doom of Babylon by itself—contained in chap. xvii. and xviii. The remarkable prominence given to this subject, shows the singular place it held in the mind of God, as deserving of his special reprobation. Babylon in many respects stood alone in guilt. Instead of correcting and reforming the world, the false church had fallen in with its corruptions and lent the name of God to these, for her own temporal aggrandisement. Therefore, her shame must be fully exposed, and her overthrow be portrayed with the greatest fulness of detail and vividness of colouring. But as this part of the vision has been fully exhibited in the preceding section, there is no need to enlarge on it here.

15. The same also may be said of the last and concluding series of this portion of the book—that which occupies the greater part of chap. xix. We have there a revelation of the final dealings with the kingdoms of the earth. The series of the vials, which has to do merely with judgments, leaves a portion of the history untold. While God's work upon Babylon, and His work also upon the beast and the false prophet, that is, the world viewed in respect to its ungodliness and corruption, comes to a close with the destruction of the evil, it is otherwise with the kingdoms of the world viewed in respect to their inhabitants. These, as already exhibited in the series of the trumpets, are to be transferred to the dominion of Christ. And so, to wind properly up this part of the marvellous history, a representation is given of the conquest of the kingdoms to Christ, which, like all His conquests over the hearts and consciences of men, is accomplished by the power of the truth, wielded by a faithful church, and rendered efficacious by the power of His Spirit. External troubles and social evils no doubt contribute to the result; but it is still the sharp sword of the word, and the spiritual energy and faithfulness of the church, by which all is more immediately effected. Thus the spirit of error and iniquity which had corrupted and destroyed the world is put down; the beast and the false prophet, as well as Babylon, are cast into outer dark-

ness; and the saints with their Divine head possess the kingdom, and enjoy together a reign of millennial blessedness and glory.

16. It remains only to notice the indications of time contained in the portion of the Apocalypse we have been surveying. These appear to be simply three, though one of them has a threefold expression. It is the period of the church's tried and oppressed condition—denoted first in chap. xi. 2, as a period of forty-two months, during which "the holy city is trodden down of the Gentiles," during which also the beast was to continue in its power to blaspheme and injure (chap. xiii. 5); then as consisting of 1260 days (forty-two months multiplied by 30 days), during which the witnesses, representatives of a faithful, but oppressed and persecuted church, were to prophesy, chap. xi. 3, and the church was to abide in the wilderness, chap. xii. 6, having a place and food prepared for her by God; and finally, as a time, times and an half (corresponding to one year of twelve months, two of the same, and an half year of six, or to forty-two months, or again to 1260 days), during which the church was to remain and be fed in the wilderness, chap. xii. 14. In Dan. vii. 25, where the expression first occurs, it is the time during which the saints of God were to be given into the hand of the power that was to speak great words against the Most High. These are manifestly but different modes of expressing one and the same period, as the state of things also to which they are applied is substantially identical, though variously represented. For the sojourn in the wilderness on the part of the faithful and proper spouse, the treading down of the holy city by those who belonged only to the court of the Gentiles, and the testifying for the truth of God by a faithful remnant clothed in sackcloth, and wrestling against error and corruption; these are obviously but different symbolical representations of the same abnormal and dislocated state of things. The other two periods mentioned are both very brief, as compared with the one just noticed. The shortest is that during which the bodies of the faithful witnesses are represented as lying dead, though unburied,

three and a half days, chap. xi. 11; and the other is the five months during which the scorpion-locusts were to have power to torment the followers of the beast, chap. ix. 5.

Now, it is scarcely possible to avoid being struck even on the most cursory inspection of these periods, with a peculiarity that is common to them all—the broken and incomplete aspect they present. A certain whole was evidently in respect to each of them in the mind of the Divine author of the vision, as that toward which the parties spoken of were aiming, but were arrested midway in their career. This is particularly observable in the largest and by much the most important number, which in every form—whether as time, times and an half, or as the months and days that make up three and an half years—is most expressive of an unfinished course, a period somehow cut off in the middle. In like manner, the three and a half days of rejoicing over the unburied corpses of the slain witnesses, betokens the same violent and abrupt termination of the course indicated; in their ungodly triumph, the adversaries could not complete more than half of one of the briefest revolutions of time—one of the smallest cycles of the whole period alloted to the ascendancy of evil. The incompleteness may appear less palpable in the five months specified for the plague of scorpion-locusts; but it will scarcely do so to those who have attended to the use made in Scripture of ten with reference to certain kinds of totality. The five is simply the broken ten.

So marked a peculiarity in the use of all these numbers is itself a strong presumption in favour of their symbolical import. It seems to stamp their value as indications of relative, rather than of absolute periods of duration—relative both as regards each other, and also as regards an ideal whole. And it will appear to do so the more convincingly the more the periods are viewed in reference to the parties mentioned, which are the entire spiritual church throughout the world, on the one side, and the whole antichristian power on the other; for in regard to such vast bodies, and their wide-reaching interests, what could such periods avail in their natural sense! They could obviously afford but a mere fraction of the time necessary for the accomplishment of the results connected with them; nor could such results in actual history be shut up into *any* periods consisting of such exact and definite measures. Another, and very powerful consideration in favour of the same view is the *place* of these historical numbers—surrounded on every hand, not with the literal, but with the symbolical. The woman that is persecuted, and the dragon who persecutes; the wilderness into which she flees, and the floods sent after her; the beast that rages against the truth, and the two witnesses who testify for it to the death; the holy city that is trodden down, and the Egypt or Babylon by whom the treading is effected; all are symbolically used, and shall the *periods* of working be otherwise than symbolical? In that case there would be the violation of one of the plainest laws of symbolical writing, and confusion and arbitrariness, as a matter of necessity, would be brought into the interpretation.[1] It is true the number seven, as applied to the heads of the beast, and the number ten spoken of its ultimate forms of separate organization, have already been found by us to possess a kind of historical verification. But this, when more closely considered, manifests an evident striving after the symbolical. For, it is to make out the number seven, that St John diverges so strikingly here from the representation of Daniel, taking in the two earlier worldly kingdoms, which Daniel had omitted, and making of the divided state of Daniel's fourth empire a separate kingdom—the seventh. Nay, even this seventh he calls in a sense also the eighth—chap. xvii. 11—although seven still is taken as the proper number, because it alone has the proper symbolical import. The beast comes into view mainly as the rival of God, and seven being the common symbol of completeness for the Divine manifestations in the world (Isa. xxx. 26; Zech. iii. 9, iv. 2; Prov. ix. 1; Rev. i. 4, iii. 1, etc)—originating, no doubt, in the sevenfold acts of God at creation—the worldly rival of God's power and glory

[1] See Part I., Chap. v., Sec. 4.

in the world is, in token of its God-defying character, presented under the same number of manifestations.[1] For a like reason the divided state of the last manifestation is distributed into the number ten. This also is often used as a symbol of completeness, on which account the ancients called it the perfect number, which comprehends all others in itself. But it commonly denotes completeness in respect to *human* interests and relations—as in the tithes or tenths (ten being regarded as comprising the entire property, from which one was selected to do homage to him who gave the whole), and the ten commandments, the sum of man's dutiful obedience. When, therefore, the divided state into which the modern Roman world fell, is represented under ten horns or kingdoms, it may well be doubted whether this should be pressed farther than as indicating, by a round number, the totality of the new states—the diversity in the unity—whether or not it might admit of being exactly and definitely applied to so many historical kingdoms. There is always some difficulty in making out an exact correspondence; and we should the less hold such a correspondence to be necessary, since even in the case of the tribes of Israel, when taken to represent the company of an elect people (chap. vii.), one tribe is totally omitted

[1] It is perhaps by a silent reference to this that we should explain the enigmatical passage in chap. xiii. 18, respecting the name of the beast: "Here is wisdom. Let him that hath understanding count the number of the beast: for it is a man's number; and the number is 666." The name must be taken here (as usual in Scripture), as the indication of the nature. Now, though the beast had been allowed to assume a sevenfold manifestation, as a kind of assumption and parody of the Divine, and though in the latter stages of its existence, its lamb-horned ally was to do much to work it into a *resemblance* of the Divine, yet as regards the realities of things, it could never reach what it aspired after—it could not attain to any development beyond the human—though it should have this in its higher form. Not the *seven*, therefore, the symbol of Divine fulness and perfection, but only the *six* highly potentialized—this six three times repeated is the utmost that could be assigned him for a symbolical indication of his nature—this is the number of his name. It is but a man's name still, not God's.

to preserve the symbolism of the historical twelve. This shows very strikingly the stress laid on the symbolical element, and strengthens the conclusion, that both in the seven and ten, as applied to the beast, and in the broken periods now under consideration, that element is primarily respected. Lastly, there is to be added on the same side the obviously loose setting of the periods; neither their starting-point, nor their termination is sharply defined. Viewed historically, indeed, one does not see how it could have been otherwise. The flight of the church into the wilderness, or the treading down of the holy city by the Gentiles, came on gradually; and appeared in different places at different times. It cannot be linked to definite historical epochs, as if at one or other of these it commenced for the first time, and for the whole church; and from the very nature of things, the termination must have a like diversity and gradation in its accomplishment. This draws a plain line of demarcation between the periods before us, and Daniel's seventy weeks, which are definitely bounded both in respect to their commencement and their close. The narrower field, and more outward character of the things they referred to, easily admitted of such a limitation; but here the world is the field, and the cause of vital Christianity throughout its borders the great interest at stake.

Giving all these considerations their due weight, we cannot avoid arriving at the conclusion, that the periods mentioned, in accordance with the general character of the book, are to be chiefly, if not exclusively, understood in a symbolical manner, as serving to indicate the times of relative length or brevity which the operations described were destined to occupy. If anything further is implied, it should only, we conceive, be looked for in some general correspondence, as to form, between the symbol and the reality, such as might be sufficient to guide thoughtful and inquiring minds to a more firm assurance of the realisation of the vision. But all precise and definite calculations respecting the periods, as they necessarily proceed upon a disregard of the symbolical character of the book, and upon a too external and political contemplation of the events to which it points, so they must inevitably be defeated of their aim in the future, as they have continually been in the past. The prophecy was not written to give men to know, after *such* a fashion, the times and the seasons, which the Father has put in His own power.[1]

The same considerations, it may be added, which have conducted us to this conclusion, in regard to the periods connected with the church's humiliation and conflict, substantially apply also to the period of her future ascendancy. The thousand years' reign of the saints must be taken, like the others, symbolically, and as such it forms a perfect contrast to the comparatively brief and broken sections of time that preceded it. It is formed of the round number of totality in earthly things, the ten; and that increased to one of its higher values, by being twice multiplied into itself ($10 \times 10 \times 10 = 1000$), still further heightened by being connected, not with days or with months, but with years. A ten times ten revolution of years, and that again increased tenfold—what a symbol of completeness! What a contrast to the three and an-half days of triumph over the slain witnesses! or even to the three and an-half years of usurped dominion on the part of the beast! Yet such is the relative continuance allotted in the decrees of heaven to the power and prevalence of the good, as contrasted with the evil: *so long* is the true church of the Redeemer destined to ride upon the high places of the earth, in comparison with the days in which she was made to see evil. What an elevating prospect! And how earnestly should she long to see it truly entered upon!

[1] Compare what was previously said upon this subject at p. 173, sq.

SECTION IV.

THE PROPHETICAL FUTURE OF THE CHURCH AND KINGDOM OF CHRIST IN THEIR RELATION TO HIS SECOND COMING, AND THE CLOSING ISSUES OF HIS MEDIATORIAL KINGDOM.

THE portions of the Apocalypse, and of other prophetical books, which have already passed under our review, reach down to what is known as the millennium, or the thousand years' reign. That the things written concerning this belong to the still undeveloped future, we entertain not the remotest doubt, and regard as utterly futile all the attempts that have been made to accommodate the terms of the description to any period of the past.[1] The very best that has yet been can be

[1] The latest of these attempts is that of Hengstenberg, who would date the commencement of the millennium from the year 800, when Charlemagne was proclaimed emperor; according to which the millennium has already reached its close, and we are now sustaining the assault of Gog and Magog. Of this view, Auberlen justly remarks, " One is at a loss to know, whether to be more astonished at the extraordinary manner in which the word of prophecy is impaired and evacuated by it, at the greatly too favourable estimate it makes of the past history of the church, or at the want of discrimination which would thus place the darkest periods of the middle ages and the Papacy alongside those of the Reformation, and treat them all as ages of gold. Was it during these thousand years, when so many sins were committed, and that, too, in the name of Christ, by Catholics and those of the national and orthodox establishments, that the devil was actually bound? Was it during those times of the Waldensian persecutions, of the Inquisition, of Huguenot wars, and Bartholomew nights, that the martyrs governed the world? Was it during those times, when princes were, indeed, styled Apostolical Majesties, Most Christian Kings, etc., yet lived in the most flagrant sins, that they were really priests of God and kings of Christ? It is truly lamentable that a man like Hengstenberg should have contributed in such a manner to mislead the judgments of men respecting the nature of the church and the world, and should have been able to derive from the prophets no

nothing more than the prelude of what may still be expected of good. But the subject of the millennium, and the closing periods generally of the world's history, have such a real or supposed connection with the second coming of Messiah, that it is necessary, in the first instance, to investigate the language of Scripture upon this point. We are the rather inclined to do so, as we are persuaded, that if the Scriptural representations regarding it were but calmly considered, there might both be more of formal agreement on the main subject, and less of confident assertion generally on some of the subordinate topics connected with it.

I. The doctrine of the Lord's coming is common to both Testaments, as the desire and expectation of it belongs to the people of God under both dispensations. It could scarcely fail, therefore, that the mode of representation employed respecting it in New Testament Scripture should bear a close resemblance to that which had been in use under the Old, and should even be in great measure coincident with it. The proper starting-point for all the representations is the entrance of sin, which brought as its necessary result the withdrawal of God's manifested presence, and laid a restraint upon His intercourse with men. Prior to that fatal period, He did not need to come, as from a distance, to do anything for man; He did it as being already and habitually at hand. Even after the transgression the fallen pair are represented, not as seeing the Lord come for the occasion, but as hearing His voice walking in the garden in the cool of the day; they knew the familiar sound of their heavenly Father's footsteps. But they were to know it thus no more. The Paradise, where God *could* so familiarly dwell with man, had now

deeper and purer insight. He substitutes what was a false anticipation of the thousand years' reign for the reign itself—external political Christianity for the real—Christianity of the name and the lip for the true and genuine." (P. 415.) In truth, the description given in the epistles to the seven churches of the kind of Christianity which alone the Lord could recognize and own, forms a strong anticipative protest against such a millennium, and repudiates it.

become to them a forfeited region; and not till the evil which then entered should have run its course, not till the works of sin should be destroyed, and the warfare with its abettors brought to a perpetual end, could the original state of things in regard to men's relation to God be again restored. Then, however—that is, when the new and better Paradise is brought in—the tabernacle of God shall be once more with men, and He shall dwell with them, in an everlasting fellowship of love. But till that blessed consummation, there can only be occasional manifestations—comings of such a nature and in such succession as may be needed to maintain the divine interest in the world, to provide the requisite means of grace and comfort to the Lord's people, and administer seasonable rebukes to His adversaries.

Now, in Old Testament Scripture there appears a perpetual struggle against this untoward state of things. Faith is ever striving to bring God out of the distance to which He has retired, and present Him in immediate connection with the deeper experiences of the soul, and the more important movements of the world's history. The Book of Psalms may be regarded as a continued exemplification of this. How often, in perusing it, do we feel as if we even heard the voice of God, and saw His shape! The soul, animated by a lively spirit of faith, and thereby raised to the higher moods of spiritual thought and feeling, moves among the things of God as among sensible realities; is tremblingly alive to whatever marks His presence or His absence; is alternately cheered by the light of His countenance, and troubled by the hidings of His face; and is conscious of all the indications of a sustained or interrupted fellowship. "Lord, by thy favour thou didst make my mountain to stand strong; thou didst hide thy face, and I was troubled." "Arise, O Lord, in thine anger; lift up thyself because of the rage of mine enemies; and awake for me to the judgment that thou hast commanded." "In my distress, I called upon the Lord, and cried unto my God: He heard my voice out of His temple, and my cry came before Him, into His ears. He bowed the heavens also, and came down." "O God, how long shall the adversary reproach? Shall the enemy blaspheme thy name for ever? Why withdrawest thou thy hand, even thy right hand? Pluck it out of thy bosom?" "Arise; why sleepest thou, O Lord? Cast us not off for ever," etc.

Such a mode of contemplating and addressing God pervading a book which is the production of so many hands, and in its several parts is connected with so many diversities of time and place, could not, it is clear, belong to a few isolated individuals, or be transient in its exercise. It must have been the natural tendency and expression of that spirit which grew out of the religion of the Old Covenant, and which it was the design as well of its symbolical institutions, as of its express promises, to strengthen and foster. Hence, also, it enters deeply into the language of prophecy. Everything of moment in the dispensations of God, is there connected with His presence and working. So, for example, in the earliest prophecy after the transactions connected with the fall, the prediction of Enoch, which is preserved in Jude, though not recorded in the original history: "Behold, the Lord cometh with ten thousand of his saints, to execute judgment upon all; and to convince all that are ungodly among them of all their ungodly deeds, which they have ungodly committed, and of all their hard speeches, which ungodly sinners have spoken against Him." The prophecy, as appears from the application made of it by St Jude, had an extensive reach, and might be understood even of the final manifestation of the Lord to execute judgment. But, from the time and circumstances in which it was spoken, there can be no doubt that it pointed more immediately to the clouds of wrath which were already gathering around antediluvian sinners, and that when these burst in the deluge there was the first realization of the Lord's threatened coming to judgment. In like manner, the next recorded manifestations of righteousness of an unusual kind—those connected with the destruction of Sodom and Gomorrah—the punishment of Egypt and the rescue of Israel—are in Scripture associated with the Lord's immediate presence and agency. He is represented as "coming down to see and hear" how matters stood; and when He saw, smiting, on the one hand, with pestilence and destruction, on the other, stretching forth His hand to protect and succour. What a vivid representation is given in the song of Moses of the Lord's appearance and working, in connection with the events of the Red Sea! It seems as if it spake of what the eye had seen and the ear had heard: "The Lord is a man of war; the Lord is His name. Thy right hand, O Lord, is become glorious in power: thy right hand, O Lord, hath dashed in pieces the enemy. Thou didst blow with thy wind, the sea covered them; they sank as lead in the mighty waters. Thou stretchedst out thy right hand, the earth swallowed them."

It is not otherwise in prophecy generally. The descriptions vary in respect to imagery and vividness of colouring; but they are alike in connecting the Lord's personal presence with events, whether of mercy or of judgment, which bore materially on the well-being of His people, or on the power and policy of their enemies. If signal judgment was to be executed upon the worldly kingdoms which sought to oppress or extinguish the covenant-people, proclamation was made of the Lord's coming to inflict it (Isa. xiii., xix., xxx. 27, etc.). When sin prevailed among the covenant-people themselves the Lord speaks of His soul departing from them, or of going far off from His sanctuary (Jer. vi. 8; Ezek. viii. 6), as He actually did when He gave them up to the will of their enemies, and laid their land desolate for a season. On the other hand, when the prospect of better times was announced, it came in the form of an assurance that the Lord would appear with salvation, would Himself even go before as a leader, or, as a protector, bring up their rere-ward (Hosea vi. 1–3; Isa. xl., lii. 12). And when the remnant from Babylon again settled at Jerusalem, they were met with the prophetic testimony that He also had returned to Jerusalem with mercies (Zech. i. 16). But were the people not taught to expect another, and, in the stricter sense, personal coming of the

Lord from heaven? Undoubtedly they were—not, however, by the simple announcement of such a coming, but by the conditions and circumstances associated with it, which were such as to require for their fulfilment a personal appearance of Godhead in the flesh. Predictions like those in Malachi, in which it was intimated that the Lord should come suddenly to His temple, that the day of His coming should be terrible, and should burn as an oven, might be paralleled by many others which had their accomplishment in events long prior to the incarnation, and were accompanied by no external displays of the Divine personality. But then in other prophecies there were particular adjuncts connected with the coming. It was to take place amid conditions of flesh and blood, of time and circumstance. There was to be a preparation of the way by a messenger going before, a birth in a definite line and at a specific place, a life and death alike marked by the most singular characteristics—all not only affording ground for expecting, but even containing terms that indispensably required, a coming of the most distinct and palpable description. It was not, therefore, so properly the coming considered by itself as the declared manner and objects of the coming, which rendered that of Messiah's predicted appearance in the flesh different from all other announcements of the Lord's coming. And if, on that account, the epithet *real* is applied to the one, and *figurative* to the other, or, if the one is designated a *personal* coming, and the others only *virtual* or *spiritual*, such modes of distinction, it must be remembered, are not derived from Scripture, nor are they strictly accordant with the truth of things.

The Lord was as really present at the destruction of Sodom, at the deliverance of Israel from the host of Pharaoh, and at the restoration of the captives from Babylon, as in the life and death of Jesus of Nazareth. There was a proper coming, and an actual presence, in the earlier as well as the later events referred to; only in the former withdrawn from human sight, and forming no part of the visible realities which made up the historical transactions of the time. It *was* there, however, as a living force, and the invisibility attaching to it was the result merely of a defect in the perceptive part of our natures, which (if He had pleased) might have been supplied by some higher intuition, or even by an intensifying of the power of spiritual apprehension. It was from no want of reality in the appearances, which betokened, on a certain occasion, the presence of the Lord and of His ministering host, but for want of the necessary discernment, that the servant of Elisha was unconscious of their existence; and when the prophet prayed that the servant's eyes might be opened, presently, we are told, he saw the mountain full of horses and chariots of fire round about Elisha (2 Kings vi. 17). In like manner, the peculiar elevation of soul which was given to Stephen on the eve of his martyrdom, enabled him to see what had otherwise remained hid,—the glory of God, and Jesus standing on the right hand of God. Jesus himself is reported to have heard with perfect distinctness a word addressed to Him by the Father, which, in the duller ears of those about Him, sounded only as a confused murmur (John xii. 28, 29); and, subsequently, in His own manifestation to Saul on the way to Damascus, Saul both saw and heard in the clearest manner what seems to have made but a faint impression upon the senses of others (Acts ix. 7). How, indeed, in the case of One who is everywhere present, without whom not even a sparrow falls to the ground, nor a single event, from the least to the greatest in any region of the universe, is accomplished; how but by a special adaptation of Himself to the existing faculties of His creatures, or by an elevation of these faculties to a nearer conformity to His own spiritual nature, can they perceive Him where He is, or descry the signs of His approach? The Son of Man speaks of Himself as being in heaven at the very time He was living upon the earth (John iii. 13), as from His essential divinity He must have been, and must also have appeared to be to the higher beings who could penetrate the region of His glory. So that, as regards the Lord's presence and coming, the real and the visible are by no means to be regarded as interchangeable;

and it is only from the accompanying circumstances and conditions that we can determine, in regard to any predicted manifestation of Himself, whether it is to be patent to the senses of men, or concealed from their view.

Such are the conclusions we arrive at on the subject of the Lord's coming from a consideration of what is written of it in Old Testament Scripture; and the presumption is, as we have already indicated, that it may not be materially different, when we pass from the Old to the New. Here it is the Messiah in His distinctly defined personality as the God-man, and in His character as the glorified Redeemer, whose coming in glory is announced as the great hope of the church. When on earth He was known as "He that should come" (ὁ ἐρχόμενος, the coming one), coming to accomplish the great salvation, and satisfy the longing expectations of spiritual minds. But this could only be done in part at the first appearance of the Lord. It was even necessary, that the work begun on earth should be prosecuted in the heavenly places, that the full number of the elect might be gathered in, and the way prepared for that final possession of the world, and that free intercommunion between God and men, which is to constitute the blessedness of Paradise restored. The agency of Christ, therefore, must be carried on within the veil, and accomplish great results among men, before He can appear in glory. And both in regard to the terminal point itself, and the intervening steps necessary to secure its being reached, we might justly expect representations to be given in the prophetic word very similar to those, which had appeared in Old Testament Scripture regarding the incarnation, and the more peculiar manifestations of divine power and glory that preceded it.

Such we find to be actually the case. There is a coming spoken of in New Testament Scripture which may be designated in the proper sense terminal, and therefore also visible; so that every eye shall see it, and every heart be filled either with joy or dismay on account of it. And there are comings of a provisional kind, which all point toward the ultimate manifestation, and differ from it only in being less palpable in their nature, and less complete and lasting in their results. The reference to both modes of coming is found in our Lord's own discourses upon the subject. In some of the parables it is presented under the aspect of a single and conclusive event; as in the parables of the talents and the pounds, where He appears as one going to a far country for a time, and leaving his servants to their several spheres of privilege and duty, with the prospect of a personal reckoning on his return; in the parable also of the wise and foolish virgins, which presents the church in its false, as well as its true portions, under the aspect of a bridal company waiting for the arrival of the proper spouse to the celebration of his marriage solemnity; and in the delineation, substantially also a parabolical one, of the appearance of the Son of Man on the throne of judgment, when He shall have come finally to separate between the goats and the sheep, and to give to every one as his works may have been. In all these representations the coming of the Lord has the aspect of a grand and culminating event, which winds up the affairs of time and ushers in the destinies of eternity. But if we turn to the parable of the wicked husbandmen (Matt. xxi. 33–43), we find a coming spoken of, which is plainly interpreted by our Lord to have had its accomplishment in an earlier, and merely provisional event. There the husbandmen are represented as consummating a long-continued course of wickedness by proceeding to kill him, who had come to them in the character of son and heir. And the question is then asked, "When the Lord of the vineyard *cometh*, what will he do unto those husbandmen?" The persons present instinctively supplied the answer by saying, that he would miserably destroy those wicked men, and let out his vineyard to others, that would render him the fruits in their seasons. On receiving this answer, and making special application of the truth it embodied, the Lord forthwith uttered the memorable words, "Therefore say I unto you, the kingdom of God shall be taken from you, and given to a nation bringing forth the fruits thereof." So that the divine procedure, which had the effect of transferring the kingdom from Jewish to Gentile soil, must correspond to the coming of the Lord of the vineyard in the parable, for the purpose of dispossessing one class of husbandmen, and installing another. But how was that transference effected? Simply by the setting up of the gospel dispensation by means of the word preached, and the Spirit bestowed among the Gentiles, along with the overthrow of Jerusalem and the dissolution of the old economy. The Lord then came and let out the vineyard to others.

Nor is this the only place in our Lord's discourses, where the same use and application is made of the expression. In the tenth chapter of St Matthew's gospel we have a full report of the address delivered by our Lord on the occasion of His sending out His apostles on a missionary tour—the first of its kind. Precisely because it was the first—the moment when the ἀποστέλλειν (the sending forth) came into force, from which the apostles derived their name—Jesus perceived in it the image of the whole future mission-work of the kingdom. Accordingly, He framed His address on the occasion so as to embrace the whole, and rendered it substantially a charge to all ministers and missionaries of the gospel to the end of time. That Jesus should have taken this wide and comprehensive view of the subject is itself an evidence of His divine greatness. For a mere man to have done so, might justly have been held extravagance or presumption; but in Him, who could see the end *from* the beginning and *in* the beginning, it was perfectly natural. And because He thus embraced in His perspective the whole future progress of His kingdom, even to the bringing in of its final results, He did not fail at the outset to deliver appropriate counsel and encouragement for the later as well as the earlier labourers belonging to it. The discourse, indeed, falls into three successive portions. The first, which reaches to the close of ver. 15, has respect more immediately to the present temporary mission committed to the twelve; as appears from their being charged to confine themselves to the house of Israel, without turning aside either to the Samaritans or the Gentiles, and also from their being instructed to take with them neither scrip nor staff, changes of raiment nor provisions—restrictions which were afterwards withdrawn, when their more general and permanent mission began (Luke xxii. 35, 36). The second part, which again begins with the "I send you" at ver. 16, has respect to a more advanced stage of the work, though one in which those apostles had still the chief burden to bear; it embraces the main period of apostolic agency. In this portion mention is made for the first time of persecutions, and such persecutions as should not be of a merely local kind, but would involve the appearance of the disciples before kings and rulers, as well as councils and synogogues, and among Gentiles not less than Jews. For the emergencies and trials thence arising the promise is also for the first time given them of the Holy Spirit, with all requisite and suitable gifts of grace. And the limitation of the period, as well as of the sphere, to which their agency was to be more especially confined, is marked in the closing words of the section, ver. 23, "Verily I say unto you, ye shall not have gone over (τελέσητε, finished, namely in respect to the great aim of the mission) the cities of Israel till the Son of Man be come." A pregnant word indeed for those first heralds of the gospel—as it already gave intimation of difficulties to be encountered among their own countrymen, which they should but very partially succeed in overcoming within the allotted period for their labours! A pregnant word also in respect to the light it threw upon the future intentions and purposes of our Lord! He announces a coming so near, that they should not have time to finish their work as apostles among the cities of Israel, till it should be brought to pass. What possibly could be meant by this but His coming to order and settle anew the affairs of His kingdom among men! Coming, not in visible personality, yet in real majesty, first to endow His followers with power from on high, and cheer them with manifestations of His presence; and then to remove by His judgments the old polity and commonwealth out of the way, which from being superstitiously clung to served only to mar the progress of the new, that the field might be left clear to the gospel of the kingdom! But the end, which was to be introduced by this coming of the Son of Man, was only the beginning of what was to constitute the end in another respect. As the spiritual kingdom then to be set up constituted the New Jerusalem in its commencement, and the Old that was to be destroyed had become a kind of spiritual Sodom or Egypt (Rev. xi. 8); so the work as a whole, with its salvation on the one side, and its destruction on the other, formed a striking image of the still more signal coming of Christ, when the old world of sin shall be finally abolished, and the new brought in with its scenes of everlasting purity and bliss. Therefore, in the last section of the discourse, our Lord proceeds to unfold what might be expected by all future labourers in His kingdom both in trial here and in recompense hereafter—what troubles and persecutions they might look for—what encouragements and supports he would be ready to extend to them—what fidelity and zeal it would be their calling to exhibit—and in what fulness of blessing and glory their service would issue, if they but continued stedfast in it to the end.[1]

There are not wanting other passages of a similar kind in our Lord's discourses; for example, Matth. xvi. 28, "Verily I say unto you, There be some standing here, who shall not taste of death, till they see the Son of man coming in His kingdom"—which, by no fair and natural exposition can be referred primarily to events and times altogether subsequent to the apostolic age; it must indicate what *some* of those then present lived to witness, viz., to the manifestation of Christ's divine power after His ascension, when introducing the new

[1] The sense put, and unavoidably put in the above remarks upon Matt. x. 23, and upon the coming indicated in the parable of the husbandmen, shews how groundless the statement of Bishop Horsley is, "that the phrase of our Lord's coming whenever it occurs in his prediction of the Jewish war, as well as in most other passages of the New Testament, is to be taken in its literal meaning, as denoting His coming in person, in visible pomp and glory, to the general judgment." The investigation on which he founds this statement is very summary, and neither of the passages above noticed are referred to.

dispensation, and formally removing the old. This is the only thing that can be regarded as coming properly within the terms of the description; and what, in effect, was it but the first movements of the stone in Daniel's vision, proceeding to displace the things opposed to it, and to take possession of the field? "The day of the Son of Man," in Luke xvii. 24, must also be viewed as having its primary reference to the same period—since if referred to the final advent, the practical exhortations connected with it would not be applicable. And in Matth. xxiv., it is impossible altogether to separate between the immediate and the final coming. To a certain extent, the two are intermingled together, and the one is contemplated as the type and presage of the other.

At the same time there can be no doubt, that the final return of the Saviour is often held forth in New Testament Scripture as the great object of hope and expectation to the church. It meets us at the very commencement of the Apostolic history, in the words addressed by the angels to those who witnessed the ascension: "This same Jesus, who is taken up from you into heaven, shall so come in like manner, as ye have seen Him go into heaven"—which manifestly gives promise of a return equally visible and glorious as the departure which had just taken place. It is again shortly afterwards, and in the most pointed manner, referred to by the apostle Peter in his second address to the people of Jerusalem, when representing it as necessary that the heavens should receive Christ only till the times of the restitution of all things. The same apostle in his second epistle describes believers not only as holding fast the promise of Christ's coming, but even as hasting toward the day of its fulfilment; and St Paul characterizes the followers of Jesus as those "who love his appearing." It is needless to multiply examples. But such passages alternate with others, in which a coming is spoken of, which is neither terminal nor marked by any outward personal display. The history detailed in the book of Acts, though formally that of the apostles, appears more as the continuation of Christ's personal agency, carried on through the instrumentality of the immediate actors, than of their own proper working. The wonders of Pentecost were exhibited as the evidence of Christ's exaltation, and the fruit of His power. The miraculous healing of the poor cripple at the temple-gate, and the no less miraculous judgment on Ananias and Sapphira in the church, were alike viewed as the results of Christ's outstretched hand; they happened because He (the Holy One whom the Father had anointed, chap. iv. 27–30), was present with the power of His Spirit to do signs and wonders. When the apostles bore to other lands the gospel of salvation, and planted Christian churches, Christ Himself was declared to have come and preached peace by them (Eph. ii. 17). On Him as a present living Saviour, they laid the foundation of a living church (1 Cor. iii. 10, 11). In the Book of Revelation, more especially, where the final coming is most conspicuously displayed, provisional and invisible comings are also most distinctly noticed. "Remember from whence thou art fallen," is the charge to the church of Ephesus, "and repent and do the first works; or else I will come unto thee quickly, and will remove the candlestick out of its place." So also to others, "Repent, or else I will come unto thee quickly," "If thou shalt not watch, I will come on thee as a thief, and thou shalt not know what hour I will come upon thee." Nay, he even speaks of himself to the church of Laodicea as standing at the door and knocking. In the subsequent parts of the Book, it is he who, as a "mighty angel," is represented (chap. x.) as coming down from heaven, and setting his feet upon the sea and dry land, as going presently to take permanent possession of both; and who again, during the currency of the sixth vial, and in respect to the things then in progress, proclaims, "Behold I come as a thief; blessed is he that watcheth and keepeth his garments, lest he walk naked, and they see his shame" (chap. xvi. 15).[1]

[1] When all these things are put together, and when it is remembered how our Lord taught a parable for the express purpose of destroying the expectation, that the kingdom should immediately appear in visible glory

From the general current, therefore, of Scriptural representations concerning Christ—from the language employed in the Book of Revelation, and in other parts of the New Testament—it is plain, that the question of Christ's second advent or His coming, not to depart again, but to dwell with His people, is not to be determined by the mere announcement of His coming. The farther question has still to be considered, for what purpose is the coming announced, and in what manner may it be expected to take place? It was Christ's promise to the disciples, before He left them, that though corporeally absent, He would still be really and effectively present with them; that He would manifest Himself to them as He could not do to the world, and would be ever coming to do works of mercy or of judgment in their behalf. In every age the heart of faith finds the realization of this promise, sometimes more, sometimes less conspicuously, though never so as to satisfy its longings, or consummate His own work, till He shall come visibly in the clouds of heaven with power and great glory. And the more particular question, whether this terminal coming is to precede the millennium, or to be subsequent to it, must depend for its settlement on the things spoken of the millennium, whether they are such as befit the manifested presence and glory of the Saviour, or are properly compatible with it. This can only be learned from a careful consideration of what is written upon the subject. We turn, therefore, to the millennium itself.

(Luke xix. 12)—when it is remembered also how the apostles, in their more specific passages, interpose a long series of operations and events between their day and the consummation of all things (as in 2 Thess. ii., and the Apocalypse)—it is difficult to express one's astonishment at the confidence with which it is still often affirmed of the apostles, that they looked for the return of Christ before their own death. If so, they must have been at once the most impracticable of learners, and the most inconsistent of writers. The real explanation of the matter lies in their singular strength of faith, with which many of their commentators can so little sympathize, and which led them, in a manner, to overleap the gulph of ages, to identify the present with the future, and to realise great events, whether near or remote, in their pressing magnitude and importance.

II. It is only in the Book of Revelation that we have any formal or explicit account of what is known as the millennium, or the thousand years' reign of Christ and His saints. The Old Testament prophets contain many delineations which point towards it, and which shall only then reach their proper accomplishment; but they are, for the most part, of a general description, and are couched under the veil of Old Testament relations. They speak, for example, of a time to come, when the knowledge of the glory of the Lord shall cover the earth as the waters cover the sea (Hab. ii. 14); when the Lord shall be king over all the earth, and His name one (Zech. xiv. 9); when men shall be blessed in Him, and all nations shall call Him blessed (Ps. lxxii. 17); when the earth, having been smitten with the rod of His mouth, and the wicked slain with the breath of His lips, righteousness and peace shall universally prevail, and there shall be nothing to hurt or to destroy in all God's holy mountain (Isa. xi. 1–9). There are many such descriptions sufficient to show that the Old Testament prophets were enabled to descry, even from their comparatively distant watch-tower, the sure and final overthrow of every form of evil in the world, to be followed by a long and happy reign, during which the truth of God should be everywhere triumphant, and the blessings of salvation shed abroad. But beyond this, nothing can with certainty be anticipated from such descriptions. Those of Daniel, however, are somewhat more specific. In the first of them the kingdom, represented by the stone cut out without hands, the kingdom that was to be set up by the God of heaven, is described as "breaking in pieces and consuming all those kingdoms, and itself standing for ever"—apparently implying, not only the ultimate success and permanent establishment of the Divine kingdom, but along with this, and as somehow necessary to it, the formal abolition and disappearance of the kingdoms, which were contrary to its spirit, and had opposed its progress. So also in the other vision, that of chap. vii., the prophet says he "beheld till the beast (the embodied representation of all the worldly kingdoms in their hostility to the kingdom of Messiah) was slain, and his body destroyed, and given to the burning flame—as if not merely the spirit that had animated it, but the very form and shape it had assumed, was to come to an end. And, again, to the like effect in the explanation, "The judgment shall sit, and they (viz., the saints, the only party of an opposite kind mentioned in the preceding verse—they, therefore, having now received power and authority to judge) shall take away his dominion, to consume and to destroy it to the end. And the kingdom and dominion, and the greatness (or power) of the kingdom under the whole heaven shall be given to the people of the saints of the Most High, whose kingdom is an everlasting kingdom, and all dominions shall serve and obey Him." If this language does not certainly betoken, it yet seems naturally to imply something more than the infusion of a better spirit into the kingdoms of the world; to indicate an actual remodelling of the state of things among men, and a fresh organization of the social fabric, such as would formally commit the administration of affairs into the hands of the Lord's people, by making personal piety and worth the essential qualification for civil rule.

The indications to this effect in Daniel are confirmed, and still more distinctly exhibited in the Apocalypse, which contains by much the most explicit revelation upon the subject. It is not simply, however, the account given of the thousand years' reign (chap. xx. 1–6), that here calls for consideration; but the manner, also, in which this is introduced, and the antecedent condition of things, out of which it is represented as emerging. Prior to this millennial reign, and preparatory to it, the worldly power in all its successive phases and forms of working, is seen to have gone down. It had passed through every conceivable species of combination and culture, from the time of the old heathen monarchies, down to the subdivided, and at last professedly Christian kingdoms of more recent times. In the course of the changes it underwent, and as the result of the contact into which it came with Christianity, it had appeared for a season to die; the stroke as of a mortal wound seemed to have befallen it; but the former vigour again returned to it, and even more than the former danger to the cause and kingdom of Christ became connected with its operations. Instead of carrying into full and proper effect the spirit of the gospel, it had only imbibed as much of the Christian element as served to render its ministrations to the flesh more perilous for those who knew not the power of godliness; on which account its Christianity had proved but a mother of abominations, and its prophecy a spirit of carnal pride, and lying divination. All, therefore, had been judged and cast out; first, the whore, or the corrupt and faithless church, which even the worldly power was at length to repudiate; and then this power itself—the beast—with his ally, the false prophet, both had been adjudged to the lake of fire, or finally put down as irreconcilably opposed to the spirit and interests of the divine kingdom. The last trial had been given to the world in what might be called its native and self-contrived organizations, to see if its authorities would submit themselves aright to the truth of the gospel, and have their administration directed in accordance with the mind of Christ. But without the desired effect. The old enmity still lurked; the opposition to God and holiness only assumed new and more aggravated forms; and the kingdoms themselves, as well as the beast that represented their ungodliness, and the false prophet that, as it were, inspirited and justified the evil, were swept away into the blackness of darkness for ever.

It seems scarcely possible to understand all this of a simple diffusion of gospel light, and a general ascendancy of the Christian element, under forms of social life and conditions of working, such as the world has hitherto exhibited. We might have conceived it would be so, if merely a corrupt and apostate Christianity, and a science and learning opposed to the gospel, were all that had been represented as going into perdition. But it is otherwise, when the beast also, and the kingdoms of the world are spoken of as sharing the same fate; for this seems to import, that the worldly powers, or forms of earthly government now and hitherto subsisting in the world, should pass away, as in their very nature incompatible with that higher state of things which is in prospect. They cannot, it would appear, be so divested of the bestial properties inherent in them, as to be capable of assuming the aspect of that kingdom, which had its proper representation in one possessing the likeness of a son of man. The transition from one to the other involves a shaking of earthly things to their foundations, that other things, which cannot be shaken —the things which are of God—may remain. And, indeed, let any one reflect on the invariable tendency of worldly power and dominion—how constantly it takes the direction of fleshly indulgence and selfish aggrandisement, becomes partial or exclusive in its operations, makes undue account of the adventitious and the temporal, while it leaves comparatively unheeded what is of primary and enduring moment; and this, not as in one age merely, or in some particular phases of political and social life, but in all: let any one reflect carefully on this, and say, whether worldly kingdoms, as such, can be conceived to perpetuate their formal existence, on the supposition of everything coming to bear the image of a living Christianity. It is one thing to overthrow evil in its more prevailing forms, but another thing to bring in and establish on a secure and permanent footing the contrary good. The progress of enlightenment, and the growing diffusion of divine truth, may of themselves expose the corruptions of a false religion, and render manifest the insufficiency or ungodliness of a mere earthly wisdom. But they may still prove wholly inadequate to the higher end of making righteousness everywhere and continuously triumphant; nay, must do so, unless the entire framework of society shall be cast anew, so as to lay open all the avenues of life for the good, and close them against the evil. Yet nothing less than this is the extent to which the change predicted shall reach. It is that the saints, not merely shall become more numerous and powerful than hitherto, but shall formally possess the kingdom under the whole heaven, and exercise its dominion. It is, that the god of this world shall be bound in his proper home, that men may not be deceived, and turned aside from the right by the lust of the flesh, the lust of the eye, and the pride of life. It is, therefore, that the spiritual shall carry it over the natural in the ordinary affairs of the world—that the grace and energy of holy principle, not hereditary place, or the adventitious distinctions of rank and fortune, shall come to bear general sway among men. And how this can be done without many organic changes being wrought in the social and political sphere, it is impossible to conceive.

The more closely the account of the millennial reign is examined, the more does it confirm us in these impressions. Thus, while we read still of the nations of the earth (chap. xx. 3, 8), we hear no more of the old worldly kingdoms, nor of the beast and the false prophet. The existing and historical forms of the world's power, and wisdom, and glory, have all disappeared. Then, the thrones which were set for judgment, and which unquestionably represented not only the actual, but also the ostensible, forces that are destined to regulate the affairs of that better age, are said to be for those who had suffered for the word of God and for the testimony of Jesus—a description which, however understood in respect to the particular occupants, and of which we shall speak presently, undoubtedly denotes such as are distinguished for the most faithful and uncompromising adherence to the principles of the gospel. These it is who are then to appear before the world as its guides and rulers; by them somehow, and by them in the recognized character of the Lord's people, the world is to be presided over and governed. Of them, as emphatically "blessed and holy," it is written, that they are the "priests of God and of Christ, and shall reign with Him a thousand years." Being, like Christ Himself, priests upon thrones, their kingly power and influence shall be based on ascertained holiness of character; all authority shall be held directly of God, and such things only shall be allowed to proceed as carry with them the divine sanction, and are fitted to promote the interests of righteousness. Happy period, truly, that shall witness the commencement of such an administration! But what a remodelling shall it not need to bring along with it of the political and social fabric! In the same direction, also, points the notice that is given of the prime agent and patron of evil. Satan, we are told, shall be bound during the thousand years' reign in the bottomless pit, so that he shall be able to deceive the nations no more. Here, again, there is a mighty gulph to be bridged over for the world, and even for the church. Outside the professing church, the field is, in a manner, all his own; he is the spirit that works in the children of disobedience, and carries them captive at his will. But even within the church his temptations are plied with unwearied diligence, and lamentable success. Under the very eye of the apostles, and in spite both of their supernatural gifts, and their unceasing watchfulness, he found it possible to deceive many; and by dint of his subtle agency, not only has there been reared a huge system of antichristian idolatry, but in the case of myriads living amid the clearest light, a worthless profession is ever being substituted for the life and power of godliness. When that agency, therefore, with its fruits, shall have been abolished, there will inevitably be a revolution, previously unheard of, in the general order and constitution of things. Governments as they now exist, the policy and business of the world as at present conducted, even the management and direction of the church, which shall then have ceased to be distinct from the world, shall be antiquated; in many respects they shall have to take another aim, and work in another manner, than they have hitherto done; because they shall have to be adapted to a state of things in which no longer ignorance, delusion, and falsehood predominate, but the knowledge and love of the truth.

Such, then, being the view of the millennial state presented to us in the twentieth chapter of the Apocalypse, taken in its plain and broad import, the question naturally arises, How is it to be brought about and maintained? What is indicated as to the means and agencies by which such extraordinary results are to be accomplished? To say nothing of the operations going before, and preparing the way for the introduction of this state—which have been discussed in a previous chapter—there are two leading features in the millennial vision itself, the two circumstances last noticed, which must be regarded as of the nature of means or agencies, and must be understood, if not themselves to possess, at least to involve in the way of inseparable accompaniment whatever of vital influence or efficient working may be necessary.

(1.) The first instrumentality referred to is the binding of Satan: "And I saw an angel," St John writes, "come down from heaven, having the key of the bottomless pit, and a great chain in his hand. And he laid hold on the dragon, that old serpent, which is the devil and Satan, and bound him a thousand years; and cast him into the bottomless pit, and shut him up, and set a seal upon him, that he should deceive the nations no more, till the thousand years should be fulfilled; and after that he must be loosed a little season." That this description is, in respect to the form, figurative, can admit of no doubt; for the actual performance of such material operations as those here connected with the key, the chain, and the seal, are obviously incompatible with the nature of the being to whom they relate. A spirit without bodily parts cannot possibly be the subject of such gross and mechanical treatment. But as a finite being, subject to the conditions of space and time, he may, doubtless, be confined within a definite region—confined as strictly as if he were actually chained in a prison-house, with the door sealed by the hand of Omnipotence to prevent the possibility of egress. And such *may* be the meaning here. The binding of Satan may denote a local and personal incarceration of the prince of darkness within the region designated by the bottomless pit; or it may indicate, that in respect to his cause and operations in the world, it shall be as if by forcible arrestment and location in such a region he were prevented from taking part in them. Which of these two senses should be preferred will depend upon the question, Whether the representations given us of Satan in this book, and in Scripture generally, are mainly of a personal or of a relative description? Whether they refer to Satan as an individual, or to the relation in which he stands through his workings to the church and the world? Now that it is the latter, and not the former, may be rendered evident by a few plain considerations.

It is in perfect accordance with the economy practised by Scripture in its supernatural communications, and the strictly moral design with which it makes them, that it should be very sparing in its intimations respecting the personal history of Satan, and should give prominence only to what concerns his power and interest among men. There is, therefore, an antecedent presumption that the knowledge imparted will be chiefly, if not exclusively, of a relative description. And when we look to the communications actually made, we soon perceive that unless they are contemplated in this light they stand in irreconcilable opposition to each other. Thus, at a certain period of our Lord's ministry, He declared that He saw Satan fall like lightning from heaven; at another and later period, He speaks of Satan being judged and cast out (viz., from the world); while in the second chapter of the Apocalypse he is represented as having his seat at Smyrna, then, in chapter twelfth, as being, in consequence of our Lord's perfect obedience unto death and ascension up on high, cast out of heaven, and brought down to the earth; yet again, in this twentieth chapter, as shut up in the bottomless pit; while in 2 Peter ii. 4, the whole company of fallen angels, inclusive doubtless of their chieftain, are declared to have been, from the very period of their fall, thrust down to hell, and under chains of darkness reserved unto judgment. It is impossible, excepting on the most arbitrary and forced suppositions, to bring such statements into harmony, if they are understood absolutely, and applied simply to the *personelle* of Satan. But viewed as symbolical representations of his position and influence in relation to mankind, the whole becomes perfectly intelligible; and the several changes of position indicated in respect to height and depth, heaven and earth, confinement and release, only mark the different stages of the power he exercises, and the cause he maintains in the world.

Such, on a still farther account, must be the view we adopt of the description given of Satan in the vision before us. In it, as in the descriptions generally of this book, a symbolical element predominates. The characters delineated in them all are representative, rather than individual and personal; and Satan is no more to be considered apart from the legions of darkness, and the instruments of evil generally, than the beast from its different embodiments in the worldly kingdoms, or the woman and the whore from the parties they respectively symbolized. Satan, therefore, comes into view here simply as the representative of the devilish power and agencies in the world; and the disposition often shown by writers on the Apocalypse, to consider the binding of Satan in a strictly personal light, is but another example of the intermingling of the literal with the symbolical, which has so greatly retarded the proper understanding of the prophetical Scriptures.

Taking, then, the description of Satan's being bound with chains, and shut into the bottomless pit, in a relative sense, we have in it a symbolical representation of the utterly prostrate condition to which at and during the millennium his interest in the world shall be reduced. It goes down, as it were, to the lowest hell. At first the adversary had appeared altogether in the ascendant; his dwelling seemed to be in heavenly places—such commanding sway had he obtained over the minds of men and the affairs of time. He is compelled to stoop, however, from his lofty elevation by the accomplishment of our redemption, and the ascension of the Son of Man to the right hand of the Father. But though thenceforth crippled in his power, and reduced to a lower sphere, he still wields a mighty influence, and sustains a vast dominion in the world. He does so partly by giving a new and more Christian-like form to the beastly power of the world, and partly by the corruption of the church through the formation of the great apostacy. Here again, however, he is destined to another downfal. The building he has laboured with such power and dexterity to raise, at length gives way under the advancement of truth and righteousness. The judgment of heaven alights on its different parts—Babylon, or the corrupt church, first going into perdition, then in close succession the beast and the false prophet. One abyss receives them all; and with their descent thither, the adversary has his dominion overthrown also upon the earth, and is consigned as to a miserable and inactive bondage in the nether world. In each stage of the downward history all is at once symbolical and relative, and is consequently framed according to the appearances of things. At every step in the process we must explain, *it was as if Satan were in such a position, as if now he were occupying such a sphere.* And hence in what respects the last stage, his place during the thousand years' reign, it is the comparative, rather than the absolute annihilation, of his power and influence that must be understood. His cause on the earth shall be gone. He shall no longer have a distinct party to represent him, or a fitting agency to ply his devices and prosecute his designs. It will be as if he had altogether lost his influence among the generations of mankind, though, since men shall still be in the flesh, and death shall still work, and a liability shall still exist to deception and apostacy, his connection with the world cannot be wholly destroyed. It will survive, but only—as the cause of God in the past times of the world's corruption—in a mystery.

From what has been said of the nature of the representation before us, it follows that the binding of Satan, when viewed in respect to millennial means and agencies, is much more of a negative than of a positive nature. It will appear in the withdrawal of manifold temptations to evil, and the cessation of plans and operations, which had for their object the encouragement of ungodliness and crime. But that very cessation and withdrawal must itself be a result. It will be the supplanting of falsehood by the prevalence of truth; the abolition of darkness by the diffusion of light; the removal of what is in itself evil, or tends to evil, by the love and practice of what is pure and lovely, and of good report. The kingdom of Satan, it must be remembered, belongs not to the physical but to the moral sphere. The foundation on which it rests is sin; and wherever the occasions and inducements to sin are resisted, there also the devil is worsted—he plies in vain his machinations, his weapons of war have perished. But to render such a resistance general in the world there will necessarily be required a direct and powerful agency of good. There must be influences from above, and, through these, states of mind, social habits, and arrangements, brought into play, which shall on every hand counterwork the wiles of Satan, and give effect to the pure and beneficent spirit of the gospel of Christ.

(2.) It is in the other feature of the description that we are to look for the more direct and positive agencies, by which the comparative perfection of the millennial state is to be secured. This, though in itself one, has a double representation in the vision. In the first instance it is described as a judging and reigning with Christ; while afterwards it is designated the first resurrection; the one aspect, however, being involved in the other, and only rendering more prominent what had been previously implied. "And I saw thrones," so the description runs in regard to the first aspect, "and they sat upon them; and [I saw] the souls of them that were beheaded for the witness (testimony) of Jesus, and for the word of God; and such as had not worshipped the beast, neither his image, neither had received his mark upon their foreheads, or in their hands; and they lived and reigned with Christ a thousand years." Now, that they are said to have *lived* and reigned, is obviously as much as, that they lived again in order to reign. It implies their previous death, and their death from circumstances the very opposite of those now associated with their state—because they had not power to reign, nor even to preserve themselves in life. The description, therefore, is plainly that of a martyr-company. It is so throughout, in the latter part as well as the first; for the whole of the parties mentioned are represented as now living and reigning, in contrast to a previous time, when they had found it impracticable alike to live and to reign. But it becomes conclusively certain, and, indeed, must cease with all fair and sober interpreters to be a disputable point, when the description here is taken in connection with earlier passages, which it merely resumes, in order to shew the reverse of the picture that had been previously exhibited. The first of those passages is chap. vi. 9–11, where it is said, at the opening of the fifth seal, that there appeared "under the altar the souls of them that were slain for the word of God and the testimony which they held"—manifestly the first company indicated in this millennial vision, who are said to have been beheaded, or slain, for the word of God and the testimony of Jesus. And in answer to the cry for judgment raised by those slain witnesses, it was intimated, that "they should rest yet for a little season, until their fellow-servants also and their brethren, that should be killed as they were, should be fulfilled." This is not less plainly the other company, who were to suffer in the later stages of the beastly power's opposition to the cause of God, and whose case is more fully represented in subsequent portions of the Book. We find it in chap. xiii. 15, where it is written of those who would not receive the mark of the beast, nor worship his image, that power was given to the second beast to kill them; and again in chap. xvii. 6, where Babylon, the antichristian power of later times, more peculiarly embodied in the papacy, is described as being even drunk with the blood of the saints, and of the martyrs of Jesus. Referring now to these previous delineations, and embracing the whole line of confessors and martyrs, the vision given to the Apocalyptist of the occupants of the millennial thrones includes such as had not worshipped the beast, nor had received his mark, together with those who, at an earlier period, had been beheaded for the word of God and for the testimony of Jesus. So that the description tells simply of the confessors and martyrs living anew, and, instead of dying as formerly for the cause of Christ, reigning with Him over a world at last brought into subjection to the truth of God.[1]

[1] This seems now to be generally admitted by those, who yet differ

In what sense, then, is it, that the martyrs previously referred to as persecuted and slain, are here represented as living anew and reigning as kings? Is the description to be understood of such persons individually and properly? or is it to be understood of them symbolically, as representatives of the cause and kingdom of Christ? Many reasons and counter-reasons have been presented in answer to these questions; of which, however, the greater part determine nothing either way. But there are two considerations, which to our own mind are perfectly decisive; and the rather so, as they are considerations which the simplest readers of the Apocalypse are capable of discovering and resting in, as well as the most subtle and learned. The first is, that if the souls of the martyrs are to be viewed in an individual, then they must also be taken in an exclusive respect. It must be held, that those, and those only, who had suffered unto death in the cause of the gospel are to rise again and reign during the millennium; for individuals of that precise class having the honour assigned them, those not belonging to it must be understood to have been purposely omitted. But then the class is so comparatively limited in number, and so palpably distinguishes those who compose it from other genuine believers by the accidents of their history, rather than by the essential characteristics of their state, that to confine the regency of the millennial age to them, were to run counter to the whole genius of the Gospel. It would exclude the apostle John himself from any share in the honour, since he was not beheaded for the testimony of Jesus, nor, we have reason to think, were the apostles gene-

widely on other points—compare, for example, Dr Brown's Second Advent, part I., chap. 10, and Mr Birks' Outlines of Prophecy, pp. 108-110. We are, therefore, the more surprised, that such a writer as Auberlen should fail here so much in apprehending the connection of the passage, and the character of the representation, as to interpret only the first part of the martyrs, and the second of all, who did not belong to the whore—true Christians generally. In one sense, no doubt, they are included, but no more in connection with the one portion of the martyr-company than the other.

rally, and the first evangelists in the church. We hold, there fore, the partial and arbitrary character of this interpretation to be fatal to it; understood of individuals the exclusive bearing of the description is as legitimate and necessary as the inclusive one, and then not Christian believers, but only Christian martyrs must be destined to live again and reign in the millennium.

There is another point, however, in this view of the description, which is still more decisive against it; namely, its contrariety to the general style of the representations of this Book, and in particular to that of the earlier portions referred to in the very terms of the description. In unison with the ecstatic condition of the prophet, and the mode of revelation, which was by vision, the scenes are throughout ideal as to the form they assume; and the characters that appear in them are in consequence described symbolically and representatively, not individually and personally. Thus the royal and conquering hero in the first seal is not the personal Saviour, but the cause and people that have Him for their living head; it is personified Christianity in all its compass and completeness. In like manner, the woman in the twelfth chapter is not properly or directly the Virgin Mary; as is plain from the woman's seed being used as a comprehensive term for the whole of the elect church; it is this church itself which can only at most be regarded as having for the moment found a concentrated representation in the mother of Jesus. That the same holds of the vision in the fifth seal respecting the souls under the altar seems so manifest, that it is difficult to understand how it should ever have been contemplated otherwise. Their position alone as seen under the altar is conclusive of the sense in which it is to be taken; it shews the description to be that entirely of an ideal scene, in which the animal souls (corresponding to the life-blood of the ancient victims) of the martyred witnesses appeared in the place of sacrifice, their righteous blood that had been poured out there crying to heaven for vengeance. It is quite frivolous, therefore, to insist upon the term *souls* being often used to denote persons;

no one doubts that it is; but the question is, can it be so taken here? In the midst of a scenic and symbolic representation, in which certainly it is not a literal altar, nor a literal cry for judgment, nor literal robes of glory that are spoken of, are the souls, that form the centre of the whole to be understood in the literal and personal sense? They manifestly cannot be so understood without arbitrarily interchanging the literal with the symbolical, and destroying all certainty of interpretation. The souls seen in the ideal region under the altar simply represent those, who during the struggling and depressed period of Christ's kingdom had to bear reproach and suffering unto death on account of it. And so, again, here, the souls once sacrificed and slain, but now living and enthroned represent the party that had been persecuted unto blood, risen at length to the dominion, not only possessed of fresh life, but invested with kingly power and authority. Should it be asked, whether the party so represented must not, however, be viewed as composed of the same individuals? We reply, that the question here is not properly of individuals, but of a collective body, and of a continuous history. It might as well be asked, whether the witnesses in the eleventh chapter, who represent the church during the whole period of her earnest contending for the truth of the gospel, were the same at the close as at the beginning? Or, whether the beast was the same in the later forms and manifestations of the worldly power as in the earlier? Or, whether the whore was the same, when she received her doom, as when she entered on her career of backsliding and apostacy? In all cases of this description there is, and must be, a continuity in the imagery employed; the future as to its essential elements must be identified with the past, in order to show that it is the same cause which is proceeding, the same interests that are involved. And precisely as here the once beheaded souls are seen rising to life and reigning, so in earlier and closely related visions the two witnesses appear as first slain, then coming to life again and ascending to heaven, and the holy apostles and prophets are called to rejoice over Babylon, as being avenged in her destruction (chap. xviii. 20), although they lived before the apostacy represented by Babylon had even assumed a formal existence in the world.

We are compelled, therefore, by a regard to the scenic and symbolic character of the representations in the Apocalypse, and by the necessity of avoiding what would otherwise war with the great principles of the Gospel, to take the souls here described as passing from the death of martyrdom to the possession of thrones, not in an individual, but in an ideal and representative sense. In their position and aspect as formerly seen by the apostle, they formed a fitting and impressive image of the church and cause of Christ, when struggling for existence and striving unto blood for the testimony they held; now, they not less fitly image the same church and cause everywhere triumphant, appearing, as they did, not under the rod of oppression, but upon thrones of judgment, not as sheep for the slaughter, but holding at command the sovereignty and dominion of the world. It is simply to mark the contrast in its full extent, that the description in the Apocalypse takes the form of the martyred host rising to life and glory. In Daniel, on the other hand, where the same representation in substance is given, but where it assumes a more general and outward form—the form of a contest for dominion between the kingdoms of earth and the kingdom of heaven, the issue of the contest naturally presents itself under the image of the judged becoming the judges, or of the saints possessing the kingdom, and exercising the dominion under the whole heaven. These saints in Daniel are no other than the martyrs in the Apocalypse; and it is only from the demands of the symbolical representations in the two places respectively, that a diversity in the form to that limited extent prevails.

But if such be the true interpretation of this part of the vision, why, it may still be asked, should such emphasis be laid on the scene described as a resurrection? "They lived and reigned with Christ," it is said of the souls, "a thousand years; but the rest of the dead lived not again, until the thousand years were finished. Blessed and holy is he that hath part in the first resurrection: on such the second death hath no power, but they shall be priests of God and of Christ; and shall reign with Him a thousand years." Why designate the event referred to so explicitly and repeatedly as not only a resurrection, but the first resurrection, and distinguish between the dead then raised and the rest of the dead, who are not to be raised till the close of the millennial era, if the description is not to be understood of definite individuals, but symbolically of the representatives of Christ's cause and kingdom among men? Simply, we answer, to mark the greatness of the moral resuscitation that is to take place, the mighty and permanent impression it is to make upon the world, and the near approach that is to be effected by it toward the final issues of the kingdom. In these respects it will be immeasurably superior to every thing that has been known or experienced within the sphere of the earthly life. In describing it the prophet must borrow his imagery from the higher life to come: it is the first resurrection, because it seemed to his illuminated eye to partake more of the immortal vigour and bloom of the resurrection-state, than of the sickliness and languor which have hitherto characterized the church on earth. Such glowing delineations of the nearer future, by the characteristics of the higher and more remote, are not unknown in prophecy. The prophet Ezekiel, when foretelling what relatively occupies the same place in his predictions with the scene before us, finds nothing suitable but the coming resurrection; it is under this image, wrought out after his peculiar fashion into manifold details, that he portrays the resuscitation that was to come upon his peeled and scattered countrymen.[1] It is under the same image that the apostle Paul, in no ecstatic

[1] Indeed the whole that is written here in chap. xx. 1-10, is but the resumption, with reference to Christian times and relations, of the predictions in Ez. xxxvii.-xxxix; where there is first the revived state imaged by the resurrection—then the happy and peaceful reign under the presidency of the new David—and, finally, the temporary interruption of this happy state of things by the invasion of Gog and His warlike hordes.

mood, depicts the result of Israel's conversion: "what," he asks, "shall their reception be, but life from the dead?" How much more, then, might such a style of representation be used of the time, when the universal church, freed at length from the thraldom of the antichristian yoke, and recovered from the slumber and filth of ages, is to burst forth in the freshness and beauty of a divine life? When all her members shall reflect the holy grace and energy of her glorified Head? and these members grown so many in number, and so powerful in influence, that every sphere of life shall be penetrated by their agency, and every region of earth be willingly obedient to their sway? When such a scene is realised, shall not the first stage of the resurrection-life seem to be reached? Shall not the world at length have the visible pledge of a blessed immortality?[1]

Viewed thus, the language of the vision has its perfect justification, both in the nature of the things described, and in the usage of prophecy. And were it not for the mistaken realism, which is ever forcing itself in upon even the better class of interpreters, and disturbing the harmony of the Divine symbolism, no material difficulty would be found in what remains of the description. Let it be only kept steadily in view, that in the apostle's account of what he saw and heard in the visions of God, we have an ideal delineation of the great and heart-stirring reality just described—such a delineation as might convey to the church beforehand, the most

[1] It is no argument against this view, to say, that the words "this is the first resurrection," are introduced by way of explanation, and cannot, therefore, be understood symbolically. For we find similar explanations constantly occurring in the Apocalypse; as in this very chapter, "the lake of fire, this is the second death;" chap. xiv. 4, "these are they which are not defiled with women, for they are virgins;" chap. xi. 8, "the great city, which spiritually is called Sodom and Egypt, where also our Lord was crucified;" chap. iv. 5, "seven lamps of fire, which are the seven spirits of God." In all these, and various others, there is a symbolical element in the explanation, as well as in the thing explained; and it is by the whole character and connection of the vision, that the precise import of the descriptions is to be determined.

correct and vivid notion of its character; and it will readily be perceived, why he should pronounce those peculiarly blessed and holy, who should have part in the first resurrection, and should also represent the rest of the dead as not living till the thousand years were finished. The change is to be so great and deep—there is to be such an inwardness and strength in the spiritual life of the millennial era, that not only a resurrection, but a resurrection of the most faithful and devoted of Christ's followers seemed necessary to characterise the event. It should be as if the flower alone of the church, her noblest exemplifications of holy zeal and self-sacrificing love had come to life again, and entered on their immortal career. Nothing any longer should appear of the lukewarm, who had hung mid-way between flesh and spirit, Christ and the world, and in times of temptation had ever been ready to fall away; far less of those who had openly espoused the cause of ungodliness, and soiled their garments in the pollutions of the world. At the millennial era there shall be no resurrection of such mongrel characters—none, at least, till the period commenced by that era shall be drawing on to its close. Then the other dead shall have their representation also; and the diversities that have appeared in the past, shall be found embodied anew in the lives and actions of professing Christians. Not so, however, during the millennium itself. Then there shall be only life in its fullest vigour and efflorescence; and the church shall present the aspect of a body fair as the moon, clear as the sun, and terrible as an army with banners. Hence the eulogium, "Blessed and holy is he, that hath part in the first resurrection, on such the second death hath no power:" that is, they shall be all visibly of the right stamp—not like men standing on slippery places, and leaving it doubtful, whether heaven or hell might at length come to be their portion; no, but men so sincere in heart, so consistent in behaviour, so clearly and transparently Christian, that no room shall be left for doubt in regard either to their blessed condition, or their glorious destiny.[1]

[1] It is only by understanding thus "the rest of the dead," who lived

This perfectly harmonizes, also, with the other part of the description, which represents the millennial worthies as "priests of God and of Christ, and as reigning with Him." Royal power shall belong to them, but not such as the world is wont to associate with the name. It will be the royalty of priests, who in their kingly administration shall do spiritual and holy service to the Lord. The ensigns of their dignity shall not be stately equipages, nor shall carnal weapons be the instruments of their sway. They shall deal with the higher elements of power, with what is fitted to reach the springs of action, rather than to direct its outward courses; and so they shall do their "great works upon the unforced obedience of men"—the noblest proof of a spiritual agency and a divine calling. But how they shall actually do so; by what steps they shall themselves attain to this priestly power; what special organizations, when attained, it may lead them to form; through what modes of influence and channels of working it may diffuse itself in the world, we can as yet form no distinct conception. It is enough for us to know, that it shall be, and that the residue of the Spirit is with the Lord, to accomplish the result. Has He spoken, and shall He not do it? Has He purposed, and shall He not accomplish it?

III. Having now considered what is written of the thousand years' reign, we return to the question, in what relation does it stand to the coming of the Lord? Of much that has been advanced upon this question, it is not our intention to take any notice; being persuaded that a multitude of things have been pressed into the field from a misapprehension of the proper nature and province of prophecy, and from a desire to extract from it an amount of light respecting the precise form and lineaments of the future, which it was never intended to give. If in the first part of our inquiry we have

not till the close of the thousand years, of *classes of characters*, that the uniformity of the symbolical description is preserved. And to interpret it of the remnant mentioned in chap. xix. 21, or of the dead generally as to their personal resurrection, is to bring in a realistic element out of place—in the midst of a symbolical delineation.

not succeeded in showing the impropriety of such a treatment of prophecy; and if the proofs which have subsequently been exhibited of the erroneous and contradictory results, to which it inevitably leads, have failed to produce conviction, nothing that could be said now on this particular phase of the prophetic future could be of any avail.

But from what has been already stated respecting the millennium itself, as well as from the kind of providences which must be necessary to bring it into accomplishment, there can be no doubt that it must be in a very special manner connected with the power and presence of the Lord. The apostles spake of Him as coming and being present, when the gospel through their instrumentality and the working of God's providence took effect in particular places, and when the kingdom of God was transferred from Jewish to Gentile soil. But the operations by which such things were accomplished, could not have afforded nearly such marked indications of His presence, or such proofs of His controlling agency and power, as must appear in the world-wide movements and changes, of which we have been treating. The subversion of antichristian falsehood and domination, the bringing to nought of the world's power and wisdom, the abolition of all that in the social and political condition of things is opposed to truth and justice, and, along with these, the formal elevation of the pious and God-fearing portion of mankind to the place of influence and authority, and the establishment through all lands of the pure and benign principles of the Gospel:—Such things, when they take place, cannot but betoken a manifestation of the presence and coming of the Lord, far surpassing what has yet appeared in the past—if we except the period of His actual sojourn among men. Besides, when we take into account what human nature now is, and how much its instinctive cleaving to the dust, together with the veil that hides from its view the realities of a higher sphere, operates as a hindrance to the work of grace among men, and to the practical ascendancy of the truth of God in the world, it cannot appear wonderful if there should be some nearer connection established in the millennial period between the two regions of the divine kingdom. Without speculating much concerning the possibilities of things, we can conceive a mode of administration not impracticable, which should bring into fuller realization than hitherto the word of our Lord to Nathanael, "Hereafter ye shall see heaven opened, and the angels of God ascending and descending upon the Son of man"—something whereby faith might become more like a living sense than it has ever been in any number of individuals, or for any length of time in the same individuals, during the past stages of the world's history. This, we say, might not seem impracticable, and might even appear needful, when we think of the difficulties to be vanquished, and the resistances to be overcome, compared with the gigantic and blessed results, that for so long a period are to be in progress. Indeed, we can scarcely understand how such results can be effected, unless supports of some sort are furnished to faith, and an insight is given into the spiritual and divine beyond what has been the common privilege of believers since the present dispensation began. But whatever may be justly anticipated in this direction, it ought to be looked for, not so much, perhaps not at all, in connection with any objective or visible manifestation on the Lord's part, but from subjective elevation on theirs. In so far as given, it will be the property of faith, not of sight, and will come as the effect of a more copious outpouring of the Spirit—an outpouring, it may be, such as shall make gifts that have hitherto been rare comparatively common, and shall raise the recipients of them to such an elevation of soul, and such nearness of communion with heaven, that all who see them shall feel as if they saw the face of an angel. There is nothing in the constitution of the church of Christ, or in the prophetic word, to prevent such an enlargement of present grace and privilege; but much rather to warrant and encourage the expectation of it. The more so, as it is plain that, entirely apart from the removal of external hindrances, or the supply of adventitious helps, there must be an operation of the Spirit of grace, of the most efficacious and persuasive kind, in order even to reconcile the world to the rule of the saints, or to give it practical effect. If there shall be power to make the people generally willing to obey, how much more of power—power to reach to the greater things of God—will be required for those who in such a time will be called to rule in the affairs of men, and ride on the high places of the earth! And if it shall be the grand reaping-time for the world in the Spirit's work, of which till then the first-fruits only shall have been gathered, what must form the essential condition of its accomplishment, so much as the nobler endowments of the Spirit, and His richer communications to the souls of men!

But that the glorified Redeemer should openly manifest Himself to the world, and in the splendour of Divine Majesty should take visible possession of the throne—that what is known as distinctively *the* advent of the Son of Man in glory, for the purpose of winding up the affairs, and bringing in the final results of His dispensation—that this is to precede the commencement of the millennial reign, and constitute its more important and distinguishing feature, we can by no means admit; for it seems to us in many respects at variance with the clearest revelations given on the subject, and incompatible with the constitution and order of things, that shall then be brought into existence. We shall only glance at some of the more leading points.

(1.) First of all, in the passage which beyond doubt contains the most explicit and detailed account of the millennium, this personal manifestation, and local residence of Christ on earth, is not mentioned. If it really were to have a place in the state of things then to exist, that place must unquestionably be a pre-eminent one; it should, one would imagine, have formed the prominent feature in the description. But it is not once distinctly named. The reign of Christ is implied, merely, as forming somehow the foundation of that, which His people are to exercise. But it is the reign of this people themselves—the thrones set for *them* to occupy—the royal priesthood *they* are to discharge—the high, blessed, and honourable condition *they* are to hold—these alone are the points, which are prominently exhibited in the delineation. When the people of Christ are thus represented as possessing the kingdom, it must be because they are ostensibly to bear sway upon the earth; the reins of government are to be in their hands. Then, no doubt, as well as now, the position they occupy shall have its root in their connection with Christ; their rule, therefore, shall not be of an independent nature, but, as it is here described, a reigning with Christ, precisely as in their present state they live with Christ, and (spiritually) sit with Him in heavenly places. As regards outward appearance, however, it is they who in the millennium are to constitute the dominant parties, while in an after-stage, the really culminating period of the world's history, when Christ *is* to appear, and shine forth in His glory, they fall comparatively into the back-ground, and He is brought prominently forward. Then by the excessive lustre of His throne, every other throne disappears; all power and authority, life and blessing, centre in Him, and diffuse their influence on every side (chap. xx. 11, xxi. 5, etc.).

(2.) A second argument against the visible manifestation and personal appearance of Christ at the millennium is derived from the account given in the Apocalypse of what is to precede and usher in the era. Its more immediate precursors are to be the execution of the doom of antichrist, the destruction of the beast and the false prophet, or the overthrow generally of the world's organised power and wisdom. The final conquest of the kingdoms that formed the earthly forces and adherents of those hostile parties had been represented in chap. xix. under the image of a royal rider on a white horse, going forth with his armies to bring the people under him. Such a rider cannot fail to suggest the thought of Christ; yet the representation is properly an ideal one, and exhibits the spirit rather than the exact form of the coming transactions. This is evident alone from the accompaniments of the chief personage—his white horse and splendid accoutrements—his band of faithful and devoted attendants—and, above all, the grand weapon employed in the conflict, the sharp sword going out of his mouth. This, we can have no doubt, is the word of truth, considered as a word of conviction and rebuke, wielded, however, as it ever is now, not by Christ directly and personally, but through the instrumentality of His faithful and devoted servants. Through them, therefore, as the immediate actors in the conflict, the victory is to be won. And so again in the overthrow of Babylon, or the destruction of the antichristian apostacy, so far from any visible and overpowering display of Christ's divine glory being required to accomplish it, the kingdoms of the world themselves are represented as having a chief hand in the business, turning, as it is said, to hate the whore and to destroy her (chap. xvii. 16). Their taking this part will by no means dissociate the event from Christ's personal agency; it will still be *His* doing, and so, in 2 Thess. ii. 8, it is expressly ascribed to the breath of His mouth and the brightness of His coming. But since even worldly kingdoms are to be actively employed in effecting it, the coming spoken of cannot be that of the final advent or any external manifestation of Christ's power and glory. It must be such a coming as took place in Pentecostal times, and the overturning that followed, through heathenish intervention, of apostate Judaism; so that whether we look to the immediate precursors of the millennium, or to the distinctive features of the millennium itself, there seems nothing in the description that requires or properly admits of the manifested appearance and abiding presence of Christ.

(3.) Thirdly, The hypothesis of the final advent before the millennium assumes an incongruous mixture of the two states of humiliation and glory, such a mixture as seems incompatible with the great principles of the divine administration. Looking either to these principles themselves, or to the exemplification that has been given of them in the past, there seems to be a gulph fixed between the two conditions. The things belonging to a state of humiliation cannot, excepting in momentary periods and partial cases, intermingle with those belonging to the state of glory. The outward frame and constitution of the world is adapted to the present condition of its inhabitants; and if the one becomes essentially changed, the other must undergo a corresponding alteration. When Jesus entered on His state of glory He could no longer dwell on earth and make Himself visible to men. Before this can fitly take place the corruptible must have put on incorruption, the carnal be changed into the spiritual. Only when He comes to make all things new, and stamps them with the perfection of His divine work, will the world be prepared as the house of the glory of His kingdom.

(4.) Again, the special acts more immediately associated in Scripture with the period of the second advent belong to the age subsequent to the millennium. Among the acts referred to must be placed, in the first instance, those of the general resurrection and the final judgment,—both of which are here placed after the millennium, and described in the latter part of chap. xx. It is as clear as language can make it, that by St John's account these events are both posterior to the millennial age, and also peculiarly connected with the Lord's manifested presence and glory; and all opinions which attempt to get rid of these conclusions must be assigned to the region of speculation, not to that of fair and unbiassed interpretation. The same order also is observed in the representations elsewhere found in Scripture. Another act of the same class is the solemnization of the bride's marriage with the Lamb. This, in the Apocalypse, is placed subsequent to the millennium, subsequent even to the general judgment. It is only after the period of conflict is entirely closed, and the final awards have been dispensed, that the holy city (as the church is now called) appears descending out of heaven as a bride adorned for her husband (chap. xxi. 2). At an earlier stage, indeed, she is spoken of as having made herself ready, and the time for her marriage is even said to have come (chap. xix. 7). But the actual and formal realization of the espousals is only introduced afterwards, and the previous notice of preparation and readiness must be understood simply of the great relative advance made toward the consummation. So marked was this at the period referred to, that farther delay, in regard to the final issue, seemed needless; the union, so far as the existing church was concerned, might be consummated at once. Hence, when we look to the representations given of it in Scripture, we find the union spoken of as one that admits of a series of matrimonial solemnities. Even the first union of believers to Christ has sometimes the aspect of a marriage given to it (Rom. vii. 4; Eph. v. 32; Isa. liv. 5). More commonly, however, the present relationship of the church to Christ is described as that of a bride to the bridegroom, contemplating the marriage-union as an event yet in prospect. But at the glorious epoch of the millennium the things that concern her seemed to take such a mighty rise—the number, the holiness, the power and influence of her members, appeared to mount so far above their former level, that the happy time for a consummation might already be said to have arrived. Yet, if the church should then seem ready, other things would not be so. The theatre of bliss would be by no means adequately prepared for the full manifestation of the sons of God, and their joint-participation with Christ in the highest honours of the kingdom. For this there is required not only a church all glorious within, but a corresponding glory also without—a new heavens and a new earth. Sin, in every form, must be put down; the powers of evil must be driven from every department of nature and every sphere of life; the whole region of terrestrial things must again become very good; and then at length will the Lord dwell with men as at first, there being nothing any more to offend the eye of His holiness, or to draw forth the visitations of His displeasure. Then will He find it possible to treat His redeemed as His proper spouse, and maintain with them a free and blessed intercourse of love. But if so only then, a pre-millennial manifestation in glory, followed by His abiding and visible presence, cannot be justly looked for.

On all these grounds the conclusion forces itself upon us, that whatever of spiritual elevation may be given to the Lord's people during the millennium, and whatever indications may be afforded them of His own peculiar nearness and presiding agency, as still the restitution of all things shall not then have fully come, so it will not be the time for the unveiled manifestation of His presence, and His face to face communications with men on earth. This belongs to the period of final deliverance from evil, when every thing in the natural and the spiritual world shall be stamped with the glory of the new creation. And between the millennium and this ultimate period of blessing and glory, there lie, according to the representations of the Apocalypse, two great acts—the one forming the last phase of wickedness on the part of man, and the other the last phase of retributive justice; what shall be emphatically *the judgment*, on the part of God.

IV. The earlier of these great acts is presented in so abrupt and abbreviated a form, as necessarily to suggest a reference to some preceding revelation. "When the thousand years are expired," it is said, "Satan shall be loosed out of his prison; and shall go out to deceive the nations which are in the four quarters (literally, corners) of the earth, Gog and Magog, to gather them together to battle; the number of whom *is* as the sand of the sea. And they went up on the breadth of the earth, and compassed the camp of the saints about, and the beloved city; and fire came down from God out of heaven, and devoured them. And the devil that deceived them was cast into the lake of fire and brimstone, where the beast and the false prophet are, and shall be tormented day and night for ever and ever." Were there not an earlier revelation, which this merely resumes and applies to post-millennial times, it would be inexplicable, that the extraordinary names of Gog and Magog should have been thus suddenly introduced upon the scene, without any thing to indicate why such names should have been chosen to designate the heads of so vast a confederacy, or what should have moved either them to undertake, or others to concur in it. It is singular, also, that in the description of their hostile movement, while they are said to come up over the breadth of the earth, and to compass the camp of the saints and the beloved city, no mention had previously been made of the saints having pitched that camp, or of their possessing such a city. These obvious blanks in the vision before us can only be accounted for by an implied reference to a fundamental passage, in which materials should be found to supply what is here defective, and which rendered more explicit statements unnecessary. That passage, we can have no doubt, is the prophecy contained in Ezek. xxxviii. and xxxix., which forms one of the most characteristic portions of Ezekiel's writings. Having endeavoured to unfold its meaning in detail elsewhere,[1] it will be enough at present to exhibit its general bearing and import, and its natural adaptation to the use made of it in this portion of the Apocalypse.

By its whole texture, the prophecy must be regarded as an ideal delineation of certain dangers and assaults, that might be expected to arise in the distant future against the cause and people of God, with the triumphant result, in which it was to terminate. Amid all that is ideal in this delineation, there are some prominent features in the great conflict it portrays, which are so exhibited as to leave no room for doubt respecting them, and which it is more especially important here to bear in mind. 1. The first has respect to the *time* of the conflict: it is not only assigned to the remote future, but is placed absolutely last in the series of struggles, through which the covenant-people were destined to pass. The prophet had represented them, in the predictions going before, as delivered from all their existing troubles, and raised above their hereditary enemies in the immediate neighbourhood. He had spoken of the very best things in the past—the things on which their recollections loved to dwell—as having returned again, with more even than their former celebrity, and being settled also on firmer foundations. The new David has established the covenant in its fulness of life and blessing; the Lord himself is known to have His dwelling among them by the abun-

[1] Commentary on Ezekiel, p. 414, sq.

dant peace and prosperity that was poured into their lot; and the one thing, that should arise to cloud for a moment the bright sunshine of future glory, was the extraordinary outbreak of hostile violence by the forces of Gog, bursting over the land like a tempestuous blast. When this has past away, the last form of evil has come and gone; the heathen are utterly perished, and it is known throughout the world, that the Lord shall not again desert His people, nor hide His face from them any more (chap. xxxix. 28, 29). Future visions speak only of the ultimate perfection and glory of the redeemed. 2. A second point in the delineation is the *condition*, in which the covenant-people were contemplated as being when this assault took place, and which in a manner provoked it. They are described as dwelling in a state of secure peace—so secure, that no thought of danger seemed to cross their minds, nor was any external preparation made to meet it: the people were seen throughout the land dwelling at rest, inhabiting towns without walls, and villages that possessed neither bars nor gates. Such a state manifestly bespoke the enjoyment of a prolonged season of repose, and the entire disappearance from their neighbourhood of any apparent elements of danger or annoyance. They had been so long and so completely freed from these, that it had seemed needless to make any formal provision against their recurrence; and so, defenceless in regard to outward weapons of assault, and strong only in resources of spiritual life and blessing, it seemed to the enemies, who had been eyeing them with jealousy, and mustering their forces for an attack, as if they should fall an easy prey into their hands. 3. Then, thirdly, in respect to the *enemies* themselves, who thus thought and reasoned, they were, as might be inferred from what has now been said, hostile powers from the distance; powers that had hitherto lain, as it were, out of sight, and now for the first time were gathered from the most remote regions, and brought up in battle array by a powerful and enterprising leader. This leader is described under the ideal name of Gog, of the land of Magog, prince of Rosh, Mesech, and Tubal; and as having in his train, beside the people more immediately belonging to his own northern latitudes, the far-off Ethiopians and Libyans, on one side; and on the other, the Armenians, the Persians, and the Cimmerians of Crim Tartary. Even the nearest of these tribes was at a considerable distance from the land of Israel; and some of them were in the very corners of the earth, alike remote from each other, and from the people of God. They were, therefore, the fit representatives of a hostile movement to be made from quarters *morally* at the greatest distance from the kingdom of God, and thence disposed to imagine, that by mere dint of carnal weapons and numerical force, they might carry it as by storm over the children of righteousness and peace. 4. Finally, the result proves them to be entirely wrong in their calculations; for as the assault was not provoked by any defection on the part of the Lord's people, so they have Him for a shield of safety; with fire from heaven He consumes the adversaries, and causes it to be known, that now the *right* must prevail, that the meek and pure, not the violent and rapacious, must possess the earth, and dwell in it for ever.

Such are the main features of the prophecy, which, with certain characteristic differences, the divine Seer of the Apocalypse resumes and applies to the period immediately subsequent to the millennium. The differences are not such as materially to affect the nature of the vision, or the relative place and bearing of the things disclosed in it. In accordance with his more advanced position, and the deeper insight possessed by him into the spiritual world, the later prophet supplies at the outset a link that is omitted by the earlier—he connects all with the powerful agency of the prince of darkness. Satan at the commencement of the new period is loosed from his prison, and goes out to deceive the nations which are in the four corners of the earth; that is, fresh opportunity and a larger scope is, by some turn in the affairs of Providence, to be given him for plying his temptations and influencing the minds of unregenerate men. And though the parties whom his wiles succeed in stirring into rebellion are not here connected, as in

Ezekiel, with any definite localities, and are represented, not as mustered and led by Gog, the prince of Magog, but as themselves collectively Gog and Magog (for the purpose, no doubt, of showing more clearly, that such names are to be understood in an ideal manner), yet the substance of the revelation entirely corresponds with that of Ezekiel. First, the *time* assigned for the fearful conflict is the remoter future—the closing stages of the present dispensation, after which nothing remains for the church but the final recompences of blessing and glory. The mighty revival and spread of living godliness destined to characterize the latter days represented by the resurrection of the martyrs, and their thousand years' reign among men, corresponding to the resurrection-scene in Ezekiel (chap. xxxvii.), with the long period of holy peace and prosperity that was to follow; this has already, in the prospective outline of St John, come and fulfilled its course: and before the final extirpation of evil, room is afforded for but one more, and, as it were, a spasmodic effort of the adversary to regain his lost ascendancy.

The general *condition*, in like manner, of the cause and people of God, in the period preceding the hostile assault was evidently one of secure and tranquil enjoyment. So complete had been the ascendancy of good, and so long the flow of outward peace and prosperity, that no thought of evil was likely to have entered the bosoms of men, or any outward munitions of defence and safety to have been provided against its possible occurrence. The followers of the Lamb have reigned for ages in their character as saints; by the moral weight of holy principle and works of righteousness, they have borne sway in the affairs of men; and, realizing on this account their connection with the omnipotent grace, and sure guardianship of Heaven, they could scarcely fail to discard from their minds all care for other means of protection. But carnal minds, if any such still existed, must be expected to judge otherwise; to their view the spiritual rule of saints, simply because trusting so much to divine supports, and intent mainly on the employment of moral agencies, could not but appear to be deficient in solid strength; and this, coupled with the joyous security, and benignant satisfaction everywhere diffused, might well be conceived enough to prompt the idea of a gigantic effort to overturn the dynasty of righteousness. The more naturally might such a project come to be entertained, if it should happen, that in process of time the power of godliness, to some extent should fall into decay, and the love of many wax cold. But this is precisely what we have already seen to be indicated in ver. 5, by "the rest of the dead living not again till the thousand years were finished."[1] It intimates that other characters than those who belonged to the highest sphere of the Christian life, who were ready alike to die for Christ and to reign with Him, should appear on the stage; that when the mighty flood of millennial zeal and devotedness should have spent its force, there should come, not, indeed, a general apostacy, or corrupt worldly admixture, as of old, but a season of comparative languor, in which many should be found to want the spiritual elevation, that as a whole is to distinguish the saints of the millennium. What more natural, then, when such a relaxation might become apparent in the higher qualities of a divine life, that the awe, in which the world had been held by such living piety and pre-eminent worth, should give way, and that the hope of regaining the ascendancy should spring up afresh in the slumbering remains of the world's ungodliness? Then, as to the quarters where these remains might exist, or by what means they might be stirred into such combined action and desperate hostility, as the words of the vision indicate, nothing very definite can be drawn from the description of the apostle. But the corresponding vision of Ezekiel entitles us to infer that they will be gathered from the outskirts—not of course the *literal* but the *moral* outskirts of the habitable globe—the regions of society or spheres of life, which even the millennial agency of Christian love shall have failed to penetrate, and win over to the

[1] See p. 467.

interests of righteousness. We cannot conceive that these would be very numerous or extensive during at least the better and brighter period of the millennial reign; but they will naturally grow with the decline of its fervour and activity toward the close, and when roused to action by the subtle malice of Satan (through what forms of delusion we know not), they will ultimately present the aspect of an innumerable host compassing the camp of the saints and the beloved city—that is, they will then virtually place the people of God throughout the world in the same relative position, that Israel of old was, when surrounded with enemies in the field, or beleaguered in their capital city. The cause of God will seem for a time to be brought by them into peril. However, it shall only be for a time; the danger shall soon pass away. Its appearance shall but serve to rekindle the zeal and devotedness of the people of God. The martyr-spirit shall once more revive in all its energy of life and action, and like hallowed fire sent down from heaven (for we cannot think of literal fire any more than of a literal camp and city, on the one side, or a literal Gog and Magog, on the other), shall consume the carnal elements, and defeat the hostile machinations, through which the confederacy of evil hoped to prevail. Thus ends the last great struggle of the adversary; and having been allowed to make his final attempt against the followers of the Lamb, and failed in doing so, his doom of utter and hopeless exclusion from the domain of earthly affairs is carried into effect. As formerly the beast and false prophet, his earthly representatives, so now the devil himself is cast into the lake of fire; the original sentence against the tempter is executed to the full, and his head utterly bruised.

V. In the midst of this general route and confusion of the adversary and his host, or immediately subsequent to it, there comes the end of all things, as regards the present frame and constitution of the world, and the fixing of the final destinies of all who have had part in its eventful history. This is introduced in the visions of the apostolic seer, by the appearance of a great white throne (emblem of the pure and glorious majesty of the divine Judge), and one sitting on it who is identified with God (ver. 11, 12). Before the face of this Eternal King, earth and heaven (the old frame and constitution of things) were seen to flee away, and the dead, small and great, stood before God to be judged by their deeds. The process of judgment is described by the books being opened, those, namely, which were viewed as containing the record of all they had done and said during their lives on earth, and along with these memorials of good and evil in the past, the book of life, wherein are recorded the names of the elect from the foundation of the world. Of the latter class, none can be allowed to perish with the wicked; they shall all have their portion in the New Jerusalem, however diversified may be their respective lots there; since these must be determined by the other things concerning them that may be found written in the books. It is impossible to understand all this of any thing short of an absolute universality: the language of symbols can have no definite meaning, if such descriptions are not to be understood as comprising the entire race of humanity in the whole of its two grand divisions of the saved and the lost. And the more so, as (in ver. 13) every region and receptacle of the dead are said to be ransacked for the purpose of having the assize complete: not the earth merely, or the world in its more conspicuous and settled parts which did not need to be particularly named, but the sea also which is identified with whatever is deep, mysterious, turbulent, and death and hades themselves—the ideal lords and possessors of the departed—wherever their realms might extend—all now are compelled to resign their charge, that the judgment of God may proceed to the completion of its work. And when these ideal powers, death and hades, as well as all whose names were not found written in the book of life, are represented as being cast into the lake of fire, it is but a symbolical way of exhibiting the awful truth, that all the forces and abettors, the agents, and the results of sin shall be doomed to remediless destruction. The accursed thing with all belonging to it, the forms it has assumed, and the instruments it has wielded, shall go into the perdition, which, from the first, it was destined to inherit.

VI. The old framework of nature, with the noxious powers and elements which had so long held possession of it, being thus brought to an end, the closing scene of the book unfolds to us the new and better constitution which is to take its place. The description can only be regarded as presenting an imperfect image, derived, like all the preceding delineations in the book, from such things in the past or present, as seemed best fitted to shadow forth the coming reality. If we should seek to ascertain from it the precise form and lineaments of the church's final condition and destiny, we shall turn it to a purpose it was palpably not intended to serve. It tells only—and relating, as it does, to things which immeasurably surpass all that eye has yet seen, or ear heard, it *could* tell only—of the relative nature and properties of what is to be hereafter. By a manifold variety of allusion and figure it exhibits this to our view as both negatively and positively perfect, alike freed from all evil, and possessed of whatever is desirable, glorious, and good. The sea, which has so often served as an image of the world's restless turmoil and disorder, is no longer seen; nor the temple, which by its own peculiar sanctity witnessed to the general pollution of the world around; night also disappears (emblem of the world's guilt and shame), and with it every thing that works abomination and causes defilement: and as the natural result of this stainless purity, there are found no tears, no sorrow, no pain, no death, for, in such respects, "the former things have passed away." Then, with this removal of all the forms and occasions of evil, there is not less prominently marked, under signs and emblems of an opposite description, the appearance of whatever might be needed to constitute a state of consummate happiness and glory. There is the radiance of a perennial lustre, the very light and glory of God, investing the whole region of the church's existence. Then the church herself, seen descending from heaven in loveliest form and most comely attire, as a bride prepared for her marriage-union with the Lamb; or, again, appearing as a city, perfect in its proportions and structure, paved with gold, built and garnished with the most precious gems—a city watered with the river of life, issuing clear as crystal from the throne of God, and bearing on its banks the tree of life, the blessed medicine of immortality; and, to crown all, the living God, as now thoroughly reconciled to the work of His hands, and beholding in all around the reflection of His own perfect nature, having His tabernacle with men, and discovering everywhere the signs of His gracious presence and working. What more is needed to complete the picture, and heighten the ideal of the coming good? It is still, indeed, but an ideal, framed out of such materials in the past and present as imagination has here at its command. It necessarily leaves undefined the exact shape and features of the glorious future. In that respect we must still say, "We know not what we shall be;" but we know, at the same time we cannot doubt, from what is here written, that all shall be very good, and that as God is the end as well as the beginning of all, so the end shall be not only like the beginning, perfect in its kind, but in that kind unspeakably higher and better—not nature rectified merely, but nature refined and glorified.

APPENDICES.

APPENDIX A, P. 6.

THE ORIGINAL IMPORT OF THE WORD נָבִיא (PROPHET), AND ITS LATER USAGE.

In what has been advanced respecting the true idea of a prophet, and the essential nature of a prophecy, no stress has been laid upon the original meaning or derivation of נָבִיא, as nothing material depends upon the precise view that may be taken of it. The difference of opinion which prevails respecting its fundamental import, turns on the point, whether it is originally of active, or of passive signification—whether it designates the prophet as the recipient, or as the conveyer, of divine communications. The former is the more common, and also, in our judgment, the more natural opinion—both because the form (קָטִיל) is one, that according to the rule is derived only from intransitive verbs, and because, understood in that sense, the word points to what is certainly the more fundamental characteristic of the prophet's calling—his relation to a revealing God. Ewald, however, still holds to the other view, and understands the word as strictly importing a speaker, who announces the mind, and utters the words of another, who does not himself speak (Die Propheten des Alten Bundes, p. 6). Practically, the two opinions coalesce; since the true prophet was always one who in the first instance received communications from above, but only that he might impart them to others; so that it was equally his obligation to speak, and to speak simply according to the tenor of what he had received. He, who might speak without having received a message to deliver, and he who might refrain from communicating the message with which he had been charged, would alike prove unfaithful to the calling of a prophet—although, when distinguishing the true from the false in prophecy, it is naturally the former deviation from the proper line, that is most prominently exhibited. (See Jer. xiv. 14, and Ezek. xiii. 2, with the remarks in my commentary on the latter passage).

Turning, however, from the etymology and original import of the word to its later and more general usage, there can be no doubt that the deliverance of the message entered as the preponderating element into the idea of a prophet. Hence the change of phraseology that took place in ancient Israel, when prophetic agency began to assume a more regular and recognized place: the term *seer*, which had more immediate respect to the inward reception of the divine communication, fell into general disuse, and that of *prophet*, which had then at least acquired a more active meaning, came in its place (1 Sam. ix. 9). The language of the prophets themselves bears respect to this distinction. Thus Isaiah, when reproving the people of his day as to their obstinate resistance to the word of God, speaks of them as those, "who say to the seers, see not; and to the prophets, prophesy not unto us right things, speak unto us smooth things, prophesy deceits" (chap. xxx. 10). And Jeremiah, when describing his own prophetic calling, represents himself as one sent in the name of the Lord to speak, and even designates himself "the Lord's mouth" (chap. i. 7, xv. 19). On this account, also, the person who simply delivered a divine message, though he had that message at second-hand—not directly from the Lord—one, therefore, who could not be called properly a seer, still bore the name of a prophet. Of such we have examples in the person whom Elisha sent to anoint Jehu (2 Kings ix. 1–4), and, we may say, in the prophets generally as regards that portion of their work, which consisted in the exercises of devotion and the re-enforcement of the law of Moses. It may be added, that the Greek term, from which our word *prophet* is derived, προφήτης, while in its original import equally comprehensive with the Hebrew, נָבִיא, having respect to *any* divine communication, not merely to the prediction of future events, gives distinct expression to this active side of the matter: it denotes one, who interprets the mind of another, who speaks for a divine person. Thus poets were called "the prophets of the Muses," and Apollo, "the prophet of Jupiter," and the Pythoness was "the prophetess of Apollo," because disclosing the mind of the parties they severally represented. So long as μάντις was used somewhat in the sense of the Hebrew *seer*, for one who possessed the spirit of divination, the προφήτης was the interpreter of the oracle pronounced. But in later times the term came to acquire the meaning of our word prophet, denoting one who had obtained a supernatural insight into the mind of Deity, and more especially one who came forth with a revelation, real or pretended, of things to come.

APPENDIX B, P. 10.

INTERPRETATION OF NUMB. XII. 6–8, AND THE PROPHET LIKE TO MOSES.

In the text, we have given the precise and literal rendering of Num. xii. 6–8. But as a different view has recently been presented of their import, and one on which some important conclusions are founded, in a treatise entitled the "Harmony of the Mosaic and Geologic Records," a few explanatory remarks are necessary. That the words in ver. 6, "If there be a prophet among you," answer with substantial correctness to the original, which more literally runs, "If there be your prophet," is so obvious, that had another meaning not been suggested, we should scarcely have imagined any other could have been thought of. The Chaldee paraphrases, "If there should be prophets to you;" and all commentators of any note give a similar sense. The connection also seems conclusive in its favour; for Aaron and Miriam were here ranging themselves against Moses, and on the side of the people; they were endeavouring to raise a popular tumult against their brother, so that the expression "your prophet," spoken generally, and in respect to the people, is manifestly equivalent to "a prophet from among you"—one, not like Moses, in a sense apart from, but out of your own number. To render —as is done in the treatise referred to—"If he (viz., Moses) were your prophet"—*i.e.*, the prophet of Aaron and Miriam, is against the preceding context, where the question is respecting a prophet from God, not to them, but to the people; and in respect to what follows, it involves a kind of absurdity. For it would represent God as intimating that he would have given visions and dreams to Moses, had he been the prophet of Aaron and Miriam. Did Aaron himself, in consequence of being a prophet under Moses, get revelations in such a way from God? We certainly read of none; and, looking at his conduct on the present occasion, we should judge it very unlikely that he had received any.

The two clauses, "I will make myself known to him in a vision, in a dream will I speak to him," explain one another. The revelation was to be made in the imperfect form of a *vision;* but as this term is of somewhat doubtful import, and does not of itself sufficiently indicate the imperfection in the mode, another clause is added, to make it more explicit—"in a dream I will speak to him." All the Jewish commentators understood a certain degree of obscurity to be implied in communications so made. And, as Baumgarten has justly remarked on the passage, "A divine revelation by dreams forms a complete contrast to revelation as made in Paradise, where Jehovah walked, and where, therefore, his appearance was made in a quiet manner, in connection with the things of the external world, and presented itself to man, while in his quite natural state." Here, on the contrary, he was to be taken out of his natural state, isolated from surrounding objects, and raised merely for the moment, in his spiritual part, into communion with Heaven. Such *was* God's ordinary mode of communicating with the prophets, usually so called, but *not* his mode of communicating with Moses—otherwise, Moses had, in this respect, enjoyed no peculiar distinction.

The distinction he actually possessed is stated in the second part of the declaration. In this part, the word rendered *vision* in the first part again occurs, מַרְאֶה, and is often translated adverbially, as in the authorised version, "apparently." "I will show him the thing as it is," is Abenezra's explanation. Rosenmuller has adspectu, and others render in a similar manner. There is no material difference in most of the explanations, nor will there be found any ambiguity in the double use of the same word, if only it is noted that in the case of the ordinary prophet, mentioned in the first part, the word was plainly intended to denote the form and method of the Divine revelation made to him; while here it has respect rather to the personal manifestation of the revealing God, "Mouth to mouth I speak to him, and appearance." What can this mean, in such a connection, but visible, open manifestation? As indeed, the last clause, which is evidently epexegetical of what precedes, renders manifest, "and the similitude or form of the Lord he beholds." Perspicuity and distinctness are the characteristics here, the employment of ordinary converse, and, as a natural consequence, the disuse of dark or enigmatical sentences. This is precisely such a distinction in behalf of Moses as the whole circumstances would lead us to expect.

In regard to the purpose for which, in the treatise referred to at the beginning of this note, a different interpretation is sought to be established, viz., to represent Moses as having got the professedly historical account of creation in Gen. i. by vision, it is open to other, and these also insuperable objections. On this point, however, we are not called to enter.

We simply state that there is no instance of what is given to the church *as* history having been communicated to the church by way of vision, except in such cases as the visions recorded in Dan. ii. and vii., or Rev. xii., where, in a dramatic representation of a connected series of events, the portion already past has also a certain place—an essentially different case, and very differently exhibited also from that of the Mosaic account of the creation. To regard this as given by vision, is to confound the real and the ideal, history and prophecy. Nor can we throw the historical narrative contained in the three first chapters of Genesis so far back as the time of Moses. The great facts there related formed the very basis of the primeval religion; and either precisely the same history, or another very much akin to it, must have been communicated to the earliest worshippers of God.

Not to dwell, however, upon such points, it is plain, from the right interpretation and clear import of this passage in Numbers, what was required to the full verification of the closely related passage in Deut. xviii. 18, "I will raise them up a prophet from among their brethren, like unto thee, and will put my words in his mouth, and he shall speak unto them all that I shall command him." From the connection in which the passage stands, there can be little doubt that it had a certain respect to the prophetic testimony in general, which was to be continued in the Jewish church. But the specific qualification included in the words *like unto thee*, leave as little room to doubt, on the other side, that nothing more than a partial and provisional fulfilment could be given to the prediction by prophets of an ordinary kind. There was a general resemblance between Moses and every prophet who received a Divine communication to deliver to the people; but along with that resemblance there was also an important difference—a marked inferiority in the case of the ordinary prophet. His communications came only in vision and by dream, while Moses received them by a waking, face to face intercommunion; so that the people of our Lord's time justly expected the prophecy to receive a higher exemplification than it had yet found in the past, and the apostles had both the import of the original, and the general feeling of their countrymen on their side, when they applied it specifically to the Messiah. It was manifestly the common understanding in their time, that the Messiah was to be emphatically *the* prophet spoken of; the only question was, whether Jesus of Nazareth was the person in whom the terms of the prediction had met with their fulfilment. That He was this, and, as such, not only *like* Moses, in that wherein he differed from the ordinary members of the prophetic order, but rising also far beyond him, must be the conviction of all who believe in His Messiahship. And though other points of resemblance betwixt Him and Moses should not be overlooked, yet when considered simply in respect to prophetic standing and gifts, it is in the particular point indicated in Numb. xii. 6–8, that the *likeness* should be viewed as more peculiarly exemplified. The prophet like to Moses, in the full sense, could only be the one who received his revelations like Moses; in the first instance, Christ, and subordinately the apostles whom He sent forth to make known His mind and will to men.

APPENDIX C., P. 13.

PROPHETIC AGENCY APART FROM PERSONAL HOLINESS.

THE cases which most readily occur, of prophetic agency in a state of divorce from personal holiness, are those of Balaam in the Old Testament, and Caiaphas in the New. Both of them were manifestly of a quite exceptional nature, and stand entirely apart from the ordinary track of God's procedure in the bestowal of such gifts. It might, without impropriety, be said that there was a doubly miraculous element in the predictions they uttered; they were miraculous, as well on account of the personages who spoke, as the Divine foresight exhibited in what was spoken. Balaam was used by

God against his own inclination to make known the Divine purposes at a peculiar crisis in the history of ancient Israel. It was a time when, with some apparent reason, their hearts were ready to faint at the prospect which was before them, and helps and encouragements of a somewhat extraordinary kind were needed to bear them through the trial. It seemed, therefore, an act worthy of the Divine interposition not only to provide the special support to faith that the emergency called for, but to do so in a way that should verify the proverb of even "making the eater bring forth meat." The more strikingly to manifest the power and faithfulness of God, in behalf of His people, a blessing is extorted for them from a child of perdition. On this account Balaam was used, though an *unwilling* instrument; and for a like reason, only in a more quiet and incidental manner, Caiaphas was used, even though an *unconscious* one. In a time altogether peculiar and extraordinary, he was made to utter a sentiment, in which thoughtful and reflective minds could not fail to perceive the overruling hand of God, since it declared a very great and important truth singularly applicable to the crisis, although not in the sense intended by the speaker. It was, we may say, the guiding of the last official representative of the priestly order enigmatically to disclose the event, which was at once to antiquate its existence, and to fulfil the end of its appointment. And this might the more fitly be done by one who knew not what he said, as the priesthood generally, at the time, had ceased to know the mystery of its own vocation.

But setting aside such cases as altogether peculiar and exceptional, the connection between the personal sanctity of the prophets and their divine communications will be found to hold as a general rule. It was not so stringent, indeed, in its application, as not to admit of occasional defections in the history of particular persons, and considerable diversity in different individuals of the prophetical order. When Jonah attempted to evade the work committed to him respecting Nineveh, by taking ship to go to Tarshish, there was undoubtedly a temporary failing in regard to the spiritual frame of mind proper to the true prophet. And to recover this, which could not be wanted in such a case—for that end primarily at least—he is subjected to a treatment alike severe and unprecedented. He is made to go down to the lowest depths, that he might there acquire the living faith and intense earnestness of soul, which would fit him for being the bearer of a divine message to Nineveh. In like manner the case of the old prophet at Bethel, mentioned in 1 Kings xiii., must be regarded in its more general aspect, as that of a prophet imperfectly sanctified. Indeed, the very fact of his residing at Bethel and remaining silent, as he appears to have done while Jeroboam was proceeding with his idolatrous innovations, was a clear sign of his having previously fallen into a state of spiritual slumber, and having become well-nigh deserted by the Spirit of God. He seems to have been at length roused out of this slumber by the report of the circumstances connected with the mission of the prophet, who came from Judah to denounce the Divine judgment against the abominations of Jeroboam, and who received in the execution of his commission, such manifest tokens of the Divine approval. The old prophet was bent on making the acquaintance of this servant of God, and claiming, as it were, kindred with him—although no mode of accomplishing what he sought presented itself but that of decoying the other back by a falsehood. In this he too plainly showed how far he still was from having attained to the proper spiritual elevation. But as the other prophet also had erred in acceding to his proposal, and thereby deviating from the prescribed path of duty, a word for the occasion was given to the old prophet to intimate the displeasure of God on the defection, and the judgment that was ready to chastise it. With the sin that mingled on both sides in the transactions, it was impossible almost for the blindest not to see, that the unbending truthfulness of God's word, and the necessity of holiness in those whom He called to His more immediate fellowship and service, received but a more impressive and awful testimony. To the idolatrous Bethelites it gave forth a peculiarly solemn warning; since if God so severely requited a comparatively slight deviation from the path of rectitude in one of His chosen servants, how much more might He be expected to chastise *their* flagrant corruptions! And to the members of the prophetical order themselves it furnished the salutary lesson, that if they would be honoured by God with His more special communications, and be fitted for the higher kinds of service in His kingdom, they must be found in heart and conduct holiness to the Lord.

APPENDIX D, P. 94.

SYMBOLICAL DESIGNATION OF KINGDOMS AS MOUNTAINS.

THE first passage, probably, in which a kingdom is presented under the symbol of a physical elevation, or a mountain, is the historical notice in 2 Sam. v. 12, where it is said of David's interest as king, "And David perceived that the Lord had established him king over Israel, and that He had *exalted* his kingdom:" it had now sensibly become a conspicuous thing, a height in the earth. Writing in Ps. xxx., and at a later period, of the vicissitudes which he experienced on the throne, he says, "Lord by thy favour thou didst make my mountain to stand strong; thou didst hide thy face, and I was troubled." In Ps. lxviii. 16, the hill of Zion, which had already been chosen as the seat of the kingdom, is taken for an emblem of it, and the other and loftier, but more remote hills, stand for images of the rival kingdoms of the heathen: "Why leap ye, ye high hills? This is the hill God desireth to dwell in; yea, the Lord will dwell in it for ever." In Ps. xlvi. 2, the mountains are spoken of as "shaking in the midst of the sea," and the figure is explained by the introduction of the reality at ver. 6, where it is said, "The heathen raged, the kingdoms were moved," or rather shook. The hill of Zion with its fortress is identified with the kingdom of God, and addressed as symbolically one with it in

Micah iv. 8, "And thou, O tower of the flock, the stronghold (hill) of the daughter of Zion, unto thee shall it come, even the first dominion, the kingdom also shall come to the daughter of Zion"—compare also Dan. ix. 16, 20. In Ps. lxxvi., the greater heathen kingdoms are denoted, not only mountains, but "prey-mountains," as being apparently raised to the gigantic height they attained for the purpose only of laying waste and destroying others. Babylon, in particular, is called by Jeremiah, chap. li. 25, "a destroying mountain, that destroyed all the earth"—not as Bishop Newton interprets, vol. i., chap. 10, "on account of the great height of its walls and towers, its palaces and temples," but from its lofty and domineering altitude among the political eminences of the world. And hence, quite naturally, in the Apocalypse, which gathers up and applies the symbolical imagery of the earlier prophets, in a whole series of passages *mountains* are used as the familiar designation of kingdoms, chap. vi. 14, viii. 8, xvi. 20, etc.

APPENDIX E, P. 96.

PROPHETICAL LITERALISM ESSENTIALLY JEWISH.

THE essential coincidence between the Jewish mode of interpreting prophecy, and that of the extreme literalists among Christians, will force itself on any one who compares for a moment what has been written by the respective parties on the prophetical future. For the most part he will find the same passages quoted by both, and the same principle of the historical sense applied to them—only, with this difference, that while both apply it to establish the necessity of a future restoration of the Jews to Palestine, and the re-institution of the Mosaic polity and worship, the Jew also applies it, and with perfect consistence, to the rejection of Jesus Christ as the Messiah. We say with perfect consistence, for the principle is as fairly applicable to the one point as to the other, and by that principle, the evidence of prophecy in favour of the Messiahship of Jesus is not *impaired* merely, but *annihilated.* The argument from prophecy as between Christians and Jews is gone; that only remains which may serve the Jew against infidels and heathens. If, for example, the literalist school of interpreters among Christians, are right in maintaining, as they do, that Christ has not yet appeared as King of Zion, or as the possessor of David's throne and kingdom, why should not Rabbi Crool (in his Restoration of Israel, which was replied to by Thomas Scott), and other Jewish writers, be equally right in contending, that Jesus of Nazareth cannot be the Messiah? The passages which both parties appeal to—such as Zech. ix. 9; Isa. ix. 6, 7; Micah v. 2—though they are expressly declared by the evangelists to have been fulfilled in Christ, yet speak of the Messiah under the very character and relations, which, it is alleged, have not yet been assumed by him: they represent him as going to appear among men, to be born at Bethlehem, to ride on an ass into Jerusalem, etc., in the character of the king of the Jews, and to the great joy of his subjects. Therefore, says Crool, and with manifest right on this principle, your Jesus cannot be the Messiah; for He did not sit upon David's throne, He set up no Jewish kingdom, and instead of finding joy and peace and union from His presence, the Jewish people only then began to experience their greatest troubles and their widest dispersions. So, of the greater proportion of prophetical passages applied in New Testament Scripture to Christ; and with equal justice on the principle of historical literalism, for they generally connect the appearance and work of Christ on earth with His destiny as the Son of David, or His relation to Zion and the covenant-people. And if certain characteristics are associated in prophecy with Messiah's birth and appearance—if certain results are described as flowing simply from His *coming,* not from His coming a *second time* to Zion or Jerusalem, and if these are not found in the person and history of Jesus of Nazareth, the plain and obvious inference is, that the promised Messiah is yet to come. In a word, the apologetic value of prophecy as regards the truth of Christianity is gone, and turned instead into a weapon of assault. So much is this felt to be the natural tendency of the line of interpretation referred to, that those who adopt it have, of late years, been withdrawing prophecy after prophecy from the number of those, which the inspired penmen and all truly Christian writers hitherto have understood of Christ. As in regard to the first great promise to fallen man, so also here, the principle of a prophetical literalism has led to the same result as its apparent opposite—a subtilizing rationalism: the one needs as much the doctrine of *accommodation* as the other, in explaining the New Testament applications of prophecy to Jesus. See this proved in Typology of Scripture, 2d Ed., vol. i., p. 50–7, against an American Literalist; See also Dr Brown's Second Advent, chap. vii., for proof of the successive abandonment of prophecies in reference to Christ, and for some able and acute remarks respecting the essentially Jewish position of the interpreters in question. Indeed, the list there given might be greatly increased. In chap. i., sec. 3, of our Second Part, when treating of the Apologetical value of Prophecy, the subject necessarily recurs again, and it is there shewn, that the literalism sought for in respect to Christ's throne and kingdom was in the nature of things impossible, and that if He be really the Son of God, the differences between the New and the Old form of things could not be otherwise than they are.

APPENDIX F, P. 111.

INTERPRETATION OF 2 PETER I. 21.

THE rendering given in the text of 2 Peter i. 21, is the strictly literal one: and as so rendered the passage exhibits more distinctly the contrast between the human and the divine in prophecy, denying it to be of the one, and affirming it to be of the other; at the same time, representing the mental state of those to whom and through whom it came, to have been of a quite supernatural description. The statement contained in the passage is given as a reason for the more general declaration which immediately precedes, that "Scripture prophecy is not of private interpretation," or, as it should rather be, "no Scripture prophecy comes of one's own solution"—literally, *loosing out*, ἐπιλύσεως. The word is peculiar, but its use here is to be accounted for by prophecy being contemplated according to its fundamental character, as an unravelling, or opening out of the secret counsels of heaven. As such it comes, the apostle tells us, from no private solving of the hidden mystery, on the part of those who uttered it; it was not of one's own (viz., the prophet's) unfolding. This seems to us by far the most natural sense of the passage; as it is also the one which fits most suitably in to what follows. It is only thus, too, that we preserve the force of the verb γίνεται, which is comparatively lost in our common version; for the real import of the apostle's statement is, not that no Scripture prophecy *is*, but that none *comes* in the manner specified; it does not so take its being and form. The question is not, as it is put by Bishop Horsley and many others, how the *meaning* of prophecy is to be made out or interpreted, but how *prophecy itself* came into existence, whence it drew its origin. And besides, to say of all prophecy alike, as such persons understand the declaration, that it is not of self-interpretation, but can only be understood as to its proper bearing when the events it contemplates have actually occurred, is not true as regards some prophecies (for example, 1 Tim. iv. 1, "The Spirit speaketh expressly"), and would virtually contradict what the apostle had said of prophecy immediately before, when he represented it as "a light shining in a dark place." With what propriety could it be designated a shining light, if itself necessarily remained without any sure interpretation, till outwardly shone upon by the events of Providence.

APPENDIX G, P. 119.

THE SYMBOLIC ACTIONS OF THE PROPHETS.

THE rule laid down in the text, founded on the distinction between the record of God's communications to the prophet, and that of the prophet's communications to the people, we have said, will generally be found sufficient to guide us in determining, whether the actions described belong to the ideal region, or to the territory of actual life. It will be so at least, if it is coupled with the considerations previously advanced respecting the essential nature of the actions themselves. This may, perhaps, be rendered more palpable, by a brief examination of the view that is presented of some of the prophetical actions noticed or referred to in the text, by writers who understand them in a realistic manner. We shall take it on the showing of one of the most sensible and judicious of the class —the Rev. Dr Turner of America. In a little work, published in 1852, *Thoughts on the Origin, Character, and Interpretation of Scriptural Prophecy*, after mentioning some instances of revelation by symbolic vision, he says:—"But the symbolic method was often employed by means of real actions openly performed. That ideas may be conveyed in this way distinctly and with perfect clearness, we know with certainty. Observation and experience have proved this beyond all doubt. In adopting this method, therefore, divine wisdom did but choose one from among various means, any of which is sufficiently well adapted to assure men of the meaning of His will. And the method chosen is sometimes the most impressive and startling that can possibly be imagined. When it is said of the prophet Isaiah, that, in obedience to the divine command, to 'loose the sackcloth from off his loins,' and to 'put off the shoe from his foot,' 'he did so, walking naked (*i.e.*, stript of a part of his clothing) and barefoot, three years, a sign and a wonder'—in other words a remarkable indication of God's judgment 'upon Egypt and upon Ethiopia;' it is hardly possible to conceive of a more direct prediction of overthrow and captivity, and of the contumely and shame to which Egypt, the world-renowned, the world-scorning, and in its own estimation all but celestial, Egypt should be exposed. And when Ezekiel is 'set for a sign unto the house of Israel,' and at the command of God 'removes his furniture in the sight' of the people, 'bearing it upon his shoulders and covering his face;' it would seem that the act itself spoke out its own meaning, and certified the miserable inhabitants, that they 'should remove and go into captivity,' that the prince should be degraded to a servile condition, carrying the most necessary articles, and hiding his face through shame for the ignominy to which he should be subjected.—Let us look at the symbolical actions of Jeremiah. On one occasion God orders him to get a potter's earthen bottle, and after a public proclamation addressed to king and people, of terrible judgments impending, and of their iniquities which occasioned them, to break the bottle in pieces in their presence, as a symbol of their utter destruction. Such preaching, one might think, could hardly need the oral comment accompanying it, which begins in these words, 'Thus saith the Lord of Hosts, even so will I break this people and this city, as one breaketh a potter's vessel that it cannot be made whole again.' At another time, he is directed to send yokes to certain kings in the neighbourhood of Judea, indicating that the Creator and owner of all had resolved to subjugate them to the Babylonian power, announcing at the same time, that Zedekiah, the reigning king of Judah, should also be compelled to submit to the same degradation. To select another illustration from the same prophet. Whilst the armies of Nebuchadnezzar are besieging Jerusalem, and its conquest by the Chaldeans is generally expected; when the death, destruction, or captivity of the inhabitants is almost morally certain, and consequently no value can be attached to property, the enjoyment or possession of which had become wholly precarious; Jeremiah, at the divine direction, buys a field within the city, pays down the purchase-money, requires a deed properly attested, has the transaction witnessed according to law and with remarkable circumstantiality, and adopts measures to secure the legal documents, that they may neither be lost nor injured. No doubt, the ungodly portion of the inhabitants, who had abandoned themselves to the despair of infidelity, must have imagined that the prophet had become insane. But all this was done to show his faith in the divine promise of a future restoration, and resettlement of the people in their own land; which took place long afterwards under the decree of Cyrus. And to adduce one more instance: On occasion of the birth of a son, Isaiah is directed to give him a symbolical name, indicative of the fact, that the Assyrians should plunder Israel and Syria, powers which were then in hostile combination against Judah. In order to give publicity to the prediction, he is required to write the name of the child on a broad roll or tablet. He does so, and has the whole matter attested by unimpeachable witnesses of high standing and character. In due time the fact takes place, and the prophecy is verified." Pp. 75–78.

We have admitted, that the action recorded in the nineteenth chapter of Jeremiah in respect to his going to the potter is so related, as to leave us in some doubt, whether it took place only in vision, or on the territory of real life. We shall, therefore, allow it to pass without particular notice; but shall make a few comments on the rest.

1. The first is the action of Isaiah, chap. xx., appointed to symbolize the coming disgrace and humiliation of Egypt and Ethiopia. What is the action, according to the description of the prophet? Not as Dr Turner and others make it, "stripping off a part of his clothing," but "loosing the sackloth from off his loins, and putting off his shoe from his foot," and for three whole years "walking naked and barefoot;" and this expressly as a sign of the people of Egypt and Ethiopia being doomed ere long to become captives, rendered "naked and barefoot, even with their buttocks uncovered, to the shame of Egypt." The thing signified was a *shameful uncovering*, or a disgraceful humiliation of those proud worldly powers, on whose support Israel was idolatrously inclined to

lean; and the sign, which was appointed to foreshadow it, was a shameful uncovering of the prophet's person. This alone *could* be a proper sign; and to talk of his putting off only a part of his garments, as if the object had been merely to lessen the comfort or gracefulness of his attire, is quite beside the purpose. Nothing less than a shameful exposure of the person was required to satisfy the conditions of the prophecy. And if the affair was conducted amid the realities of daily life, the prophet must necessarily have made himself a spectacle of aversion to every right-thinking person. In the very act of fulfilling his mission, he must have given a shock to the interests of piety; such, nay greatly more than was done in our own land by the early Quakers, who were led by a mistaken view of this and similar passages in the prophetical writings, to exhibit in actual life what had been transacted by the prophets in vision. The universal disgust produced in Edinburgh by some of that sect running through the streets without clothing, and crying out that they were "the naked truth," or by one in Aberdeen (Andrew Jaffray) who, stript to the middle, and with filth in his hand, walked about proclaiming himself to be "a spectacle and a sign among the people," on account of the offensiveness of their sins, may convince us how impossible it was for God to have commanded His servant Isaiah to present himself in such an attitude to the people, even for a day, to say nothing of three whole years. Besides, if such painful results could any how have been averted, an action of the kind specified, when spread over so many years, and seen, if seen at all, only in fragmentary portions, and by a few individuals, must have lost nearly all its effect in the performance. And then the action itself left its own bearing undefined. How should any one, who might have seen the prophet walking in his shame, have known to transfer the image to Egypt and Ethiopia? It must have been from an accompanying word, explaining the action, that they were enabled to do so. So that it still was the prophetic *word*, to which they were mainly to be indebted for the information of their minds; and the rehearsing of the action as done in the visions of God—done in the peculiar sphere of the prophet's spiritual agency—along with the explanation of it, was on every account the mode best fitted for reaching the end; the only mode, we may affirm, actually possible.

2. The other action of the prophet Isaiah referred to by Dr Turner—the last of the cases specified by him—not less imperatively demands the same interpretation. We have again to notice the slurring over the main features of the transaction, as presented by Dr Turner; he speaks of it as simply consisting in the ceremony of giving a symbolical name to a child of the prophet. This, however, was the smallest part of the matter. The *existence* of the child, much more than his name, was what formed the embodied prophecy; the name merely served to explain the symbolic meaning of the child himself. And how was this child to come into being? Not properly as a member of the prophet's family; but the prophet was to "go to the prophetess," who was thereafter to conceive, and bring forth the son, that was to bear the symbolic name; and not only to go, but to take with him witnesses of the whole transaction, that there might be no doubt respecting any part of it (chap. viii. 1–3). Can anything be conceived more entirely at variance with the essential character of a true prophet, if understood of what was to be done in real life, or that would more palpably have identified his procedure with the worst practices of self-inflated visionaries? For, the prophetess to whom Isaiah was to go, and with whom he was to have carnal intercourse, can with no propriety be understood to be his own wife; she is represented as one standing apart from him, and with whom his connection was to be quite special, so as to require even a formal attestation. An ideal person, therefore, she must be considered, and the connection one that existed only in the ideal sphere—if the prophet is to be vindicated from the charge of pollution in the very execution of his mission. Indeed, the mode of designating her, clearly indicates as much: *the prophetess*—what prophetess? We have heard of none before, and we

hear of none afterwards in this connection. Such a designation can be understood only if viewed as the form into which God threw His communication to the prophet, and, as such, confined to the higher sphere of his immediate intercourse with heaven. An assurance was to be given to the people of the approaching certain overthrow of the enemies of God's covenant—the combined powers of Samaria and Damascus. And for that purpose there is given forth an account of an ideal transaction, through which the prophet is spiritually conducted by God, and in which he, the prophet, is described as going to the prophetess, that by the conjunction of a twofold prophetical character in the parentage, there might be a birth in the fullest sense prophetical—a son so strikingly predictive of the coming overthrow, that before he should be able to cry, my father, both Syria and Damascus should have fallen under the stroke of Assyria. Viewed thus, merely as a sensible form, though confined to the ideal sphere, under which God made known His fixed determination to the people, one can easily perceive the propriety of what is recorded; but no otherwise can the history it seems to delineate be vindicated from the gravest charges. It may be added, that in this case, too, as in the preceding, it could not have been the outward reality (even if it had taken place, and had been liable to no moral imputation), on which must mainly have depended the assurance given of the intended result: the chief ground for faith to rest upon, still was the word which accompanied and explained the transaction. And for this it was substantially one, whether the word was connected with an action in vision, or an action in ordinary life.

3. The case of Ezekiel, at the Divine bidding, removing his furniture in the sight of the people, and going forth with covered face, and only an exile's implements (chap. xii.), is particularly unhappy for the realistic interpretation. Dr Turner seems to have regarded it as one of the most telling examples, as if the act itself spoke its own meaning. But he forgets where the prophet was when the supposed action

was performed before his countrymen. Both he and they were already in exile on the banks of the Chaboras, and the impression that would naturally have been produced upon their minds by the sight of such a symbolic action would have been, not that the day of exile, but rather that the day of escape from exile was at hand. The persons whose exile was foreshadowed in the prophecy were the king and people far off in Jerusalem, not those who should have witnessed the transaction had it been outwardly performed. So that for those whom the prophetic action *immediately* contemplated it must, of necessity, have been not the actual sight of what was done, but only the rehearsal of it, that was to tell upon their minds. And surely, in that case, it mattered little whether the sphere of the transaction might be the ideal or the real world; while for those in the immediate neighbourhood of the prophet, it so far mattered that, if it had outwardly taken place before them, it would have tended to convey a false information.

4. It is needless to dwell upon the two instances (besides the one already considered) connected with the prophetical agency of Jeremiah. They are both of them confined to what respects God's communications to the prophet, and so belong to the higher sphere in which direct communication was held with heaven. One of them may be said to have been beset with impossibilities, if considered as an action in real life. We refer to the bonds and yokes which Jeremiah was commanded in chap. xxvii. to make, and not only put upon his own neck, but also to send to the kings of Edom, of Moab, of the Ammonites, of Tyre, and of Sidon, and to do so by the hand of the messengers who were coming to Zedekiah, as a sign that all those countries were to be brought into subjection to the king of Babylon. Such persons, we may be sure, would neither carry such a symbol to the different kings mentioned, nor the message that was appointed to accompany it. And the prophecy itself was for the people of Jerusalem rather than for those surrounding nations. It only took the form of a message to them, in order, more distinctly,

to show the fixedness of God's purpose regarding the issue of the struggle in which Zedekiah was engaged with the king of Babylon. The rehearsing by the prophet of the command he had received, to make the yokes, and send them to the different parties, was what properly constituted the prophecy. And though Jeremiah appears, from what is related in chap. xxviii., to have had yokes actually on his neck, yet this seems rather to have been done for the purpose of calling attention to the prophecy than the necessary condition of its announcement. Nor is anything said in the historical part of the sending of yokes to the surrounding nations. In regard to the other instance, that recorded in chap. xxxii., the whole has the aspect of a continuous stream of communications between God and the prophet; and the prophetical action about the buying of Hanameel's field is most naturally regarded as of a piece with the rest, an action in vision. There are other reasons, also, against its being taken as an actual transaction, for, being a priest, Jeremiah could scarcely have entered into any such transaction for the purchase of land; and if he could, yet, as he had predicted that a desolation was at hand, which was to last for seventy years, the transaction would, in his case, have been a kind of extravagance, since long before the purchase could have been of any avail he must have been numbered with the dead, and all the old landmarks practically abolished. Only as an ideal action in the peculiar region of the prophet's spiritual activity does it admit of a natural and fitting interpretation.

Thus, when more nearly considered, the instances appealed to in proof of the symbolic actions having taken place in real life, are found to support the principle of interpretation we have sought to establish. The striving after outward reality in such things, on the part of modern commentators, has chiefly arisen from forgetfulness respecting the fundamental law of prophetic revelation, that it was to be by vision. Had this been sufficiently borne in mind it would have seemed quite natural (as no doubt it did to those by whom, and to whom, the word of prophecy came), that in accounts of

Divine communications, things done in the sphere of the prophet's ecstatic elevation should have been described as real transactions; for to the prophet's own consciousness, and as symbolic representations for the people of the mind and purposes of God, they had all the force and value of realities.

APPENDIX H, P. 245.

ST PETER'S DISCOURSES IN ACTS II., III.

THE view given in the text of Peter's discourses in the Acts puts no strain upon any of the expressions, but takes them all in their natural sense and connection. Strange liberties are resorted to by those, who espouse the Jewish theory of the future, and in part also by some who adopt only the semi-Jewish. The question of the disciples to Jesus on the eve of his ascension, about restoring the kingdom to Israel, is usually made, not only to commit Jesus to the fact of such a restoration, but also to rule by its carnal sense the whole of the subsequent expressions. It is assumed, that Peter's views of the kingdom *after* the descent of the Spirit, continued the same as they were *before;* and that, however it might be in other respects, on this subject he gained nothing in depth, spirituality or clearness of discernment. It is usually farther assumed, that in those invitations to press into the kingdom, addressed to men far and near, as many as the Lord might call, he never thought of any but Jews as having a right to the blessings of the kingdom—although the Lord had in the most explicit manner charged the apostles to include the whole world in their ministrations. They were, He said, to be "His witnesses both in Jerusalem and in all Judea, and in Samaria, and unto the uttermost part of the earth:"—a regular gradation, but only in respect to order and time; first Jerusalem, then the country around Judea; next Samaria, the kind of intermediate region between Jew and Gentile; and finally, the most remote and distant territories. Nay, the original charge, as given in Mark, chap. xvi. 15, was that they were to "go into all the world, and preach the gospel to every creature"—precisely, as in the first parable, "the field is the world." So that if Peter and the apostles still thought only of Jews as entitled to a place in the kingdom, they must have been most strangely inattentive to their Lord's instructions. That they did not open the door at once to the Gentiles, arose simply from their views respecting circumcision and the law; they thought these were still to remain in force, and consequently that the Gentiles must enter the Messiah's kingdom by passing under the Jewish yoke. But this had respect merely to the mode of admission; it did not touch the fact, that the Gentiles had an equal right to enter, but simply that they had to enter as the Jews; both alike must go in by the legal door. And in this very circumstance we have an answer to the statement made by many—among others by Baumgarten—respecting the sense attached by the apostles to the expression "the restoration of the kingdom to Israel," as necessarily meaning both with them and with Christ the revival of Israel's external power and splendour as a nation; because "their honest and childlike minds clung to the *what* and the *how* that the prophets had written of." The apostles no doubt did this, they did so in this matter only too long, and in respect to circumcision, as well as the kingdom; but the issue proved in the latter case, that their spirit, however honest and childlike, needed enlightenment, as the style of Peter's future discourses showed that it had also done in respect to the other.

The passage in chap. ii. 30–36, seems alone quite conclusive of a change of view respecting the kingdom. In one part there is a diversity as to the proper reading, and the two best MSS. A, B, omit the words in ver. 30, rendered in the common version, "According to the flesh, he would raise up Christ." There are good reasons for supposing, that these words were not in the original; so that the passage should stand thus: "Therefore [David] being a prophet, and knowing that God had sworn with an oath to him, of the fruit of his loins to make to sit upon his throne, foreseeing this, he spake concerning the resurrection of Christ, that his soul was not left in hell, neither did his flesh see corruption. This Jesus God has raised up, whereof we all are witnesses," etc., and, after quoting Ps. cx. 1, 2, he concludes, "Therefore let all the house of Israel know assuredly, that God hath made that same Jesus, whom ye have crucified, both Lord and Christ." The passage is plain enough without the omitted words, and unless it is a piece of false logic, and the conclusion does not cohere with the premise, it explicitly affirms Christ's present possession of the throne of David. The position from which Peter sets out is, that "God had sworn with an oath to David, of the fruit of his loins to make to sit upon his throne;" and the conclusion at which he arrives is, that that same Jesus who had been crucified and had ascended to the right hand of God, "*has been made* both Lord and Christ." In such a connection, what can the being made Lord and Christ mean, but sitting upon David's throne? What other inference could the public audience Peter addressed (who had neither time nor taste for subtle ingenuities, but naturally took the words in their plain and obvious meaning) draw from the statement? They *must* have felt, that, according to the apostle, the word to David respecting the possession of his throne by a son had now reached its fulfilment. As contemplated by them, the being made Lord and Christ in any other sense would not have been to the point.

The words uttered in common by the apostles in an address to God, as recorded in chap. iv. 25–27, clearly express the same view. They quote the first verses of the second Psalm, which speak of the rulers combining and standing up "against the Lord and His Christ" (anointed); and then, applying the testimony to present times, they add, "For of a truth, against thy holy child Jesus, whom thou hast anointed, both Herod and Pontius Pilate, with the Gentiles and the people of Israel, were gathered together." In such a connection to call Jesus the person, whom God had anointed, could only mean, what is more fully expressed in the second Psalm, by being anointed as king and set on His holy hill of Zion. In any other sense the application of the terms must have been irrelevant, and fitted to mislead; unless, indeed (for that is the only means of escape from the conclusion), the apostles acted on the rationalistic principle, and merely accommodated the words of David to Jesus, on account of certain resemblances between the two cases.

The other passage referred to in the text, chap. iii. 19–21, is the only one in those addresses of Peter, which distinctly points to the future. Here the correct rendering undoubtedly is: "Repent ye, therefore, and be converted, for the blotting out of your sins; in order that seasons of refreshing may come from the presence of the Lord, and that He may send Christ Jesus, who was before appointed to you (or, the Christ before appointed to you—Jesus); whom the heavens, indeed, must receive, till the times of the restitution (ἀποκαταστάσεως), of all things, of which God hath spoken by the mouth of His holy prophets from the beginning of His world." Such persons as can see nothing here but Israelitish prospects, and nothing more in the restitution of all things than what was meant to be expressed at chap. i. 6, by the restoration of the kingdom to Israel, must be swayed by other reasons than are furnished by a natural exposition of the apostle's words; and they do him, besides, the manifest injustice of making his views, before the descent of the Spirit, rule and determine those which he entertained afterwards. Discharging all preconceived notions, and taking the passage in its most obvious meaning, it seems plainly to indicate a series of progressive stages: first, a present duty in order to a present blessing (repenting and being converted for the sake of obtaining forgiveness of sin); then, on the ground of this repentance and forgiveness, the just expectation of seasons of refreshing—seasons like that of Pentecost, which those only who have become forgiven and accepted in the Beloved, can rightfully expect, but which they may confidently look for. These, however, are not the ultimate things of redemption—there is a stage higher and better still, for which they but tend to prepare the way and hasten forward the consummation. This is denoted by the sending of Christ Jesus from heaven, and the times of the restitution of all things; for though, did the sense absolutely require it, the seasons of refreshing (καιροὶ ἀναψύξεως), in ver. 20, might be identified with the times of the restitution of all things (χρόνοι ἀποκαταστάσεως πάντων) in ver. 21, yet the natural supposition is, that they point to different epochs, as they also seem to indicate different results. Times of refreshing may come from the Lord's presence, while the Lord Himself is not visibly manifest; and in no proper sense can they be called, when they do come, complete restitution-periods; they are rather the occasional showers of blessing sent to invigorate the strength and cheer the hearts of faithful labourers before the final harvest. That harvest is a nobler thing—not something sent from the Lord merely, but the sending of the Lord Himself—not a present refreshment, but an ultimate and universal restitution—a restitution which has been spoken of, not by the peculiar prophets of Israel alone, but by all prophetic men from the foundation of the world. Such a restitution, and so spoken of, must transcend every thing local and temporary; it can be nothing less than that bringing back of all to the order and perfection of God, which from the first, has been the great purpose of Divine grace, and the hope it has awakened in the heart of faith. Formally this restitution comprises the whole burden of prophecy, but not really; for the bringing back to what was, carries in its train an indefinite elevation. It involves the rise of all to another and higher sphere of being; for He who stands at the head of it is the Lord from heaven; and while He restores, He at the same time refines and glorifies. Why should not this thought also be extended to the other expectation, and determine what *should* be understood by the restoration of the kingdom to Israel? This restoration, too, may still be spoken of; but if so, it should be as connected with a glorious elevation. In Christ, David's throne has become allied with Godhead, and the kingdom assumes of necessity a far loftier position and embraces an immensely wider domain. It becomes, indeed, co-extensive with the world; and hence the two points, when rightly understood, coalesce; the final re-adjusting and ordering of the affairs of Christ's divine government shall be at once the restoration of the kingdom to Israel, and the restitution of all things to the world. Hence also, what in the prophets generally, who spoke in the midst of Israel, and from the Israelitish point of view, is predicted under the aspect of the full and perfect re-establishment of David's kingdom, appears in Daniel, who by his position was led to contemplate the matter in its broader relationship to the world at large, as the setting up of the kingdom of heaven in the hands of one like a Son of Man. They are but different modes of exhibiting the same great truth; intimating that the kingdom, which belongs to Christ as Son of Man or Son of David, when conducted to its final issues, shall bring along with it the restitution of every thing on earth to perfect order and blessedness.

APPENDIX I, P. 268.

WHO ARE THE SAINTS, THAT IN DAN. VII. 18–22, ARE SAID TO POSSESS THE KINGDOM.

THE representation given in the text of Daniel's vision proceeds on the assumption, that in the kingdom of Messiah, as there disclosed, there is no distinction of tribes and races, and that its subjects are simply the righteous as opposed to the wicked—"the saints of the Most High." The words themselves and the whole character of the vision seem to make this plain enough. But interpreters with Jewish leanings cannot so view it; the warping influence of their opinion as to the future ascendancy of Israel induces them to impose on the passage a limitation, of which there is no trace in the passage itself. Their literalism is exchanged here for the most unwarranted licence, and the saints of the Most High shrink into merely "the people of Israel." Thus Auberlen, who belongs to the Hofmann and Delitzsch school, in his work on the prophet Daniel and the Apocalypse, writing of this vision, says at p. 219, "By the people of the saints of the Most High, to whom the dominion is to be given, Daniel could manifestly have understood only the people of Israel, as contradistinguished from the kingdoms and peoples of heathendom, who up to this time are to reign; so that we also with exegetical right and propriety can think of nothing else, therefore not immediately of the church." Here, in the first place, we have a groundless assumption—that Daniel could only understand by the expression, the people of Israel. What Daniel understood is not stated, nor generally are we informed of the prophets how far their insight carried them into the real import of the visions given them. It, no doubt, differed in one prophet as compared with another; and also in the same prophet with respect to different parts of the communications he received. Of them, therefore, as of the ancient believers generally, it cannot be said with certainty in any particular case, how far precisely they understood the meaning of their predictions. But, secondly, whatever their understanding might be—if Daniel here, for example, understood by the saints of the Most High simply the Jewish people, that is no reason why we should hold such to be what was properly meant. We are no more obliged or warranted in such a case to abide by his understanding, than we ought to abide by the partial and mistaken senses, which the apostles often put upon our Lord's words up till the day of Penetcost. The words are not so properly the words of Daniel as those of the Spirit of God, and to ascribe to them a certain sense, different from what they naturally bear, as not only that put on them by him, but because so put, their only valid and proper sense, is to embrace the old rationalistic principle, which treated the prophetical writings as simply the productions of men, incapable of bearing any other or higher sense than the men themselves fully understood. Such a principle is utterly at variance with the proper inspiration of prophecy, and with the real circumstances of the prophets of the Old Testament. In regard to the things which were given them to make known concerning the Christian dispensation, they themselves saw through a glass darkly; they had consequently to search, as St Peter tells us, chap. i. 11, what in certain respects the Spirit of Christ which was in them did signify. The very search implied a measure of darkness in the prediction, and of ignorance in the prophet; and in regard to the opinion itself, to which this search in any particular case conducted, we have, in the first place, no certain means of knowing what it was, and, in the second, even if we knew it, we should not be bound to abide by it, the judgment of the prophet, as Horsley has justly said, "must still bow down to time as a more informed expositor." This holds particularly in respect to such a prophecy as the one now before us, in which Daniel merely reports what he saw in vision and heard in a dream. Neither the matter nor the words of the prophecy are in any proper sense his own—not his own, that is, as to the ultimate meaning and intention of them. They were his only in so far as they accurately described what he saw and heard; but for all that this pointed to, and required for its proper realization, Daniel was merely on a footing with other believers, and far less favourably situated for understanding it than believers now are. The very absence of any peculiar reference to Israel in the words of the prophecy is clear evidence that none was intended.

APPENDIX K, P. 360.

THE TENDENCY OF PROPHECY TO DESCRIBE THINGS ACCORDING TO THE REALITY, RATHER THAN THE APPEARANCE OR PROFESSION.

The interpretation which has been given in the text of the strongest terms in the apostle's language respecting the antichrist, by understanding them of a *virtual*, in contradistinction to a *formal and avowed* assumption of blasphemous prerogatives, is so much in accordance with the general style of prophecy, and so plainly demanded by the connection, that we cannot refrain from expressing our wonder, at finding interpreters of note still pressing the opposite view. Their doing so must be regarded as another instance of that tendency to literalism, which has wrought such confusion in the prophetical field, and which, at particular points, returns upon some, who in general have attained to a correct discernment of the characteristics of prophecy. The practice of describing things by their *real*, as opposed to their professed or apparent character, is one that peculiarly distinguishes the Apocalyptic imagery. Thus the worldly kingdoms, both in Daniel and the Revelation, are represented as beasts—not that they actually were, or gave themselves out to be such, but because they pursued a course which partook largely of the bestial nature; they were, one might say, virtual beasts. And the false, seductive power designated Babylon, the mother of harlots and abominations, we may be sure, was not going to proclaim her own shame by declaring herself to be what those epithets import. Beyond all doubt, she is described according to what she really was, not by what she should profess, to be. In like manner, the names of blasphemy on the head of the beast indicate a real rather than a professed dishonour to the God of heaven; for open profanity and avowed atheism have, with few exceptions, been studiously avoided by the worldly power. It has almost uniformly striven to associate with its different forms of government, and political aims, the name and sanctions of religion. Even in the more prosaic parts of the Apocalypse we find the same characteristic prevailing—as when it describes the soaring spirit of the gnostic teachers, by their knowing the depths of *Satan* (not those of God, which they themselves rather affected to understand), and designates them by such epithets as Nicolaitans (people-destroyers), followers of Balaam, Jezebels—which they were so far from professing to be, that they laid claim to the highest gifts and the most honourable distinctions. Nor could it be otherwise with the wolves, of whose coming St Paul warned the Ephesian elders (Acts xx.); they were not going, when they appeared, to avow their own wolf-like character, but would, doubtless, aspire to the place of guides and shepherds of the flock. All prophecy, indeed, abounds with examples of this mode of representation; for, speaking as with Divine intuition, it ever delights to penetrate through showy appearances, and to strip deceivers of their false disguises. Thus the self-deifying pride of the Chaldean conquerors has its representation in the prophet Habakkuk, by their being characterised as successful fishers, sacrificing to their own net (chap. i. 16); and the corruption of degenerate Israel is exhibited with singular boldness by Ezekiel, under the form of their having had an Amorite father and a Hittite mother (chap. xvi. 3); and by Isaiah, under the announcement, as from themselves, that they had made a covenant with death, and come to an agreement with hell (chap. xxviii. 15.) By a still bolder figure the prophet Amos calls the tabernacle in the wilderness the tabernacle of their Moloch, because the idolatrous and unsanctified spirit which still clung to them rendered it practically an idol-tent rather than that of the true God (chap. v. 26). These and many similar representations are obviously designed to set before us the real state and character of the parties described, though entirely different from the outward profession and appearance. On any other principle it were impossible to render much that is written in prophecy either intelligible in itself, or consistent with the facts of history.

The violation of this principle in regard to the passages which treat of the antichristian apostacy, by adhering to a mistaken literalism, is the more to be regretted, as it is doing with this portion of the prophetic Scriptures what it has already done with those which have respect to the promised Messiah—it is altogether destroying in the hands of its abettors their apologetic value. As, with the one class of predictions, Jewish Rabbis find themselves backed by Christian literalists in denying the fulfilment of some of the clearest prophetic intimations in the history of Jesus of Nazareth, so Romish controversialists are sheltering themselves under the wing of Protestant interpreters of the same school, in rebutting the application of the Scriptural antichrist to Popery. Thus, in a small volume recently published on "The End of the World, or the Second Coming of our Lord and Saviour Jesus Christ, by the very Rev. John Baptist Pagani," a very adroit use is made of the name of the late Mr Faber. An astonishment is first expressed that any intelligent person could ever have thought of identifying the Pope of Rome with the antichrist of Scripture, especially that this could be done in so enlightened a country as England; and then a passage from Mr Faber's "Calendar of Prophecy" is quoted to show how a sensible Protestant writer exposes the absurdity of the idea. In the passage referred to the argument is thrown into what is considered both by Mr Faber and by his Catholic admirer a conclusive syllogism. "I shall throw my argument," the writer says, "into the form of a syllogism, and if any person be able to confute me, I shall be very ready to own myself mistaken. According to St John, he who denies the Father and the Son, this is the antichrist. The line of the Roman Pontiffs did not deny the Father or the Son; therefore the line of the Roman Pontiffs is not the antichrist." Embracing with satisfaction this triumphant syllogism, Mr Pagani proceeds to give it additional strength by affirming, that so far from denying the Father and the Son, the Roman Pontiffs have always maintained the doctrine of the Trinity against Deists, Sabellians, Unitarians, and other heretics; that they have uniformly held, that Christ has come in the flesh; that they have also been remarkably distinguished for their humility, taking for their ordinary title, "unworthy ministers of Christ," "servants of the servants of God," whereas antichrist is to exalt himself above all that is called God. P. 41, sq.

One might go through a considerable portion of prophecy with this sort of syllogism, and ask in vain for any thing in the transactions of real life, that would answer to the terms of the predictions. What, on such a style of interpretation, could be made of the passages to which we have been adverting? Must we suspend the veracity of one prophet on the question, whether the proud Chaldeans actually hung up a net in some temple, and did sacrifice to it? Or that of another, on the similar question, whether the Israelites literally bore about during their long sojourn in the wilderness an idolatrous tabernacle in impious rivalry to that of Jehovah?[1] Or must we have credible testimony to the fact, that the great worldly monarchies, as they successively arose, did each proclaim their own bestial and blasphemous character? Or, finally, shall

[1] Even Hengstenberg has given too much countenance to this utterly groundless and extravagant idea, when, in discoursing upon this passage of Amos in the first volume of his work on the Pentateuch, he thus unfolds the general sense of the announcement: "The great mass of the people had, for the larger part of the time during their march through the wilderness, given up honouring the Lord by sacrifices, and instead of Jehovah, the God of hosts, had set up a spurious king of heaven (the Egyptian Pan), whom with the rest of the host of heaven, they honoured with a spurious worship." It is against all probability, that such an openly idolatrous worship, as is here supposed, should have been practised by the mass of the Israelites during their stay in the wilderness. Occasional defections there no doubt were, but we have no reason to think more—at least, nothing approaching to such a regular, systematic, and general idolatry. We are told even of the comparatively smaller and isolated offences of a public nature—such as the gathering of sticks on the Sabbath, and the blaspheming of God's name—being capitally punished; and can it be imagined that an idol-tabernacle should have been allowed to be carried about, and openly frequented? Assuredly not. It is of the state of the heart, of its still unsanctified and idolatrous spirit, that the prophet speaks; this *practically* turned Jehovah's tent and worship into the interest of heathenism; in God's sight it belonged to Moloch rather than to himself. When thus viewed, also, there is no need, with Hengstenberg, of rendering "your king," instead of "your Moloch;" indeed to do so rather obscures the meaning. The prophet is seeking to identify the idolatrous spirit of his own day with that of earlier times; they were then going after Moloch: and so, says the prophet, you have always been substantially doing. You did so through your forefathers in the wilderness; even then you bore the tabernacle of your Moloch, and sacrificed to strange gods, and the old doom must return upon you. It is, therefore, the *later* form of idolatry, which is used to characterize the earlier, not (as Hengstenberg would have it) the earlier the later.

we hold, that nothing can verify the description given of the mystic Babylon, which does not set itself openly to establish and avow the prostitution of all righteous principle? If such be the kind of expectations, with which we proceed to examine the prophetic word, we may certainly lay our account to meet with few instances of fulfilment; we know not where they are to be found in the past, and are afraid they may not soon be found in the future. But surely, if the apostle in his day knew persons in the Christian church, whom he could declare to be the "enemies of the Cross of Christ," even while they were avowedly looking to that cross for salvation, the pontiffs of Rome might justly enough be characterized as denying the Father and the Son, if they should be found claiming prerogatives, and upholding a system of error and delusion, which virtually subvert the revelation given of the Father and the Son in Scripture. Let it just be granted, that in the descriptions of the collective antichrist, the apostles had their eye on the realities, not on the mere appearances of things—no very extravagant postulate surely—then the proper syllogism will stand thus: the antichrist, according to St John, is he who denies the Father and the Son; but the line of the Roman pontiffs, by their own blasphemous assumptions, and by their system of legalized falsehood and corruption, utterly opposed to the spirit and design of the Gospel, have denied what is revealed of the Father and the Son; therefore the line of the Roman pontiffs is antichrist. This we take to be a truer form of syllogism than Mr Faber's. But it only meets one fallacy involved in the interpretation. There is another in its taking for granted, that the representations in John's epistles, are to be regarded as comprehensive of all that was to characterize the spirit and conduct of the antichrist. He merely points to one of the first forms and manifestations of the evil—that which took shape under the hands of the gnostic teachers. By and by this was to lead on to others, of which not less distinct intimation was given elsewhere in the New Testament writings. The antichristian spirit was to assume different phases, according to the peculiar influences of the time, and the changing fortunes of the church. But they were all to have one thing in common: under a profession of Christianity, there was to be something in doctrine or practice, which in effect made void the Christian truth and life. This in *every* form was to be the characteristic of antichristianism as contradistinguished from atheism, heathenism, or undisguised worldliness. And hence, so far from expecting that the Popes, or any other embodiments of the antichrist, should formally assume what is predicted of this power, we should rather expect the reverse. We should expect a studious effort to disguise the truth of the case, though such an one as should only impose upon the ignorant or the corrupt. And precisely as the *Servant of servants* can in lordly arrogance place his foot upon the necks of princes, and claim the ascendancy over all earthly power and authority, so under a boastful proclamation of the doctrine of the Trinity, and the conversion of the Cross into a magic charm, may there be found the most substantial denial of the Father and the Son. In a word, the question is, not what Popery *pretends* to be, but what it *really is;* with this alone we have to do in determining its relation to the prophetic delineations of Scripture. And when the subject is viewed in this light, he must be strangely blinded or unhappily biassed, who fails to perceive the striking correspondence between the one and the other.

INDICES.

I.

PASSAGES OF SCRIPTURE MORE PARTICULARLY REFERRED TO AND EXPLAINED.

II.

AUTHORS AND SUBJECTS.

A